# THE PLAYWRIGHT AS THINKER

# ERIC BENTLEY

## DRAMATIC WORKS
### COLLECTIONS:

RALLYING CRIES: THREE PLAYS (*Are You Now Or Have You Ever Been*; *The Recantation of Galileo Galilei*; *From the Memoirs of Pontius Pilate*), *1977*

THE KLEIST VARIATIONS (*Concord*; *The Fall of the Amazons*; *Wannsee*), *1982*.

MONSTROUS MARTYRDOMS (*Lord Alfred's Lover*; *H for Hamlet*; *German Requiem*), *1985*.

### PLAYS:

ORPHEUS IN THE UNDERWORLD (*opera libretto*), *1956*.

A TIME TO DIE, *1970*.

A TIME TO LIVE, *1970*.

THE RED, WHITE AND BLACK, *1971*.

ARE YOU NOW OR HAVE YOU EVER BEEN, *1972*.

THE RECANTATION OF GALILEO GALILEI, *1972*.

EXPLETIVE DELETED, *1974*.

FROM THE MEMOIRS OF PONTIUS PILATE, *1977*.

WANNSEE, *1979*.

THE FALL OF THE AMAZONS, *1980*.

CONCORD, *1981*.

LORD ALFRED'S LOVER, *1981*.

GERMAN REQUIEM, *1985*.

H FOR HAMLET, *1985*.

ROUND 2, *1987*.

## CRITICAL WORKS

A CENTURY OF HERO WORSHIP, *1944*.

THE PLAYWRIGHT AS THINKER: A STUDY OF DRAMA IN MODERN TIMES, *1946*.

BERNARD SHAW: A RECONSIDERATION, *1947*.

IN SEARCH OF THEATRE, *1953*.

THE DRAMATIC EVENT, *1954*.

WHAT IS THEATRE? A QUERY IN CHRONICLE FORM, *1956*.

THE LIFE OF THE DRAMA, *1964*.

THE THEATRE OF COMMITMENT, AND OTHER ESSAYS ON DRAMA IN OUR SOCIETY, *1967*.

THEATRE OF WAR: COMMENTS ON 32 OCCASIONS, *1972*.

THE BRECHT COMMENTARIES, *1981*.

THE PIRANDELLO COMMENTARIES, *1986*.

THE BRECHT MEMOIR, *1986*.

THINKING ABOUT THE PLAYWRIGHT, *1987*.

## ANTHOLOGIES

THE IMPORTANCE OF SCRUTINY, *1948*.

FROM THE MODERN REPERTOIRE (*3 volumes*), *1949–1956*.

THE PLAY: A CRITICAL ANTHOLOGY, *1951*.

SHAW ON MUSIC, *1953*.

THE MODERN THEATRE (*6 volumes*), *1955–1960*.

"LET'S GET A DIVORCE!" AND OTHER PLAYS, *1958*.

THE CLASSIC THEATRE (*4 volumes*), *1958–1961*.

THE GENIUS OF THE ITALIAN THEATRE, *1964*.

THE STORM OVER "THE DEPUTY," *1964*.

THE BRECHT-EISLER SONG BOOK, *1966*.

THE THEORY OF THE MODERN STAGE (*2 volumes*), *1970*.

THE GREAT PLAYWRIGHTS (*2 volumes*), *1970*.

THIRTY YEARS OF TREASON, *1971*.

THE DRAMATIC REPERTOIRE (*4 volumes as of 1987*).

## AS EDITOR-TRANSLATOR

PARABLES FOR THE THEATRE: "The Caucasian Chalk Circle" and "The Good Woman of Setzuan," by Bertolt Brecht, *1948*.

NAKED MASKS (*Plays by Luigi Pirandello*), *1952*.

"RIGHT YOU ARE (IF YOU CARE TO THINK SO!),"
by Luigi Pirandello, *1954.*

"THE BRUTE" AND OTHER FARCES, by Anton Chekhov,
*1956.*

SEVEN PLAYS BY BRECHT, *1961.*

"FILUMENA MARTURANO," by Eduardo de Filippo, *1964.*

"THE WIRE HARP," by Wolf Biermann, *1968.*

"INSPECTOR" AND 3 OTHER PLAYS, by Nicolai Gogol,
*1987.*

## RECORDINGS

BENTLEY ON BRECHT, *1963.*

BRECHT BEFORE THE UN-AMERICAN ACTIVITIES COM-
MITTEE, *1963.*

"A MAN'S A MAN," by Bertolt Brecht, *1963.*

"THE EXCEPTION AND THE RULE," by Bertolt Brecht,
*1965.*

SONGS BY HANNS EISLER, *1965.*

"THE ELEPHANT CALF" and "DEAR OLD DEMOCRACY,"
by Bertolt Brecht, *1967.*

BENTLEY ON BIERMANN, *1968.*

ERIC BENTLEY SINGS "THE QUEEN OF 42ND STREET,"
*1969.*

I believe above all in the future and in the universal need of serious things . . . the time is ripe for the DRAMA OF THOUGHT.

ALFRED DE VIGNY

The serious thing about drama is not the ideas. It is the absorption of the ideas by the characters, the dramatic or comic force which the characters give to the ideas.

HENRY BECQUE

# THE PLAYWRIGHT

## A STUDY

# ERIC BENTLEY

# AS THINKER
## OF DRAMA IN MODERN TIMES

WAGNER  IBSEN  STRINDBERG  SHAW  PIRANDELLO  SARTRE  BRECHT

**HARCOURT BRACE JOVANOVICH, PUBLISHERS**
San Diego  New York  London

Requests for permission to make copies of any
part of the work should be mailed to:
Permissions, Harcourt Brace Jovanovich, Publishers,
Orlando, Florida 32887.

The Introduction by Richard Gilman first appeared, in slightly
different form, in *The Play and Its Critic: Essays for Eric Bentley*
(Lanham, MD: University Press of America, 1986), a festschrift
commemorating Bentley's seventieth year, edited and introduced
by Michael Bertin. The Introduction also appeared in *American
Theatre* magazine, a publication of the Theatre Communications
Group (New York: October, 1986). Reprinted by permission.

The photograph of Eric Bentley on the back cover of this edition is
by Gene Bagnato.

Library of Congress Cataloging-in-Publication Data
Bentley, Eric, 1916–
    The playwright as thinker.
    Reprint. Originally published: New York : Reynal &
Hitchcock, 1946.
    Bibliography: p.
    Includes index.
    1. Drama—19th century—History and criticism.
2. Drama—20th century—History and criticism.
3. European drama—History and criticism.    I. Title.
PN1851.B4    1987        809.2        87–17601
ISBN 0–15–172042–8
ISBN 0–15–672041–8 (pbk.)

Book designed by Harry Ford

Printed in the United States of America

First edition

A  B  C  D  E

FOR MAJA

# CONTENTS

Parts of this book have already appeared in the "Kenyon Review," "Accent," "Partisan Review," and the "Rocky Mountain Review."

# ACKNOWLEDGMENTS

I WISH TO THANK GORDON K. CHALMERS AND JOHN CROWE RANSOM, through whose interest and generosity I was able to work on the book for some months while serving as a consulting editor of the *Kenyon Review*.

In a more general but no less sincere way I have also to thank friends who in conversation and correspondence gave me information or criticism by which this book has benefited: Bertolt Brecht, Berthold Viertel, Frederic Cohen, Ernst Krenek, Alrik Gustafson, Heinrich Jalowetz, Lionel Trilling, Philip Rahv, Francis Fergusson, G. Wilson Knight, and Harry Levin. Arthur Mizener read the first draft of the MS and gave me helpful criticisms. Jacques Barzun read the MS at two later stages and wisely urged more and more revisions.

I shall take this opportunity to express my gratitude to those who first gave me an adult interest in the theater: Miss Norma Wilson of the British Broadcasting Corporation; Nevill Coghill of Exeter College, Oxford, who, by theory and practice, by lecture and production, teaches what drama can be if we have knowledge, taste, humility, and undergraduate actors; John Gielgud, Thea Holme, and Esme Church, whose services to British theater are for one pupil outweighed by the personal debt incurred by acting in productions of theirs. Lastly I wish to express good will to those with whose ideas I quarrel in this book, the more so since several of them—George Beiswanger, Allardyce Nicoll, Mrs. Edith J. R. Isaacs—have shown me nothing but benevolence.

E. B.
Winter, 1946

# INTRODUCTION

## BY RICHARD GILMAN

A MAN IS WALKING ALONGSIDE ME WHOM I RECOGNIZE FROM a few photos I'd seen on dust jackets or in the papers. He's taller than I'd imagined, a lot taller than was Brecht, after whom he's vaguely (and, it occurs to me, as a sweet sort of tribute) modeled his appearance, to the extent, anyway, of wearing his hair in bangs. It's a beautiful late summer afternoon and Commercial Street, the main drag of Provincetown, is crowded with strollers, some of them going back and forth, as in a Mexican paseo. A celebrity alert is in effect, and to me he's one of the biggest celebrities of all.

As he pulls ahead of me I tell the people I'm with who he is and that I've decided to introduce myself to him. So I do. I rush forward, step in his path and say, "Mr. Bentley, it's a pleasure to see you here." Then I tell him my name and add, "I've admired your work for a long time."

Not that long, if the truth were known. This was the summer of 1962. I had been writing about the theatre only since the fall of the previous year, having been asked (on the strength of my style, one review of some new translations of Ibsen and, I suppose, a faith in my capacity to learn) to be the drama critic of *Commonweal*.

I was an unlikely choice. I hadn't formally studied drama or theatre; my only practical "experience" lay in having acted in some nondescript plays in school and summer camp. Until a few years before I hadn't even any particular interest in the stage. In this respect I resembled the great majority of my intellectual contemporaries, for whom drama, as we'd encountered it in this country, was an art distinctly inferior to fiction or poetry. We might, of course, make an exception for a Shakespeare or a Chekhov, but we saw their work more as literature than as theatre (the way it's still seen by English or Comp. Lit. departments). Besides, they survived from a past that had somehow been able to spawn a true dramatic art; that no longer existed, we thought in our airy sophistication, seeing so-called "modern" drama as pretty much a wasteland.

So what I wrote about and thought about, too, when I started to do those things professionally, were poems, stories and novels, as well as general cultural ideas. It may be too much to say that Eric Bentley's books, especially *The Playwright as Thinker*, singlehandedly made me open my eyes to the aesthetic and intellectual possibilities of the stage (seeing *Waiting for Godot* in 1954 also played a big part in my awakening), but his writing was surely among the chief propulsions I had at the time.

He was what we didn't then call a "role model," and whether or not my becoming a drama critic was an accession to the culture, I haven't any doubt that Bentley had the same kind of revelatory effect—an effect like a clearing of vision, light entering where murk had been—on many others that he had on me: students of the arts, ordinary literate persons and even, presumably, in time, hardened theatre professionals.

Is it surprising that the latter group put up the strongest resistance to letting themselves be enlightened? I didn't read *The Playwright as Thinker* when it was first published in 1946, for that was during the extreme phase of my unconcern for theatre, but some years after I did read it and was so greatly inspired that I did a little research into the book's contemporary reception.

It was scarcely a publishing "event," though it got a few respectful, and one or two laudatory, notices. The responses it mostly aroused within the theatre universe and its satellite universe of journalistic theatre coverage ranged from the scornful, shocked and appalled to, at best—maybe at worst—the condescending. If I remember rightly, the reaction in the academy wasn't much warmer.

I'm taking some liberties with the actual language of what we might call the establishment rejoinder to *The Playwright as Thinker*, but the burden of it was this: How can this man's approach be right? How can playwrights be thinkers, when everyone knows that they're *feelers*? They deal in emotions, not ideas—don't they? Well, don't they?

No they don't, not the way you mean. More than any other critic, Bentley gave to the theory and observation and potential practice of theatre in this country—he certainly gave it to me—a means of overthrowing so wrongheaded and baneful a distinction. Francis Fergusson added to the work of demolition and reconstruction, but Fergusson was much narrower.

Mind and body, thought and feeling, ideas and emotions—such crude and injurious antitheses have a long history of causing intellectual blight in America, nowhere more flagrantly and debilitatingly than in the theatre. In his quirky way, Edgar Allan Poe was the first to hint at the malady; Henry James (whose drama criticism is still too little known) refined the diagnosis and prescribed for its cure; and Bentley carried the understanding into our own time and expanded it.

The points he was making in *Playwright* and that he elaborated on in the writing that was to follow are, in essence, that drama is, or has been, an art as dense or supple or reverberant or mysterious or vigorous or disturbing as any other; that like other artists, dramatists *think* in the ways proper to their art; that thinking in art is the process by which raw, unmediated emotion—with its treacheries and deceitfulness, its inducing of blindness—is made present to the mind, placed, explored and brought into relation with both experience and imagination. Brought, in other words, into *consciousness*.

When Pirandello said that what was "new" about his plays was that in them he had "convert[ed] intellect into passion" (he might equally well have said that he had bound them together, made each an aspect of the other), he may have been overstating his originality. He had had great predecessors, but the remark, and the action it described, were accurate and startling enough in the conditions of the theatre in his day.

Intellect and passion had always been complementary, reciprocal; but the received wisdom of the theatre, even in its admiration for the "classics," persisted in seeing them as contrarieties. This is what lay behind Walter Kerr's infamous dismissal of *Godot* as a "philosophy lesson" not a play; and it's what lay behind the established opinion, widely disseminated in my youth (and still hanging on here and there), that, for example, Ibsen was all intellect or "ideas" and no passion, Strindberg all brute feeling and no mind, and Chekhov, well, the comfortable, silly notion had it, he was neither passion nor thought but some drowsy, moody, "bittersweet," wispy thing in between.

Pirandello, Ibsen, Strindberg, Chekhov, Brecht, to a lesser extent Shaw—these were the playwrights of the modern era whom Bentley's book rescued for me from obscurity, misreading, obloquy or, maybe deadliest of all, the academic. In its pages, too, I came for the first time upon their great neglected nineteenth-century ancestors (all Germans as it happened): Kleist, Grabbe, Büchner supremely; and dramatists I'd only known as novelists or poets: Zola, Yeats, Lorca. For that matter the book introduced me to theoreticians and practitioners I hadn't known or had barely heard of: Appia, Gordon Craig, Antoine, etc.; and critics: Stark Young, Shaw and Beerbohm in that aspect of their careers. I was educated by *Playwright*.

The book holds up remarkably well, and though *The Life of the Drama* may be a better book—certainly it's better organized and more assured—it can't displace *Playwright* from the center of my affections. Something else occurs to me, which is that the book seems to have served (as Bentley said *Brand* and *Peer Gynt* did for Ibsen) as the "quarry" from which he drew the materials for most of what he would later write.

Over the years I've read just about everything Bentley has published, having had to catch up with the books that appeared during my time of indifference to the theatre. I haven't always been persuaded (the book on Shaw didn't convince me that its subject had done quite what Bentley said he did), and I've sometimes found myself dissenting from some theoretical propositions—about the nature of melodrama, for instance. But I've been wonderfully instructed, made wiser about drama and the stage.

I think of that series of chronicles he published in the '50s—*In Search of Theatre, The Dramatic Event, What Is Theatre?*—his weekly criticism between covers, along with some occasional pieces. Has there ever been journalistic reviewing in America so supple, witty, deep and unaccommodating? His was the chief voice of reason in—or about, or against—the American theatre during those years; he was its tireless, learned policeman, as Shaw described one of the critic's tasks.

I start to reach for the books, which I always keep on a shelf near my desk, but then I realize that I don't need to refresh my memory, for it can readily offer me any number of exemplary pieces. I think first of "Trying to Like O'Neill," still the shrewdest estimate I know of our (alas!) best playwright. Then they start crowding up: "Doing Shakespeare Wrong"; "The China in the Bull Shop" (a witty tribute to Stark Young, a predecessor at *The New Republic*); "Craftsmanship in *Uncle Vanya*"; "The Stagecraft of Brecht"; "Tennessee Williams and New York Kazan" (a finely balanced assessment of the playwright and an equally astute evaluation of the director's virtues and delinquencies); "The Broadway Intelligentsia" (mostly the people who think playwrights are feelers); "Is Drama an Extinct Species?," with its prescient remarks on film as an aesthetic threat to the stage.

When it came time for me to write my own book, *The Making of Modern Drama*, I was dismayed to find myself with the impulse to quote Bentley on every other page. So I did a volte-face; falling deeply into the Anxiety of Influence I kept shutting him out of my mind. Although Eric wasn't old enough to be my biological father, spiritually, intellectually he was my progenitor, and if I couldn't kill him, even metaphorically, I could at least keep thrusting him away. Still, hard as I tried to do this, I remember my editor commenting mildly on the frequency with which comments of Bentley's did turn up in my text, and my replying that there simply were cases where I wasn't able to say better, or with any degree of originality, what he'd already said.

Eventually the times outdistance us all, so it isn't surprising that in recent years Bentley has dropped away from what we call "developments" in the theatre, or they've skipped beyond him. Then, too, much of his energy has gone into his own plays and performing: the critic stepping down into the arena after watching it for so long with an eye that nothing escaped. Politics have occupied him more directly than before, political reality, whose presence in drama had been one of the uncomfortable truths he had unearthed and laid before a theatrical world which would much rather not have seen it.

Though my political values aren't that far from his, I don't share all his particular positions and I sometimes find myself irritated by his diatribes. But he's earned them, and it's all right. Everything's all right. He's over seventy now and I want to tell him, and as many readers as I can garner, how much he's meant to me. With all the awards our self-congratulatory theatre is forever bestowing on itself, there ought to be one for him. But, then, he'd probably turn it down; in his high-pitched, hesitant voice he'd say something elegantly wry, maybe paraphrase Brecht to the effect that any institution that needs heroes is in bad shape. Well, we were in bad shape and we needed him.

THE PLAYWRIGHT AS THINKER

# FOREWORD

BEFORE TURNING TO THE GREAT PLAYWRIGHTS OF THE PAST—the recent past—who are the chief subject of this book, it may be advisable to bring to mind the current state of the theater. If the past often helps us to understand the present, it is the present which establishes our historical perspective. The present is every historian's point of departure. But the trouble with the present is that we know too much about it—or think we do. There is the danger of spending so much time on the point of departure that we never actually depart. We are thus bound to select infinitely fewer facts than we leave out. With the limitations of such a proceeding in mind, I propose to establish a point of departure by commenting briefly on a few current plays, some of which have been successful on Broadway, and all of which have been offered to the reading public. They are rewarding reading.

There are some, I know, who believe that plays are no more suited for silent reading than musical scores. Unlike music, however, drama is conceived and recorded in words. Since every reader of a play is a self-appointed director with a theater in his own mind, I shall assume that the well-equipped reader can experience and appraise the play in his study, and that a play which is altogether bad to read is altogether a bad play. Good literature may be bad drama. That is obvious. But does the converse hold? Can good drama be bad literature? This is a question to bear in mind throughout this book; we shall take it up again later.

Here I shall prepare the ground to the extent of requesting a little skepticism about accepted views and unacknowledged assumptions. Of these none should be more suspect than the idea that great drama need not be great literature. Perhaps when we make such an assumption we are dimly remembering some such argument as Charles Lamb's, when he contended that Shakespeare was too big—spiritually speaking—for the stage. It would follow that drama of the right size must be something spiritually smaller. From this conclusion it is but a step to the equation of good drama and bad literature, good literature and bad drama. The literary man begins to use the term "theatrical" as a reproach; the man of the theater learns to despise the "literary."

It is perhaps curious that the "nonliterary" and thoroughly theatrical plays which succeed on Broadway or in the West End of London are invariably given to the public in book form as well. The printed play may of course be offered partly as a memento of an amusing evening, like those illustrated souvenirs which the ushers thrust at one in the lobby. But, however explained or explained away, the Broadway play is supposed to be interesting in print and is read in the provinces by many who will never see it staged. In short, the fact that a play is printed is sufficient warrant for judging it as literate—which is only to say again that it is a form of art presented in words. Might we not also assume that the printed play is a fair challenge to a dramatic critic? It prevents him from airing his usually obtrusive knowledge of actors, electricians, designers, directors, producers, and box-office managers. The only man now to be praised or blamed is the one who on Broadway is happily protected or unhappily buried by all these: the playwright.

This book is about the playwright, the forgotten man of the modern stage. Forgotten? I shall be told that he is so far from forgotten that he occupies a recognized place in an industrial hierarchy. Here we must distinguish between imaginative playwrights and those committees of businessmen and script manufacturers who put together Broadway and Hollywood shows on their intellectual assembly lines. In other words we must distinguish between art and commodity in the theater. This book is concerned with art. But it can be admitted at the outset that the relation of art to commodity is seldom simple and that, particularly in the theater, art has seldom or never flourished in absolute independence of commodity. Indeed, it is well known that dramatic art has most often had to exist in the commodity theater or not at all. If by now the public is so specialized in different directions, so stratified and diversified, that independent art theaters are possible and desirable, this is a new and unprecedented situation. Let us postpone the analysis of it until after we have perused the modern stage more thoroughly. What we should acknowledge from the start is that the commodity theater constitutes—on the most modest estimate—a tremendous pressure upon the drama as a whole. Perhaps at some periods of history this pressure can be regarded as on the whole salutary. It may provide a firm convention, a necessary habitat for the playwright to operate in. But circumstances alter cases. The pressure of commercial theater may also become a tyranny. In that event the artist can know but one relationship to it: the relationship of antagonism. In such an era the playwright is either a rebel and an artist or a yes man and a hack.

I am afraid that the present is such an era. The nature of modern drama, therefore, is comprehensible only to those who can see the sharp difference between modern and earlier cultures. One example will suffice. Until the modern period great drama has possessed not only those deeper and subtler qualities which reveal themselves to the careful analyst and which constitute its greatness, it has also possessed more generally available qualities. It has appealed on different levels. It has appealed to the connoisseur *and* the amateur, the critic *and* the public. It has functioned as mere entertainment for some and as the highest art for others. A great deal of modern art, however, including drama, does not possess this double appeal. It appeals only to those who can discern high art, just as modern entertainment frequently appeals only to those who are satisfied with mere entertainment. Scandalized, our spiritual doctors call on the entertainers to be artistic or on the artists to be entertaining. The one class is censured for its "low-browism," the other for its "high-browism." Whatever the proposed solution, wherever the blame is to be placed, the facts themselves are inexorable. A peculiar, problematic, and perhaps revolutionary situation exists. Art and commodity have become direct antagonists.

What are the characteristic products of this situation? Who are the characteristic playwrights of today?

Perhaps Mr. Oscar Hammerstein is a fair specimen. His work *Oklahoma!* (the exclamation mark is his own) has been "hailed" as establishing a new genre, praised in at least one literary quarterly, awarded a Pulitzer Prize by special dispensation, and compared, not unfavorably, with *The Magic Flute*. It was the outstanding theatrical success of the war period; and it is entirely representative of current trends. In fact, it belongs with the "new Americanism" in being folksy and excessively, ostentatiously wholesome; also in being trite, cocksure, sentimental, and vacuous. On the stage it is decked out in gay color and from time to time enlivened by tricky dancing. But in all drama (I do not say in all *theater,* for ballet and opera are theater) color and dancing are only embellishments; in this case they are the embellishment of a scarecrow.

It may be beside the point to apply any critical criteria. After seeing *Oklahoma!* on the stage I read it in an anthology edited by Bennett Cerf and Van H. Cartmell, who in their foreword endorse Mr. Lee Shubert's remark that "the box office never lies." They continue as follows: "It is fashionable to poke fun at public taste, and to hold that no really good play can be a financial success. The record, spread out on the following pages, does not support such a theory." Spread out on the following pages are some of the worst plays I have ever read, such as *East Lynne, Rip Van Winkle,* and *The Bat.* Of their three most recent choices—*Life with Father, Arsenic and Old Lace,* and *Oklahoma!*—the editors write: "That they are, from any viewpoint, the soundest and most thoroughly representative of their type is an encouraging augury to lovers of the theater." Consequently, "American playwrights and American audiences can face the future with high hopes and light hearts." Has any voice more authentically Philistine been heard since that of the Victorian quoted by Matthew Arnold as praying that "our unrivalled happiness may last"? With light hearts and heavy purses the one-hundred-per-cent American playwrights and the one-hundred-per-cent American audiences are to enjoy the best of all possible theaters. The box office never lies, and when asked how good these three plays were it replied with aplomb: two million dollars apiece.

To move from Mr. Hammerstein to Mr. S. J. Perelman and Mr. Ogden Nash is to move one rung up the cultural ladder. But only one. If *Oklahoma!* is Broadway's idea of folk art, such a work as *One Touch of Venus* is Broadway's idea of sophistica-

tion. If the word "folksy" connotes the adulteration of the folk
spirit, does not our current understanding of "sophistication"
imply an adulteration of the comic spirit? Is not the sophistication of *One Touch of Venus* the cleverness of the half-educated?
Is it not crudity ill-concealed by quasi refinement? Is it not a
guffaw suppressed to a snigger? *One Touch of Venus,* as the
title alluringly hints, deals with sex, or rather, to retain the
original innuendo, it touches on sex, and nothing reveals its
character more than the way it fingers Venus without coming to grips with her. Nothing in the realm of humor is
more acceptable than bawdry; nothing to my mind is less acceptable than the Broadway sophistication which pleases old
ladies by avoiding outspokenness and at the same time titillates
young ladies by insinuation. We may find it funny to hear a
woman sing:

> Venus found she was a goddess
> In a world controlled by gods
> So she opened up her bodice
> And equalized the odds.

But the very next stanza tells us:

> Look what Beatrice did to Dante,
> What DuBarry did to France;
> Venus showed them that the pantie
> Is mightier than the pants.

And after that there are forty more lines of it. As to Mr. Perelman's prose, it consists of humor of this order:

> RODNEY. You're practically naked! I can see your—*form!*
> VENUS. Don't you like my—form?

The idea is to mention sex as often as possible because sex is
very funny, and not to call anything by its name because that
wouldn't be very nice. Perelman, Nash, and their audiences are

nothing if not knowing. Why, they even know who Dante and Beatrice were!

This brings me to a second point about *One Touch of Venus* —the nature of its burlesque. Burlesque or parody may be aimed at the most august object, but surely it must imply an understanding of that object. Unhappily we get the impression that Perelman and Nash and the kind of audience they address do not. The humor of

> Giotto and Watteau
> Were obviously blotto. . . .
> Cézanne and Modigliani
> De-glamorized the human fanny

betrays, not quite intentionally perhaps, the hostility to culture which is a leading theme, overtly or not, of New York wit. The audience recalls having heard those queer French and Italian names in college, and how silly they sound when shown up by artists whom the veracious box office approves! The burlesque humor of Perelman and Nash is polysyllabic and allusive in form; its gist, its ground base, is a bronx cheer to culture.

On the next rung of the ladder we find plays in which some attention is paid to certain perennial tasks of the drama, such as telling the truth about people's lives and problems. My specimen is a play which has been called "the most important event in our native American drama in twenty years"—*Anna Lucasta*, by "an extremely successful writer in Hollywood," Philip Yordan. Mr. Yordan doesn't always tell the truth but he does take a look at people and their problems. A Harlem family plans to get the money of a young Negro just arrived from the South by marrying him off to one of their number who has hitherto been a prostitute. Being a "romantic" whore, she falls in love with the boy in earnest. The wedding day arrives, but before nightfall the father has revealed the whole story of Anna to the boy's family. In despair Anna returns to her whoring without waiting to consult her bridegroom. A tragic ending is indicated. But Mr. Yordan learned all about endings in Hollywood. The public, which after all is barely one remove from the box office, demands happy ones. Clearly the hero of the play should be "romantic" too. He must still want to marry Anna in spite of everything, and her attempts at suicide must fail. The plays ends on the customary note of hope.

It would be no use telling Mr. Yordan it won't do. He knows it will. He knows the truth from the one who never lies. A critic called the play "a combination of *Anna Christie* and *You Can't Take It with You.*" And what a combination that is! All the pleasures of the sordid with no morbid, mournful, "modernistic," conclusion. And can Mr. Yordan write slick dialogue? A machine couldn't do it better. And does Mr. Yordan love the Negro people? His original choice was a Polish-American milieu but, says the jacket, "eventually he was persuaded to shift the locale to Harlem." And can Mr. Yordan see the importance of persuasion? Negroes are lovable. They're nasty too, and you can put coarser words in their mouths than Broadway would otherwise accept. And they're always marrying prostitutes. Oh yes, Mr. Yordan knows the truth.

On the next rung is the late Franz Werfel. He knows more about life than Mr. Yordan and probably wouldn't tell so many deliberate lies about it; his specialty is not deceiving others but deceiving himself. Mr. Werfel is therefore the first author so far mentioned who might conceivably be considered high-brow. By some he is still considered an important artist. At least he is one of the few contemporary writers of whom professors of German have heard. A long time ago he wrote a play about a monster, a play which, being unrealistic, invited high-brow attention and settings by the best designers. Mr. Werfel was once known for such lyrics as the one that opens: "My only wish is to be related to Thee, O Man!" Today he is known for *Song of Bernadette, Embezzled Heaven,* and a philosophical work in which Mr.

Werfel depicts himself as uncomfortably suspended *Between Heaven and Earth.*

The Werfel play of the times is *Jacobowsky and the Colonel,* adapted to Broadway by S. N. Behrman, who is obviously cut out for the job, and later published in a professional translation which shows that Mr. Werfel is no better than Mr. Behrman. The printed play adds to the Broadway version a symbolic interpolation of St. Francis and the Wandering Jew, two gentlemen whom Mr. Werfel loves to pose as. Adapted or restored, acted or printed, it is a dreadful play. It is that most irritating of artistic phenomena: an utterly banal and sentimental piece that parades its pretensions to art in successive bursts of artiness. Only the subtitle—Comedy of a Tragedy—is apt, for one is embarrassed throughout by all this fooling and footling in the midst of death. I never would have thought—till I witnessed it— that an audience could so enjoy the fall of France.

On the next rung—if I may blaspheme against the box office —I would like to specify two writers whose most recent works have either failed on Broadway or have not appeared there at all: William Saroyan and. J. B. Priestley. For all the evident differences between them, these two playwrights are fundamentally of the same caliber. Equally energetic, talented, missionary, they are faced by the same dilemmas, the dilemmas of the writer who is gifted but not supremely gifted, the man who, being a small artist, knows he might be a great entertainer, the man whose seriousness is all too easily compromised by his knowledge that he will reach a broader public if he is not *too* serious.

Mr. Saroyan tries to sell his work by direct self-advertisement and by disclaiming high intentions. *"Get Away Old Man,"* he writes, "is an American play and nothing else. It was conceived, written, and produced solely to entertain." It closed after thirteen nights on Broadway.

In presenting to the American public four recent plays, none of which Broadway has produced, J. B. Priestley takes the opposite line of protesting that "New York deliberately prefers to produce what is left of our [*i.e.* British] drawing-room stuff instead of bolder and more original work." Obviously both Mr. Saroyan and Mr. Priestley wish to be at once entertaining and artistic, and nothing could be more laudable if, in their desire to please everybody, they were not ignoring the cultural stratification of modern society—the rungs of our ladder. This is no mere error in their publicity. It is a mistake that vitiates most of their work. If a certain earnestness prevents them from stepping down to the lowest rungs of the ladder, a fear of minority culture, a yearning to be taken to the bosom of the public, limits their thinking and their sensibility. Occasionally, as in the movie *The Human Comedy,* Saroyan does step down to the lowest rungs. And when he hops back into place he is bewildered and unsure: his latest play even has a bitter ending! All Saroyan's work is soft inside, sentimental at the center, because he is in his work a moral and aesthetic appeaser. Choices are refused. Distinctions are obliterated. All substance melts into the ocean of sentiment. "The whole world's gone mad," says the protagonist in *Get Away Old Man,* "and no man knows who is innocent or guilty." What a staggering lie! To know *nothing,* according to Saroyan, is to forgive everything.

Mr. Priestley finds what may be the only exit into speculation that is open to a certain class of mind: occultism. In the early thirties he wrote phony plays about eternal recurrence as expounded by the English magician J. W. Dunne. Today he offers us a play about "an extrasensory or second-sight relationship" and three socio-political plays calculated to make us feel cheerfully "progressive." Anyone interested in the drama of ideas should compare them with Bernard Shaw's plays. In Shaw ideas flash, roar, and reach the target in one long fascinating battle fought with the most efficient ordnance from the poison phial to the bomb. In Priestley they fizz and flop like damp fireworks.

The inadequacy is at once imaginative, intellectual, and, probably, moral.

Mr. Saroyan and Mr. Priestley are two prime instances in the dramatic world of "high-brows" trying to be "low-brows" without losing caste. Hence their exaggerated hominess, their forced simplicity, their overdone patriotism and insistent local color, their chronic fear of the esoteric. It seems to me that the result of their attempt to speak to everybody on everybody's behalf is that they speak to the lower-middle classes (socially *and* culturally speaking) and that they express a lower-middle-class mentality.

Now in ascending as high as Mr. Saroyan and Mr. Priestley we are already too high for Broadway. That is perhaps the main point I want to make about the current condition of the theater. Even if my brief appraisals are not all acceptable, I hope these notes on commercial theater have made it clear what kinds of playwright this book is *not* about. It is not about playwrights who could never have risen above the commercial theater. It is not about playwrights whom the commercial theater has spoiled. Nor is it about playwrights whose sole merit is their rejection of commercial theater. It is about great playwrights and about playwrights who—if they are not great—are highly original. For there is another sort of artist who is important besides the great artist who finds and fulfills. That is the original artist who seeks and suggests. This kind of artist is of special importance in a revolutionary period. "In our time," said Ibsen, "every new creative work has the task of shifting the boundary stakes."

The fact, then, that many well-known contemporary playwrights are not discussed in this book is not necessarily an aspersion on their work. My account of modern drama limits itself—for the sake of clarity and simplicity—to certain key figures. Sometimes when there was no obvious key figure I realize that another name would have done as well as the one I chose.

There are three American playwrights in particular whom I would like to have said more about: Eugene O'Neill, Clifford Odets, and Thornton Wilder. One reason I did not say much about them is that all of them are expected to bring out "major" work early in the new postwar period. Since I regard the earlier work of all of them as chiefly *promising,* rather than great, I propose to wait for the new work before discussing them at length.

The fact that I put even O'Neill in the class of the promising, and not in the class of Aeschylus where his friends put him, will suggest another reason why many well-known playwrights are not discussed in this book: it is that I do not admire them very much. We have been fooling ourselves into believing that the period 1920-1940 was a great period of drama, particularly of American drama. It was not. The period has its important experiments and its important achievements; but the experiments are only notorious and the achievements still almost unknown. The drama that our best actors lent their charm to and that critics and anthologists lent their support to was—as I think we shall soon be discovering—much overrated. I do not refer only to reputations of the moment like Hammerstein and Yordan, nor only to slicksters troubled with immortal longings like Werfel and Priestley and Saroyan. I refer to some of the most serious of contemporary playwrights—certainly the most "high-brow" that Broadway can offer—such as Elmer Rice and Maxwell Anderson. *The Adding Machine* and *Street Scene,* which Mr. Rice wrote in the twenties, showed a brilliant talent; but the talent—and this is the story so often in American theater—had no soil to grow in and consequently never grew. Mr. Anderson is also brilliant. He has the gifts of a first-rate melodramatist; but he wants to be all this and Shakespeare too. How good *Winterset* would be without the poetry and the would-be "tragic" significance! . . . To write about playwrights like these is to write about the crippling effects of a sick theatrical culture on honest talent.

That is why I shall *not* write about them. For this is not a book about the corrupting forces which turn artists into willing slaves or imagined Shakespeares. It is about those who were not corrupted.

I pick on the American theater because I am writing in America. I am under no illusion that things were at all times better elsewhere. Soviet Russia has had the liveliest popular theaters in the world but latterly the standard of her plays has seemed to be falling steadily to the Broadway level. Nazi Germany maintained the theatrical organizations of Weimar Germany, or substituted new ones, but had to rely on nineteenth-century drama for productions of any quality. Scandinavia, like America, turned out competent plays but little that was original and nothing to approximate Ibsen or Strindberg. After the deaths of Garcia Lorca and Pirandello, Spain and Italy had to be content with the histrionics of Franco and Mussolini. France had her experimental theater but, already before 1940, it seemed to be languishing. The two art theaters of Dublin have had, perhaps, a smoother history than other such ventures, yet Sean O'Casey was turned down and Denis Johnston, greeted as O'Casey's successor ten years ago, has apparently written nothing recently. As to Britain, drama is there reduced to the status of opera: all the best energy goes into revivals of classics. There seem to be only two dramatists of consequence in England: O'Casey who is not improving and Bernard Shaw who is not getting any younger. Such is the record down through the thirties.

It is not a very good record. But then, as Bernard Shaw once told his biographer, "The theater is *always* at a low ebb." The modern high drama, in which my readers and I are interested, exists—if at all—in the nooks and crannies of a graveyard called the show business. It feeds—if at all—necrophilously upon the body of the theatrical monster. It succeeds—if at all—by flukes and irrelevances (by sexiness, by violence, by winning the patronage of a star actor). The present situation differs from that of, say, twenty years ago chiefly in the comparative fewness of the flukes. Add to all this the annihilation of good European theater by the Nazis, the increasing stress on sentimental propaganda in Russia, the apparent lack of important younger dramatists in all countries; add above all that time marches on, and that—in the economic sphere—the pressure of the big business upon the small business increases. High theater is a very small business. It is constantly bought out by Hollywood and Broadway, which need its talents for their own very different commodities. Hence the pilgrim's progress—or was it a Gadarene stampede?—from *Waiting for Lefty* to *None But the Lonely Heart*. If Lefty is in Hollywood growing yearly more spiritual and more wealthy we may have to wait a long time yet.

Some ebbs are lower than others. The past few years have seen the almost total extinction of artistic drama in the commodity theater. This is "no time for comedy"—or for tragedy either. Can we speak as confidently of a coming dramatic renascence after this war as our fathers did after the last war? The last war was preceded by Ibsen and Strindberg; the postwar generation forged ahead on *their* steam. Between the generations such a man as Max Reinhardt was (for all his foibles) an essential link. This time the links, or most of them, have been broken. One might be tempted to say that the theater at present fulfills only one precondition of renascence: it is dead.

Would this be an overstatement? We need not prejudge the issue. And even if the theater *is* dead, we can comfort ourselves with the thought that only when a man is dead can we review his career with any semblance of detachment and comprehensiveness: a lull in the history of drama is a good time to review the situation. We can now look back upon a period—the later nineteenth century and the earlier twentieth—when high drama somehow managed to make its presence felt. Much of the drama that is known as Modern can now be seen in perspective and at a distance. To our fathers, Ibsenism was new and, whether shocking or exhilarating, seemed to them more the beginning of something than the end of something. To us the birth of Ibsenism, and of Expressionism, too, was a process at which we did not assist. The "new spirit in the theater" as advertised twenty years ago is already extinct, the "theater of tomorrow" as advertised by adventurous stage-designers is already the theater of yesterday, an aspect of the Bohemian twenties. Even the Federal Theater belongs to a Roosevelt Era that already seems far away.

Nevertheless history does not so easily close its doors. Nothing with life in it is easily shut out. Great artists live on by their greatness when they can not survive by some more negotiable coin. Many who are not supremely great live on by the continued fruitfulness of their work. Some great modern dramatists have scarcely yet begun to fructify: Strindberg is one of these. Others have been heeded only where they collided with our grandparents' ethics: of these Ibsen is the chief. Another —Bernard Shaw—we have often heard from but seldom listened to. Yet another—Richard Wagner—we have disputed over in musical and political argumentations without heeding what Nietzsche long ago told us: that Wagner was first and foremost a man of the theater.

Looking back over the whole long span of drama since 1850, a few such figures as the above detach themselves from the crowds with whom they mingled. We would no longer care to discuss Ibsen *and Björnson* or Shaw *and Galsworthy*. We would no longer care to have a Henry Arthur Jones lecture us on the revival of the theater at the hands of Henry Arthur Jones. (Some of my readers, without being the worse for it, will not even know who Henry Arthur Jones was.) If a William Archer made the anti-Ibsenites sound old-fashioned, what could be more so now than Archer's championing of Pinero? Whoever wishes to share the less exhilarating sensations of an Egyptologist rifling a tomb should read the drama books of forty, thirty, even twenty years ago. Which is a chastening thought for the writer on drama today.

Yet we must use the perspective of our own point in time for what it is worth. What follows is an attempt to do so, an attempt motivated by a deep concern with dramatic art and its fate in our civilization, by a feeling that something is wrong which might—at least partly—be put right. There would of course be nothing new in urging that the money-changers should be driven out of our temples with whips. What I shall urge is that the temples be left to the money-changers to wallow in; the true faith must survive—if at all—elsewhere. The hope of the theater—I shall maintain—lies outside the commercial theater altogether. Not that we can forget the money-changers. They are fat and influential. They have the scribes and Pharisees on their side: in plain words the scholars and critics of the theater —or at least a high proportion of them—have sold themselves to the managers. The academicians are determined to be unacademic.

So much the worse for them. If it is academic to see plays in their concrete context of thinking, feeling, and doing, rather than in the context of footlights and box offices, then there is much to be said for academicism. I should be happy to oppose the antiacademicism of even the best of the regular theater critics, George Jean Nathan, who holds that a good play is not a thing that can profitably be examined in detail and that criticism of great drama is therefore fruitless or impossible. My own conviction is that any good thing is a *very* good thing and that any good work of art can bear the closest scrutiny. The better, the closer. The most revolutionary tenet to be advanced in this book is this: the drama can be taken seriously. "A play," as Oscar Wilde said, "is as personal and individual a form of self-expression as a poem or a picture." It follows that the playwrights must have a self to express. Our commercial playwrights have none. They are as nearly as possible nobody. The imaginative playwright is somebody.

If, then, we seek out the mind and art—the real identity—of our imaginative modern playwrights, we shall at the close be in a better position to confirm, reject, or qualify our impression that the theater is dead.

A play Is a slice of life artistically put on the boards.

JEAN JULLIEN

This trompe-l'oeil [i.e. the "slice of life"] which is doubtless suitable to the cinema is the exact opposite of dramatic art.

GUILLAUME APOLLINAIRE

# 1. THE TWO TRADITIONS

# OF MODERN DRAMA

## I

A COMMUNIST CRITIC HAS ARGUED THAT THE SEARCH FOR new forms which has taken place in all branches of the arts during the past hundred years is a vain attempt to arrest the decline of a culture. This argument might be acceptable if the critic did not go on to imply that all would be well if artists merely waited for a socialist revolution, after which one correct form—Socialist Realism—would establish itself to the exclusion of all others. Experimentalism in the arts always reflects historical conditions, always indicates profound dissatisfaction with established modes, always is a groping toward a new age. Modernist experiment is no longer so young that it has nothing but freaks and abortions to show. In poetry, in the novel, in painting and music and architecture, a distinctively modern style has for some time now had its very considerable achievements, as the names of Rilke and Joyce and Picasso and Schoenberg and Gropius testify.

I would tend, though not so violently as our communist critic, to pooh-pooh the idea that any of the experimental modes of drama is the one mode of the future. Discovering *the new* anything is the business of fashionmongers, and we had better leave it to them. On the other hand if we are to make sense of modern drama we must try to evaluate some of the various quests after new form. *"Materia appetit formam ut virum femina,"* our medieval forefathers believed, "material seeks a form as woman seeks man." Each time a work is written a proper form has to be found. Form is a fluid but not an arbitrary thing. It corresponds to the mind of the artist, which in turn is in part molded by place and time. Although, therefore, an age may bring forth many forms, all of which represent its nature as well as the nature of the individual poet, there may well be one or two particular forms which are predominant. Thus we think of the classical tragedy as profoundly characteristic of Louis XIV's France. Thus we classify a whole era as Classical—and another as Romantic. In such categories there is danger of distortion in the beginning and meaninglessness in the end. There is never more meaning in such terms as Romantic and Classical than the critic can distill from the concrete facts and experiences that underlie them. Having all this in mind, I am going to suggest that the dominant mode of the nineteenth century—perhaps even of the twentieth—is naturalism, and that this is important in interpreting modern drama.

What is it we notice if we pick up a modern play after reading Shakespeare or the Greeks? Nine times out of ten it is the *dryness*—I do not mean the *dullness,* for none of the dramatists to be described in this book is dull, but the sheer modesty of the language, the sheer lack of winged words, even of eloquence. Such a play as Karel Capek's *R.U.R.,* Mr. Kenneth Burke acutely comments, is little more than a scenario for Shakespeare. And *R.U.R.* is not a Naturalistic play, is not, so to say, an experiment in dryness. It is Expressionist. It aims at liberating the theater from the prosaic deliberateness of Naturalism. The failure of Expressionism to do this, the failure of so many attempts to restore poetic drama, is the most convincing evidence of the triumph of naturalism.

So much is obvious. What is not so obvious is that the triumph of naturalism is a positive achievement. Mr. Burke's comment conveys the stock attitude of the literary world: naturalism is seen as a deficiency because only the things it does not do are noted. Many people think of naturalism as necessarily a desiccating and trivializing influence. They have in mind such things as externality, lack of selectivity, or dirty-mindedness. But that is only the negative side. On the positive side we should recognize that naturalism has presented the facts of man's life and environment in a quite new and rich explicitness. It signifies the conquest of a great area of human experience previously ignored, understressed, if not altogether taboo in art. Its justification lies both in the permanent widening of our horizons and in the masterpieces of a Tolstoy, a Dostoevski, or a Proust. Naturalism was not the result of an itch for the new at all costs. It was the result—or concomitant—of the urbanization and mechanization of life, which, however it is appraised, cannot be ignored. It was the result—or concomitant—of democratic reformism, of the new concern with the condition of the people. It was the result—or concomitant—of the rise of the physical sciences which aimed at controlling nature by knowing its processes. The destined receptacle for naturalism was the novel, which had been shaped by the same forces. The novel, one might almost say, is *per se* naturalistic, and even the best "non-naturalistic" novelists, such as Franz Kafka, are virtuosi of the naturalistic manner. The novel is also the dominant literary genre of latter days and its influence is therefore exercised upon all other genres. By this time naturalism is so much the air we breathe that in popular usage "style" now means "non-naturalistic style," while "naturalistic style" is—well, just "natural."

What is labeled Naturalism in the narrow sense of belonging to a literary movement around 1880 is a species of the genus we have been discussing. (Throughout this book the genus is written with a small, the species with a large *n*.) Naturalism as a genus embraces a much larger body of writing in which the natural world is candidly presented. Admittedly such a definition—if it can be called a definition—will infuriate the logical reader. The trouble with literary terms is that in proportion as they become impressive they become useless, in proportion as they become exact they become inapplicable. A literary term is a shifty creature. It changes color while you watch it. The only rule must be to watch it very carefully. It must not be imagined, for example, that the word naturalism could ever be a summary of a good writer's work. The term will not include one hundred per cent of his art, nor will his art include one hundred per cent of the meanings of naturalism. Terms like these can obviously be abused. A textbook can construct an edifice of verbiage that has little relation to literary experience. On the other hand, such terms are useful enough to those who know their limitations. The rule here is to use them only where they clarify more than they mystify. The definitions are rough. But we have in our own artistic experience and knowledge a court of appeal.

If this is understood there need be no grumbling at the fact that we must frame our descriptions of naturalism roughly and tentatively. *The candid presentation of the natural world* is the first formulation we have hit upon. From Defoe to Faulkner and Hemingway we can observe the kind of presentation referred to. It is exact and detailed. And this leads us to a second fact. The attempt to be closer to the actual texture of daily living produces its own technique and manner. Thus we have, for example, the particular technique known as "the stream of consciousness" in the last chapter of *Ulysses*. In general there is a turning from all forms of elevated discourse to simple and colloquial discourse. When we have seen the leading intention of naturalism and its consequent need of special techniques, we may then choose to incorporate both within a larger historical or philosophical framework—which will be that of some form of modern scientific empiricism.

An increasing closeness to objective facts; special techniques for their reproduction; an empiricist outlook—these are naturalism. The historian will observe that there are naturalistic elements in the literature of all periods, but it is particularly since the eighteenth century that the world about us, man-made and God-made, has been the absorbing interest of imaginative writers. Dr. Johnson still regarded the numbering of the streaks of the tulip as unpoetic. He was denounced for this by a school of writers, frequently but not very helpfully represented as anti-naturalistic, the Romanticists. The naturalistic and super- and preternaturalistic coexisted in the Romanticists in undifferentiated union. A more one-sided development came around the middle of the nineteenth century with the so-called Realists, who weighted the scales in favor of the dull and prosaic. This Realism is one species of whàt we are calling naturalism. Among playwrights the term is usually applied to the French well-made plays and thesis plays of the period between 1850 and 1880. The Naturalism of the textbooks was a further development of Realism and a rebellion against Realism. It conforms well enough with our descriptions since its intention is certainly a candid account of the world about us; it has a special technique —to present a slice of life instead of a carefully constructed plot —a technique, that is, which keeps us close to the raw flesh of life itself; and it adopts a particular form of empiricism—a philosophy of scientific determinism based on the "facts" of heredity and environment.

This special form of Naturalism claims forebears in Balzac, Flaubert, and the brothers Goncourt, as well as in scientific writers and in the social conditions of the time. Its apostle was

Emile Zola who, if he was not the greatest, was yet among the most influential of modern writers—as the new American tradition from Dreiser to Farrell may serve to remind us. Zola fathered theatrical Naturalism by adapting his *Thérèse Raquin* to the stage in 1873 and writing a prefatorial manifesto to go with it. The play was successful neither artistically nor commercially, but the opinions of a great seminal mind remained. Since Zola's words apply, *mutatis mutandis,* to the trend of the drama in Europe generally, they may be cited at some length:

> . . . I am absolutely convinced that we shall next see the Naturalist movement imposed on the theater and bringing to it the power of reality, the new life of modern art.
>
> . . . The drama dies unless it is rejuvenated by new life. We must put new blood into this corpse. They say that the operetta and the fairy play have killed the drama. That is false. The drama is dying its own fine death. It is dying of extravagances, lies, and platitudes.
>
> . . . I defy the last of the Romanticists to put upon the stage a heroic drama; at the sight of all the paraphernalia of armor, secret doors, poisoned wines and the rest, the audience would only shrug its shoulders. And melodrama, that middle-class offspring of the romantic drama, is in the hearts of the people more dead that its predecessor; its false sentiment, its complication of stolen children and discovered documents have finally rendered it despicable, so that any attempt to revive it proves abortive. The great works of 1830 will always remain advance-guard works, landmarks in a literary epoch, superb efforts which laid low the scaffoldings of the classics. But now that everything is torn down and swords and capes rendered useless, it is time to base our works on truth . . .
>
> . . . the experimental and scientific spirit of the

century will enter the domain of the drama, and in
this lies the only possible salvation of the drama . . .
we must look to the future and the future will have to
do with the human problem studied in the framework
of reality. The drama will either die or become modern and realistic.

These words bore fruit in the following decade when Henry
Becque wrote his two great plays, when Ibsen's *Ghosts* made
him a European figure, when André Antoine founded the
Théâtre Libre expressly for the production of Naturalist plays.
This is the beginning of a "modern movement" in the drama.

The success of the new theater movement of the nineties was
the success of Naturalism. The little theaters in European capi-
tals where the new plays were shown nearly all came into existence for the production of Naturalistic plays. The drama became
a fighting issue. The challenging ideas of the young were in these
plays thrust in the faces of the old. The three great areas of
taboo in middle-class culture—sex, religion, and economics—
were all displayed rather freely on the stage. There were battles
with the censor or the public about plays by Hauptmann, Shaw,
Wedekind, Brieux, and the rest. The prim and respectable
Ibsen was called crazy, cranky, nasty, stupid, consistently dirty,
deplorably dull. The *London Daily Telegraph* printed an article describing *Ghosts* as "this mass of vulgarity, egotism,
coarseness, and absurdity" and an editorial further describing
it as "an open drain, a loathsome sore unbandaged, a dirty act
done publicly, a lazar house with all its doors and windows
open." Like all powerful literary movements, Naturalism was
not chiefly aesthetic but ethical. Like all ethical movements, it
was somewhat right and enormously self-righteous. Zola announced with characteristic magniloquence: *"Dans l'enfante-
ment continu de l'humanité, nous en sommes à l'accouchement
du vrai."* Writing of his own Naturalism, Bernard Shaw said:
". . . what we wanted as the basis of our plays and novels was

not romance but a really scientific natural history. Scientific natural history is not compatible with taboo; and as everything connected with sex was tabooed, I felt the need for mentioning the forbidden subjects, not only because of their own importance, but for the sake of destroying taboo by giving it the most violent possible shocks." The idea that the "scientific truth" about humanity has at last been learned is so premature that one understands how a Zola or a Shaw can be quickly dismissed by those who have heard them only in this vein. But one should not overlook what lay behind the ebulliency of these Naturalists. It is the ebulliency of men who have found something. Perhaps they have not found what they think they have found. Discoverers nearly always think they have found *the* truth. What they have actually found is at best *a* truth, *a* formula, *a* new and fruitful approach. Zola had found the kind of truth that was to fascinate an era, he had found a formula for the modern novel and the modern play, he had found the modern approach.

Without Naturalism there would not only be no Zola and no Becque, there would be no Shaw, no Chekhov, no Schnitzler, no O'Casey, no Odets. The later Ibsen, as we shall see, though in form naturalistic, was no out-and-out Naturalist. Yet even he was not immune from the pressure of the dominant mode. It was this pressure that turned him away from poetic drama— which we may well regret. Yet it was this pressure too that gave us the subtle quasi naturalism, the disguised symbolism of the last great plays. Even Strindberg, none of whose work is Naturalistic in the popular sense of drably photographic, was made by Naturalism. From the promptings of his own mind, and later from Zola and the brothers Goncourt, he learned a thoroughly Naturalistic approach. The great preface to his play *Miss Julia* presents the early Naturalistic view of staging in words that would have warmed the heart of the Duke of Saxe-Meiningen and the pioneers of the Naturalistic stage. Even Strindberg's dream plays depend to a great extent on Naturalistic factuality and detail. That is what distinguishes them from the abstract plays of the German Expressionists. Ibsen and Strindberg are good illustrations of the fact that Zolaist Naturalism may be very important in the work of writers who are on the whole not Naturalists. To search out all the Naturalism in modern drama we would have to look almost everywhere.

## II

Although naturalism has long been the dominant mode of modern drama, there are two inventions which could—and, according to many authorities, should—put an end to naturalism in the theater. One is the cinema. The other is the electric lamp.

Just as the abstract painter argues that photography removed the need for representational painting by doing the job much better, so, it is argued, cinematography removes the need for naturalistic theater. Now about the same time as the cinematograph came into use—around 1900—the electric lamp began to replace the gas lamp on the stage. It revolutionized the theatrical medium. It created magical new worlds. At the same time as the stage was outdone by the movies in the representation of objects, it received, by way of compensation, a new power over the non-naturalistic realm through electricity. Playwrights, accordingly, should—so the argument is clinched—unlearn naturalism, revive poetic drama, or make new styles for the new settings.

Since it is clear that physical changes in the theater and in society have many times in the past modified and even revolutionized the art of drama, it is fair to give these two recent inventions our best attention. First, the cinema. What effect does it have on the art of drama in general? And does it, in particular, render stage naturalism obsolete?

When the nineteenth-century invention of the cinematograph led to the twentieth-century invention of the cinema there arose a new art, not to mention a new business, which in many respects could carry out the aims of certain types of dramatic performance much more fully than the theater. Some felt from the beginning that the motion picture would be the dramatic art of the twentieth century, and this opinion was not hard to support even in the days of the silent screen. Before the talkies were a decade old, even the kind of people who had earlier despised the screen began to see in it the successor to the living actor. In this belief, for example, Mr. Clifford Odets left Broadway for Hollywood: the drama was a thing of the past, the future belonged to the motion picture. A more subtle analysis of the relation of stage and screen was given by the distinguished head of the Yale Drama School, Professor Allardyce Nicoll, in his interesting and informative book *Film and Theatre*. He tries to find a place for both stage and screen by assigning to each its proper style. The style of the screen is naturalism, he says, the theater should accordingly be non-naturalistic. The argument is worth quoting at length:

> If we seek for and desire a theater which shall possess qualities likely to live over generations, unquestionably we must decide that the naturalistic play, made popular towards the close of the nineteenth century and still remaining in our midst, is not calculated to fulfill our highest wishes.
>
> Of much greater importance, even, is the question of the position this naturalistic play occupies in its relations to the cinema. At the moment it still retains its popularity, but, we may ask, because of cinematic competition, is it not likely to fail gradually in its immediate appeal? The film has such a hold over the world of reality, can achieve expression so vitally in terms of ordinary life, that the realistic play must surely come to seem trivial, false, and inconsequential. The truth is, of course, that naturalism on the stage must always be limited and insincere. Thousands have gone to *The*

*Children's Hour* and come away fondly believing that
what they have seen is life; they have not realized that
here too the familiar stock figures, the type characterizations, of the theater have been presented before them
in modified forms. From this the drama cannot escape;
little possibility is there of its delving deeply into the
recesses of the individual spirit. That is the realm reserved for cinematic exploitation, and, as the film
more and more explores this territory, does it not seem
likely that theater audiences will become weary of
watching shows which, although professing to be "life-
like," actually are inexorably bound by the restric-
tions of the stage? Pursuing this path, the theater truly
seems doomed to inevitable destruction. Whether in its
attempt to reproduce reality and give the illusion of
actual events or whether in its pretense toward depth
and subtlety in character-drawing, the stage is aiming
at things alien to its spirit, things which so much more
easily may be accomplished in the film that their exploitation on the stage gives only an impression of
vain effort.

Is, then, the theater, as some have opined, truly dying? Must it succumb to the rivalry of the cinema?
The answer to that question depends on what the theater does within the next ten or twenty years. If it
pursues naturalism further, unquestionably little hope
will remain. . . .

These are weighty sentences, but are they really unquestionable? One might question whether the drama has always been
incapable of delving into those "recesses of the individual
spirit," whether the movie, even in the best hands, has in fact
shown itself any more capable? But my prime interest is in
Mr. Nicoll's remarks about naturalism. A generation of movies
has given to naturalism a popular success such as no dramatic

style has ever had before. *A Tree Grows in Brooklyn,* movie version, is, one might say, pure Zola. Mr. Nicoll's strongest point, perhaps, is that the screen gives the illusion of actuality itself. The screen actor is not thought to act. He does not act. He is himself and, the argument runs, rightly so, since the screen must seem to be life itself. Such is the power of the camera. In support of his argument Mr. Nicoll adduces the fact that plays fail on the screen, and that movie actors haven't a style that can be parodied as Henry Irving had. The screen play, more than any other form of art, is just such a "slice of life" as the Naturalists had always wished to cut.

This is Mr. Nicoll's argument, but does it all ring true? After all, we *do* praise acting on the screen; many of the screen's best actors are also stage stars and they are not always so very different in the two mediums; they *can* be parodied, and a parody of Charles Laughton the filmstar is not very different from one of Charles Laughton the actor; and good plays—witness Shaw's *Pygmalion*—have been successfully transferred to the screen with little alteration. Nor do audiences believe that what happens on the screen is really happening or that it has happened—at least no more than theater audiences do. After all, it was in the theater that the proverbial man in the gallery told Othello to leave the lady alone, and it was on the radio that the announcement of the end of the world was taken literally. These are abnormal responses. Normally an audience does not give full credence to fiction on the air, the stage, or the screen. I have known a movie audience to catch its breath at the sight of wounded soldiers in a newsreel and to be quite unperturbed by the same sight in a fictional movie.

In short, and Mr. Nicoll to the contrary notwithstanding, I think there is no radical distinction between stage and screen illusion. At best the difference is one of degree. The usual Hollywood product does seek to be a convincing illusion of actuality, but so does the usual Broadway product. This is a matter not of stage or screen, but of the style chosen by the director or author or producer. On either stage or screen he may choose, with great effectiveness, to be naturalistic or the reverse. It is also a matter of audience. An untrained audience, an audience of children, might want to save Desdemona's life in the theater, as at the movies it might believe that it is actually present in Greta Garbo's bedroom. That is the trouble with being untrained and childish.

What Mr. Nicoll says is true of current movies and of many audiences, but not of all possible movies and all possible audiences. At present, it is true, we go to the movies to witness certain illusions and to share them. We do not go for imaginative experience. Years ago the Lynds found out how the movie magnates appealed to Middletown, via the *Saturday Evening Post*, in such advertisements as this:

> Go to a motion picture . . . and let yourself go. Before you know it you are *living* the story—laughing, loving, hating, struggling, winning! All the adventure, all the romance, all the excitement you lack in your daily life are in Pictures. They take you completely out of yourself into a wonderful new world . . . Out of the cage of everyday existence! If only for an afternoon or an evening—escape!

This is not Zola's Naturalism in subject matter and aim, for it is frankly "romantic" and remote from everyday life. It is the naturalism of the movies. It is Mr. Nicoll's naturalism. And it stems not, as Mr. Nicoll thinks, from the medium, but purely from social factors. The movie is an extension of gossip and daydream. It influences life as no art ever has because it influences not as art at all but as suggestion, almost as hypnotism. Clark Gable is found to have no undershirt on, and the underwear trade of America suffers a fifty-per-cent loss for a year. Ingrid Bergman has her hair cut short, and the women's hairdressers of the nation have to send for more scissors. Not that the theater, on its part, has held aloof from such nonartistic matters.

Actors and actresses have often been foci of mass emotion and sometimes leaders of fashion. All that Hollywood has done in this, as in so many other matters, is to systematize what had been haphazard and to make a mania out of a tendency.

The escapist naturalism of the movies is only that of most popular art. William Dieterle's movie *The Hunchback of Notre Dame* is not different in kind from Sardou's play *Patrie*. What is new is that we have in movies an art form so exclusively given over to Sardoodledom that a Yale professor thinks that Sardoodledom is ingrained in the celluloid. Sardoodledom—or escapist naturalism—always consisted of concealing flattering, sentimental hokum in a setting of the most solid and beefy reality, thus conferring upon hokum the status of the actual and the real. This, it is very true, the film can do even better than David Belasco, because its realism can be at once more varied and more intimate. The camera can find the needle in the haystack and the fly in the ointment, and, above all, the camera—like Mr. Lee Shubert's box office—cannot lie. Aided by the camera, and abetted by popular prejudice in favor of the tangible the director is able to wrap the maximum of nonsense in the maximum of verisimilitude, a combination as dangerous as the atomic bomb.

We must distinguish between the predilections of Hollywood and the nature of the medium. If the screen is able to be more naturalistic than the stage, it is also able to be more fantastic. If the Hollywood director is a super-Belasco, the Disney cartoon is a super-Punch-and-Judy, and Eisenstein is a super-Gordon Craig.

Mr. Nicoll makes the movie so completely natural that it is no longer art. He takes the "slice of life" theory too seriously. If we want life, we have it without making works of art at all. We need not pay our fifty cents for it; we necessarily pay in our hearts' blood. The *theory* of Zolaist Naturalism has nearly always been astray here, though Zola himself was prepared to define art as "a part of life seen through a temperament" and the last three words are an important proviso. There is art only if the material of life is selected and intelligently arranged. Such arrangement is of course artificial. It imposes form on the formless. And the understanding of art depends upon a prior understanding of this fact. Nothing, therefore, that we take for reality can we also take for art. In a good movie, as in any good work of art, we *are* aware of the "artificial" elements—structure, selection, characterization, cutting—or rather, we can be. In actual fact very few moviegoers are aware of any of these things; but the same is true of novel readers and theatergoers.

A more astute way of arguing that film and theater are utterly different is by pointing to the conditions of production. A movie is manufactured in little bits, the bits forming a jigsaw puzzle which is put together later; on the stage the unity of a single complete performance is the director's chief end in view. This distinction between the two media, like the others we have examined, is not a necessary distinction. It is to equate the present doings of studios with the exigencies of the medium. The degree of decentralization that exists in Hollywood is not a technical necessity. Many Russian directors, for example, have done their own cutting. And, for that matter, joint authorship, in the form of impudent revisions perpetrated by hacks and businessmen, and lack of integration in the directing and producing of plays—these are the bane of Broadway as well as Hollywood.

What then *is* the difference between film and theater? Or should one not rather ask: what are the differences? Let us be content with the reply that the screen has two dimensions and the stage three, that the screen presents photographs and the stage living actors. All subtler differences stem from these. The camera can show us all sorts of things—from close-ups of insects to panoramas of prairies—which the stage cannot even suggest, and it can move from one to another with much more dexterity than any conceivable stage. The stage, on the other hand, can be revealed in the unsurpassable beauty of three-dimensional shapes, and the stage actor establishes between himself and his audience a contact real as electricity. From these basic differences one might elaborate many others. Here I wish only to reiterate that there is no such difference as is suggested by the antithesis of naturalistic film and non-naturalistic theater. One cannot say, with Mr. Nicoll, that undecorated reality suits the screen, and fine words the stage. Such a belief is a hangover from the days of silent films. On the talking screen the aural is not necessarily subordinate to the visual. One could just as easily argue that the stage should stick to the natural, since on the stage the possibilities of fantasy are physically limited, while the screen should go in for poetic fantasy, since it can show anything in this world or the next with its cameras and can reproduce the merest murmurs and the subtlest intonations with its sound apparatus. All such distinctions are arbitrary. The truth is that dramatic art is possible on both stage and screen. On both it could fulfill its function of presenting an account of human experience deeply and truly. On both it would require the services of an artist—I think we may say a dramatist—to plan the whole work as a unity beforehand and of an interpreter or director to see that the unity is faithfully reproduced.

Is the film the dramatic art of the twentieth century then, or is it not? If as yet it is not, could it still grow to be so? My answers to these questions, which we started from, must now be evident. The movies as a whole, like plays as a whole, are a matter of business, not of art at all. The occasional artistic movie, like the occasional artistic play, is one legitimate and welcome form of twentieth-century art. It is not the only one. Moreover, while playwrights have demonstrated to us for centuries the potentialities of the stage, the screen is as yet an only partly explored territory. We have still to learn what its possibilities are. I have acknowledged that they are different from those of the stage, especially in certain kinds of emphasis. But they may not be as different as many have supposed. And there is no reason to assume that the art of the screen is a threat to the art of the stage, naturalistic or otherwise. Let us question Mr. Nicoll's unquestionable proposition. Although the movie industry can threaten the theater industry, the one *art* cannot be threatened by the other. So long as an art is alive it will be cherished and kept going by the minority that is interested in the arts. The answer, Mr. Nicoll said, "depends on what the theater does within the next ten or twenty years. If it pursues naturalism further, unquestionably little hope will remain. . . ." About ten years have passed since these words were written. Today one of the few live spots in the drama is the Epic Drama of Bertolt Brecht, which is—in some respects—a new naturalism. That the Epic dramatist believes also in combining the use of stage and screen in the theater is an additional sign that the two media need not part company according to the prescriptions of the doctors.

# III

What of the electric lamp? It was perhaps a prime factor in the creation of a nonrealistic theater. It brought Richard Wagner's conception of the *gesamtkunstwerk*—or Composite Art Work—much closer to realization than the maestro himself had ever been able to bring it. The theory of the Composite Art Work, of the drama as a grand mixture of all the most lavish arts of the theater, was completed, years after Wagner's death, by the Swiss stage designer, Adolphe Appia, who was perhaps the first man to see the infinite possibilities of electric light on the stage. He worked out most of the possible differentiations between blurred and defined lighting, flat and three-dimensional lighting, floods and spots. He set about studying color combinations under artificial light. He suggested that light might have a psychological function. (In *Tristan,* he said, let the lights change when King Mark enters.) He analysed stage procedure in terms of four plastic elements: perpendicular scenery, horizontal floor, moving actor, and lighted space. He was probably the first theorist to insist on the director as a separate yet co-ordinating force in the theater.

Some years before the First World War, light became the prime mover in the development of an antinaturalistic movement. Since drama consists of "theater arts" and not merely of "script writing," it is therefore, said the new generation, to be constructed and put across by theater artists. This conception found its most famous and most pompous spokesman in the son of Ellen Terry—Gordon Craig. Brought up in the shadow of actor-virtuosi, Craig seemed to develop a certain resentment against the essentially dramatic part of the theater, its playwrights and its actors. A poor actor himself, he took to directing. Finding even this irksome, he finally settled down to bringing out a magazine in Italy and drawing pictures of beautiful productions that would never be staged, some of which indeed, as Mr. Lee Simonson has shown in his delightful book *The Stage Is Set*, could not be staged in any theater that is not also a skyscraper. "The theater," Craig wrote, "must not forever rely upon having a play to perform but must in time perform pieces of its own art." If we ask what this art will be, Craig improvises about masks and imaginative space and symbolic gesture and marionettes: "Why, there are tremendous things to be done. We haven't yet got near the thing. Über-marionettes and wordless plays and actorless dramas are the obvious steps to a far deeper mystery." Obvious? In all the years since Craig started writing, even the obvious steps have not been taken and the mystery is more mysterious than ever.

Craig is perhaps more symptom than cause. Antoine's Naturalism was born in the eighties. It flourished in the nineties. In the nineteen-hundreds came the particular reaction with which Craig's name is connected, a reaction toward a theater that was to be more spectacular and artificial. This was the decade when the great Russian Naturalist director, Stanislavsky, lost the support of brilliant younger men like Meyerhold, who went the new way. The "modernistic" staging of the latter was later to be regarded as the fruit of Bolshevism, alike by those who hated modernism and the Bolsheviks and by those who approved of them. Actually the theater of Meyerhold and Tairov was part of the European "high-brow" theater of which the supreme representative was Max Reinhardt.

In the nineties Reinhardt had been a young actor under the great Ibsenite Otto Brahm, the Antoine of Germany. Reinhardt himself never "abandoned naturalism." He was eclectic. He excelled in all modes, and like Wagner he was fond of fantasy in very solid, not to say elephantine, form. It was not the greatness of a style that Reinhardt stood for, nor, after a few years, was it zeal for any particular plays or playwrights. It was the greatness of the stage itself. As Mr. Vladimir Horowitz seems to love the piano more than music, so Reinhardt seemed to love the stage more than drama. Not that there is anything unique in this. It is true of most directors. What was unique about Reinhardt was the time when he came to the front and the alacrity —perhaps the genius—with which he responded. Reinhardt was one of those men who first seize on the possibilities of new machines, in his case the electric switchboard, the revolving stage, and the like. And not only of machines. In rethinking, as he did, the whole art of staging, he was prepared to take any device from any place or period and make it his own. Up to Reinhardt's time, each place and period had had its own separate way of doing things. Reinhardt's eclecticism meant rummaging all through history for ideas that might be revived. He used all three basic types of stage—the circus ring, the apron stage, and the peep show which modern audiences are accustomed to—and even mingled them. He revived the mass theater of the Greeks, and recreated the intimacy of private theatricals in his Chamber Playhouse. He replaced stardom and virtuosity in acting by building a repertory company in which every actor was a star by the time Reinhardt had finished with him.

Reinhardt was a great man. But his theatricalism made him more and more a great showman and less and less a great servant of the drama. The depression that followed the First World War dispersed his repertory company. No longer confined to Berlin, Reinhardt's activities spread over the old world and the new. Every few months some new prodigy was born. He was producing plays in the Hofburg or in Salzburg Cathedral, he was amazing London and New York with *The Miracle,* he was in Hollywood filming *A Midsummer Night's Dream.* . . . When books were written on the Theater of Tomorrow and the New Spirit in the Theater their authors may have been thinking of the ideas of Appia, but in the realm of practice it was Reinhardt of whom they thought. The books they wrote are still impressive, since they contain good pictures. They are a beautiful mausoleum to the idea of a theater made out of electric light.

## IV

Naturalism was not to be overthrown either by the cinema or by electric lamps. Like all persistent creeds it has, of course, been declared dead at regular intervals. Mr. Allardyce Nicoll wrote of the end of naturalism in 1936. In 1891 the *Echo de Paris* had sponsored a questionnaire, asking: "Is [Zolaist] Naturalism sick? Is it dead? Can it be saved? What will it be replaced with?" Anatole France categorically answered: "Naturalism is finished." Rémy de Gourmont wrote: "The trend of the new generation is rigorously anti-Naturalistic. It is not a matter of partnership; we simply depart with disgust from a literature whose baseness makes us vomit. . . . Villiers de l'Isle-Adam is our Flaubert! Laforgue and Mallarmé are our masters. And Huysmans, having become conscious of his personal value and mission (after having outdone the Naturalists in their strictest formulae) has cut loose by his *A Rebours,* and thus liberated a whole new literature. . . ." The Parisians were very advanced. 1891 was the year when *Ghosts* horrified the elders in London. At this time Naturalism in the theater—in the special form of Zolaism—was but beginning its famous career. But then, among literary people, declaring a movement finished is only a way of expressing dislike. Naturalism has been heartily disliked. But it survives dislike. Wave after wave has lashed against this fortress in vain.

Naturalism not only survived. It always returned in full vigor. In the heyday of Expressionism—the early twenties—Sean O'Casey wrote his *The Plough and the Stars,* one of the great naturalistic masterpieces. (The point could be reinforced by comparing the play with one of the same author's much less successful non-naturalistic plays, such as *The Star Turns Red.* Similarly: Eugene O'Neill, in a fit of antinaturalism, wrote *Lazarus Laughs,* stipulating a chorus wearing forty-nine different kinds of masks; he had been much more effective as a simple naturalist in the little plays of the sea.) Of the art theaters of the first generation, the Abbey Theater, Dublin, was probably the only one not born out of the spirit of Naturalism. The Abbey was the child of the Neo-Romanticism of W. B. Yeats. Its highest achievements, however, were the peasant naturalism of J. M. Synge and the urban naturalism of Sean O'Casey. In the nineteen-thirties both Neo-Romanticism and Expressionism seemed *vieux jeu.* No longer were there ambitiously experimental and non-naturalistic stages in Moscow and Berlin, nor did the younger playwrights in New York seek to maintain the earlier vogue. In America the slogan was Social Theater, as in Russia it was Socialist Realism. In the background was Bertolt Brecht's Epic Drama, a type of theater that, for all its originality, for all its eclecticism, owed its greatest debt to the naturalistic tradition.

Protests against naturalism are, however, just as characteristic a part of modern drama, and of modern culture, as is naturalism itself. If naturalism survived, so did the animus against naturalism. Naturalism reigned, but the insurgent movements had achievements of their own. At the time of the First World War the theater of electric light passed from its Impressionist phase, the phase of Craig's Celtic mists and dim Gothic towers, to its Expressionist phase, the phase of abstract, geometrical design. More fruitful than either Expressionism or the brilliant non-naturalistic staging of the Russians was perhaps the theater of the French *avant-garde*—of men like Jacques Copeau among directors and Jean Cocteau among playwrights—which will be discussed in a later chapter.

I propose to speak of the modern drama in terms of the two traditions which we have identified as naturalistic and anti-naturalistic. This dichotomy, though a rough one, cuts below most of the usual divisions into schools and types. It underlies such antitheses, as useful as they are misleading, as:

| | | |
|---:|:---:|:---|
| slice of life | vs. | convention |
| realism | vs. | fantasy |
| social | vs. | individual |
| political | vs. | religious |
| propagandist | vs. | aesthetic |
| prosaic | vs. | poetic |
| objective | vs. | subjective |

It follows from my remarks about critical terms and the term naturalism in particular, that a writer may well be in the right-hand column in some respects and in the left-hand column in others. Nor are the pairs mutually exclusive. Yet, although neither naturalism nor any of its conceivable opposites could possibly exist alone, we do find throughout the history of modern drama a naturalist wing and an antinaturalist wing—His Majesty's Government, so to say, and His Majesty's Opposition. And, since the eighteenth century, when naturalism first invaded the stage, antinaturalism has existed in conscious protest against it, in conscious anxiety to preserve or recover the poetry and the grandeur that seemed lost. As fast as some playwrights tried to clothe their muse in modern dress, others fought to clothe her in a fancy dress that might recall Sophocles, Shakespeare, or Racine.

In the next two chapters I shall examine the history of tragedy—or pseudo tragedy, if that is what it is—since the eighteenth century: first, the "tragedy in modern dress" of the naturalists; then, the "tragedy in fancy dress" of their opponents.

The bastards of Shakespeare have no right to ridicule the legitimate children of Balzac.

EMILE ZOLA

# 2. TRAGEDY

# IN MODERN DRESS

## I

What happens to tragedy, which has generally been regarded as the major dramatic genre, in an age of naturalism?

If we trust popular parlance, tragedy is still flourishing under the auspices of Broadway. If on the other hand we ask the experts, they usually tell us that high tragedy disappeared with aristocratic society and that middle-class and democratic societies are lacking in tragic sense. Tragedy, they say, shows the heroic stature of man and the justice of the gods while naturalism shows man either as the impotent victim of a hostile world or as a justified rebel against divine order. If we follow this line of argument the tragic and the naturalistic are polar opposites.

Let us look at some of the facts. Let us look specifically at some attempts that have been made to create a kind of drama that is naturalistic and at the same time in the tragic tradition.

The story begins with the establishment in the early eighteenth century of a genre midway between the older tragedy and comedy, a genre that was called *tragédie bourgeoise*—"bourgeois tragedy"—when it tended toward tragedy, and *comédie larmoyante*—"tearful comedy"—when it tended toward comedy. It is this middle genre that has often been taken as primary evidence for the death of tragedy by analysts of eighteenth-century society, philosophy, and culture. The social analyst can represent the new genre as the genre of the rising middle class, a class which lacks alike the taste of an aristocracy and the spontaneity of a populace, a class whose optimism and love of comfort can be regarded as utterly antitragic. The philosopher, if he belongs to the same school of thought, can accuse the eighteenth-century *philosophes* of naïve illusions, of too ingenuously assuming that human nature is benevolent, of too confidently expecting steady progress and human perfectability. The literary critic and cultural historian can speak of a dissociation of sensibility, of a growing reflectiveness and spirit of rumination, of the unpoetical character of the age, an age—he may complain—which at the same time boasted of Reason and indulged a debilitated palate with Young's *Night Thoughts*.

Such critics and historians have for the most part been content to quote instances of sentimentality, schoolmarm didacticism, and simple-minded adulation of the new genre. Here are three quaint specimens:

> 1. The passions of Melpomene are violent, carried to the extreme; ours are repressed by education and by social practices. The vices that tragedy depicts are crimes, ours are weaknesses.
>
> 2. To be an author is already considerable, but to be a useful author, to have an influence on the conduct and customs of one's fellow citizens, to purify

them in the flame of morality, is to seize the most
beautiful privilege of human nature.

3. It lies in the nature of the *genre sérieux* to fur-
nish a more appealing interest, a more immediate morality, than heroic tragedy, and a deeper morality than
light comedy.

There are interesting assumptions behind these statements.
The dramatist is morally to influence his audience. His audience is to consist of his fellows ("one's fellow citizens") not of
his patrons. And since education and the newer mores have
checked the passions and eliminated crime, the *genre sérieux*
is better fitted than either tragedy or comedy to accommodate
the only defects now left to humanity, "weaknesses." At least
these views are revolutionary. The older tradition of critical
comedy was to show human nature as difficult if not depraved;
high tragedy had shown that even an heroic nature was not
quite adequate to the demands of a human situation. When
the man of sentiment relaxes into contentment with average
human nature as it is, the old tragedy and the old comedy are
at an end. . . . But—in spite of the experts whose views I have
been citing—I shall maintain that something which might well
be called a new tragedy was in the making.

The middle genre which resulted from these attitudes was
at first a minor genre. "Tragedies" like *George Barnwell* and
*The Gamester,* "comedies" like *The Conscious Lovers* and
*Mélanide,* can only be read for purely historical interest or revived for unintended mirth. The originality of Lillo and his
compeers consisted, not in the greatness of their art, but in the
courage with which they acted on the Christian-democratic assumption that merely to be a man is a tragic fact. If this was
not the view of the older tragedians, it might yet be that of the
future towards which the new tragedians of the eighteenth century were striving. Even the excessive sensibility which ruins
the *tragédie bourgeoise* had its positive functions. In it we

should see not only a subterfuge and a falsification but a fresh, though fumbling, grapple with the passions which Reason was seeking to make taboo. The emotional gaucherie of eighteenth-century tragedy is comparable to that of the early Elizabethans.

The achievement of the middle genre was the discovery of a new tragedy, the tragedy of modern life. It was probably Lessing who first saw that the solid citizen *(der Bürger)* and his family were the hub of a new culture (though in his day society was still outwardly aristocratic) and who located the tragic experience there. Schiller went further and connected the family crisis with society generally by making a point of class antagonism. Nevertheless the middle genre remained inadequate throughout the eighteenth century and, for example, the dramatic catastrophe was a sheer accident, not just outwardly, as in *Hamlet,* but inwardly too. Schiller's *Kabale und Liebe* seems to be *about* class difference and yet there is no connection between this theme and the disaster which winds up the play.


## II

The task of giving tragic substance to the middle genre was left to a later generation. Each of the four great men of the German theater who were born in 1813—Richard Wagner, Georg Büchner, Friedrich Hebbel, and Otto Ludwig—had his own way of remaking drama, and the way of Hebbel and Ludwig—at least *one* of the ways of Hebbel and Ludwig—is a development of the middle genre. Both were acutely aware of the defects of the existing plays of the genre; both were convinced, however, of the possibilities of naturalism, that is, of the intimate presentation of bourgeois life, provided that the play be given a strict and logical form and that it be informed by a poetic imagination. Ludwig thought that such a modern naturalism would be more authentically Shakespearean than the Shakespearionics of Schiller and his epigones. But Ludwig's descriptions of Shakespearean drama—written in the forties, fifties,

and early sixties—sound to us like a description of Ibsen's
naturalism of the seventies and eighties. They body forth a fully
mature middle genre such as Ludwig himself never quite succeeded in writing.

The gist of Ludwig's rich theory is that modern tragedy
should be "a genre of poetry which springs organically not from
the passing hour but from the whole complex of actual life."
The play should be one catastrophe motivated by characters and
situations; its exposition and dialogue generally should be analytic, that is, should carry forward the action and acquaint us
with the preliminary facts at the same time; the ideal plot is a
simple one in which not too many persons, contrasted in motive
and temperament, are brought together in the smallest possible
space. If all this were not sufficiently Ibsenite, we seem to hear
the very voice of Ibsen in such observations as Ludwig's dry
comment: "It is no little thing to keep your eye on eight fellows
all at the same time." And when Ludwig advances what has unhappily come to be considered the most heretical of dramatic
doctrines—that action is merely a suitable occasion for dialogue
—we are on the threshold of Shavianism.

With Ludwig, his rival Hebbel had really much in common.
Both men helped to carry dramatic art through the hard years
of the midcentury. Both did it in the name of a revolt against
Schiller, yet both had learned so much from Schiller, and had
so deep a relation to him, that their attitude has aptly been hit
off by Egon Friedell, a prince among commentators on the
drama, as an Oedipus complex. Like Ludwig, and in line with
Schiller, Hebbel stressed the fact that language is the essence
of all poetic art, including drama. At the time when the theater
was suffering the first great onslaught of bourgeois entertainment, Hebbel, like Ludwig, and unlike the other dramatists of
western Europe, understood the requirements of great drama.
At a time when a Kotzebue and a Scribe had taught a generation of dramatists how to show effects without causes, character

without complexity, and history without dialectic, Hebbel described a drama which could embody a world:

> At its every step there throngs around it a world of
> views and relations, which point both backwards and
> forwards, and all of which must be carried along; the
> life-forces cross and destroy one another, the thread of
> thought snaps in two before it is spun out, the emotion
> shifts, the very words gain their independence and re-
> veal hidden meaning, annulling the ordinary one, for
> each is a die marked on more than a face. Here the
> chaff of little sentences, adding bit to bit and fiber to
> fiber, would serve the purpose ill. It is a question of
> presenting conditions in their organic totality. . . .
> Unevenness of rhythm, complication and confusion of
> periods, contradiction in the figures, are elevated to ef-
> fective and indispensable rhetorical means. . . ."

Omitted from Barrett H. Clark's standard anthology of dramatic theory, Hebbel's criticism is both more perceptive and
more closely linked with the history of high drama in Europe
than that of any of his contemporaries. That such men as he
and Ludwig are unknown even to devotees of the theater is one
token among a thousand of our deep ignorance of modern
drama. Types of drama and dramatic theory seem to be regarded by many as a congeries that can be arranged in any order
and taken up each according to its ability to amuse the critic.
But the drama has a history that has been omitted by the dramatic historians, many of whom seem to know nothing but
drama or nothing but literature. And drama is after all only
a portion of a complex historical whole. A great dramatist may
occupy a place in history more like that of Socrates or Karl
Marx than like that of David Belasco or Victorien Sardou.

Hebbel is the first great dramatic critic and practitioner to
show the explicit influence of that historical imagination which
is one of the great novelties of modern times, a novelty whose

influence was already writ large upon Goethe's great dramatic poem and upon prose fiction. Those who think of history and tragedy as necessarily antithetic would assert that Hebbel wrote dramatic histories and not tragedies. For history is his very mode of vision. Influenced like all his generation in Germany by Hegel, Hebbel described the history of the drama in Hegelian-sounding terms. Great drama, he maintained, occurred at the transition from one epoch to the next and expressed the clash of *Weltanschauungen*—"world-views." So far Western history had known two such crises. The first was when the antique world shifted from simplicity to reflection, from belief in gods to belief in fate. The second was when the medieval order was shaken by the individualism of the Protestants. (Hence, says Hebbel, the "terrible dialectic" of Shakespeare's characters.) The third crisis (as usual with such formulations) is that of today when some "new form of humanity" (a great nineteenth-century longing from Shelley to Nietzsche) hovers just out of sight. In the drama of the first world crisis we see a conflict between man and what Hegel called the Idea, that is, between the individual and the manifest part of the Idea, namely, political, religious, and moral institutions. In the second crisis the conflict is within the individual. (Hebbel evidently has *Hamlet* in mind.) In the third crisis the problem is placed directly in the Idea—in our institutions. When, therefore, Hebbel says that problem is of the essence of drama, he is much more than a prophet of our "problem plays." He refers not only to plays about immediate social abuses, but also to all plays which grapple with political, religious, and moral institutions. He is the prophet not only of the socialist but also of the "mystical" Ibsen.

How does Hebbel's version of tragedy connect with the tradition of the middle genre? Being an historical mind, Hebbel says that eighteenth-century sentimentality would only successfully be replaced, not by a return to the seventeenth century, but by a nineteenth-century discovery. Instead of advocating a neo-Shakespearean drama, as so many writers from Schiller to Lud-

wig had done, he sought the conflict within the Idea—*i.e*, in political, social, and religious conflict. He gave drama a backbone
of dialectic—according to the Hegelian formula, some will say,
though Hebbel made of the dialectic of history a tragic, not a
merely logical or meliorist, development. This is an admirable
misunderstanding of Hegel and the cornerstone of Hebbelism.
Into the abstract Hegelian molds he poured—with whatever philosophic impropriety—a poetry of his own. For him the antithesis
which confronted the thesis was a Divine Antagonist, a social
manifestation of the Idea which became a new sort of fate. That
Hebbel's conception is a direct encounter with his material and
not an academic rehash of older tragedy is best shown in his
view of the tragic catastrophe. Those who reflect lovingly upon
tragedy, as opposed to those who create it out of the agony of
their hearts, are apt to stress the beauty of tragic reconciliation.
Not so Hebbel. "There is no reconciliation," he wrote. "The
heroes fall because they are overweening." Hebbel rediscovered
tragic horror: "all tragedy lies in destruction and proves nothing
but the emptiness of existence." This of course is too crude and
cryptic. In a more explanatory mood he would explain that
while there was no reconciliation among the characters, no individual compensation, no poetic justice, there was a "reconciliation of the Idea," a vindication of the larger law to which
the individual is subordinate. This is demonstrated in its narrower, Prussian sense in the sacrifice of his Agnes Bernauer to
the state. It is more subtly demonstrated in *Maria Magdalena*.

This play is justly famous as at once the continuator of the
eighteenth-century middle genre and the starting point of Ibsenism. The nature of these connections, however, is not so evident. Hebbel objected to the existing bourgeois tragedy because
its dialogue was still too inflated and unreal and because of the
arbitrariness of the catastrophe, not to mention lack of integration in other parts of the action. He determined to follow
Lessing's lead in locating the tragedy in the family and Schiller's lead in playing on the theme of class difference. But in

one respect Hebbel stood the middle genre on its head. The genre had been evolved by the middle class for the adulation of the middle class. Hebbel makes the stifling atmosphere and prejudice of middle-class mentality into an all-enshrouding fate. As Büchner is the first dramatist of the *little* man in his marvelous naturalistic tragedy *Wozzeck,* so Hebbel is the first dramatist of the *middle* man, the type in which Ibsen would find the symbol of our society and our era. Ibsen wrote: "The character of the average man is in no way trivial from the artistic standpoint; as an artistic reproduction it is as interesting as any other." Hebbel had already written: "One need only be a man, after all, to have a destiny." It was such reflections that made of the politically conservative Hebbel, who insisted that he did not wish to overthrow existing institutions but only to give them a better foundation, a revolutionary who could look forward to a "new flight" in the history of drama and even a "new form of humanity."

## III

Ibsen professed surprise that the Germans could be so taken with his work when they already had their own Hebbel, yet the fact is that Hebbel never carried his theories to their fullest conclusion either in *Maria Magdalena* or in his later invention of a modern symbolic drama. But he indeed rebuilt the foundations, and after such an operation it is not so easy as he supposed to retain the superstructure. A young German scholar who had long talks with Hebbel in Rome in 1844 wrote a little book six years later in which he at the same time praised Hebbel as the founder of a new drama and tempered his praise with the admission that Hebbel had not fulfilled the promise of his essays and his early plays. The little book—*Das moderne Drama,* by Hermann Hettner—was read very soon after its publication by the young Henrik Ibsen, author at that time of little besides a verse tragedy about Catiline. In it Ibsen read:

In the struggles of our inner character-development,
in the secrets of a family life which has been shaken
right down to its innermost foundations, in the vol-
canically undermined soil of our social conditions lie
at this moment the deepest deeps of the moral spirit
(*des sittlichen Geistes*). But where there are deep moral
struggles there is also fate, great and gigantic, and
where there is a great, that is, an inwardly necessary,
fate, there also is pure tragedy.

Already around 1850, then, we find a partly developed tragedy in modern dress, that is, in terms of modern life, and a fully
developed theory of such a tragedy. The Ibsenism of Ibsen's
predecessors was, moreover, a complete Ibsenism which embraces
not only the social and technical features of *A Doll's House*,
but also an Ibsenite emphasis upon poetry and symbol. Reduced
to formulas, Ibsen's massive play *Emperor and Galilean* is pure
Hebbel: its stuff is historic myth; the myth is rooted in its own
geographic and chronological soil; it presents the clash of two
eras and in so doing establishes a clear relationship with the
present.

It would be foolish to make of Ibsen a purely Hebbelian, a
purely German dramatist, though of the three springs from
which Ibsen drank—the Norwegian, the French, and the German—the last has been most overlooked in non-German countries. He drank equally deeply of all three, and his synthesis of
Norwegian romance, French naturalism, and the spirit of Hebbel is the first fully realized "bourgeois" tragedy. It is also the
last. The ground for tragedy is seldom fully prepared; and even
more seldom is the man present to occupy it. 1580 would have
been too early for Shakespeare and 1620 too late; 1914 would
have been too late for Ibsen and 1830 too early. Or so it seems.
For a brief time, if every preparation has been made, a Shakespeare may stand on the shoulders of his predecessors and reach
down *Hamlet;* an Ibsen can reach down a *Peer Gynt* and a

*Master Builder.* Some would push the analogy of Ibsen and Shakespeare even further, applying to him what Otto Ludwig wrote of Lessing: "The form is French, but the substance is Shakespearean." This is unhistorical thinking. In those plays of Ibsen which have a French form—the outwardly naturalistic plays, from *Pillars of Society* on—the substance is Shakespearean only in being genuinely imaginative and poetic. Of course Ibsen did write an immature play after *A Midsummer Night's Dream;* he did become the rich poetic dramatist of *Peer Gynt;* he did recreate the grandeur of Elizabethan histrionics in *Hedda Gabler;* he did recreate a sort of tragic hero at least in *The Master Builder* and *John Gabriel Borkman;* and, like Shakespeare, he wrote tragedies of waste in which deep despair over the human lot is overcome only by even deeper faith in human potentiality. But unless we define tragedy so narrowly as to exclude everything but one school of tragic practice, we are bound to expect from *every* tragedy at least the very broad qualities which we find in both these playwrights. This is not to subscribe to the view that all great tragedy is fundamentally the same, that each great poet digs down to a level where human nature is always and everywhere alike; in arguing so the champions of eternal verities reduce diverse and rich phenomena to depressing sameness in the manner of the very scientists whom they hate. All tragedy, so I would be inclined to state it, is a broad and deep account of the life of the individual, and, at least by inference, his fellows, in which neither man's problems nor his ability to cope with them is belittled. Tragedy cannot be extreme optimism, for that would be to underestimate the problem; it cannot be extreme pessimism, for that would be to lose faith in man. At the heart of tragedy is a tough dialectical struggle in which the victory of either side is credible. That the doom of the hero is in many types of tragedy "inevitable" is an irony; for this very hero who has no chance of winning is in the end the spiritual winner. The case of tragedies—so various as *Le Cid* and *Faust*—which end happily reminds us that tragedy is not the opposite of comedy. It is a way of looking at things. In comedy we see and criticize man's life; in tragedy we sense and appraise his fate.

Now life, that is, morals, ideas, characters, is not immutable either on the surface or on the deepest levels of consciousness; nor is the battle which man fights in carving out his destiny forever the same; the fact that two events are both called battles or that two beings are both called men is not a proof that they are fundamentally alike. Once the almost universal assumption of the timelessness of art is discarded, we shall see that historical interpretation is not merely an apparatus to help us fill out the details of our understanding of Shakespeare or Ibsen; we shall find that Shakespeare's individuality lies in his *Elizabethanness* and not in his timelessness. Obviously Shakespeare is not to be enjoyed merely by "an age" but by "all time," yet that is not to say that posterity cannot enjoy the Elizabethanness of Shakespeare. There has been much confused thinking on the point, and the historical scholars have contributed to it by remarks on the eternal Shakespeare which reduce their own researches to insignificance. The arts are fragments of the time and place which produced them and cannot be comprehended either conceptually or imaginatively, outwardly or inwardly, without a knowledge and imaginative understanding of their context. The great generalities which unhistorical critics produce are the inevitable product of their ignorance of the relevant particularities. In tragedy we find an image of the deepest conflicts in the life of the time. Hebbel was among the first to see this, but he diagnosed the conflicts with too little empirical knowledge. Tragic conflict in Shakespeare is not always, as he assumes, within the individual. But Hebbel's suggestion that behind Shakespeare is the clash of the medieval and the modern eras is something you might read in the latest book on Shakespeare today.

As one great historical opposition—that of medieval convention and the Renaissance individual—underlies Elizabethan tragedy, another—that of mass organization and the modern individualist—underlies modern tragedy. The analogy should not of course be made too much of. Shakespeare did not have to choose between the medieval and the Renaissance ideas. His work *reflects* the conflict between them. In line with the more philosophical and partisan reasoning of modern art, the modern playwright regards the conflict as a challenge. Which side shall he take? The Italian futurists boldly and brashly took the side of the machine against the organism. A conservative like Hebbel, or a Marxist like Mr. Erwin Piscator, can take the side of the collective against the individual. In that case the theme will be that the individual must be sacrificed to the general good. Even a skeptic, taking neither side, will not in these days attempt Shakespeare's godlike comprehensiveness of vision. Torn between rival allegiances, Ernst Toller expresses in his play *Masse-Mensch*—"Masses or Man"—his agonized inability to decide for either course. Most often, perhaps, the modern tragic writer sides with the individual against the mass and sees the struggle as one between greatness and mediocrity, the living and the petrifact. Is not this the position of Nietzsche in his quasi-tragic *Also Sprach Zarathustra* and of T. S. Eliot in his quasi-tragic *Waste Land?* Is not this the position of Ibsen?

For the expression of this sort of conflict Ibsen tried many modes and in three achieved greatness: the dramatic poem on the pattern of *Faust;* the naturalistic play on the French pattern; and the symbolic drama which was Ibsen's late variant on the French pattern. In contrast with most of the modes in which Ibsen was not so successful, these three modes are all tragedy in modern dress, and not merely in modern *dress* but in a modern *spirit.* Unlike Eugene O'Neill, Ibsen would never have dressed up ancient tragic heroes in modern clothes. That is too easy a road to sublimity and it is to rely too confidently on the classicist's assumption that human nature is constant and that it was once and for all interpreted by the Greeks. Ibsen assumes that everything changes, that one must write from one's own experiences, and therefore about one's own age. In his letters he makes a point of the fact that *Peer Gynt,* often assumed to be unmodern in source and treatment, is a distinctly modern tale perfectly adapted to Ibsen's experience of the mid-nineteenth century.

*Brand* (1866) and *Peer Gynt* (1867) are twin pillars of Ibsenite tragedy; all later works are made up of bits of stone cut off from them. *Peer Gynt* is a counter-Faust. It shows the other side of Faustian striving, the striving of modern careerism with all its vast implications. In his gay unscrupulousness, his adventurous egoism, and his amiable immorality, Peer Gynt is the Don Quixote of free enterprise and should be the patron saint of the National Association of Manufacturers. If Peer Gynt is the opportunist, Brand is the fanatic. The pair are Scylla and Charybdis for modern character: the man of no principles and the man of one principle, the heretic and the bigot. The good man of one principle, that man of the formula who is with us today more than ever, Ibsen consigns to an avalanche, rejected, like the original Pharisees, even by the God of love. The feckless man of no principles is saved by an act of rebirth through love, the procreative principle. Ibsenite tragedy can end happily or not. In one of his little speeches, Ibsen declared that he was a pessimist insofar as he did not believe in any *unum necessarium,* but that he was an optimist in his adherence to the procreative principle. Philosophically, Ibsen is a pragmatist denouncing fixed dogma, a vitalist denouncing the bodiless idea. But his work is more tragic than polemical, and the new life according to Ibsen comes only after conflagration.

Ibsen is not a Sophocles (though he is in many respects a Euripides). He does not hew out the positive and sublime sculptures which are what one usually thinks of as tragic portraiture. Like most other great men of the period, he felt that modernity did not permit grandeur, and so after his bold beginnings, he progressively narrowed down his art till it was about almost nothing but himself. He perfected a "bourgeois tragedy" but it was an uneasy perfection, and the longer Ibsen lived the further he retreated. The work of his last period, from *The Wild Duck* (1884) at the earliest or from *The Master Builder* (1892) at the latest, is the tragedy of his retreat, the tragedy of a repentant Axel. The thesis and antithesis of his tragic dialectic are life and death, the meaning of which, as later in *The Waste Land,* is ironically and tragically reversed. T. S. Eliot's use of an heroic past contrasted with an ignoble present is a theme of only one Ibsen play *(Hedda Gabler)* but, as in Flaubert, it is implied as between one work and another. Such early works as *The Warriors at Helgeland* are not the most important Ibsen, but they should co-exist in one's mind with the plays of modern life. The viking plays are related to the modern plays as Flaubert's ancient and medieval studies are related to *Madame Bovary*: Emma Bovary and Hedda Gabler would have had scope for their energies and their dreams in those earlier worlds. As history this is not a very plausible theory. But in Flaubert, Ibsen, and Eliot it is, let us prefer to believe, as a hypothesis of unmechanized, though not unconditioned, life that the heroic age is offered to us. It is a picture of a noble kind of life in a concrete setting of human passion and wrongdoing, rather than in an abstract, futuristic paradise. It is the life thesis to which the antithesis is the living death which Flaubert called muckerism.

Ibsen resembled his admirer James Joyce in one respect: he made of his art so specialized and so personal a thing that those who came after could copy it, they could isolate a part of his method and copy that, they could start on a new path under his inspiration or in revulsion against him, but they could not go further along the road which he himself traveled. The Naturalists borrowed from one drawer in Ibsen's cabinet, the Neo-Romanticists from another. Only one of the post-Ibsen generation—Gerhart Hauptmann—produced good drama in the tradition of the "bourgeois tragedy," and even he fell short of greatness for lack of originality of conception. But there was one

dramatist whose tragic drama was not simply a personal variation upon a general decline: August Strindberg.


## IV

The break between nineteenth-century drama, of which Ibsen was the crown and culmination, and Strindberg might be
considered the abruptest break since that between the seventeenth century and the age of sentiment. Ibsen represents at
their best the ideals, techniques, interests, and attitudes of the
nineteenth century as they had expressed themselves from the
Romantic Revolt on. Strindberg too was a child of the nineteenth century, and he went through phases of allegiance to
several of its chief faiths. But he was at home with none, and his
ardent desire to find something to supersede secular liberalism,
feminism, socialism, indeed all the creeds which were still
thought "advanced" in his day was of a piece with his sense of
chaos and his striving after new forms to express the new state
of soul. Let us see what Strindberg did for "tragedy in modern
dress" with reference to his celebrated play, *Miss Julia*.

When Strindberg sent a copy of *Miss Julia* to the archnaturalist Zola, the latter's comments make it quite clear that
what Strindberg called a Naturalistic Tragedy was not authen-
tic Zolaism. In such a play, to be sure, we see the twin Zolaesque
forces of heredity and environment combining to make a catastrophe, and an old theme of the middle genre—the clash of the
classes, the lady in love with the servant—is here revamped.
What Strindberg actually made of these themes, however, is as
far removed from the prosaic literalness of extreme Naturalism
as it is from the *kitsch* piquancy of "love interest." His desire
and ability to go beyond these and restore tragic passion and
tragic guilt are implied in his words: "The naturalist has wiped
out the idea of guilt, but he cannot wipe out the results of an
action." This from the preface of the "Naturalistic Tragedy."
The word Naturalistic here can only mean that this is no revival

of an ancient muse, but the procreation of a modern Melpomene. It is an ironic answer alike to the optimists and to those
who thought that a middle-class era was incapable of tragedy.
Strindberg portrays a man-hating half-woman who is modern,
he says, not in her fundamental disposition but in that she has
become vocal and aggressive on behalf of her disposition. "The
type is tragical," the preface continues, "offering us the spectacle of a desperate struggle against nature. It is also tragical as
a Romantic inheritance dispersed by the prevailing Naturalism,
which wants nothing but happiness: and for happiness strong
and sound races are required." The era of happiness will destroy the survivors of the previous era. The nontragic era will
open tragically. And perhaps in the Nietzschean statement that
"for happiness strong and sound races are required" there is the
tacit irony that the era of happiness will not be so untragic—or
so happy.

"I have tried to modernize the form," Strindberg announced.
The great preface tells how he has destroyed the French "well-
made play" which had been the technical basis of later Ibsenism. Dialogue and stage setting are to be jagged and asymmetri-
cal. Monologue, pantomime, and dance are to be reintroduced.
The theater is to be small and intimate. With a new technique
goes a new tragic conception. As in most bourgeois tragedy there
is no hero, but while much naturalistic work had suffered from
sheer lack of any imaginative conception of character, Strindberg makes of herolessness a positive point. People in real life,
he often insisted, are not "characters," and his own stage personages he defines as "conglomerates, made up of past and present stages of civilization, scraps of humanity, torn-off pieces of
Sunday clothing turned into rags—all patched together as is the
human soul itself." That is Strindberg's psychology, and his idea
of modernism is implied in the statement: "Because they are
modern characters, living in a period of transition more hysteri-
cally hurried than its immediate predecessor at least, I have

made my figures vacillating, out-of-joint, torn between the old and the new."

The philosophy out of which Strindberg makes a new tragic conception is a nihilistic brand of relativism, than which no philosophy seems artistically less promising. Tragedy, Strindberg assumes, means pity and terror. The pity depends solely on your feeling that the fate of the heroine might have been yours. The terror stems from "the sad circumstance that the hawk eats the dove and the flea eats the hawk," as to which circumstance Strindberg asks: "Why should it be remedied?" From the pity and terror together comes tragic exultation: "We shall receive an unconditionally good and joyful impression from seeing the national forests rid of rotting and superannuated trees. . . . I find the joy of life in its violent and cruel struggles."

Herolessness and a modern mentality turn the Aristotelian elements topsy-turvy. Classic pity was not relief at one's own immunity; classic terror was not a Darwinian reflection upon the struggle for existence; classic exultation was not a fascistic celebration of the destruction of the weak. In making a kind of serious parody of classic theories of tragedy, Strindberg elevates the Naturalistic theory of Zola to the level of imagination and in so doing parodies Zola too. The world which science coolly and objectively reveals, so Strindberg implies, cannot be coolly and objectively regarded. To think that it can is the error of Zolaism. Actually it shows life to be tragic. *Miss Julia* is the tragedy of the Darwinian ethos. The concepts in it are through and through Darwinian, but the tragic interpretation is itself a critique of Darwinism. Within this irony is another, the central irony of the piece. Strindberg uses the most notorious notion of nihilistic relativism—the notion that all perspectives are equally true—for artistic purposes, for the purpose, in fact, of setting up a deliberate dissonance, a dissonance behind which, however, one hears—or not quite hears—mocking laughter:

> And what will offend simple brains is that my action cannot be traced back to a single motive, that the

viewpoint is not always the same. An event in real life
—and this discovery is quite recent—springs generally
from a whole series of more or less deep-lying motives,
but of these the spectator chooses as a rule the one his
reason can master most easily, or else the one reflecting
most favorably on his power of reasoning. A suicide is
committed. Bad business, says the merchant. Unre-
quited love, say the ladies. Sickness, says the invalid.
Crushed hopes, says the shipwrecked. Now it may be
that the motive lay in all or none of these directions.

*Miss Julia* is not itself meaningless; meaninglessness is Strindberg's subject. As other ideas of Strindberg are better known
to an unenlightened generation in O'Neill and O'Casey, not to
mention the Expressionists, this idea, this approach, is often
thought to be the gift to modern culture of Luigi Pirandello.

Strindberg came to regard Naturalism as something he had
outgrown. But he was never really a Zolaist. A moral difference
separates his "Naturalist" from his later "Expressionist" plays.
In the former the fantastic element is merely a demonic force
which wrecks lives; in the latter it is also the creative fancy and
imagination which are associated with religion: in them the
irrationality of life leads not to the frightening joy in living of
*Miss Julia,* but to religious resignation. Naturalism and Expressionism, the twin poles of the Strindbergian mind, are two answers to the challenge of a Darwinian world. They are not
philosophies. They are the two archetypal patterns of defeat in
the modern world: defeat at the hands of a naturalistic nihilism
and defeat at the hands of a compensatory supernaturalism.

In Strindberg modern tragedy is in process of dissolution.
*Tragédie bourgeoise* began with respect for the solid character
of the burgher; in Strindberg's *Dream Play,* "the characters
split, double, multiply, vanish, solidify, blur, clarify." For
Strindberg there cannot even be those Pastor Rosmers and Mas-

ter Builder Solnesses whose quest for integrity had had a certain grandeur. The burgher, as Strindberg sees him, is not only sick, he is prostrate. His prostration is shown either directly, in dream plays where the central character is bowed with guilt, or in reverse, in the "Naturalistic" dramas where the enterprise of the burgher shows itself only in eruptions of destructive malignity. (Ibsen reflects a society of Gladstones, Strindberg is premonitory of Hitler's society.) The dream plays spelled Expressionism and the evaporation of tragedy. Now in the early Tudor period our first tragedies arose from medieval preoccupation with the humiliation of great men, which taught contempt for the world. With Strindberg tragedy returns to the medieval womb.

## V

The tragedy of the bourgeois epoch which culminated in Ibsen, and which was overthrown and superseded by Strindberg, had an aftermath in some dramatists of whom none are more symptomatic—in distinct ways—than Frank Wedekind and Eugene O'Neill.

In Ibsen and Strindberg we grow accustomed to a *fin de siècle* weariness. But Strindberg prophesied a "re-entrance of the powers" and in his lurid vision is a hint of the kind of realm in which twentieth-century barbarism is real. If Ibsen and Strindberg represent the decline of the burgher and his morality, Wedekind invents a world in which there are no burghers and no morality. The powers re-enter, and the Nazis (this around 1900) are on the stage. "Instead of the title *Erdgeist*," Wedekind wrote in a note on his extraordinary play, "I could just as well have written *Realpsychologie,* in a similar sense to *Realpolitik.*" *Realpolitik* is politics stripped down to the horrifying moral nakedness of the jungle. Wedekind strips the individual similarly. His objection to Ibsen was that the latter presented the higher animal, man, and not lower animals in human costume as Wedekind boasts of doing in the prologue to *Erdgeist*:

*Was seht ihr in den Lust—und Trauerspielen?*
Haustiere . . .
*Das* wahre *Tier, das* wilde schöne *Tier,*
*Das—meine Damen!—sehn Sie nur bei mir.**

Schigolch, Casti-Piani, Marquis von Keith, Hidalla, Morosini, Tschamper, Veit Kunz, Oaha, and dozens of other Wedekind creations form the most fatal and fabulous human menagerie outside Goya and Daumier. Wedekind has a satirist's draughtsmanship. But his standpoint is not reason, or common sense, the often rather stolid pragmatism of the comic writers from Aristophanes to Molière. It is religious. But like Baudelaire, Wedekind is only negatively religious. He is not a believer, and his vision is solely of evil. Those who are unacquainted with this cultural phenomenon simply have to take Wedekind's word for it that his aim was to unite holiness with beauty.

In some of Wedekind's plays there is a tragic element from which we can learn something. For instance, *Tod und Teufel.* The plot of this one-act play, like nearly all Wedekind's plots, is absurd. A lady representative of a society for the abolition of white slavery visits the macabre procurer, Marquis Casti-Piani, and falls in love with him. The confrontation of the woman who believes in the spirit of orthodox morality and the marquis who believes that "the flesh has its own spirit" is magnificent. Supposedly Wedekind sides with the marquis. But when the marquis learns from an experienced daughter of joy that the ecstasies of the flesh grow ever harder to attain, that the pursuit of sensual pleasure is ultimately self-defeating, his diabolonian scheme of values is upset and he shoots himself. The play ends with the lady kissing his dead lips, closing his eyes, and crying: "This last disillusionment you may well never have let yourself dream about in your frightful *Weltschmerz*: that a *virgin* closes your eyes for you!" The kiss will recall Salome, and the whole

* What do you see in comedies and tragedies? *Domestic animals* . . . The *true* animal, the *fine wild* animal, that, ladies, you see only at my place.

story sounds clumsily "decadent." But that is to reckon without Wedekind's treatment of his plot. I will pick out one feature in his remarkable transmogrification of hokum. From being at her first entrance a typical caricature of a lady moralist, Elfriede uncannily changes until, even in Casti-Piani's brothel, we feel sympathy for her. Yet she is not a Saroyanesque good woman. She is a virgin in whom such tremendous sexual passion is awakened that she puts the commerce of sex to shame. This strange triumph of the human in the midst of physical and moral death is *almost* tragic.

The distortions and involutions of Wedekind's moral symbols are an early objectification of the same spiritual sickness which later outcropped in surrealism after one fashion, in D. H. Lawrence and Henry Miller, and after a different fashion in Franz Kafka. In all these diverse figures there is a deep consciousness of chaos, a longing for the numinous, for that mystic and mysterious part of experience which the modern imagination has so often overlooked. Wedekind is surrealist in his shock technique, his atmosphere of nightmare, his mastery of the sexual-grotesque. In his moral stand he is Lawrentian. Unlike all these men, his imagination functioned in theatrical terms, and occasionally in tragic, or, more correctly, pseudo-tragic terms. Perhaps his most celebrated pseudo tragedy is *Lulu,* as the double drama of *Erdgeist* and *Die Büchse der Pandora* is generally known. The first part of the play, of which Wedekind wrote: "I wanted to exclude all ideas which are logically untenable, such as love, loyalty, gratitude," ends when Lulu shoots her man. In the second part, where Wedekind attempts to bring the piece to a tragic culmination, the Countess Geschwitz, till now a ridiculous Lesbian lover of Lulu's, is slowly transformed until—without many of the critics' noticing it—she attains a sort of tragic grandeur by expressing love, loyalty, and gratitude. Lesbianism is not sentimentalized. The Countess is made Lesbian to give her virtue the most abnormal origin. In our world only a twisted virtue can triumph. Such is

Wedekind's version of poetic justice. *Lulu* is the epitaph of bourgeois tragedy.

Since Wedekind, not a few playwrights have courted Melpomene without noticing that the lady is dead. John Masefield's *Tragedy of Nan* (one of the best English plays of this century) shows what happens when a man tries to construct a tragedy out of mere knowledge of what poetic tragedy used to be like. Among the untragic tragedians the most spectacular and instructive is Eugene O'Neill. At everything in the theater except being tragic and being comic he is a success. What other American dramatist has his technique, his agility in using ideas, his earnest mind, his interest in big things? In our time O'Neill is one of the most gifted men who has tried to make tragedy in modern or any other dress.

The critic Joseph Wood Krutch, who seems to follow Heine in the belief that the bourgeois world is antitragic because undignified, thinks that O'Neill has come much nearer than Ibsen to the recreation of tragedy. Ibsen's plays he calls "sociological treatises" which, he says, "mean something" whereas Sophocles, Shakespeare, and O'Neill only mean that "human beings are great and terrible creatures when they are in the grip of great passions." Furthermore, Mr. Krutch argues, O'Neill is tragic in a modern way: "Like every great tragic writer, O'Neill must accept the premises of his audience, and it so happens that those premises are not the premises of ancient Greece or Elizabethan England but the premises of modern psychology."

O'Neill's beloved psychology has proved as dazzling to many as the modernity of his stage techniques. Another modern touch is his professed belief that the only big subject is the conflict between religion and materialism, in which the victory of the former was foreordained, though not actually announced till 1933. All this Mr. Krutch calls "finding a modern equivalent for Aeschylus and Shakespeare," a quest not strange to readers of Hebbel or the despised Ibsen. But the assumption, harmlessly present in Hebbel, that the heart of tragedy lies at a deeper level than the historical, at an unchanging, metaphysical level, leads in O'Neill out of the tragic realm, perhaps out of the imaginative realm altogether. "Most modern plays," O'Neill says, "are concerned with the relation between man and man, but that does not interest me at all. I am interested only in the relation between man and God." Making every allowance for the creative writer's blarney, and doing O'Neill the favor of not taking his assertion literally, we might still claim to find in this confession one of the sources of O'Neill's weakness. In his later plays O'Neill is increasingly indifferent to the stuff of life, of society, of history, as it has fascinated the masters of tragedy, and he has courted the abstraction Man and the archabstraction God. Tragedy is transported to the intense inane. What the philosopher Georg Simmel said of the Expressionists is even truer of O'Neill: They attempt to seize life in its essence but without its content.

O'Neill always provides outer conflict and a simple conflict of ideas. The tension that is missing in his work is inner tension. This is what distinguishes him from Ibsen and Strindberg. Ibsen always insisted that even a world conflict in a play should be a projection of something that the playwright has lived through. "And as regards the thing which has been lived through," he declared, "that is just the secret of the literature of modern times." Strindberg knew the secret. The kaleidoscopic visions of his later fantasies express the manifold forces tugging at his heart and head. And when Strindberg is more interested in God than in the relations of men he does not make the mistake of attempting tragedy.

In comparing *Mourning Becomes Electra* with *Hamlet* and *Macbeth,* Mr. Krutch observes of the former: "One realizes that it does lack just one thing and that that thing is language— words as thrilling as the action which accompanies them." For many of us this is giving away the case. Surely, a drama not verbalized is a drama not dramatized; the subordination of the words to other theatrical factors is death to the drama. If a play lacks "just one thing and that . . . thing is language," we shall miss more than thrills. We shall miss tragedy. A tragedy is a kind of poem. O'Neill is adept at putting together a great deal of sexual emotion and a modernistic technique. In fact his main intention seems to be to give a "modern" shell to an "eternal" nut. But poetic synthesis is more than putting two and two together. We must also be able to say that—in just as legitimate a sense—the nut is "modern," and the shell "eternal." O'Neill's mistake is an old one. He seeks greatness by imitating and exploiting the great, and he sees the permanence of art as a by-passing of the local and the temporal. But permanence is paradoxically achieved by a deep penetration of the present, and the greatness of the classics is best emulated, as Horace and Pope told us, by our being as independent as classical writers were.

O'Neill's early plays of the sea prove that, had he avoided tragedy, he could have been a highly satisfactory dramatist. For in his failure to rival Shakespeare we are probably justified in seeing more than personal incapacity or a mistaken dramatic theory. Is it mere smug wisdom after the event if we assume that O'Neill's time was not one of the few which are ripe for tragedy, though there has been high drama of a nontragic, noncomic sort from Chekhov to Garcia Lorca and Bertolt Brecht? From the limited perspective of 1946 it seems plausible to regard *Strange Interlude* and *Mourning Becomes Electra* as a grotesque aftermath of "bourgeois tragedy." Unlike Wedekind and Strindberg, O'Neill has not as yet been able adequately to represent the bourgeois world as the nightmare which in the twentieth century it became, though his portraits of neurosis and decay are a labored and overconscious striving in that direction. O'Neill's more powerful, *unconsciously* symbolic tendency was to try to flee the bourgeois world, not like Wedekind by standing it on its head, but by trying to deny its existence, by proclaiming exclusive reality for the eternal. It was O'Neill himself who stood on his head.

So ends the *tragédie bourgeoise*. What we see in its history is not only a chapter in the history of the bourgeoisie. It is a fascinatingly intricate instance of the changing fortunes of an art form which, at least in the plays of Ibsen, told the tragic truth about an epoch, thereby winning the only immortality. What the modern novel has done we know. And we are aware of the reach of modern poetry and more vaguely of music and art. Of drama many of us have only known that Ibsen is ponderous and Shaw frivolous. That is worse than knowing little, for it is to know what is not so.

The main difference between Shakespeare and Schiller is this: in Shakespeare the inner development is the main thing and the outer tragedy, i.e. the action, the event, occurs as a necessary consequence and at the same time as a symbolic externalization of the inner development, while in Schiller the opposite is the case.

OTTO LUDWIG

# 3. TRAGEDY

# IN FANCY DRESS

## I

THE "BOURGEOIS TRAGEDY" WAS THE MOST DIRECT TRAGIC EX-pression of a middle-class epoch. But for the greater part of its history it seemed, perhaps, no more than an eccentricity or sport of nature, so few were the plays in the genre, so powerful was the prestige, if not the continued achievement, of orthodox high tragedy still solemnly disporting itself in alexandrines, heroic couplets, or blank verse. The history of orthodox high tragedy after 1700 is an uninterrupted decline, and that, if we believe those who harp on the littleness of modernity and our untragic indignity, is the end of tragedy in the modern world. Nevertheless we do find a significant and by no means fruitless series of attempts to find for the drama a form as lofty and poetic, as overtly sublime, as poetic tragedy. Of these attempts three, perhaps, are outstanding: the attempts of the German *Klassiker* Lessing, Goethe, and Schiller; the attempt of Richard Wagner; and the attempt of so-called Neo-Romanticists at the end of the nineteenth century.

It was Lessing who turned the efforts of tragic poets into new tracks. How much this meant in boldness and originality will be clear if we remember that even so courageous and enterprising a mind as Voltaire was content to write tragedies in the old manner (though he did suggest some alterations of the old patterns). As Lessing's criticism cleared the ground for every sort of new endeavor, as his domestic plays converted the bourgeois drama from an experiment into a genre, so his *Nathan der Weise,* itself no great tragedy, indeed no tragedy at all, inaugurated an era of high drama oriented in a tragic direction such as has not since been matched: the era of the great German masters Schiller and Goethe, of which the French Romantic Drama was an aftermath, and the plays of Kleist an extraordinary off-shoot.

The dramatic achievements of Goethe and Schiller have been praised and appraised at length by generations of scholars and even, in Germany at least, by critics. They are remarkable and complex achievements. Yet if we ask what new form of tragedy they gave to the world—or even what old form they continued or revived—the answers do not come easily. Goethe is perhaps in this connection—and in this connection alone—the more straightforward case. What are we to make of him as a dramatist?

His astonishing all-round endowment made it inevitable that Goethe should try his hand at the drama. Circumstances made him director of a court theater with Schiller for a colleague. Nevertheless Goethe was not a master of the drama. His *Goetz von Berlichingen* has histrionic power and tempo; one would tend to regard the young man who could write such a piece as a born man of the theater; yet Goethe thought of it as a play for reading and was not interested in developing his theatricality. *Egmont* has charm and the kind of social-revolutionary ardor that makes good theater; but, considering the richness of Goethe's genius, the texture is surprisingly thin and the construction so flimsy that it could hardly have received his attention at all. More and more the drama became for Goethe a mere formal convenience. *Tasso, Iphigenie,* and above all *Faust,* are nondramatic poems in dramatic form. The matter is further complicated, and the discussion of drama and poetry further confused, by the fact that these poems do contain some dramatic scenes.

In this as in all dramatic subjects which he touched upon, Egon Friedell's opinion is illuminating. According to Friedell, Goethe was dissatisfied with even the most necessary theatrical conventions. He created so full a life for his people that, so to speak, the fourth wall which the theater manager tactfully omits from the stage is put back into place, and the auditorium is shut off. Really theatrical characters, Friedell implies, are not complete human beings; they partake of the nature of the theater; they exist in rooms—literally and figuratively speaking—with one wall missing.

If Friedell's theory of theater sounds to our ears too much like the arguments of our contemporary champions of the theater against drama, or too much like, say, George Jean Nathan's notion that drama is not to be taken too seriously, it nevertheless helps us to distinguish Goethe from Schiller. Goethe, one might almost say, is antitheatrical. He turns his back on the audience. Schiller is theatrical alike in the good and in the bad sense. He knows and respects the theatrical medium. He can think in terms of stage spectacle and stage movement. His notes, his stage directions, his work in the theater, not to mention the main body of his drama, bear witness to an interest in the effects of actual production upon actual audiences. And he goes too far. Had Schiller not become an official classic—a process which means the solemnification and therefore the ossification of any genius—he would be famous for unscrupulous showmanship. We have seen that the ending of *Kabale und Liebe* is accidental. Alternative endings for several of Schiller's plays were made, and some of them were Schiller's own work. His mastery of intrigue, of poison and passion, was something that Scribe or Hugo might have envied. *Don Carlos* may have a more skillful and intricate plot than *Un Verre d'Eau* or *Hernani*. It is not a jot less disingenuous.

At this point one might interject: "Lurid intrigue, passion, and crime—they prove nothing against Schiller. Aren't Shakespeare's plots the luridest?—Not to mention Webster's *Duchess of Malfi*." The reminder that Shakespeare and Webster utilized preposterous fables prompts the question whether Schiller too "does something" to his plot, whether he, like Shakespeare and Webster, makes it an instrument of a higher purpose? Certainly Schiller does not revive the spirit of Elizabethan tragedy. Yet he can be defended. And the defense would be based on the affirmation: Schiller is a playwright of ideas.

Idea is a vague concept. In one sense there are ideas in all words and therefore in all drama. Tragedy has always suggested ideas concerning the significance of human life. Comedy has suggested ideas of right and wrong conduct. Seldom, however, have ideas been the lifeblood of drama. Even in Molière it is only in a retrospective sketch like the *Critique de l'Ecole des Femmes* that the idea is all. Though *Le Misanthrope* may be an exception to this, as to so many other rules, Molière may be said to *use* ideas but not to make his drama out of them. Again setting *Le Misanthrope* aside, it may be suggested that Molière uses accepted ideas, lets his characters embody them and fight it out. The characters fight, the ideas lie still and unmolested. In a drama of ideas, on the other hand, the ideas are questioned, and it is by the questioning, and could only be by the questioning, that the ideas become dramatic, for seldom or never is there drama without conflict. Lessing must surely be the first major writer to see quite clearly that, since it is conflict and not outward action upon which the drama depends, there could be a drama in which the basic conflict was one of ideas, and that such a drama might be peculiarly appropriate to a world without a common faith, philosophy, or idea. Accordingly Lessing chose precisely the lack of a common faith as the theme of his pregnant drama *Nathan,* in which the dialectic of the theme is one with the dialectic of the dramaturgy: the different strands of the drama, drawn together by the unity of the structure, are identical with the different faiths which by tolerance—the leading idea of the play—are revealed as one.

Where Lessing promised, Schiller tried to fulfill. By *Don Carlos* and *Wilhelm Tell* he won himself a name as a political dramatist and wrote lines which the Nazis had to censor more than a century later. He would be greeted by liberals as a forerunner and by Nazis as a *kampfgenosse.* He would be sneered at by leftists as a bourgeois liberal and by rightists as a humanitarian. In Marquis Posa and Wilhelm Tell he justified reform, toleration, and tyrannicide; yet he was no callow enthusiast; he carefully makes Posa declare that his eighteenth-century ideas are ahead of the sixteenth century in which he lives; Tell's tyrannicide he hedges round with a dozen provisos calculated to safeguard the heads of kings.

I have suggested that being a classic prevents the lighter qualities of a work from being perceived; it also prevents its faults from being acknowledged. *Don Carlos* is not only long. It is cumbersome. Schiller has tied and untied enough knots to supply the intrigue for several plays. He has then added Posa and his ideas without attempting to integrate the whole. Though *Don Carlos* would have to be mentioned in any consideration of modern tragedy, it is not a tragedy at all but a clever melodrama rendered into a college classic by legerdemain, an elevated tone, and forensic eloquence. And in the end, like several of Marlowe's plays, which also were full of nonsense, it is irresistible; Marlowe and Schiller exercise a fascination that can scarcely be explained by their addiction to hocus-pocus.

More satisfactory than *Don Carlos* is *Wilhelm Tell*. Lacking the exuberance, the complication, and the hokum of the earlier play, *Wilhelm Tell* is a successful fusion of idea and event, character and deed. Is it a tragedy? It will not matter that the ending is happy, if the play has the temper and scope of tragedy. But has it? Seriousness it has in abundance. It has a hero too, and it *tests* him to the uttermost, as tragedy is wont to do. Is the testing tragic? Tell's first choice is between death and shooting at an apple placed on his son's head. He chooses death until he learns that the son will be killed with him. The choice then shifts to sure death for both, or Tell's running the risk of killing his son. This—Tell's ultimate choice—is surely not tragic, for it is really no choice at all. There is only one thing to do: to try to save both lives by shooting. Tell shoots, and later he kills the tyrant Gessler who had forced him into shooting. Both actions are splendidly heroic. But they constitute something closer to a success story than to tragedy.

Those who miss the ambiguity of the famous climax and *coup de théâtre* must be baffled by the length and discursiveness of the sequel, and indeed there has been endless complaint—tempered by the nervousness due to a classic—against it. The shooting scene is in Act Three. In Act Four Tell kills the villain, but the deed is swift and almost perfunctory. Most of the act is talk. Two great speeches in Schiller's best bravura manner—Attinghausen arguing for a united front and Tell justifying his murder of Gessler—are the twin supports on which the act stands. But by this time critics and directors have had enough. They learned in school that the word drama originally meant action. Undeterred, Schiller defies etymology and the critics in another long act, the fifth, again almost entirely devoted to argument. Another tyrant-killer comes to Tell as to a brother. Schiller's thoughts on the subject are driven home when Tell repudiates the man who has murdered the emperor from personal motives and not from public necessity. Tell says:

> *Nichts teil ich mit dir—Gemordet*
> *Hast du, ich hab mein teuerstes verteidigt **

and then the play ends with a pleasant pastoral scene celebrating the merits and beauties of Switzerland. *William Tell* therefore is many things: oratory, debate, idyll, adventure, apologia, folk tale, document. As poem, as theater, as lesson, it is very rich. Is it churlish to suggest that as tragedy it does not exist?

Had we to compress the iridescent world of Schiller's theater into historical formulations our conclusion might run something like this: While in one play—*Kabale und Liebe*—he successfully essayed the new middle genre, he elsewhere sought to renew the high tragic tradition by returning—above the heads of the classicists, French and German—to Shakespeare. But an influence from a past age is inevitably assimilated to the later. The Shakespearism of Schiller is exactly two hundred years distant from Shakespeare. When Schiller translated *Macbeth* he replaced the porter's bawdy prose by a dignified song, a substitution that has been thought academic, Teutonic, and so forth. Actually the alteration is shrewd and genuinely theatrical. The better audiences, in my experience, are embarrassed by Shakespeare's scene; the worse giggle at it. Yet Schiller's version is desperately un-Shakespearean. It shows a readiness to compromise with an audience and a concern with dramatic sequence—a song at dawn following a murder—reasonably figured out rather than imaginatively grasped. Schiller was more of a thinker than Shakespeare. Where the latter presents things, Schiller writes *about* things. His Shakespearism is in the first place a stimulus to independent work of his own and in the second a matter of externals, such as his adoption of the long, many-scened, open plays of the Elizabethans as against the concise, triply unified, closed plays of the French. The spirit and meaning of Schiller is un-Shakespearean.

* Nothing will I share with you—*you* murdered, *I* protected my dearest possession.

However we take Schiller's outlook—stressing the influence of Rousseau or Kant or Goethe—we shall agree that it is very much of his time, and hence that it is—on any orthodox view— untragic. His muse, we might be tempted to think, is not Melpomene but Clio. What is his *Wallenstein,* we might say, but a by-product of his history of the Thirty Years' War? What is his most original act, one critic says, but to bring onto the stage corporate as well as individual life? These are valuable hints. If he looks enviously back to Shakespeare or the Greeks, Schiller also looks forward to a drama of social ideas. Alfred de Vigny when he wrote of a *"drame de la pensée,"* Friedrich Hebbel when he wrote of a drama founded in the Idea, were carrying on where Schiller left off. In this respect Schiller may undoubtedly be judged a pathfinder. He was hardly a recreator of tragedy.

The nineteenth century saw many attempts to do what Schiller had not succeeded in doing. Nearly every major poet—not to mention the minor ones—tried his hand: one tends to forget that Byron was once chiefly admired for such things as *Cain* and that even Keats had Shakespearean longings. Benjamin Constant wrote a French adaptation of *Wallenstein;* Dumas *père* pored over Schiller, and Victor Hugo's brigand-hero Hernani is the heir of Schiller's robber Karl Moor; not least important, the Germans led the French Romanticists back to Shakespeare. After which it is depressing to note that French Romantic Drama is a portentous failure, that *Hernani* is a schoolmaster's classic far inferior to anything of Schiller's (not to compare it with Shakespeare, as Matthew Arnold did), and that the plays of the French Romanticists succeeded best, when they succeeded at all, on the operatic stage for which God, if not always their authors, intended them. Much more considerable are the efforts of Kleist and Hebbel, the eccentric Grabbe and even the rather academic Grillparzer. A history of the high tragic tradition could not omit them. But in this place there is one man of the theater who clamors for consideration. Because he offered an entirely different solution to the problem of tragic drama, a theory and a practice greeted with such cries of joy and rage as never before had greeted any artist, Richard Wagner commands our attention.

## II

If there is anything that a Wagnerite and an anti-Wagnerite can agree upon, it is that Wagner was first and foremost a man of the theater. Drama was to Wagner the highest art, and if he is best known as a musician that is because he tried to approach the drama by way of music, an art in which, contrary to his desires, he was more gifted. Wagner was as fully aware of the plight of the theater in his time as was the amazing Friedrich Hebbel. He gave a full account of recent stage history in his essay "German Art and German Politics" (1867). As early as January, 1846, he had been writing to the critic Hanslick: "I regard my present and forthcoming works as mere experiments to see if opera be possible." Soon the "mere experiments" grew to a full-blown claim to "an art work which, thoroughly as it differed from both opera and modern drama, yet should rise above them simply by carrying to their end the choicest tendencies of either, and uniting them in one ideal and unencumbered whole."

The Wagnerian art work, which Wagner at first called *musikdrama* and *gesamtkunstwerk* and later simply opera, was essentially another attempt to create a high drama of tragic scope in the modern world. "By opera alone," Wagner wrote, "can our theater be raised again." Yet, though he set great store by his libretti, Wagner did not believe with Gluck and Hugo Wolf that the musician should simply underscore the words. The idea that he did so is one of the chief popular errors about Wagnerism. But it was Wagner himself who wrote: "The union of music and poetry must always end in . . . a subordination of the latter." It was not literature but theater that Wagner believed to be "the one indivisible supreme creation." One of the founders of the now popular philosophy of drama according to which the words of a drama are a mere "script," a mere fragment of an immense structure, Wagner is fundamentally antiliterary. In his essay on actors and singers he insists that the author participates in a play only to the extent that he anticipates the effects of stage presentation. In itself this is a sound idea, though the people who promote it are almost always people who regard poetry as untheatrical.

It has been said that while Lortzing wrote libretti to his own scores, Wagner composed scores to his own libretti. The epigram is not true if it suggests that Wagner was more of a writer than a composer. It *is* true that Wagner's imagination was pictorial and theatrical. His first full-length work was a juvenile neo-Elizabethan tragedy. His first and most formative enthusiasms were theatrical. It was a performance by the famous Madame Schröder-Devrient that showed Wagner the possibilities of his own sort of heroic singing and acting. "When, twenty years back," Wagner wrote in 1861, "I stayed in Paris for a considerable time, the consummateness of musical and plastic *mise-en-scène* at the performances of the Grand Opera could not fail to produce a most dazzling and stimulating impression on me." As for libretti, Wagner wrote that Eugène Scribe's would "for long serve as models." Though the older Wagner professed to despise Scribe, the younger Wagner had written: "What a colossus Scribe's genius must be," and "Without Scribe, no opera, no play, no genuine amusement." Scribe, it will be remembered, was the Noel Coward of the nineteenth century: a man who knew nothing of "drama" and nearly everything about "theater."

Even without Wagner, the early and middle nineteenth century was more successful in opera than in nonmusical drama. Spoken drama seemed indeed to be threatened with extinction. What Wagner planned to do was to confirm this victory of the opera by infusing into it all the theatrical ingenuity of Scribe.

And more. He would add tragic dignity. The dramatic stage would be able to do nothing which the opera could not do better and all in one glorious mélange. Now the operatic tradition had not been tragic. The operas of the old masters Mozart and Gluck, and of the young master Spontini, ended untragically. Some of the new Romantic operas had a catastrophic close without any aspiration to tragic import. The following is Wagner's description of what Meyerbeer, Scribe's musical collaborator, required from a libretto: he "wanted a monstrous, piebald, historico-romantic, diabolico-religious, fanatic-libidinous, sacro-frivolous, mysterio-criminal, autolyco-sentimental, dramatic hotch-potch, therein to find a material for a curious chimerical music." It sounds like the later Nietzsche on Wagner! (The earlier Nietzsche had more generally acknowledged that Wagner wanted to restore tragedy.) In his rearrangement of Gluck's *Iphigenia* Wagner put back Euripides' tragic ending. The Romantic type of opera which he himself began to practice he tried to redeem partly by his allegorical interpretations of myth, but most of all by injecting drama into the music itself.

Otto Ludwig, perhaps one of the few important philosophers of drama, said that drama in essence was the marriage of two arts, acting and poetry. Wagner substituted the formula, acting and music. "Here the infinitely potent orchestra," he wrote, "there the dramatic mime; here the mother-womb of ideal drama, there its issue borne on every hand by sound." You can hear less of the libretto in a Wagner opera than in any other: the meaning is supposed to be transferred to the orchestra. The usual question asked about the resulting dramatic music is: what is it like as music? What we have to ask here, however, is: what is it like as drama?

Critics of the poetic drama of the Elizabethans have asked us to see not only the "linear" pattern of the plot, but also the "spatial" pattern in which mood, attitude, and versification are artfully disposed. Wagnerian music drama consists almost exclusively of such patterns of contrast. One of Wagner's best-known ideas is that the symphony is a development from the dance tune; dramatic action he believed to be a developed form of the dance itself. We are again reminded of our contemporary champions of theatrical arts who stress all elements in drama except the literary elements. The drama becomes a problem in visual and auditory form. And Wagner is thoroughgoing. As one of his best interpreters, Paul Bekker, has observed, the music dramas are of two sorts: the chordal dramas (*The Fairies, Rienzi, The Ring, Die Meistersinger*) and the chromatic dramas, of which *Tristan* is the great example. In the one set of compositions the basic pattern is that of a pure harmony repeatedly broken up by dissonance; in the other it is that of repeated resolution of discords; in both it is an endlessly repeated device that is the basis of the type. Some listeners are understandably infuriated. As the composer Busoni noted, Wagner's music consists of crescendos which rise quickly to a climax, and then have to be followed by a diminuendo and another crescendo and another climax, and so *ad infinitum*. Moreover, the character of the music is determined by nonmusical considerations; modulation is facilitated by rapid changes in dramatic mood, and purists are scandalized at the default of purely musical construction. Dramatically considered, the music becomes an astonishing agent of mood and psychology, an amazingly swift and direct conductor of feeling. No wonder that inveterate Wagnerites, caught in this tidal wave, have thought "literary" drama a paltry rivulet.

"Wagner as musician is reckoned among painters, as poet among musicians, as artist generally among actors": Nietzsche's hostile words are not far from Wagner's own professed theory. Even a judicious Wagnerite could admit that Wagner was primarily an "actor," a man of the theater, and that he seeks an ironic interplay in his work by interchanging the functions of the arts. As Bekker says: "Upon the stage walk sounds, not people. They do not speak but sing words, do not think but feel.

Similarly, in musical form, people, not notes, move about, not sounding but conversing in tonal relations, not forming patterns but acting." The natural ideality of absolute music Wagner turns to its opposite: the concrete reference of program music, the very corporeality of stage performance which he had tried to reverse by the magic of a mythological subject, modern staging, and a new type of theatrical building in which a unified, dark auditorium and a "mystic abyss" created by a proscenium-arch and a covered orchestra all played a part.

In this way Wagner intended to be at once a Shakespeare and a Beethoven. He would make tone visible and light audible. Uniting sound and light, invisible and visible, subject and object, he would create a higher drama. "Beethoven's melodies," he wrote, "convey the same truth as Shakespeare's phantom figures: the two would be one could the musician command not only the sound world but the light world." To learn how Wagner did this one need but see one of his works performed; to understand what he intended, which is quite another matter, one must trace further one of the arguments of his little book, *Beethoven*. The worlds of Beethoven and Shakespeare, Wagner says, differ "only by the laws of expansion and movement which govern them. . . . A perfect art form, accordingly, must start from the point at which these laws coincide." With never-failing readiness to answer the most unanswerable question, Wagner declares that "the point at which these laws coincide" is: the world of dreams. The reply does not make clear sense, but one assumes he means that while the mode of expression of poets and musicians is different, their fantasies and feelings may be similar. In the back of Wagner's mind was probably also his love of phantasmagoria, that realm which his combination of program music and otherworldly story seemed best fitted to conjure up. Wagner's operas differ widely from each other, but they have one thing in common: an atmosphere of phantasmagoria. The attempt to be both Beethoven and Shakespeare very naturally produced something utterly unlike either.

Wagner could probably see that no pattern of mood expressed in musical sound could constitute a tragedy, and he occasionally tried to adumbrate a fully tragic theory which had some *prima facie* plausibility. As Hebbel toyed with Hegel after a poet's fashion and completely altered Hegel's meaning, so Wagner toyed with Schopenhauer and arrived by Schopenhauerian lingo at an un-Schopenhauerian view. Schopenhauer's philosophy of music was much more favorable to absolute music than was Wagner's, but Wagner dimly remembered the high compliments which Schopenhauer had paid to the art which eliminates the subject-object relation and brings you face to face with the Idea. In Schopenhauerian fashion he found the phenomenal world to be an illusion, but an illusion that can be unveiled and thus destroyed by music. Unhappily Wagner had in mind *dramatic* music, that is, music which depicts the very phenomenal world which is supposed to be an illusion. The theory is confused, but in it we descry a hazy notion of a Shakespearean tragic conception which sees the world as a battle of living human feeling against fate and time. In *Tristan* time and fate seem in a transcendental sense to be conquered, as in *Antony and Cleopatra*, by the grandeur of a high and sacrificial passion. The transfiguration of Cleopatra by poetry is of course hard to interpret, since one is not meant to assume that the queen of Egypt is a great Elizabethan poetess, or that, even if she were, her fate would be less harsh. But, it might be argued, what the mood of her last great speech does for Cleopatra, the mood of her last great aria does for Isolde.

Yet Wagner is un-Shakespearean not only in belonging to an era in which tragic significance was to be differently discovered (by Ibsen), and not only in being Shakespeare's inferior. He had thought to add to Shakespeare (S) the genius of a Beethoven (B), but instead of being S + B he was W, a third entity. The essential distinction is that between drama and opera. Music is one of the least limited of the arts in the expression of every kind of affect. Drama, being presented through the medium of words, deals not only with affects, not only with objects (some of which are within the scope of program music), but also with concepts which music cannot touch at all and which a libretto cannot very freely handle. The distinction I have in mind came home to me very forcibly when I saw Shakespeare's *Othello* and Verdi's *Otello* almost at the same time. To many who cannot accept Wagner, Verdi's opera is acceptable as theater, yet try as one may it does not communicate a tragic experience. When *Otello* is sung—and it would be the same if the actors sang the very words of Shakespeare's play—we no longer accept the substance of the play directly. The performer sings, so it seems, *about* Othello; he cannot *be* Othello. The singer is a narrator; the text is something cited. Hence one can see that music might be appropriate to the dramas of Bertolt Brecht, who uses music precisely to give the affect of quotation and distance; but in non-narrative tragedy where we identify ourselves with a protagonist, music is an intrusion.

It is also a handicap. It subordinates poetry, as Wagner himself admitted. And every dramaturgic practice that subordinates the words to any other medium has trivialized the drama without giving full rein to the medium that has become dominant. Painters, choreographers, and musicians have more scope outside drama altogether—in pageantry, ballet, and opera. Instead of adding the merits of one art to another, Wagner set the muses quarreling. Thalia, Melpomene, and Euterpe fight an interminable battle. There were technical difficulties in the way of Wagner's grand schemes: to set a play to music is almost to double its duration and thus to change all its tempi; even then, no singers ever communicate their words unbrokenly to the audience. Above all, music performs its dramatic functions very inadequately. Though Wagner and Richard Strauss have carried dramatic music to extraordinary lengths, they not only cannot, as the latter wished, give an exact musical description of a tablespoon, they cannot do anything at all with the even more baffling world of conceptual thought. They cannot construct the complex parallels and contraries of meaning which drama demands. On the stage the death of Hamlet is moving, despite all the indignity of actors simulating death agonies, because of the meanings—the ideas with all their connotations and interrelations—that Shakespeare's lines have fixed in our minds. The death of an operatic hero—a Tristan, an Otello, a Boris Godunov—may be impressive in many ways but it is not a supreme event. It is the decoration of an event. We appreciate very openly the skill with which the event is circumvented, and when the actor pretends to fall dead we applaud.

*Tannhäuser* and *The Ring*, *Tristan* and *Parsifal* fail to be great tragedies not because the tenors are fat or because the orchestra is too loud or because Wagner was a proto-Nazi; such things, if true, are beside the point. These works fall short of Wagner's intention because—I am inclined to think—opera cannot be tragic. They have many dramatic, and even more theatrical, elements in them. They tell stories that would serve for tragic purposes; and the libretti, studied by themselves, reveal much conscious and unconscious allegory. But knowing that a libretto is not a tragedy and hoping that he might make an opera into one by dramatizing the score, Wagner wrote libretti that were thinner and more repetitious than those of some other composers. The result is that at the end of his dramas we have a conclusion to the story but no *tragic* close. To overcome or conceal the difficulty, Wagner grew accustomed to ending his works with even more than his usual musical virtuosity. There is the superb *mild und leise* of Isolde and the weaving together of all the "leading motives" at the end of the *The Ring*. This is musical genius. It is not tragedy. To investigate the tragic intention we have to go not to the opera itself but to the libretto as elaborated by Wagner and the Wagnerites.

Such is Wagnerism. Our study of it will be resumed in the next chapter, where Wagner's method of redeeming the drama is contrasted with Ibsen's. For the present we should be content with certain elementary distinctions.

There are three main ways of combining music and drama. The first might be called Music with Dramatic Interludes. This is the more vulgar sort of opera in which dramatically sensational narrative operates as the bridge between musically sensational arias. The second way is Drama with Musical Interludes. This includes all drama—such as Shakespeare, the Greeks, or our own Sean O'Casey—in which music plays an important but subordinate role. It includes the theory though not the practice of Gluck. The third way is Drama by means of Music, which is what Wagner wanted, which is indeed what most major operatic composers have wanted, and which we might call Opera Proper.

We have seen how Wagner went wrong. As a musician to be reckoned a painter, as a poet to be reckoned a musician, is to have blurred and confused the arts, not to have united them. Furthermore I have ventured the suggestion that in attempting tragedy by musical means Wagner attempted the impossible. Opera cannot be tragedy. It was perhaps ill-advised even to define opera as "drama by means of music." However convenient this formula may sometimes be, it is confusing, since the potentialities of opera are really so different from those of spoken theater that it is misleading to call them both drama. Music Drama is a misnomer and a misconception. It led Wagner not only to gloss over the real differences between the arts, but also to imagine that the work of one could be done by another. Hence the gigantic error of his believing that drama could be *replaced* by opera.

Today I think we would rather stress the legitimate differences between the arts. Their territories may be adjacent, but they are not identical. Undoubtedly we do not know very clearly even now what opera can do. But we can learn from failures, however glorious, what it can *not* do. The Wagnerian experiment did not succeed in handing over the art of tragedy to the musicians. Even Nietzsche, who began by thinking the enterprise possible—he argued that tragedy was born out of the spirit of music—was disenchanted by a visit to Bayreuth.

## III

Toward the close of the nineteenth century came the New Drama and with it other serious efforts to create a genre with the depth, dignity, and lyric power of tragedy. I do not allude to lyric poets such as Tennyson, who continued the futile tradition of pseudo-Shakespearean poeticism by which so many had tried in vain to achieve drama, nor yet to such more modern flights as those of D'Annunzio, who essayed tragedy with fancy dress but without the muse. Looking back over the New Drama today, one is inclined to overlook the catalogues and categories of its historians and to pick out from that motley crowd, in which a Stephen Phillips jostles a Bernard Shaw and is therefore taken for his equal, one or two who deserve to stand when the rest have fallen by the wayside where only graduate students will ever pick them up. Among all the attempts to clothe Melpomene grandly again, none is of more special and intricate interest than that which we find in certain plays of the Belgian Maeterlinck, the Russian Andreyev, and the Swede Strindberg. The dream plays of these writers—and we may adopt the term Dream Play for a whole cluster of dramas which seek their effect through the evocation of mental states believed to be dreamlike—reflect the conviction that not only the "bourgeois tragedy" but also most non-naturalistic tragic drama in the modern period had been too external. The essence of tragedy is inner experience, and these plays, followed by those of the Expressionists from 1912 on, probe man's soul for tragic meaning. Whether they can be said to have found it is another matter.

In his *Treasure of the Humble* Maeterlinck has given us a concise and eloquent statement of his theory. His essay there entitled "The Tragical in Daily Life" suggests to our minds the leading idea of "bourgeois tragedy"—that ordinary life is tragic. Nor are Maeterlinck's characters necessarily in the aristocratic mode and grand manner of traditional tragedy. They may be in modern costume (though they usually are not) since to Maeterlinck the physical is nothing and the soul all. So far the theory is only a rather unusual mixture of usual ingredients. Nor are we unduly surprised when Maeterlinck informs us that action is unimportant. It is a common enough view. The unusual element in Maeterlinck's theory is his further assertion that dialogue itself is nothing—at least in its literal denotations. Silence, he says—and he does not mean merely dramatic pauses—is more eloquent than words. What matters is a mysterious unspoken dialogue that is somehow implied. We may retort that since the unspoken dialogue must to a great extent be suggested by the spoken dialogue, the latter is important after all. But Maeterlinck still has a point—that drama, as Eugene O'Neill has rephrased it, must suggest forces "behind life." The most revolutionary and most dubious part of Maeterlinck's theory is its denial of the necessity of conflict. Drama, he insists, the tragic experience itself, can be felt as pure stasis. Here the word-play is less defensible than it was in the discussion of dialogue. To be sure, the final tragic experience might be described as pure stasis. But this is the repose following violence, the synthesis that accrues from the clash of thesis and antithesis. To be sure, tragedy does not absolutely require physical and overt conflict. But even *Interior* and *The Intruder,* which are the extreme examples of Maeterlinck's views in practice, have an element of opposition, contest, or dialectic, and therefore of tension—otherwise it is not clear how they could register in our minds as unified and meaningful experience. The longer plays, such as *Pelléas et Mélisande,* have so much obvious and outward struggle in them as to remove them from the debate altogether.

In a "Letter on the Theater," dated 1914, Andreyev stated a theory very similar to Maeterlinck's. He wrote that action was not necessary in drama "inasmuch as life itself, in its more

dramatic and tragic moments, departs ever further from outward action, only to go into the depths of the soul, into that
quiet and internal immobility of living experience, the intellect." Andreyev proceeds to develop a historical theory. Our
consciousness has changed in recent centuries, he argues. The
life of a Benvenuto Cellini, all action and external event, is a
thing of the past. Modern man is much better represented by
Nietzsche, whose biography is purely spiritual. "Life has gone
within," Andreyev continues, "and the stage has remained outside. Life has become psychological, if one may express oneself
so, has become aligned with primitive fears. Along with the
everlasting heroes of the drama, love and hunger, comes a new
hero, the intellect. Neither love nor hunger nor ambition:·
thought, human thought, with all its sufferings, joys, and struggles—there is the true hero of contemporary life!" The idea that
thought should have a prime place in the modern drama is not
a contribution of the 1900 generation  It had been championed
or implied by Schiller, Vigny, Hebbel, and Ibsen. It is the
peculiar associations of thought—with suffering and joy, with
struggle and primitive fears—that is characteristic of the later
time. It prepares us for Pirandello and O'Neill. Such a drama
would inevitably be attacked by the Philistines as "intellectual." But the emphasis is on the agony of the intellect, upon the
intellect *in extremis,* not upon its supposedly arid cerebrations.
Admittedly such a subject is beyond even the high-brow end of
Broadway. Admittedly also it is a leitmotiv of modern culture.

There are large differences between Maeterlinck and Andreyev. Although the latter was in theory committed to the
doctrine of the static, the "quiet and internal immobility," he
likes to tell wild, macabre stories; he taps a vein of Dostoevskian
savagery. Maeterlinck, on the other hand—at least the Maeterlinck of the theory—prefers the nuance, the half-tone, the sigh,
the whimper, and the wistfulness. What Maeterlinck and Andreyev have in common is their central teaching: that there is
real tragedy in modern life and that it is to be found deep

within the individual ego. They echo Edgar Allan Poe's cry: "The terror of which I speak is not of Germany, but of the soul." They complete what had been a long process in the history of drama, namely, in the words of a dramatic historian: "a shifting of the scene from that which is without to that which is within." C. E. Vaughan, the author of these words, represented this process as the chief line of development indicated by the whole history of drama. An interesting formulation, to which we shall return.

Maeterlinck's theory was derived, in part at least, from none other than the greatest writer of tragedies, not in medieval, but in modern dress: Henrik Ibsen. In his own words:

> Some time ago, when dealing with *The Master Builder*, which is the one of Ibsen's dramas wherein this dialogue of the "second degree" attains the deepest tragedy, I endeavored, unskillfully enough, to fix its secrets. For indeed they are kindred handmarks traced on the same wall by the same sightless being, groping for the same light. "What is it," I asked, "what is it that, in *The Master Builder*, the poet has added to life, thereby making it appear so strange, so profound, and so disquieting beneath its trivial surface?" The discovery is not easy, the old master hides from us more than one secret. It would even seem as though what he has wished to say were but little by the side of what he has been compelled to say. He has freed certain powers of the soul that have never yet been free, and it may well be that these have held him in thrall. "Look you, Hilda," exclaims Solness, "look you! There is sorcery in you too as there is in me." It is this sorcery that imposes action on the powers of the beyond. . . . Hilda and Solness are, I believe, the first characters in drama who feel, for an instant, that they are living in the atmosphere of the soul. . . . Their conversation

resembles nothing that we have ever heard, inasmuch
as the poet has endeavored to blend in one expression
both the inner and outer dialogue. . . .

August Strindberg hated Ibsen, whom he called the Norwegian bluestocking, and would probably never have confessed
to learning anything from him. But he read Maeterlinck. Reading him at the time of his own naturalistic plays, Strindberg
was not impressed. Coming back to him at the turn of the
century, when, following his destiny and the Paris fashion set
by Huysmans and his beloved Péladan, he was turning toward
religion and the occult, Strindberg enthusiastically placed Maeterlinck among the greatest writers. For a time he bubbled over
with Maeterlinckism, as we see from his play *Swanwhite*. Later
he came to think that Maeterlinck could not be imitated but
only absorbed, and we can thus regard Maeterlinck as one of
the formative forces that went to the making of Strindberg's
later fantasies, of which the chief are *The Dream Play, The
Road to Damascus,* and *The Ghost* [or *Spook*] *Sonata.*

"*The Dream Play,*" Strindberg wrote, "is a new form which
is my invention." With greater clarity and penetration than
Maeterlinck or Andreyev, he saw that what they needed as the
container and frame of such visions was: the dream. And just
how fully Strindberg understood the possibilities of the dream
is shown by a program note which he added to *The Dream
Play* lest his audience think him capricious:

> In this dream play, as in his earlier one, *The Road
> to Damascus,* the author has tried to imitate the dis-
> jointed but apparently logical form of a dream. Any-
> thing may happen: everything is possible and probable.
> Time and space do not exist; on an insignificant ground-
> work of reality, imagination spins and weaves new pat-
> terns: a mixture of memories, experiences, unfettered
> fancies, absurdities, and improvisations.

The characters are split, doubled, and multiplied: they evaporate and are condensed, are diffused and concentrated. But a single consciousness holds sway over them all—that of the dreamer; for him there are no secrets, no inconsequences, no scruples, and no law. The dreamer neither condemns nor acquits: he merely relates; and since a dream is usually painful, less frequently cheerful, a tone of melancholy, of sympathy with all that lives, runs through the swaying narrative. Sleep, the liberator, often plays a painful part, but when the pain is at its fiercest comes the awakening to reconcile the sufferer with reality, which, however agonizing it may be, is at that moment a joy compared with the excruciating dream.

This sounds post-Freudian, and indeed it was written several years after *The Interpretation of Dreams,* but it does not seem that Strindberg had read Freud, much as he had been interested in the latter's pastors and masters—Charcot and the Nancy school of psychiatry. But, if we know any cultural history at all, we know that such confluences of opinion need not be discussed, and could not be explained by the influence of one thinker on another. More curious and significant than influences is such a fact as Darwin's and Wallace's arriving simultaneously and independently at the same conclusion. So it is with Strindberg and Freud. Or to phrase it differently: the same forces which at the close of the nineteenth century drove Freud to the study of dreams in the psychiatric field drove Strindberg toward the same study in his investigation of tragic experience. Artists have known about dreams from time immemorial, but they had seen them as divine messages or merely utilized them as a convenient frame for an improbable story. Strindberg is Freudian in that he finds human significance, as well as an artistic opportunity, in the substitutions, inversions, and telescoping of the dream work. These, he thinks, are the way to the inner core of tragic experience. This discovery—which Strindberg seems chiefly to have made for himself, though under pressure from the *Zeitgeist,* to which, like his kindred spirits, Kierkegaard, Dostoevski, and Nietzsche, he was abnormally sensitive—is the theory of his dream plays.

Ibsen, more than any other dramatist, had presented on the stage the individual soul. Maeterlinck, more than any other dramatist, had presented the haze of dreaminess. If Strindberg pushed Maeterlinck's dreaminess much further, creating a highly complex and explicit dream drama, he also may be said to have pushed Ibsen's psychological intimacy much further, until his dramas are completely subjective, not to say confessional. Both these developments, which Strindberg united in his dream plays, are extraordinary adventures far from the track of all drama as we learn about it in books and on Broadway. Drama is the most solid of the arts; it presents objects to the eyes; it is commonly supposed to be somewhat crudely physical. Strindberg transports it to the dream world. Drama is objective, external; the dramatist is supposed to create a world of characters with their own separate existence and with each a separate identity guaranteed by the visible separateness of his body. Strindberg, even more than Ibsen, introduces sheer subjectivity upon the stage. Every tragic artist must have written autobiographically to some extent. Sophocles, we may say, *was* Oedipus, and Shakespeare Hamlet. Yet Master-Builder Solness is Ibsen much more explicitly, to such an extent indeed that we may barely understand the play without reference to his lifework if not to his life. How much more is this true of Strindberg's dream plays! They carry symbolism well over the borderline of the public and intelligible into a private realm to which we need a biographer's passport. The tragic muse has never worn a fancier dress.

C. E. Vaughan presented the increasing inwardness of the drama as a sort of progress, and a later theorist cites Maeterlinck's views as the latest and most encouraging reach of dramatic enterprise. All of which was some years ago. Today we cannot see why it is necessarily so encouraging. Consider the career of Maeterlinck himself. As a dramatist he has become more and more conventional. As a leader and maker of opinion he has moved from the vanguard to the rear, and today we find him praising Clare Boothe Luce to the *New Yorker's* reporter and writing on the value of spirituality for business magazines. So ends the man who once made so strong an impact upon men like Debussy, Rilke, Yeats, and Strindberg. Not only has he himself deteriorated. Maeterlinckism bore no fruits after 1910. Andreyev's work too seems to have been the exploitation of a cul-de-sac.

But we would hardly need history to tell us this. Is it not evident that we cannot go indefinitely behind life? The aim was to find the essence of life; the result was—it is barely a pun —leaving life behind. Maeterlinck, even in the most Maeterlinckian plays, abuts on the false and the foolish. Andreyev falls into rhodomontade and arty uplift. There is a parallel between Maeterlinck and Gordon Craig. They are one in their attempt to create a high, tragic drama of atmosphere, and they are one in imagining that it can be made *out of* atmosphere. How far they leave life, and therefore drama, behind is clear from their substitution of marionettes for actors. A fine future for the theater if this is the drama of tomorrow! If this is inwardness we begin to long for outwardness. For we are people, as Théophile Gautier put it, for whom the external world exists.

It is not always clear what we mean when we announce that a given form or manner is exhausted. Yet in studying Maeterlinck and Andreyev it is impossible to resist the impression that what may have looked like a beginning forty years ago today looks more like an ending. Strindberg is a more complex case. There is plenty in him that belongs to an era that was closing when his last plays were written. But there are also hints, hunches, and ideas which could help to create new schools of drama. As an influence (and in many other ways) Strindberg is ambivalent. What might be regarded as his healthy influence will be described in a later chapter. The Strindberg who concerns us in this chapter was perhaps not so healthy a force. I am thinking of the Strindberg who inspired another generation of would-be tragedians, the Strindberg of strained postures and forced spirituality, in a word, the Expressionist Strindberg. Not that the unhealthiness of the influence was altogether his fault. Most often it was the fault of those who chose to copy inessentials and lacked the genius to supply the essentials themselves. The Expressionists were not a band of great men in revolt like the early Romantics. On the contrary. With them the modern crusade for high tragedy in the grand manner comes to an end "not with a bang but a whimper."

The term Expressionism was originally chosen—around 1900 —as an antithesis to Impressionism in painting. In drama the term was not current before the First World War, and the Expressionist tendency was not widely known until the twenties, with which it is still identified in our minds. Actually the chief Expressionist plays were written between 1910 and 1920.

The first recognized Expressionist playwright was Reinhard Sorge (1892-1916). The youthful Sorge was steeped in the literature of the time. At first a Nietzschean, later a Catholic, he was always in rebellion against Zolaist Naturalism and dissatisfied with the Neo-Romanticist reaction against it. If Zolaism was life without art, Neo-Romanticism was art without life. A new synthesis was needed that would acknowledge both the earthly roots and the celestial longings of mankind. From this intention the Expressionists proceeded to make a new literature which has so many individual variations that the main theme is hard to find. Lost in the maze of disorderly facts, we may appeal to the comforting Six Points of a scholar who was professionally compelled to say exactly what Expressionism is. First, he said, it is subjectivist and represents the emanations, the *ausstrahlungen,* of the individual ego. Second, it seeks, not an *im*pression of actuality, but an *ex*pression of the inner man, the unconscious, the dream world. Third, it seeks the spiritual, the elemental, the ecstatic. Fourth, it works by means of lyricism and musical counterpoint. Fifth, it is a search for the divine. Sixth, it asserts the dignity of man.

In the present context there is no need to track down each Expressionist to his lair. The Six Points are enough to suggest the tragic intention which was common to Expressionists such as Sorge and Kornfeld, Kokoschka and Stramm, Kaiser and Hasenclever, Capek and Toller, even if there were more things they did not have in common. I offer the following generalizations about the whole movement.

Expressionism, as Simmel put it, was an attempt to seize the essence of life without the content of life. In this it reflects the anxiety, the soul-searching, the sense of crisis and insufficiency, sometimes the hysteria of a generation. Dramatic Expressionism has three roots: Strindberg, adolescent despair, and electric light. Though it too was offered to the world as the drama of the future, it was more obviously an aftermath. It reproduced the *externals* of Strindberg's manner as Schiller had reproduced the externals of Shakespeare's manner. It was the last of the attempts described in this section to express tragedy by seizing the soul, so to speak, by the hair. Ibsen and Strindberg (and Maeterlinck and Andreyev at their best) had maintained an interplay between the outer and the inner, objective and subjective, naturalistic and non-naturalistic. The Expressionists cut loose from the object altogether; and one end being cut, the whole rope flops. Helplessly the Expressionists gesticulate and shriek and moan. The necessary twoness of artistic experience—irony, if you will—is absent.

Expressionism might never have become a large dramatic movement at all but for the intellectual wooziness of the war generation and, even more important, but for the New Staging with which the name of Reinhardt is identified. Here the most fundamental development—as we have seen—was the first full use of electricity on the stage. No greater technical change than the introduction of the switchboard had ever been known, and for a generation theater people were, to mix the metaphor, drunk with electricity. New shapes and colors hovered before them. Theater came to be thought of in terms of light and, even more perhaps, in terms of shadow. The theater maniacs were the making of Expressionism. They needed a drama without substance, so that light and color and design could have pride of place. The result is recorded in all those lovely picture books of the drama, dated between 1918 and 1930, in which a New Theater is ecstatically announced. Poor Expressionists! Their plays were only too eagerly taken off their hands by the rapacious zealots of the scene. The tragic muse went out in a blaze of light.

Wagner made a step beyond the poet of "Hamlet." To the reflecting, depicting, understanding, to the directly perceiving eye, he added the revelation of music from the unseen world of the inner man.

HOUSTON STEWART CHAMBERLAIN

After Shakespeare I unhesitatingly place Ibsen first.

LUIGI PIRANDELLO

# 4. WAGNER AND IBSEN:

# A CONTRAST

## I

Drama as a high art has appeared only sporadically. Music, for example, has had in the modern world a much more distinguished and continuous history. So have some literary forms, such as the novel and even lyric verse. The theater is a stepchild. Look through any good critical journal and you will find stringent, zealous, and expert criticism of all the arts with the single exception of drama, for there is at present no significant theater, and even the better dramatists of yesterday—say, Schnitzler, Chekhov, or Synge—are to a large extent forgotten, while their contemporaries in the novel and poetry—James, Proust, the Symbolists—maintain and even enhance their reputation. The dramatic criticism that does exist is divided into two equally insufficient departments: the technical, which embraces everything from academic history of the drama to studies of the various paraphernalia of the theater, and the journalistic, which even at its best seldom amounts to more than scattered witticisms and fragmentary *aperçus*.

Perhaps an art receives the criticism it deserves. Has there been a supremely great dramatist since Racine and Molière? At least we may allow that since 1700 it has been a question whether there could be theater as high art at all. First-rate minds have applied themselves to the theater, but often—one thinks of Goethe, Schiller, and Hebbel—something first-rate is written for the theater which is not first-rate theater. Goethe succeeds far better with the lyric and the dramatic poem. Schiller, for all his eloquence and intellect (greatly overlooked in English-speaking countries), is never entirely great as a playwright; his genius is more reflective than tragic, more forensic than dramatic. Hebbel's case is even more revealing. He was a poet whose lifelong ambition was to serve the theater and whose theoretic understanding of the state of dramatic art in the modern world was the most searching in his generation. But his plays, for all their real poetic and dramatic ingredients, are all somehow off center, incomplete, queer, and unsatisfying.

Whether or no these examples convince, it will be agreed that many great artists have written for the modern theater without producing great dramas. Indeed there is hardly an important modern writer—not Auden, nor Joyce, nor Lawrence, nor Henry James—who has not fancied himself as a dramatist with largely unhappy consequences. The list could be extended back through the nineteenth century to the earliest Romanticists, nearly all of whom (Wordsworth, Coleridge, Keats, Shelley, Byron) wrote bad plays in verse. Nor was the eighteenth century very much luckier.

Now I do not believe that we can answer such questions as: why was there no great drama in Victorian England? with complete finality. We can no more explain why genius does not occur at a certain time than we can explain why it does occur at another time. There is an element of chance, of the imponderable, or at least of the as yet unknown, in the matter, and Spenglerian or other patterns which attribute such things to inevitable degeneration are a futile half-wisdom after the event. On the other hand, one can partly explain why when genius did occur and did try itself so persistently in the drama it persistently failed. The partial explanation is, negatively stated, that the old tragic attitude to life had disappeared, and with it the old high tragedy, hitherto the major dramatic form. Schiller, Victor Hugo, and D'Annunzio use the forms of this kind of tragedy—as we saw in the last chapter—after the substance has gone. The comedy of Molière and Congreve was also a product of a kind of awareness which disappeared, and even the best of eighteenth-century comedy, that of Beaumarchais, Goldoni, and Sheridan, is a pale ghost of the earlier variety.

Even more directly than the other arts—or more crudely—the drama is a chronicle and brief abstract of the time, revealing not merely the surface but the whole material and spiritual structure of an epoch. Hence the necessity of historical criticism. The history of drama since the eighteenth century is the history of attempts to represent upon the stage the material and spiritual structure of a new age, an age inaugurated by political, economic, and technological revolutions of unprecedented and only half-realized scope. Today we have comfortably taken care of the three revolutions with the three words Democracy, Capitalism, and Industrialism.

There have been many attempts to body forth that new world in drama. Of these, four seem to me incomparably vaster than any others: the attempts of Wagner, Ibsen, Shaw, and Strindberg.

A quotation from Hebbel's journals will lead us into the subject. "The new drama, if such a thing comes into being," Hebbel wrote, "will differ from the Shakespearean drama, which must now be definitely abandoned, in that the dramatic dialectic will be injected not only into the characters but also directly into the Idea itself, so that not alone the relation of man to the Idea is debated, but also the validity of the Idea itself." Hebbel's words have nothing directly to do with the "drama of ideas" as commonly understood. He writes as we have noted, in roughly Hegelian terms and for "Idea" or "that part of the Idea which is embodied in actual society" we can simply read "institutions and conditions." Indirectly, therefore, Hebbel's theory has much to do with the drama of ideas, since he is saying, among other things, that the new drama will ask not only if men live according to moral laws but also whether their moral laws are valid. The stage is a tribunal. In future it will pass, says Hebbel, not only on individuals but on institutions and on the laws themselves. Hebbel wrote this passage in 1843. The next generation was that of Wagner and Ibsen. The next was that of Shaw and Strindberg. Hebbel's words were being realized.

For their contemporaries our four playwrights were each of them highly controversial figures, whom one might with equal assurance worship or despise. Even today some veteran despisers may be shocked to have one or the other of them singled out from the multitude of the relatively accomplished. Yet I think most people would agree to the selection if they were to go over the ground. Whether we think of the merit of their compositions or of the potency of their effort to make a great modern theater, Wagner, Ibsen, Shaw, and Strindberg are by far the most important men of the theater during the past hundred years.

In the preceding chapters we saw how Wagner tried to rescue the drama by means of music and how Ibsen tried to rescue it by means of modern speech. Wagner is the great exponent of tragedy in fancy, Ibsen of tragedy in modern dress. The two men are avatars of the two traditions of modern drama, the antinaturalistic and the naturalistic. In the present chapter I shall try both to retail more of the facts about them and to push the analysis of their work a little further.

## II

First, Wagner. Though the exceptions are better known than the rule, the main operatic tradition before Wagner was one of serious theater, that is, of plays which were a serious interpretation of life, not frivolous displays in which, as Wagner said of Meyerbeer, effects appear without their causes. The tradition of serious opera stretches from Monteverdi to Mozart in the secular opera, and from Schütz to Handel in sacred opera or oratorio. Even the subordination of the music to the words had been advocated. In the second half of the eighteenth century Gluck wrote: "I endeavored to reduce music to its proper function, that of seconding poetry by enforcing the expression of the sentiment and the interest of the situations, without interrupting the action or weakening it by superfluous ornament." Rather earlier the composer Mattheson wrote: "In my opinion a good opera theater is nothing but an academy of many fine arts, where architecture, painting, the dance, poetry . . . and above all music should unite to bring about a work of art." Mattheson is even closer than Gluck to a Wagnerian theory of a Composite Art Work (*gesamtkunstwerk*).

Schiller was perhaps the first important dramatist to think that the future of drama might lie in opera. "I had always placed a certain confidence in opera," he wrote to Goethe in 1797, "hoping that from it will rise as from the choruses of the ancient feasts of Bacchus the tragedy in a nobler form." Goethe replied impressively: "The hopes you placed in the opera you would find fulfilled to a high degree in the recent *Don Juan*" —Mozart's *Don Giovanni*. The operas of Mozart are commonly considered musical more than dramatic; Mozart himself wrote that in opera "the poetry must be altogether the obedient daughter of the music"; and Wagner thinks that Mozart did not take drama very seriously. Nevertheless Goethe was right, and the fusion of music and drama in Mozart's operas is closer to the Wagnerian ideal than is the subordination of music to words in Gluck's theory. Mozart's three operatic masterpieces are the greatest achievement of the eighteenth-century theater and the greatest operas of all time.

But neither they nor Gluck's *Orfeo* and *Alceste* are what we are after: the expression of the *modern* world in theater. They are the expression of the *ancien régime*, at the latest the expression of the *ancien régime* under fire. Though the music of *Don Giovanni* in its stern grandeur, its tempestuous exuberance, its subtle psychology, and its modulated mood-painting, belies current notions of "classicism," "rococo," and "enlightenment," yet the world depicted is, internally as well as externally, the world of Joseph II and not that of Bismarck.

Between Mozart and Wagner—with the possible exception of Hector Berlioz—there is no "music dramatist" of the first rank. What is the road that leads from *The Magic Flute*, which, Wagner held to be the cornerstone of German national opera, to *Lohengrin?* The question of Wagner's origin is a vexed one. Some have regarded his art as springing fully equipped from the head of the maestro. Others have assailed him as an ungrateful plagiarist. Perhaps Wagner was about as derivative as most good artists—that is to say, very derivative indeed. Outstandingly, he developed three conceptions which were already in existence. These could be called:

1. The national idea.
2. The symphonic idea.
3. The theatrical idea.

1. *The national idea.* Lacking the national unity of France and England, the Germans lacked also a national culture. The result since the eighteenth century has been a degree of overcompensation which has shocked—and rocked—the world. In the drama Lessing managed to put German comedy on its feet, while the pompous Johann Christoph Gottsched championed the idea of a German national drama. The age of Schiller went further than this in disseminating the idea that the theater

could be the guiding light of a whole culture. In the operatic field *The Magic Flute* was followed after a generation by Weber's *Der Freischütz,* which is as important a landmark of German Romanticism as *Hernani* is of French (in a sense *more* important, since Weber's Romanticism is real and substantial, Hugo's symbolic and accidental).

One of the many elements of Romanticism is a renewed interest in local tradition and thus in national folklore. Nowhere was this interest stronger than in Germany where the ballad and the *märchen* were unearthed and imitated by succeeding generations of Romanticists, from the great compendium *Des Knaben Wunderhorn* (1808) on. As interesting in this connection as *Der Freischütz* is an essay written in 1844 by the critic Friedrich Theodor Vischer, entitled "Suggestion for an Opera." German opera, Vischer said, had had in Mozart its Goethe, but still lacked its Shakespeare. Moreover Mozart was an *Italian-feeling* German, while what was wanted was a *real* German. For the expression of Germanism in music an ideal subject would be the Nibelungen story, which was Germanism chemically pure. And anyway the realm of saga was too elemental for communication in mere words; it must speak in the elemental language of music. "It is as if it were made for opera," Vischer wrote of the Nibelungen myth. "It wells up out of the most splendid musical motives; it has long awaited its composer and now imperiously calls to him."

Four years after Vischer's essay appeared, Richard Wagner turned to theorizing on the same subject in a treatise called: "The Wibelungen, World History in Saga." According to mere historians the Wibelungen are the Ghibelins and take their name from Waiblingen, where Frederic Barbarossa was born. According to Richard Wagner, for whom the difference between an "N" and a "W" was slight, they were the Nibelungen of the sagas. As Ernest Newman puts it: "In some mysterious way, it appears, the Nibelungen Hoard became identified in the minds of Charlemagne, his successors, and the German peo-

ple with the idea of universal kingship. With Barbarossa, the
Hoard became essentially one with the Grail; and that last
excursion of his into Asia, in which he lost his life, was made,
says Wagner, in obedience to a mystical impulse to grasp the
Hoard, that had now 'ascended' spiritually into the Grail."

In such ways did the Wagnerian mind play with the idea of
a national symbolism. In Wagner's theoretical works of this
period—*Art and Revolution, The Art Work of the Future,* and
*Opera and Drama*—the national character of the new art is
emphasized *ad nauseam.* Art is *of* the Folk, *for* the Folk, and,
since the artist is a magical mouthpiece, *by* the Folk. As Wagner
grew older his nationalism took on the color of the times and
he became a Reich-German, anti-French, anti-Semitic, and
"proto-Nazi."

A Nazi critic once wrote that Bayreuth was Nazi Germany
in little, and indeed there is a true, though indirect, connection
between the demagogue of Bayreuth and the demagogue of
Berchtesgaden. The idea of a national German art begins as
lofty idealism and has ended—for the present—with Nazism. But
Bayreuth has more significance than that. Eighteenth-century
opera had catered either directly to the court or to other similar
groups in a courtly society. Bayreuth was an attempt to give
social function to the opera in "a century of vile bourgeoisie."
Despite the blandishments of the Bavarian king, Wagner knew
that to be a court musician in 1870 was to be the lackey of a
lackey. Despite the apparent loss of status which the artist was
supposed to have undergone in the nineteenth century, Wagner
resolved to be more of a monarch than poor King Ludwig.

The Romanticists had claimed primacy for the artist in the
ideal world; Wagner proceeded to realize their ideal in actuality. The Romanticists had called themselves unacknowledged
legislators of the world; Wagner would be an acknowledged
legislator. It is rightly said that Wagner made only too solid and
tangible what Romantic poets had left to the fancy. The theater
at Bayreuth is itself a Romantic fancy made solid and tangible.

It is not only a nationalist symbol but also a symbol of aestheticism, the Palace of Art, Axel's Castle, the ivory tower itself. If in 1942 German soldiers on leave from the Russian front were taken to Bayreuth, it was as much to help them forget as to help them remember. Here (and everywhere you have him) Wagner is an ambiguous figure, imperialist and escapist, *real politiker* and aesthete. For Wagner is both Parsifal and Kundry; Bayreuth is Wartburg and Venusberg in one.

2. *The symphonic idea.* In opera the chief musical considerations are, first, the melodic lines of the voices, second, the harmony of voice with voice and of voice with orchestra, third, the relation of voice to orchestra, and, fourth, the relation of musical to dramatic theme.

Where did Wagner get his musical theories? Musicologists love to tell us that he took this or that from Marschner or Spontini or from some other composer whom we never have a chance to hear. Musicologists are always right. Yet, surely, the main ideas of Wagnerian music are present in the major composers too. The Wagnerian conception of melodic line, for instance. When Gluck abandond the *secco recitativo* for accompanied recitative, when Mozart composed the passionate recitatives, alike melodic and dramatic, of *The Magic Flute,* the way was prepared for Wagner's conception of a continuous melodic line to extend from the beginning of an opera to the end. The phrase "endless melody" is of course a Wagnerian hyperbole, for even in mature works like *Die Walküre* and *Tristan* certain passages inevitably detach themselves from the context like any Italian aria. Yet *Tristan* as a whole does not fall into many interrupted sections between which the audience takes a breath and applauds. It moves in a series of great waves, all of which seem to merge in one enormous floodtide.

There are two types of music, absolute music and dramatic music. Wagner's is hyperdramatic. But, although in recent years Wagner has always had to bear the brunt of attacks on program and dramatic music generally, he invented neither the one nor the other. There are programmatic elements in the music of almost every well-known composer, and there are dramatic elements in the music of every great classical composer. Mozart, for instance, uses tonality for purposes of characterization: a given key is identified with a certain mood, theme, or person. Wagner experimented endlessly with changes of key until in the *Tristan* we have that chromaticism which is at least a step toward the complete atonality of Schoenberg. Now, in absolute music, harmony and tonality are structural; the disposition and variation of harmonies is the architecture of the music. With Romanticism, however—and perhaps that includes Mozart as well as Beethoven—harmonies come to be used for their flavor, atmosphere, or "color." This is particularly clear in parts of Beethoven's Sixth Symphony and in some of Schubert's songs, where the harmony remains unchanged through a considerable passage. In such passages, and the opening of *Das Rheingold* is the most striking, interest in harmonic progression is inevitably nil. Atmosphere is all. Such is the dramatic use of harmony. The orchestra becomes a sublime stage effect.

As to the relation of voice to orchestra, Wagner's chief reform is celebrated if not notorious. He enlarged the orchestra, and changed the ratio of certain tone colors. Enthusiasts report that he is the founder of modern orchestration and of modern conducting; anti-Wagnerites complain of his vulgar confusion of size and merit. The real meaning of the enlarged orchestra is the real meaning of Wagnerian musical technique generally: *Wagner brought the romantic symphony into the opera house.* So striking is this fact that Ernest Newman concludes that Wagner was not a man of the theater turned musician, as is often held (and as I, with reservations, hold), but a musician who often pretended to be a man of the theater. Actually Wagner's symphonic idea is not antidramatic. Every good play has a rhythmic structure and a symphonic unity. Wagner's introduction of a symphonic pattern into music drama is the redramatizing of opera by genuinely musical means.

The symphonic idea in opera means that much of the onus of the drama is transferred from the action and the dialogue to the orchestra. The orchestral score becomes one long tone poem. Now many dramatists have known the value of repeated catchwords, and many musicians have known the dramatic force of repeated melodies, and from the existing idea of dramatically repeated musical themes comes the Wagnerian leitmotiv, which relieves the dialogue of a considerable burden and helps to bind a whole work together. In one work of Wagner, *The Ring,* (and critics should not speak as if all Wagner's works were the same) the leitmotiv becomes a principal element in the structure of the piece, an element that is tiresome and mechanical if one hears a large part of the cycle at once. But we are now on the threshold of the next topic, which is

3. *The theatrical idea.* In his essay *Opera and Drama* Wagner has expounded his pseudo ideas of theater. Ignoring his arbitrary "Teutonic" antitheses and the involutions, at first baffling and in the end disgusting, of his argument, we can extract from this document the assurance that Wagner was abundantly aware of the unsatisfactory status of the theater in modern life, that he saw that even Goethe and Schiller had not really succeeded in the theater, and that he shared the hope of those who saw a future in "music drama" with mythological subject matter. Myth, Wagner thinks, is always true; it is elemental; it springs from the Folk; it can be expressed in "tone-speech," that is, in language that is meant to be musically enunciated (as against verses which happen to be set to music later). The Wagnerian "music drama" has a more closely knit dialogue than the despised Grand Opera. It avoids pretty songs and pretty stanzas. In "music drama" with no recitatives the dialogue is continuous like the melodic line, and because of this Wagner slows down his voices and gives the impression of speed with his orchestra. Hence the typically Wagnerian pattern of slow vocal melody against a complex, often bewilderingly fast and tempestuous, symphonic background.

Wagner proposed to replace the Grand Opera of Meyerbeer and Scribe with the Composite Art Work, and for that reason one prime fact has been overlooked by all but the anti-Wagnerites: Wagner's own theater technique is to a great extent that of Meyerbeer and Scribe. Eugène Scribe, who never produced a first-rate work of art, is one of the pioneers of cultural history. Ibsen helped to direct Scribe plays at Bergen; Wagner actually consulted Scribe on at least one occasion. Scribe is, in a sense, the father of both the Wagnerite and the Ibsenite theater. Neither Wagner, who ended with *Parsifal*, with its distasteful mixture of sensualism and moralism, nor Ibsen, who in his last plays still used the Scribean pattern of the buried scandal, outlived Scribe's influence.

Wagner's objections to conventionality and artificiality are not so much objections to Scribe as to the late classicism of the eighteenth century, which Scribe had previously rebelled against. Wagner wished to simplify the drama of his operatic predecessors, to reduce it to bare essentials, to organize and centralize it, so that the effect might be strong and direct. That had been Scribe's idea too. Scribe's libretti had been "constructed," "well made," crude, full of action, earnest but shallow, full of suspense but empty of subtlety. So were most of Wagner's.

There is, of course, a difference of tone. Scribe had been wholly a commercial hack, and that was the last thing Wagner would ever have confessed to being. His "Teutonic" high seriousness, his theoretical lucubrations, and his grandiose mythological material give him a status as librettist, partly justified, partly the product of a confusion between pomposity and real seriousness, which Scribe could never have attained to. Ibsen poured a Scribe plot into an ancient Norse setting in *The Feast at Solhaug*. Wagner pours Scriberies into his Germanic material. Nietzsche maintained that Wagner remained essentially a late French Romanticist. If so, he was a Romanticist nearer to the level of Scribe or the elder Dumas than to that of the great Romantic poets.

## III

If operatic history since the death of Mozart is a search for the opera of the modern world, the fruit of the search is the mature work of Wagner. His early works, as far as *Tannhäuser* and even *Lohengrin,* are still Grand Opera of a kind that the audiences of Scribe and Meyerbeer would understand, at least dramatically (though the vehement criticism all Wagner's works met with shows that they had something in them more challenging or at least more puzzling than the Scribe-Meyerbeer commodity). Yet, just as Ibsen did not devise the genre which he thought most representative of his world till he had reached middle life, so Wagner did not produce a full-fledged Wagnerian "music drama" till *Der Ring des Niblungen.* For all its longueurs and needless repetitions, for all the flaws and inconsistencies which mar the final libretto, *The Ring* is one of the most significant products of the nineteenth century, at once a criticism and a mirror of the age, less great than *Faust* or even *Peer Gynt,* yet less of the closet and more of the theater than either of these.

Wagner's greatest works are *Tristan* and *Die Meistersinger,* for only in these is the conglomeration of elements a real synthesis. *Tristan* is a great drama, and it is great music; but it is marred by a diffuseness which would have ruined a work of lesser genius. In each of his works Wagner creates a special and unmistakable atmosphere appropriate to his conception; even when he works at several operas at once, he keeps them as far apart in atmosphere as separate worlds. That is one of the great things about Wagner. Now none of Wagner's manners or atmospheres is as markedly peculiar as the manner of *Tristan.* It can be recognized wherever you drop the phonograph needle. The *Tristan* manner consists (among other things) of regularly and rapidly undulating waves of sound, developed chromatically, and sweeping or fading into space. The result is very curious. So much does one feel the manner as an endlessly repeated pattern that *Tristan* seems overrepetitious and long *however much you cut it*. Even the so-called uncut version at the Metropolitan Opera House lacks several hundred bars. The fact that nobody notices such and even larger omissions is at least a partial condemnation of a work of art, which can properly be only the right size, neither more nor less.

The astonishing thing is that *Tristan* is great all the same, great not as an expression of the "eternal truth of myth," but as an expression of European nihilism, one of the deepest trends in nineteenth-century thought and sensibility. In its symbolism (it is one long representation of the sexual act), in its equation of love and death, its apotheosis of darkness and its renunciation of light, it is the Anti-Faust, the decadent poem *par excellence*.

If *Tristan* is the favorite of the Wagnerites, *Die Meistersinger* is the favorite Wagnerian opera of the non-Wagnerites. Yet *Die Meistersinger* is just as essentially Wagnerian and just as authentically of the period. Let me explain.

The nineteenth century saw the ascendancy of the middle class, and as all the champions of genuine culture realized, this meant an ascendancy of the middle-class mind. It meant the apotheosis of mediocrity. In nineteenth-century literature, therefore, we find, since the artist is by nature an aristocrat in the sense of a seeker after excellence, a series of portraits of mediocrity, a type which had not previously been common in literature. Aristotle had defined the tragic character as being above life size, and the comic character as being below life size, and literary tradition had been chiefly concerned with these two types. The nineteenth century, especially through the novel but also in drama, was interested in the middle-sized or average man. In Hjalmar Ekdal, Ibsen portrayed the type in all its ambiguity, its grandiose illusions on the one hand, its coarse *gemütlichkeit* on the other. Wagner does not portray the type; he embodies it; he is its mouthpiece; through his genius, lack of genius becomes vocal; which means (and this is Wagner's "betrayal" of culture) that he confers upon mediocrity the favors of its opposite, genius. Hence Nietzsche's hostility to his former friend and idol. Nietzsche found out that Wagner was the spokesman of the new age in its most negative aspects. *Tristan* is grandiose illusion; *Die Meistersinger* is incarnate *gemüt-lichkeit,* the middle-class substitute for serenity. Hitler, we hear, was equally at home in both worlds, and that is interesting, for fascism has had a strong appeal to both impulses involved. It has appealed to the middle man, the man with half-suppressed dreams of grandeur and destruction, the man who loves to dream also of the thatched cottages of old Germany, idyllic medieval towns, shoemakers who sing at their work, who generously give the girl to someone else, and whose not-so-*gemütlich* religion is German nationalism.

Wagner is the prime instance of a compromised genius, of one who in criticizing his age came to terms with it, of one who in his very denunciation of falsehood himself proved a liar. His gifts were extraordinary. The potency of his magic is unsurpassed in the history of music. That, Nietzsche maintained, made him all the more dangerous. None saw Wagner's merits more clearly than Nietzsche, even after the breach of friendship. For Nietzsche thought that Wagner was the only man who, uncompromised, might have brought grandeur and sublimity back to the world. "I had no one," he lamented, "but Richard Wagner." Nietzsche saw not only Wagner's potentiality but also his nature and his historical meaning: "I understand perfectly if today a musician says: 'I hate Wagner, but I cannot endure any other music.' But [? And] I would also understand a philosopher who explained: 'Wagner epitomizes modernity. It can't be helped, one must first be a Wagnerite.' " To follow Nietzsche in the matter, and it is wise to do so, is not to become a rabid anti-Wagnerite; it is to see very sharply the pro and the con; it is the pro and the con for a whole complex of ideas and meanings.

Nietzsche, the enemy of compromise, the champion of culture and all excellence, rejected Wagnerism. And there is another great enemy of compromise, another champion of culture and excellence, another advocate of an either/or choice and the categorical imperative, a man who tried a quite different path to a modern type of drama. Though Henrik Ibsen lived in the very capital of Bavaria at the time of Bayreuth's early triumphs, he ignored Wagner. He inhabited the same province as Wagner but a different universe. Nietzsche excoriated in Wagner a part of himself; he was not only the greatest critic of Wagner, but the greatest Wagnerite, and we read of his asking insistently for Wagner's music in the year 1888, the year he wrote his most pungent anti-Wagnerite works, the last sane year of his life. The antipode of Wagner is not Nietzsche. It is Ibsen.

## IV

If a consideration of Wagner carries us back to Gluck and Mozart, a consideration of Ibsen carries us back to Lessing and Diderot. Taking a hint from the English dramatist George Lillo, who resembles Scribe alike in the extent of his influence and in the paucity of his talent, two of the most representative and gifted men of the eighteenth century turned their minds to the creation of a new type of serious drama. Lessing's *Miss Sarah Sampson* and Diderot's *Le Père de Famille,* though better than Lillo's *George Barnwell,* are not good plays, but they are a new genre, the "bourgeois tragedy"—which, as we have seen, was later to yield the remarkable *Kabale und Liebe* of Schiller, the *Maria Magdalena* of Hebbel, and the plays of Ibsen's "modern" period.

Although the "bourgeois tragedy" did not rise to the heights of the best eighteenth-century opera, it does stand in somewhat the same relation to nineteenth-century drama as Gluck and Mozart do to nineteenth-century opera. Wagner learned from Gluck and Mozart, but he learned more from the Romanticists, both from the best, like Beethoven, and from the next best, like

Meyerbeer; Ibsen is in the tradition of "bourgeois tragedy," but he learned more from Romanticism, both from its high poetry and from its popular manifestations. We should stress the debt of Wagner and Ibsen to popular romanticism: Eugène Scribe and all he represents stand between the eighteenth century on the one hand and Wagner and Ibsen on the other. When Ibsen was appointed theater poet at Bergen in 1851 he proceeded to direct 145 plays, of which more than half were light plays from the French, 21 being by Scribe himself.

Ibsen's first play came out in 1850, his last in the last month of the century. The fifty years of his creative life were planned with the skill and precision of a master builder. Half of them were spent in trying out different styles, from Shakespearean fantasy to Roman tragedy, from light verse comedy to "world-historical drama," from Scribean "well-made play" to philosophic-dramatic poem, from prose satire to national myth. I have claimed that two of the "experiments" of this period —*Brand* and *Peer Gynt*—form a kind of bank for Ibsen to draw on in all his later plays. Although *Peer Gynt* is perhaps Ibsen's greatest work, it can, in relation to his career, be regarded as an experiment, for Ibsen came to consider the style of *Peer Gynt* quite wrong for himself and the age. "Verse," he wrote in words whose assertiveness may indicate diffidence, "has been most injurious to dramatic art. . . . It is improbable that verse will be employed to any extent worth mentioning in the drama of the future; the aims of the dramatists of the future are almost certain to be incompatible with it. It is therefore doomed." There could be no clearer proof of the strength of naturalism in late nineteenth-century culture, nor of Ibsen's desire to be naturalistic—or at least to make his peace with naturalism—in a naturalistic age.

The second quarter-century of Ibsen's work—beginning with *Pillars of Society* (1877) and *A Doll's House* (1879)—is a steady development of the naturalistic form of play. The Ibsen of these plays—and of *Ghosts* (1881) and its angry appendix *An Enemy of the People* (1882)—is what one of his best commentators calls the "modern Ibsen." This is the Ibsen that scandalized Europe, the Ibsen that chimed in with the Zolaist temper of the younger generation, the Ibsen of the *avant-garde* theaters of the nineties, the Ibsen, in a word, of Ibsenism, championed by Bernard Shaw for its positive values in *The Quintessence of Ibsenism,* and satirized by Bernard Shaw for the less sincere goings-on of its adherents in his first original comedy *The Philanderer.* The Ibsenite Ibsen seemed to belong not only to the general natural-ist army, but to its extreme wing—Zolaist Naturalism. Calling attention to the rotten bottoms of ships, the subjection of Vic-torian wives, the ravages of syphilis, and the corruption of mu-nicipal politics and journalism, he made himself the father of the reformist drama of the end of the century—the drama of Brieux in France, of Galsworthy in England. But it is only by false association with these gentlemen that Ibsenism can be con-sidered the quintessence of Ibsen.

Ibsen adopted a naturalistic form of play, and it is this natu-ralistic form that gives the "modern Ibsen" his character of an Anti-Wagner, a prosaic, restrained, dry-spoken, hard-bitten iron-ist. It gives him the opportunity for those clever expositions by innuendo and developments by nuance which many readers to-day find excessively elaborate or even completely gratuitous. To write *The League of Youth,* a heavy, creaking prose comedy in the manner of Scribe, *after* writing *Peer Gynt,* could give the impression that Ibsen had abandoned dramatic art for the com-mercial theater. It could rejoice those who wish playwrights to come to terms with their time as much as it could annoy those who want the artist to stick to art. The rejoicing and the annoy-ance would, however, be equally premature. The truth is that, after the initial fumbling of two plays—*The League of Youth* and *Pillars of Society* (to which I am tempted to add *A Doll's House*)—Ibsen made out of his naturalism an instrument as per-sonal and subtle—if not as attractive—as the Romanticism of

*Peer Gynt.* In fact he made out of his naturalism a new and much less overt Romanticism.

This is not juggling with terms. If no art, and no artist, can be *wholly* naturalistic, it is always important to see in a work of naturalism what the non-naturalistic elements are. When the "modern Ibsen" is on the stage we see the heavy Victorian furnishing, the heavy Victorian costumes, the heavy Victorian beards and coiffures. These things, plus a sordid subject matter and technical virtuosity, are what many people think of as Ibsen. These things, however, are obviously not what make of Ibsen's plays the crowning glory of tragedy in modern dress. No. The paradox of Ibsen's naturalistic tragedy is that it depends so much on the non-naturalistic elements for its success. Inside the skins of these prim-looking women and beefy-looking men lurk the trolls and devils of *Peer Gynt,* that is to say, the trolls and devils of Norse folk tale, the trolls and devils of Ibsen's inner consciousness. Ibsen may pretend to be an utter Realist in the manner of midcentury France or a Naturalist in the manner of late-century France. He began, however, as a Romanticist—and not a Romanticist out-of-season, not a Neo-Romanticist either. In Ibsen's youth—a generation after the Romantic Revolt in western Europe—Romanticism was still fresh and flourishing in Scandinavia, for Norway is a suburb of Europe and there is a lag between the mode in Paris and the mode in Oslo. It is true that Ibsen was later embarrassed by the provinciality of his native land. He doffed his Romantic viking robes and began to think of himself as a cosmopolitan. He drew heavily on the resources of French and German culture. But his Romanticism was no less persistent for being driven underground. It was only concealed, not eliminated, by Victorian costume, upholstery, and conversation, and by the techniques and subject matters of the boulevards. The Ibsen Secret, if there was one, was that the archnaturalist remained to the end an arch-Romanticist too. In some early verses he had stated his literary ambitions as follows:

I will build me a cloud castle. Two wings shall shape
  it forth,
A great one and a small one. It shall shine across the
  north.
The greater shall shelter a singer immortal.
The smaller to a maiden shall open its portal.

If it is easy to refer these words to such early projections of
Ibsen's as Brand and Agnes, Peer Gynt and Solveig, it is not
much more difficult to refer them to Rubek and Irene, the hero
and heroine of Ibsen's last play.

Friend and foe alike failed to understand. The first generation of critics (with solitary exceptions such as the Dane Georg
Brandes) were shocked; the next lot were thrilled by Ibsen's
revolutionism; when, finally, it was discovered that he was a
Mystic, Ibsen was done for. But nothing in this whole development was accidental. The secretive genius had brought it upon
himself. For if there is anything that the general run of critics
cannot understand, it is that an artist should be secretive and
difficult. Is it not his duty to tell them his secrets and to
make life easy for them? The critics assume so, and if this is the
assumption of literary critics what can be expected of dramatic
critics? In the nineteenth century it was so far axiomatic that a
play should be transparent that even the great master of subtlety, Henry James, described dramatic technique as throwing
the cargo overboard to save the ship, and James' refusal to burden his own comedies with imaginative cargo is the reason for
their inadequacy. The critics expected plays to be simple. A
representative critic of around 1900 wrote: "If the spectator be
confused, baffled, irritated, or bored, or any of these, he has a
legitimate complaint against the dramatist." If we ask: who is
the spectator? another critic of the time answers: "No well-
written play is above the understanding of the boy in the gallery." One would like to think that such generous inanities were
today extinct, yet in the minds of many who would not sub-

scribe to them in full still lurks a suspicion that, in view of the theater audience, drama should be obvious if not crude. It is a well-intentioned view, but it would lead to the condemnation of most plays acknowledged to be great—whether the best of Ibsen or *Le Misanthrope* or *Hamlet*. If there is any difference with respect to difficulty between modern and earlier high drama, it is not that the latter was simple but that it—unlike the former—could be enjoyed on the surface as well as in the depths. The older dramatists addressed their audience on several levels. *Hamlet* can be sincerely relished on the level of the schoolboy and the newspaper critic *or* on the level of Coleridge and A. C. Bradley. To discover the reasons why modern dramatists—like modern poets—often appeal on the deeper levels alone, we would have to analyze modern culture in general (as is sketchily done in Chapter X below).

Ibsen is difficult. He pretends to be easy, and is hard. He pretends to write a dull, characterless dialogue. He pretends to be utterly usual in his plots, dishing up a "well-made play" (*An Enemy of the People*), a Naturalistic version of heredity (*Ghosts*), a sensational study of a *femme fatale* (*Hedda Gabler*) or anything at all which an enthusiast for Dumas *fils* or Zola would have required. In his last years he became, outwardly, an almost official figure in Norway; he attended banquets, wore decorations, and was the cultural father of his country. During all this he wrote works which were more and more subjective and difficult and which bore within them a concealed condemnation of modern men, including the poet himself. Yet when *Little Eyolf,* the most involuted and reticent of his plays, was given Philistine interpretations precisely contrary to its meaning, Ibsen did not protest. He sat and waited for his state funeral. Wagner, the rebel, embarked upon his last work, *Parsifal,* with the reflection that if the public wanted something religious, he would discover religion. Ibsen, the conformist, ended his artistic career with a portrait—in *When We Dead Awaken*—of an elderly sculptor at a health resort. The project

seemed so inoffensive that no one winced when the sculptor
spoke of the naturalism of his portrait busts:

> . . . it amuses me unspeakably. On the surface I give
> them striking likenesses, as they call it, so that they all
> stand and gape in astonishment (*lowers his voice*) but
> at bottom they are all respectable, pompous horse-
> faces, and self-opinionated donkey-muzzles. . . . And it
> is these double-faced works of art that our excellent
> plutocrats come and order of me. And pay for in good
> faith—and in good round figures too—almost their
> weight in gold . . .

This passage is the best available statement of Ibsen's own
attitude to Ibsenite naturalism. It also suggests an attitude to
the public. Ibsen, just as much as Wagner, made himself famous in his own lifetime; but upon different terms. Ibsen preserved his integrity with such marvelous vigilance that he could
even see the dangers of losing integrity by obsession with
integrity—one of the themes of *The Wild Duck*. The only obsession Ibsen did suffer from was the fear that he was a virtuoso,
a merely clever representative of current trends. Accordingly,
he who knew that all his art was the outcome of experiences
which he personally had lived through pressed the self-analysis
ever closer; but he wrote no fake autobiography as Wagner did;
he was even embarrassed if anyone recognized him in one of his
characters. Self-analysis was for him a sort of purgation, even
an expiation, not exhibitionism. He wrote no novels, no mani-
festos, no memoirs, only—in addition to a scattering of lyrics,
letters, articles, and all-too-brief speeches—some twenty-five full-
length plays, the fruit of twice as many years of concentrated
work. Although he actually described his life as "that rare fairy-
tale fate which I have had," he pretended to be pretty much of
a bore. But the meaning of this pose leaks through—in his naturalistic prose for instance. Ibsen pretends to write flat dialogue,
but the opaque, uninviting sentences carry rich meanings which

are enforced only by their context. An Ibsenite sentence often performs four or five functions at once. It sheds light on the character speaking, on the character spoken to, on the character spoken about; it furthers the plot; it functions ironically in conveying to the audience a meaning different from that conveyed to the characters (and it is not merely that the characters say things which mean more to the audience than to them, but that they also say things which, as one senses, mean more to the characters than to the audience); finally, an Ibsenite sentence is part of the rhythmic pattern which constitutes the whole act. The naturalistic prose, then, is not there for its own sake. It is not there to display Ibsen's ability to write "natural" conversation. It is as rich in artifice as the verse of *Peer Gynt*. Its very naturalness is the final artifice, the art that conceals art. It is—above all—a way of giving concreteness and immediacy to themes that might have led a lesser artist into grandiosity and abstraction. It is anti-Wagnerite.

Ibsen adopted the dramaturgic patterns of the fashionable French theater. He wrote of the French plays, however: "These works have for the most part a perfected technique and therefore they please the public; they have nothing to do with poetry and therefore perhaps they please the public still more." In other words, Ibsen did not reject poetry when he rejected verse. He had no illusions about the French drama or about the middle-brow public. If he seems to write at the level of that drama or that public, it is because we choose to read him at that level (as we might read Shakespeare below his level) or because we do not read him at all. The irony of *Hamlet* arises partly from the interplay of the crude story (which had been crudely told much earlier by other writers) and the final Shakespearean poem, between the face of Elizabethan sensationalism and the heart of tragedy. Ibsen's sources are no cruder than Shakespeare's. If we tend to equate Ibsen with his sources it can only be because his naturalistic techniques have taken us in.

## V

Ibsen's naturalistic period, say the textbooks, begins with *The Pillars of Society* in 1879, his "Symbolism," his "Neo-Romanticism" with *The Master Builder* in 1892. But the symbolism which is the most tangible sign of the antinaturalistic or Romantic Ibsen is present in each of the naturalistic plays. Not to mention the rather rudimentary symbolism of the titles *Pillars of Society* and *A Doll's House,* the ships in the former play and the tarantella in the latter are symbols central to the theme. The title *Ghosts* is a much better guide to the play than any discussion of syphilis. Nearly every "naturalistic" play of Ibsen's contains a central symbol whose significance spreads over the whole play.

From *The Wild Duck* (1884) on, Ibsen becomes more and more what has been called mystical—meaning, I suppose, edifying though unintelligible. The truth is that the world of trolls and goblins comes thronging back into his work, that the naturalism becomes less the substance and more of a mask, that a complex, shifting symbolism is employed—to the dismay of those who expect symbolism to be either purely decorative or purely allegorical. A generation before Ibsen had begun to seem solid, Victorian, and safe—something, perhaps, to set up against the precious, obscure, and pessimistic moderns. The first generation of Philistines—such men as Ibsen named Manders, Kroll, or Brack—tried to break Ibsen with their hatred; the second generation almost did kill him with their friendship. One should turn freshly to the plays of Ibsen's last period to rediscover a tortured, introverted, clever, repellent, oblique, and subtle genius.

*The Master Builder,* for example, shows exactly what kind of a playwright Ibsen is and is not. The starting point is a ballad which Ibsen wrote in the folk manner. "He" and "she" lose a jewel in a fire which burns down the house. Even if they find the jewel, says Ibsen, "she" will never recover her faith, nor "he" his happiness. The symbols are characteristic of the man who spoke of torpedoing the ark, of a corpse hidden in the cargo, the man who kept as a pet a poison-spitting scorpion. The ballad is indeed the nearest thing to an Ibsen play in all earlier literature. A ballad celebrates a recent disaster. An air of fatality broods over it. It is compressed. It is all catastrophe. Upon such a mythic pattern Ibsen built a naturalistic superstructure.

The base and the superstructure interact like significantly juxtaposed colors. It would be impossible to say which is more important, or which is the prime meaning of the play, for one takes meaning from the other. On the natural level, the play is about an aging architect who, growing jealous of his younger rivals, is egged on by a neurotic young woman to an athletic feat which proves his downfall. It could be a story by a French realist. If we add that the young woman's sexual life seems to have been perverted by first experiencing orgasm from the autoerotic experience of seeing the Master Builder climb a tower, we have a story for a clinical Naturalist. Ibsen adds the myth. Underlying the play is the theme of *hubris,* the heroic rashness of ancient tragedy which brings retribution to the hero. Hilda Wangel, the neurotic young woman, represents the troll world, the world of the chaotic, tempestuous Id; she is a counterpart of the male troll who haunts her mother, who is Ibsen's main character in *The Lady from the Sea.* Hilda is not immoral, for she disapproves of Solness' harsh treatment of his assistant. She is amoral. She is a daemonic force playing upon the *hubris* of the hero.

Mythic theme and clinical story combine in Ibsen not as a vast Composite Art Work but as a highly specialized study of a very limited subject, the mind of Ibsen. Solness is the aging playwright who feels his powers slipping away, who wonders if in being so wholly an artist he has ceased to be a man, or if in appointing himself preceptor of mankind he has not built higher than he himself can stand. Cowardice or avoidance was

Ibsen's besetting sin or at least his besetting fear, as we first see at the time when he declined to fight in the war against Bismarck in 1864. The fear is projected into *The Master Builder,* split into many colors like a spectrum; and the result is a symbolic drama that is rich, complex, strange, and by no means to be dismissed as mysticism.

*The Master Builder* and *When We Dead Awaken* are about Ibsen and nothing else. Does this mean that they are limited and narrow? Limited in their appeal they will always be. They are too difficult for any conceivable large audience to follow and enjoy. Even those who most admire the "modern Ibsen" are embarrassed by the increasing improbability of his fables. Was not Ibsen the man who recalled drama to the stern realm of reality? In that case what is he doing in symbolic towers and on symbolic mountains? In *When We Dead Awaken* not only verisimilitude but also physical possibility is scouted. The man who taught playwrights the new dramaturgy was forgetting his own lesson and returning to almost Shakespearean inconsistencies of plot. It was enough to start all the Ibsenites apologizing for their master; they thought him senescent.

Limited in their appeal, are these increasingly subjective plays limited in their value, limited, that is, by their very subjectivity? No. Ibsen's subjectivity is not a failure to communicate. Nor is it egotism. It springs from his belief that "the highest attainment possible to a human being" is "so to conduct one's life as to realize one's self." The artist, Ibsen believed, should limit himself to what he has experienced. "All that I have written these past ten years," he told the Norwegian students, "I have mentally lived through." This is the individualism which has won for Ibsen the label of "petty-bourgeois" from some Marxists. And it is true that Ibsen attached immense importance to individual character. As fervently as Nietzsche or Stefan George, he called for a new nobility, not, as he put it, of birth or wealth, or even of ability or intelligence, but of will and character. Hence his deep concern with men like Rosmer and John Gabriel Borkman, whom our revolutionaries would have given short shrift to. Hence his concern with such ideas as retribution and atonement, which have little meaning for the politician.

Yet Ibsen did not stop at the individual. To his statement to the students he added: "But no poet lives through anything isolated. What he lives through all of his countrymen live through together with him. For if that were not so, what would establish the bridge of understanding between the producing and receiving mind?" Ibsen's introversion stops far short of that of Proust and Joyce. In fact the individualist Ibsen, like the individualist Shaw, was also a good collectivist, a believer in social, and even socialist organization. Hearing of the young Shaw's lectures on Ibsenism, the Norwegian commented: "I was surprised that I, who had made it my chief task in life to depict human characters and human destinies, should, without conscious intention, have arrived in several matters at the same conclusions as the social-democratic moral philosophers had arrived at by scientific processes."

The modern intellectual oscillates between the two extremes of self-absorption and self-abandonment. Ibsen felt the pull of both, and, like Walt Whitman, he managed to avoid alike the fear of self that produces the sickly, eager radicalism of the carpet communist, and the fear of society and history that reinforces the natural egoism of the aesthete. The commissar-type he portrayed—not unsympathetically—in Peter Mortensgaard. He himself was Rosmer and Solness and Rubek. Or rather, the creation of these men was the way he purged himself of their faults. As one threw himself into a millrace and another fell headlong from a tower and the third was swept away by an avalanche, Ibsen could say: There but for the grace of God go I. And so it comes about that the late subjective plays are broadly significant, perhaps more broadly significant than anything Ibsen had written since *Peer Gynt*. After a performance of *The Wild Duck*, the poet Rilke wrote in a letter: "There was something very great, deep, essential. Doomsday and judgment. Something ultimate. And suddenly, the hour had come when Ibsen's majesty deigned to look upon me, for the first time. A new poet to whom we shall go by path after path now that I know one. And again a man misunderstood in the midst of fame. An entirely different person from what one hears." Exactly!

## VI

What was Ibsen's relation to his time? For many people nineteenth-century drama means Ibsen, but except insofar as he is the *best* dramatist of the century, this is a misleading opinion. Ibsen used many current modes and methods as every artist does; but he twisted them out of shape, imposed his own different meaning upon them. *An Enemy of the People* is a "well-made play," but entirely different in temper from Dumas. *Ghosts* is Naturalistic, but entirely different in meaning from Zola. *When We Dead Awaken* is Symbolist, but entirely different from Maeterlinck. The more one studies Ibsen the more one finds him standing apart from the drama of his time. Neither his predecessors nor his disciples bear him more than a superficial resemblance. He carried his aloofness with him like a charm, and it is no accident that two of the most zealous Ibsenites were Irish writers who have also stood aloof from literary movements in solitary self-confidence, Bernard Shaw and James Joyce.

Ibsen is not "the man who gave drama back to the people," who "brought back life to the popular theater." His popularity was the accident—like Joyce's—of a *succès de scandale*. It is true that the eighteen-eighties were the occasion of a great renewal of the culture of the theater, and that the motive force of the renewal is usually taken to be Ibsen and Ibsenism. But what was the nature of the renewal? It was not popular. The new plays were most often performed privately, on special occasions only, before literary clubs, on Sunday evenings. Very few enjoyed

even a short commercial run; many were given single performances. The exceptions to this are due either to the "scandalous"
element in the play or to the presence of an Eleanora Duse in
the cast. So, far from taking drama out to the people, Ibsen
drew it in to himself. As he grew older he went to the theater
less and less often; and his work, as we have seen, became more
and more subjective. Ibsen would fit better in Edmund Wilson's *Axel's Castle* than in lectures to women's clubs by popularizers of the classics or in paeans to Primary Literature by Mr.
Van Wyck Brooks.

The dramatic "renaissance" of the period was perhaps mis-
named. There were good plays, but they were not the plays of a
new and youthful age; most of them were patently the work of
an old and diffident civilization. Outside Ibsen and Strindberg,
perhaps the most gifted dramatists of the end of the century
were Shaw, who set his axe at the root of contemporary culture,
Chekhov and Schnitzler, who wrote exclusively of social decay,
and Wedekind, whose nihilism is already almost surrealist.

Much of the most genuine work of the era 1880-1920—including Ibsen's—was introspective, oblique, tough, in fact the kind
of literature which Mr. Brooks has hastily called secondary. Although it was in some respects a period of beginnings,
for every period is both seedtime and harvest, it was in more
respects a period of endings. And Ibsen knew it. He said in
1887:

> It has been said that I, and that in a prominent man-
> ner, have contributed to create a new era in these coun-
> tries. I, on the contrary, believe that the time in which
> we now live might with quite as much reason be char-
> acterized as a conclusion and that something new is
> about to be born.

Talk of a New Drama was therefore as ill-advised as talk of a
Music of the Future. Both phenomena were very much of the
late nineteenth century. As surely as Mozart and Schiller are

of the eighteenth, Wagner and Ibsen are of the nineteenth century. In the twentieth century, it is worth noting, there has been much Wagnerism and Ibsenism, but no real development on Wagnerite or Ibsenite lines.

## VII

With the foregoing sketch of the work of Wagner and Ibsen in mind, what can we make of the juxtaposition of the two names?

Ibsen and Wagner belong to the same society and have therefore—as men—many outward things in common. They were active, much-traveled men of Europe. Neither was highly educated or widely read. Both directed their whole lives to art, and lived to win enormous prestige in the society they had assailed. Such resemblances are superficial. In essentials the two men were poles apart. Wagner was a Bohemian, an egoist, an expansive, infinitely talkative man, a fiery and changeable lover, a voluminous, muddled, and humorless thinker. If Ibsen was an egoist, he was also reserved and almost superhumanly self-critical. Like his plays he was outwardly orthodox, well dressed, and respectable; like his plays he was inwardly agitated. Though he enjoyed being a national figure as much as Wagner did ("His entire people," Ibsen said, "a poet should have around him . . ."), his urgent sense of the dangers of prestige is a leitmotiv of the last plays. Ibsen's married life was (outwardly, at least) as smooth as Wagner's was stormy; Fru Susannah seems to have been at once homelier and more intelligent than the egregious Frau Cosima. Ibsen's letters, in their austere yet simple sincerity, their dry sagacity, and their untheatrical vehemence, are a refreshing contrast to the campaign oratory of the Führer of Bayreuth.

What of the vehicles which Wagner and Ibsen chose for their art—the "music drama" and the naturalistic drama respectively? They have important things in common. They both accept the nineteenth-century theater as it is: the picture-frame stage, the dull realistic settings, the darkened auditorium, the "mystic gulf," as Wagner termed it, formed by the proscenium and orchestra pit. They both imply therefore the passive audience which "surrenders" to the play, captured by illusion, suspense, and surprise, transported to a more or less phantasmagoric world. In other respects the Composite Art Work is diametrically opposite to Ibsenism. Wagner undoubtedly fell a victim to the vulgar heresy of quantity before quality. He once argued that since music appeals to the heart, speech to the intellect, and dance to the body, the best work of art would combine all three. But artistic experience is not quantitative. Ibsen's highly specialized, "narrow" and "limited" drama meets much more nearly the criterion of the arts, which is perfection.

As to content, the stuff of Wagner's dramas is Teutonic myth, that of Ibsen's, modern incidents culled from newspapers or from direct contact. Though in this Wagner seems to be deep, and Ibsen trivial, the real difference emerges from their interpretation of the material. Actually many themes are common to both artists: the theme of a general guilt (or loss of innocence) in the industrialist-capitalist world; the theme of redemption; the theme of the Eternal Feminine; the theme of the twilight of old values; the theme of nobility versus mediocrity. But we see the difference between the two men in their different treatment of common themes. *Tristan* and *Rosmersholm* both end with a love-death, yet where Wagner only shouts hurrah for love and hurrah for death, Ibsen concentrates in this final incident the whole meaning of two complex destinies. Wagner and Ibsen differ as dramatists above all in their utterly different presentation of human nature. Wagner is not interested in the individual; Ibsen is seldom interested in anything else. Wagner's characters are incarnations of qualities and instincts, or representatives—such as the Teutonic Elsa and Siegfried or the not quite Aryan Mime and Beckmesser—of groups. Humanity comes into Wagner only through the musical presentation of crude impulses, chiefly sexual. For Ibsen on the other hand, the individual is not indeed all, but he is certainly the beginning and the end.

Ibsen and Wagner, one might almost say, are positive and negative poles of the nineteenth century. As thinker and artist, Ibsen represents the spirit of man fighting for its rights—nay, for its existence—in a mechanized world, though the materialistic, prosy, manipulating Ibsen of general misconception seems more like a docile product of that mechanization. Wagner, on the other hand, who announces himself as the champion of the spirit against money and materialism, to a great extent embodies the destructive forces themselves, though by a fantastic stroke of genius or devilry he confers upon them the status of art.

Returning to our original problem of tragedy in modern and in fancy dress, one might say that Ibsen, the great man of the modern and naturalistic tradition, was perhaps even more deeply a Romanticist, and that Wagner, the great man of the fancy and antinaturalistic tradition, was at heart a rather crude naturalist. In different terms, Ibsen was a realist outside, a fantasist inside; Wagner was a fantasist outside, a realist inside. On the whole Ibsenism worked better. Realism, controlled by fantasy, gave us the supple strength, fine irony, and rich polyphony of *The Wild Duck* and *John Gabriel Borkman*. Fantasy, controlled by realism, was fantasy mechanized and therefore partly spoiled. The disturbing thing about Wagner's Valhalla is that if you scratch it you find the Crystal Palace underneath. Wagner's ardent spirituality masks a mercenary instinct. His overanxious idealism conceals cynical compromise. The enemy of "Victorianism" is himself an arch-Victorian. The drab naturalist, on the other hand, conceals a flame of Romantic inspiration, the seemingly materialistic sociologist conceals a delicate spirituality, the man who seems now a midcentury optimist, now a midcentury pessimist, surpasses both extremes in a flexible pragmatism close to that of William James. "It has been said of me on different occasions," he declared, "that I am a pessimist. And I am insofar as I do not believe in the everlast-ingness of human ideals. But I am an optimist insofar as I firmly believe in the capacity for the procreation and develop-ment of ideals." These words bring one close also to the mod-ern playwright whom William James probably admired most: George Bernard Shaw.

. . . it would seem that what is called wit is a certain "dramatic" way of thinking. Instead of treating his ideas as mere symbols, the wit sees them, he hears them, and above all makes them converse with one another like persons. He puts them on the stage, and himself, to some extent, into the bargain. . . . But if wit consists, for the most part, in seeing things "sub specie theatri," it is evidently capable of being specially directed to one variety of dramatic art, namely, comedy.

HENRI BERGSON

# 5. BERNARD

# SHAW

THUS FAR OUR ATTENTION HAS BEEN CONFINED TO THE TRAGIC
tradition in drama. But in the minds of most of us drama is
divided into two parts: tragedy and comedy. Since Strindberg,
of course, this division has been less clear, and new mixtures of
comic and tragic elements have been made. Comedy might almost be said to be extinct in the twentieth century or at least to
have reached the same stage of senility that tragedy is in. But
George Bernard Shaw is not a post-Strindbergian artist. I in-
tend no aspersion when I say that he is a great *nineteenth-
century* artist. What Ibsen is to the tragic, Shaw is to the comic
tradition.

If there is still a mound of misconception over the dead Ibsen,
Bernard Shaw may be said to be already buried, though alive,

137

under a heap of witticism, vituperation, and anecdote. Although some of the spadework was performed by Shaw himself, it is largely the fault of the public, "high-brow" and "low-brow," that one of the major minds of the epoch can still so often be dismissed as an irresponsible jester. When great men remonstrate earnestly with the human race they are crucified. When, in a better humor, they laugh at its foibles they are dismissed as irresponsible jesters. This has been the fate of Bernard Shaw. Those who dislike him think him outmoded, flippant, superficial, vain, naughty. Those who like him like him for his most dubious qualities—his gift of gab, his excessive cleverness, and above all, his famous Puckish Humor. The Shavians with their fondness for puckish humor and the like have damaged Shaw's serious reputation as much as the Ibsenites with their fondness for social problems damaged Ibsen's. Every teacher has to be saved from his disciples.

Friends and foes of Shaw share the belief that he is so funny that he cannot be taken seriously. Accordingly I want the reader to imagine that the following lines were written by one of our latter-day long-faces who is so unfunny that we think him very important. The long-face says:

> . . . I must warn you, before you attempt to enjoy my plays, to clear out of your consciousness most resolutely everything you have ever read about me in a newspaper. Otherwise you will not enjoy them: you will read them with a sophisticated mind, and a store of beliefs concerning me which have not the slightest foundation either in prosaic fact or in poetic truth. In some unaccountable way I seem to cast a spell on journalists which makes them recklessly indifferent not only to common veracity, but to human possibility. The person they represent me to be not only does not exist but could not possibly exist.
>
> Now it may be that a pen portrait of an imaginary

monster with my name attached to it may already have taken possession of your own mind through your inevitable daily contact with the newspaper press. If so, please class it with the unicorn and the dragon, the jabberwock and the bandersnatch, as a creature perhaps amusing but certainly entirely fabulous. If you are to get any good out of me you must accept me as a quite straightforward practitioner of the art I make my living by. Inasmuch as that living depends finally on you as reader or playgoer or both, I am your very faithful servant; and I should no more dream of pulling your leg or trifling with you or insulting you than any decent shopkeeper would dream of doing that to his best customers. If I make you laugh at yourself, remember that my business as a classic writer of comedies is "to chasten morals with ridicule." . . .

In this passage—by Bernard Shaw, it is to be feared—I wish to underline the phrase, "my business as a classic writer of comedies," and the sentence, "I seem to cast a spell on journalists." And now I want to set forth the theory and practice of Shavian drama as forthrightly as possible, for, since there has been so much writing about Shaw that is brilliantly or unbrilliantly impressionistic, the most serviceable approach will perhaps be one of heavy-footed sobriety. I have accordingly drawn up a list of questions for Shaw critics, especially for those who report Shaw productions in the press. The rest of this chapter is made up of my own attempts to answer them.

*Question I: What is Shaw's theory of the drama?*
What has Shaw himself said on the subject? A great deal, almost everyone would be inclined to say. Yet in fact only a very small portion of Shaw's thirty-odd volumes is devoted to dramatic criticism and little of that is devoted to dramatic theory. From the earliest prefaces to the preface to *Saint Joan*

(1924) we find complaints of a lack of seriousness in contemporary theater and in contemporary criticism, and we find discussions of censorship and the like, but for more general judgments one must go to two chapters added in 1912 to *The Quintessence of Ibsenism,* to the Preface to *Three Plays of Brieux,* and to Archibald Henderson's biography. From these sources—and of course from many remarks up and down the collected works—one can piece together a body of dramatic theory that runs somewhat as follows.

The nineteenth-century theater, consisting of the rags and tatters of Shakespeare and the cheap new feathers of Scribe, is decadent. It presents not life but daydream, not thought but sentiment, not experience but conventional surrogates. Two men—Ibsen and Wagner—have struggled against the tide, and their efforts have been so successful that Shaw can say: ". . . there is, flatly, no future now for any drama without music except the drama of thought." That Shaw in the nineties wrote a book on each of "the two greatest living masters of their respective arts," as he called them, was more than a critical, more than a crusading venture. Shaw had his eye on his own creative work. Was he not a third great living master? He would begin as the apprentice of the first two. Receptively Shaw was probably more moved by Wagner; as a creative artist he was to follow in the footsteps of Ibsen—or of a Shavian creation known as the Quintessence of Ibsenism.

For Shaw the quintessence of Ibsenism was that Ibsen was preoccupied with morality, and that morality was in Ibsen something to be discussed and worked out, not something given. Morality is not only to do right but to discover what *is* right; immorality is not only the doing of certain things, but the deception of self in refusing to see what should and should not be done. In the drama of fixed morality there is no moral questioning at all. Hence the need of much outward action. We must see the hero in many situations, facing right and facing wrong. He must be put to tests of fire and water. Such is the nature of what Shaw calls "the tomfooleries called action" or, more explicitly, "vulgar attachments, rapacities, generosities, resentments, ambitions, misunderstandings, oddities, and so forth." Once the moral problem is one of sincerity and conscience and not merely a test of one's power to live according to moral laws, outward eventfulness becomes superfluous and therefore vulgar. Shaw denounces "crimes, fights, big legacies, fires, shipwrecks, battles, and thunderbolts" as "mistakes in a play, even when they can be effectively simulated."

Since our morality is not given, we do not know who is a villain and who is a hero. This fact is both true to life and dramatically interesting. The villain cannot only *seem* virtuous —as he always did. He can actually *be* what most people (however wrongly) think virtuous. This too is true to life, and it is dramatically striking because it establishes between author and audience the unusual, ironic, and Shavian relationship of antagonism. It is true that most of the audience will, after a time at least, make exceptions of themselves and assume that Shaw means everybody else. But Shaw does not mean everybody else, and the irony is redoubled. We must therefore conclude that there are more to the shock-tactics of Shavian drama than high spirits or even reformism. Shaw's preaching has aesthetic as well as moral point. Preaching is an art, and an art distinguished by the special attitude of the preaching artist to his audience: the preacher chides his audience and does not pretend to sympathize with their faults. When Shaw proposed a drama of ideas he did not mean a drama deprived of all dramatic elements except witty conversation. He meant, in his own words, "the substitution of a forensic technique of recrimination, disillusion, and penetration through ideals to the truth, with a free use of all the rhetorical and lyrical arts of the orator, the preacher, the pleader, and the rhapsodist."

The theory of Shavian drama is, on the positive side, a defense of the drama of discussion and, on the negative side, an assault upon all other drama, for when the artist turns literary

critic he nearly always generalizes his personal positions and
arraigns all the traditions with which he is not in rapport. Since
Shaw was not averse to attacking Shakespeare, and even to sug-
gesting that he was inferior to Shaw, the latter was somewhat
naturally accused of megalomania. What we should remember
is that Bardolatry—which does little to help the true understanding of Shakespeare—has always been one of the chief ob-
stacles to the development of modern drama. In the eighteenth
century Herder complained to Goethe of this fact. In the nine
teenth Zola had to defend his Naturalism with the angry quip
"The bastards of Shakespeare have no right to ridicule the legit
imate children of Balzac." Even after the Naturalist onslaught
the great Shakespearean actor Henry Irving preferred any
pseudo-Shakespearean rubbish of the late Victorian poets to the
work of Ibsen and Shaw. And those who try to create a drama
that is as expressive of our time as Shakespeare was of his invariably find Shakespeare and the Shakespeareans in their way. As
objective appraisal Shaw's Shakespeare criticism is unimportant.
As polemic, as part of his own theory, it is consistent and significant. If he ridiculed some plays which had been thought
sacrosanct, he called attention to the fascination of other plays,
such as *Troilus and Cressida,* which modern critics would later
claim to have "discovered"; he observed that *Hamlet* was lauda-
bly un-Shakespearean in that here was real moral doubt and
questioning of conscience and inner tragedy; he was privately
a great Shakespeare fan, and in Shakespeare discussion resembles an atheist who in religious controversy turns out to know
and relish the Bible more than the godly.

But Shaw's major critical offensive was against the pre-
Ibsenite drama of the nineteenth century. The shadow of Eugène Scribe darkened the sky. Shaw fumed. He would annihilate this cardboard monster! If this was technique, he would
annihilate technique! Hence his polemics against the "well-
made play": "Your plot construction and art of preparation
are only tricks of theatrical talent and shifts of moral sterility,

not the weapons of dramatic genius." Or again: "The writer who practices the art of Ibsen therefore discards all the old tricks of preparation, catastrophe, dénouement. . . ." Once the *mode* of these polemics is understood, Shaw's disparagement of dramaturgy in his own work can also be understood for the blarney that it is. Shaw boasts of using the comic tricks of the sixties in *Arms and the Man;* in *The Devil's Disciple* he declares he has used those of the next generation; what the critics take for brilliance and originality, he explains, consists only of the "tricks and suspense and thrills and jests" which were "in vogue when I was a boy." How little these remarks really describe the Shavian dramaturgy we must try to discover later.

*Question II: What is Shaw's case against the Shakespearean and the Scribean traditions?*

It is that both are romantic. In the Shavian use of the term —which is the popular use and not that of my last chapter, when Ibsen was called Romantic—romanticism means hocus-pocus, pretentious and deceptive artifice, the substitution of flattering but unreal and foolish conventions for realities. The theory is that Zola, Ibsen, and Shaw (and perhaps one should add the later Dickens and Samuel Butler) had made it their business to destroy romanticism by laying bare the realities. Zola made a fine beginning, says Shaw, by trying to replace romantic or stagey logic with a correct natural history, but unfortunately he formed a romantic attachment with morbidity. Ibsen made a monumental contribution, but unhappily retained the catastrophic ending in his plays; the natural historian of modern society knows that the real tragedy of the Hedda Gablers is precisely that they do not commit suicide. Shaw gives Chekhov some credit for this insight, and emulates his method in *Heartbreak House.* (It was actually no "insight," for Chekhov was not discovering the "real tragedy" of the Hedda Gablers, but asserting a preference for nontragic drama.) The mediocre French playwright Eugène Brieux, Shaw appears to regard as the most perfect exponent of "natural history." Again we should discount the Shavian appraisal but recognize the *arrière-pensée* which, here, is to justify a *naturalistic* form of comedy.

This brings us to the positive side of Shaw's dramaturgy. Shaw's theory is not that everything in traditional drama should be scrapped except talk and then the residue called the New Drama. "Rhetoric, irony, argument, paradox, epigram, parable," he writes, "the rearrangement of haphazard facts into orderly and intelligent situations: these are both the oldest and the newest arts of the drama." These words include a good deal more than clever or even profound talk. They include a good deal more than we usually associate with "problem plays" and the "theater of ideas." Attention should be paid to the phrase, "the rearrangement of the facts into orderly and intelligent situations," and to the word parable. The preface to Brieux contains an assertion that drama does not merely photograph nature, but attempts a "presentation in parable of the conflict between man's will and his environment: in a word, of problem." This is indeed an old and new theory of drama, old as the Greeks, new as Ibsen who had characterized his leading theme as "the contradiction between effort and capacity, between will and possibility, the tragedy and at the same time comedy of the individual and of mankind."

*Question III: What are the broader implications of this theory?*

Shaw's defense of a theater of ideas brought him up against both his great bugbears—commercialized art on the one hand and Art for Art's Sake on the other. His teaching is that beauty is a by-product of other activity; that the artist writes out of moral passion (in forms varying from political conviction to religious zeal), not out of love of art; that the pursuit of art for its own sake is a form of self-indulgence as bad as any other sort of sensuality. In the end, the errors of "pure" art and of commercialized art are identical: they both appeal primarily to the senses. True art, on the other hand, is not merely a matter of pleasure. It may be unpleasant. A favorite Shavian metaphor for the function of the arts is that of tooth-pulling. Even if the patient is under laughing gas, the tooth is still pulled.

The history of aesthetics affords more examples of a didactic than of a hedonist view. But Shaw's didacticism takes an unusual turn in its application to the history of the arts. If, as Shaw holds, ideas are a most important part of a work of art, and if, as he also holds, ideas go out of date, it follows that even the best works of art go out of date in some important respects and that the generally held view that great works are in all respects eternal is not shared by Shaw. In the preface to *Three Plays for Puritans*, Shaw maintains that renewal in the arts means renewal in philosophy and not in anything artistic, that the first great artist who comes along after a renewal gives to the new philosophy full and final form, that subsequent artists, though even more gifted, can do nothing but refine upon the master without matching him. Shaw, whose essential modesty is as disarming as his pose of vanity is disconcerting, assigns to himself the role, not of the master, but of the pioneer, the role of a Marlowe rather than of a Shakespeare. "The whirligig of time will soon bring my audiences to my own point of view," he writes, "and then the next Shakespeare that comes along will turn these petty tentatives of mine into masterpieces final for their epoch."

"Final for their epoch"—even Shakespearean masterpieces are not final beyond that. No one, says Shaw, will ever write a better tragedy than *Lear* or a better opera than *Don Giovanni* or a better music drama than *Der Ring des Niblungen;* but just as essential to a play as this aesthetic merit is moral relevance which, if we take a naturalistic and historical view of morals, it loses, or partly loses, in time. Shaw, who has the courage of his historicism, consistently withstands the view that moral problems do not change, and argues therefore that for us modern literature and music form a Bible surpassing in significance the Hebrew Bible. That is Shaw's anticipatory challenge to President Hutchins and St. John's College.

*Question IV: What are we to make of these views?*

We have seen that most of Shaw's critical prose is polemic and is not therefore to be submitted to the same kind of analysis as a more objective criticism. Even when arguing for science and natural history as against romanticism and artifice, Shaw writes in a prose that is at once artistic, artful, and artificial. He is a poet of polemics, as Einstein seems to have felt when he compared the movement of Shavian dialogue to Mozart's music. His polemics are therefore the more dangerous, for polemics are nothing but the art of skilled deception. A prime device of polemics is the either/or pattern, against which so much has been said in recent times, often by great polemicists. Shaw is a great polemicist in his skilled deployment of antitheses. He always forces upon his opponent an alternative which the opponent never wanted to be confronted with and sometimes did not deserve to be confronted with. Watch how he pushes not only the Scribeans but also the Shakespeareans into a corner! He condemns not merely melodramatic action but apparently all outward action as "tomfoolery." Of course the condemnation has some substance (it is the art of the polemicist to avoid untruths, and exploit half-truths) in that not much of the history of the world can be convincingly represented on the stage. Shaw knows that the stage can only show the effect of history on a few individuals and that it is much better suited to talking than to fighting and doing. That is the true half of this remark. But he loads it with a lie in order to attract attention. He feels that the weakness of the "well-made play" can only be revealed if all plot construction is ridiculed. The absurdity of melodrama can only be demonstrated by debunking tragedy. Shaw cannot always resist the temptation to remove the unoffending nose with the offending wart.

We cannot, therefore, feel wholly satisfied with Shaw's contributions to dramatic theory, brilliant as some of them are. The terms of the theory are too crude. Technique and plot cannot be isolated from the rest of a work of art in so facile a manner. More explanation would be needed to make the antithesis of romantic logic and natural history convincing. Shaw's criticism, which so many think overexplanatory, and which many assume to be voluminous, is actually reticent to the point of evasiveness. As his pose of conceit hides a considerable shyness about himself, so his volubility is, among other things, a way of avoiding certain issues, chief among them the aesthetic issues. Shaw refuses to lecture on dramaturgy on the grounds that he is a practitioner, and in this he is of course entirely within his rights. Many a creative artist would support him. The peculiar thing about Shaw is that we have the impression that he has explained everything—"I am nothing if not explanatory," he once said—though he always stops short in personal and aesthetic matters. Hence we can often learn more from an *obiter dictum* of Shaw's than from an extended statement. When, for instance, in 1934 Shaw defends one of his plays "simply as a play" we wonder what has happened to the didactic criterion. And we learn much about the art of Shaw when we read of his writing his roles for particular actors, of his own histrionic talent, of his work in actual production. Plays, he remarks casually, can be considered as exhibitions of the art of acting. Of this conception he wrote: "As I write my plays it is continuously in my mind and very much to my taste."

These are valuable hints, but they remain hints and are never developed into a critical system. Shaw's critical writing is to some extent camouflage. He has himself, consciously or not, spread the notion, recently reiterated in Mr. Hesketh Pearson's biography, that he is most interesting as a person, slightly less interesting as a sage, and least interesting as a playwright. Shaw has said that art must be subordinate to other things, and his readers have applied the theory to Shaw. But the Shavian

view is that the subordination of art to morals should make
the artist better as an artist. To say that beauty and happiness
are by-products not to be directly aimed at, is to alter our
method of attaining beauty and happiness. But beauty and happiness remain the ultimate goal even though we reach them by
doing something else. And the critic is entitled to judge for
himself whether beauty has been attained or not. By no amount
of polemic can Shaw evade the aesthetic touchstone. Not one
exceptional case only, but all his plays must stand or fall "simply as plays."

*Question V: What of Shaw as a practicing playwright?*

One or two of Shaw's generalizations about drama help us to
an understanding of his plays. One is that there are only two
dramatic characters, the long-haired aesthete and the clown.
The statement is naughty, for it is either too vague to be exactly
applicable or too dogmatic to be true. Yet it opens the door to
an understanding of Shaw's characters, at least the male characters, and the way they are contrasted. A still more pregnant
remark is that the drama, though now degenerated to a rant
and a situation, began as a dance and a story. Shaw has brought
dance back into the drama, not directly, to be sure, but in the
lively rhythm of his lines and in the rhythmic and musical,
rather than "well-made," structure of his scenes; and, precisely
by minimizing plot, he has brought back stories to the stage by
way of lengthy narrations.

The well-made play, Shaw correctly observes, is built on the
scheme: exposition, situation, unraveling. *A Doll's House,* he
more dubiously adds, is built on the scheme: exposition, situation, discussion. Discussion is to Shaw the crucial technical innovation which accompanies the changes in outlook of which
Hebbel was one of the first to be aware. The Shavian play—
everyone agrees—is a discussion play. People sit in their chairs
and talk everything over. The talk is good. And that, according
to many, is Shaw.

But, in the first place, Shaw's plays, though more like each other than any one is like any non-Shavian piece, are not cut to one pattern. Indeed his plays are so various, and there are about thirty important ones, that classification is extremely difficult even on chronological lines. Yet, though Shaw's dramatic career is not so clearly periodized as, say, Ibsen's, certain groupings do suggest themselves. A major break occurred with the First World War. The plays prior to that compose a single group which in turn may be cut in half at about the turn of the century. Dividing the postwar period also in half, we have two main periods, with two subdivisions:

   I.  i.  1892-1899  *Plays Pleasant and Unpleasant,* and
                      *Three Plays for Puritans.*
      ii.  1901-1912  From *Man and Superman* to *Pyg-*
                      *malion.*
  II.  i.  1913-1924  From *Heartbreak House* to *Saint*
                      *Joan.*
      ii.  1929-1939  From *The Apple Cart* to *In Good*
                      *King Charles's Golden Days.*

The plays of the nineties are chiefly simple inversions of current theatrical patterns, such as Victorian melodrama *(The Devil's Disciple),* the heroic play *(The Man of Destiny, Caesar and Cleopatra),* musical comedy *(Arms and the Man),* and farce, *(You Never Can Tell).* But from *Man and Superman* (1901-1903) on, Shaw makes his own patterns. These are the years of *Getting Married* and *Misalliance,* which are the extreme instances of Shavian discussion drama, of Shaw's toughest dialectical dramas, such as *Major Barbara* and *The Doctor's Dilemma* (two of the best and most original of Shaw's plays), and of his most controlled and effective fantasies, such as *Androcles and the Lion.* If *Fanny's First Play* and *Pygmalion* are, like the early plays, variants on conventional patterns, they are at once subtler and tougher variants than those of the nineties.

The play which Shaw was at work on from 1913 to 1916—

*Heartbreak House*—marks a departure in technique and mood. The socialist optimism of *Major Barbara* and the Bergsonian optimism of *Man and Superman* are gone. For the current stage of civilization, Shaw finds a metaphor which is still to be with him in 1933: civilization is a ship on the rocks. From now on, most of Shaw's plays are to be fantasies or extravaganzas in which the disappointment of many liberal hopes is announced and the apartness of Shaw from the new generation is implied. Even *Back to Methuselah*, which so anxiously tries to be optimistic, is most impressive in the extravagant satire against Lloyd George and Asquith and in the pathetic tragedy of the elderly gentleman confronted with a new generation. Even *Saint Joan*, which might seem to be aloof both from the postwar generation and from Shaw, has as its theme the homelessness of genius. Among other things it is a commentary on Shaw's autobiographical remark: "I was at home only in the realm of my imagination, and at my ease only with the mighty dead."

Whether it is fair to stress, to the extent that Mr. Edmund Wilson has done, the subjective element in the later plays of Shaw, it is evident that these plays, from *Heartbreak House* to the end of the roster, do compose a separate group which we can now see as a whole. Two of them Shaw calls Political Extravaganzas, and the name might be extended to the five plays which are a fantastic chronicle of the interim between the two world wars: *The Apple Cart, Too True To Be Good, On The Rocks, The Simpleton of the Unexpected Isles,* and *Geneva.* Are these plays inferior? From a natural tendency to say that what a famous writer does today is not up to what he did twenty years ago, and from a natural feeling that so old a man must be in his dotage, critics have on the whole damned this last cycle of Shavian plays. To be sure, they do not have the galvanic energy of *Man and Superman* or the tough dialectic of *Major Barbara.* But they are not failures. They would be enough to establish a great reputation for any new dramatist. Moreover, the Political Extravaganza is not only a new form in drama, it is in some ways the form in which Shaw's genius has been most at home. Shaw's career might be regarded as a search for a form which would fully express his genius. The Political Extravaganza is such a form, though Shaw perfected it only after he had passed his prime and written his greatest plays. The Political Extravaganza is definite enough and free enough, fantastic enough and realistic enough, uproarious enough and serious enough. It is Shavian form.

*Question VI: What is to be said for Shavian comedy? What are its merits? What is its nature?*

It is the dialogue of Shavian comedy that has attracted most attention. It was praised by Max Beerbohm and G. K. Chesterton forty years ago, and it is praised by Edmund Wilson and Jacques Barzun today. The point is that Shaw's talent is not merely for conversation but also for dramaturgy. In all justice it should be said that Max Beerbohm pointed this out in a retraction of his earlier view that Shaw was a writer of conversations, not plays. This view, says Beerbohm, collapses when you actually see Shaw in the theater: "To deny that he is a dramatist merely because he chooses, for the most part, to get drama out of contrasted types of character and thought, without action, and without appeal to the emotions, seems to be both unjust and absurd."

But these words of Beerbohm's, written in 1905, have not been heeded. In histories of the drama Bernard Shaw has been relegated to a humble role beside now forgotten mediocrities. Most of those who discover the artistry of Shaw discover the prose style much more than the dramaturgy. Even Beerbohm's praise is left-handed in its assertion that Shavian drama is "without action and without appeal to the emotions." It is curious that almost on the same page Beerbohm speaks of the splendid emotional crisis in the second act of *Major Barbara,* and has shown himself the first critic, so far as I know, to note the delicate spirituality of Shaw. It is curious, because it shows how a man can revert to the cliché conception of Shaw—"a giant brain and no heart," to cite one of the critics in *Fanny's First Play*—after a momentary escape from it. Heine once spoke of thinking with the heart and feeling with the head. The saying applies to Shaw. His intellect and his passions are alike all that one could expect of an artist-philosopher. But there is something perpetually astonishing about the way they mix.

The allegation that Shaw's plays are "without action" is more plausible but still wrong. Most of the plays from *Arms and the Man* to *The Millionairess* entail every bit as much action as other authors' plays and for the good reason that many of them are other authors' plots. The misapprehension comes about because Shaw *toys* with the plots instead of gratefully accepting them for what they are, because also he has in his prefaces railed so often against the tomfoolery of action, and because of the interpenetration of action with discussion. Look for a moment at two of the most actionless of Shaw's plays, *Getting Married* and *Misalliance*. Even these are not static dramas of a sort to win the approval of a Maeterlinck or a Chekhov. In both there is enough plot for an ordinary Broadway play. (It is amusing that Shaw has to be defended by such an argument.) In *Getting Married* the destiny of a fair number of characters is not merely discussed but settled, and the routine of boy-meets-girl is given a Shavian performance. In *Misalliance* there is all the violence and tomfoolery that anyone could wish. An aviator—and this in 1910—crashes into a greenhouse; the aviator's passenger turns out to be a lady whom Mr. Sidney Hook would have to term at once eventful and event-making. In *Getting Married* there is a coal-dealer's wife who makes love to a bishop through the mails under the name, Incognita Appassionata; in *Misalliance* there is a gunman. It is not the lack of action but the presence of intelligent dialogue which is too much for many directors, actors, critics, and audiences.

*Question VII: So much for technique. An artist who is a critic of morality and society must also submit to a moral and social criticism. What are Shaw's values?*

In reply to this question one might point to the most extended of his philosophic works, such as *Back to Methuselah,* or one might maintain that Shaw has capriciously chopped and changed. Now he is a social democrat, now an antidemocratic pessimist. Now he is a Huxleyan champion of science against religion, now a metabiological champion of religion against science. He can be represented as merely a disciple of Marx, or of Shelley, or of Samuel Butler. Mr. Edmund Wilson concludes that he is just confused.

This might not—though again, it might—be a damaging criticism of a lyric poet, but it is certainly a damaging criticism of a moralist; and one cannot be quite happy about Mr. Wilson's approval of Shaw the artist when it is qualified by so strong a disapproval of Shaw the philosopher. Of course it can be maintained that Shaw's argument against the pure artist is a deceptive strategy to trick us into believing that he is a philosopher. Even so a confused satirist is a bad satirist, and thus a bad artist.

Perhaps Mr. Wilson is wrong. What he finds inconsistent—for instance, that Shaw can be at the same time a social democrat and an admirer of Stalin—will not seem inconsistent to everyone. Mr. Wilson says that Shaw's thinking is on three levels—the level of everyday life, the level of politics, and the level of metaphysics—and that the three are never integrated. To be sure, it is no answer to this that *all* men think on these three levels without a successful integration of the three, for Shaw as an artist-philosopher must be expected to succeed where others fail. The answer is that, to a great extent, he does succeed. Of course some of Shaw's works are less optimistic than others; but a waning confidence in the immediate success of a belief is not necessarily a betrayal of that belief.

I have tried elsewhere to demonstrate that Shaw's integration

is not so incomplete as is supposed. Here it is enough to state
that Shaw is sometimes accused of betraying beliefs which he
never held. He is often suspected of trying to be much more
systematic than he ever intended to be. If he is not utterly
systematic, he is at least roughly consistent. His attitude to beliefs has been, in the main, pragmatic. This is perhaps what
most clearly differentiates Shaw from satirists of previous ages,
such as Chaucer with his catholic criteria or Voltaire with his
deistic criteria. It is at once Shaw's greatest title to originality
as an artist and his greatest title to representing his age.

Shaw's adaptability is not mere opportunism. He has often
sponsored an unpopular cause which was later recognized to be
right. He has believed in what might as justifiably be called
Romanticism as the hocus-pocus of popular novelists, namely,
in the continuity of the ideal and the real, the spiritual and the
physical, the theoretic and the practical. He is a Marxist in his
hatred of hypocritical ideologies, of religions which are opiates;
money, he says, echoing Samuel Butler, is the most important
thing in the world, and you are damned without it. On the
other hand, Shaw probably agrees with Hotchkiss in *Getting
Married:* "Religion is a great force: the only real motive force
in the world." The Shavian will see no final contradiction between the two attitudes. Religion is for Shaw a natural fact, not
a supernatural fact; just as economics is for Shaw spiritual
enough to be the subject of high comedy.

The great problem of Shaw's plays—we have examined one
instance in some detail—is the relation between ideals and
reality, and thus the relation between idealism and realism.
There is, according to Shaw, a wrong realism and a right realism, a wrong idealism and a right idealism. A wrong realism is
exemplified in Undershaft, whose realistic and absolutely correct vision supports only egoism. Idealism, on the other hand,
may be worse. It may be the conscious mask of a realist, as it is
in the propaganda of Undershaft's factory or in the gifts of
Bodger the brewer to the Salvation Army. It may be self-decep-

tion, as it is in Barbara before she sees quite clearly that she is combating liquor with a brewer's money. In either case, idealism is painted in more horrible colors by Shaw, as it had been by Ibsen and for that matter by Jesus Christ, than is Machiavellian realism. The conclusion of *Major Barbara* is that the high purpose of the idealist should be linked to the realist's sense of fact, power, and possibility. Where practical genius is found in a lofty mind Shaw approves. His Caesar is a realist with a soul, a realist who values his own life as nothing beside the high destiny of Rome. His Joan is an idealist with a head, an idealist who can see the simple facts better than the soldiers, the politicians, and the clerics put together, a visionary whose hallucinations sometimes have more validity than the philosophic ideas of the learned.

Ibsen's Brand, striving to "live the vision into deed," says:

> Daily drudgery be one
> With star-flights beyond the sun.

Perhaps this outlook could more legitimately be called Romanticism than the cheap escapist literature which Shaw designates by that term. I have suggested that the naturalistic tragedy of Ibsen is Romantic; so is the naturalistic comedy of Shaw. In the one playwright, as in the other, an intention deeply influenced by naturalistic dramatists and inspired by a Balzacian desire to write the natural history of modern life was combined with Romantic aspiration, Romantic fancy, and Romantic imagination. Through Ibsen Romanticism came to flower in Scandinavia; through Ibsen, Shaw, and others Romanticism was renewed after a generation of anti-Romanticism. Now the doctrine of religious-materialism or materialist-religion, of idealist-realism or realistic-idealism is one of the themes of Romanticism from Blake to Shaw. It is a leitmotiv of Shavian drama turning up in the pseudo-flippant form of his late Political Extravaganzas. In *Too True To Be Good* (1929), man is described as having higher and lower centers, as in D. H. Lawrence. But

Shaw is not the spokesman of the lower centers; nor is he, as many assume, the spokesman of the higher centers. He attributes our troubles to the separation of higher and lower. "Since the war," says his preacher, "the lower centers have become vocal. And the effect is that of an earthquake . . . the institutions are rocking and splitting and sundering. They leave us no place to live, no certainties, no workable morality, no heaven, no hell, no commandments, and no God." Or, as the studious Sergeant in the same play puts it, in speaking of the sexual ethics of the twenties: "But when men and women pick one another up just for a bit of fun, they find they've picked up more than they bargained for, because men and woman have a top story as well as a ground floor; and you can't have the one without the other."

Shaw's Romanticism, which is also Ibsen's Romanticism, is a more highly developed philosophy than the Romanticism of the first generation. Philosophically one should look for its affiliations less with "mysticism" or "materialism"—the two systems commonly associated with Shaw and Ibsen—than with the pragmatic pluralism of William James. The attitudes of pragmatic pluralism are part and parcel of Shaw's art as well as of his thought. Nowhere in dogmatic communist writing does one have a sense of dialectic and antithesis as keenly as in a Shavian play. Shaw's mind is well stocked, as everyone knows, and he is famous for the number of things he can mention on one page; but all this would mean nothing if he could not marshal his facts ironically. The chief mark of Shavian prose is its use of ironic antithesis and juxtaposition. Contrary to what one expects from a propagandist, Shaw not only shows the liberal's sense of the other man's point of view. He has a sense of every conceivable point of view, and can pack all the points of view into one long sentence, which climbs by parallelisms and antitheses to a climax, and then sinks with the finality of a conqueror to a conclusion which Shaw will not allow you to evade. In its course the Shavian sentence, still more the Shavian paragraph, looks in all possible directions. For Shaw sees the world as what James called a multiverse, and that is unusual in a satirist, who is customarily something of a monomaniac.

It is a fact of curious interest that William James, who thought Shaw "a great power as a concrete moralist," hit upon one of the essentials of Shaw, to wit, "the way he brings home to the *eyes,* as it were, the difference between 'convention' and 'conscience.'" Such a statement would often be the cue for a discussion of Shaw as puritan and protestant. But there is more to it than that. The difference between convention and conscience is certainly a moral matter, but Shaw is a *concrete* moralist, a master of parable, who has worked out for the presentation of his protestant pragmatist morality a new dramaturgy. Shaw is one of the few artists whose grasp of political, moral, and social forces is really professional; in political, moral, and social territory he is not a mere expropriator. But he is a genuine dramatist in that he brings his matter home to the eyes, which is something that neither the historian nor the sociologist, the poet or the novelist, need do .All these bring visions before the mind's eye; none, except the dramatist, has literally to unfold his vision before the physical eye. Appreciators of Shaw's dialogue have explained to us what Shaw has done for the ear; those who appreciate his dramaturgy know that he addressed himself also to the eye, not indeed in giving separate attention to the eye by way of spectacle, but in fusing the elements into the one kinetic picture which is stage production. William James's statement that Shaw's genius is much more important than his philosophy is true, if by it we understand that genius is a synthesizing power which obliterates barriers between thought and technique and gives evidence of both in a particular mode of presentation. The Shavian mode is drama.

A comedy only, and nothing else but a comedy, "is" a comedy.

HENRY JAMES

# 6. VARIETIES OF

# COMIC EXPERIENCE

## I

THEORISTS HAVE THOUGHT OUT ALL MANNNER OF QUASI-FINAL definitions of comedy. The procedure is either to legislate *a priori*, "The essence of comedy is A, B, and C," or, if the inductive method has more scientific associations, to generalize from a particular school of practice—the one the theorist likes best—and to say: "The essence of comedy is D, E, and F." Both methods give an assured answer, and that is a sufficient reason for adopting neither. Nor shall we find a key to the art of comedy in the psychology of laughter. Henri Bergson's splendid little book, it should be recalled, is entitled *Laughter*. Its primary subject, accordingly, is not comedy but a common by-product of comedy. Its primary aim is the analysis of human nature, not the evaluation of works of art. What is comedy as a

159

dramatic art? To answer such a question we would have to ponder the various phenomena which have been called comedy and consider what they have in common, if anything, that justifies their common name. Critical terms can never be more than approximations and conveniences. When they become battlegrounds, when someone wants to know which of the varieties is the *real thing*, we have tumbled from rational discourse into superstition.

Thinking over a large number of plays known as tragedies and comedies, we can see much good sense in one of Bergson's dichotomies. The tragic writer has generally been concerned with last things, with death, with the meaning of life as a whole, with "destiny" or "fate," with Man in relation to the universe and under the aspect of eternity. In relation to such concerns, at any rate, we could analyze the tragic endeavors of Sophocles, Shakespeare, Strindberg, and O'Neill. Comedy on the other hand has dealt more with the social, the historical, the temporal. Where the tragic writer has sought to portray the individual and to see in him universal Man, the comic writer has tried to portray types, groups, and classes, and therefore to display differences among men.

From such divergencies of preoccupation we might elaborate two opposing schemes of life, the one religious, or quasi-religious, postulating an ultimate meaning in life, the other secular and ethical, postulating an immediate moral meaning in life. Tragedy, we might say, begins with calamity and ends in beauty, reconciliation, and hope; comedy begins with laughter and ends in judgment, reproof, and perhaps bitterness. . . .

Such elaborations could be illustrated from many major plays; they possess the merit of clearing things up for us a little; but I hope we can see also the danger of elaborating them too much. The further we go, the richer and more alluring our rationale of tragedy and comedy becomes. The more, also, we exclude. *Macbeth* has always been reckoned a tragedy. Does it affirm the hero's life? Does it end in reconciliation, beauty, and hope? Obviously not. Tragedy is a topic that lures the critic into talking beautiful nonsense. On this subject even more than on others he tends to generalize from a favorite example or merely to play high-minded cadenzas. The trouble always is that tragedy has been a different thing for every major practitioner. And if anything is more elusive than a correct description of the tragic it is a correct description of the comic.

If we turn to the historical record we find comic elements almost everywhere and high comic achievement almost nowhere. It is even rarer, perhaps, than high tragedy. Nor can one easily discern any such coherence or continuity as we found in the history of tragedy. Our industrial society is not perhaps the most congenial home for the comic muse. Indeed the dominant class of this society, the bourgeoisie, had for centuries been the butt of satire precisely because they themselves seemed unwitty, unhumorous, unclever, and uncultured. Kings had laughed at M. Jourdain's attempts to be aristocratic, but now M. Jourdain was on the throne and aristocratic manners were not needed to keep him there. George Meredith's *Essay on Comedy*, for all its phrase-making and affectation and arbitrariness, first made clear to many of us the social basis of high critical comedy. The comedy of a Molière or a Congreve, we might conclude, presupposes a compact minority of ruling aristocrats who are cultured without being bookish and intelligent without necessarily being speculative. They are a group for whom conversation is the chief means of expression and whose values are therefore what Samuel Butler would have called Laodicean, that is, worldly though not necessarily egoistic, easygoing yet graceful, lax but not unreasonable, satiric but not necessarily sharp. . . .

If this social analysis is even half true, we have not far to look for an explanation of the decline of high comedy. A Sheridan and a Goldoni, in whom the spirit of classical comedy survived into the eighteenth century, are uncharacteristic of their age not only in their genius but in their ·adherence to the earlier formula. And there is Holberg to remind us that the analysis is

not wholly true and that the Molière tradition means not only
Louis XIV and Versailles but also the common touch in high
comedy. Perhaps the most barren period in the history of comedy is the first half of the nineteenth century. We might have
wished that Goethe, so zealous a reader of Molière, had turned
his hand to comedy. We might almost think we have found the
creator of a modern comedy in Alfred de Musset, whose little
plays, at first so inconspicuous beside the "high-brow" monstrosities of Victor Hugo and the "low-brow" monstrosities of
Scribe, later emerged as the most charming French dramatist
between Beaumarchais and Rostand. Or we might rediscover
the genius of Gogol's *Inspector,* in which Molière seems to live
again. But neither Musset nor Gogol is large enough as a playwright to stand in our minds as the maker of a new comedy.
Whatever rebirth we may claim for comedy must be dated—
with the general "rebirth" of drama—toward the close of the
century. The master of a new comedy, if he was to come at all,
would have to be modern as well as classic, must indeed find a
niche for comedy and the comedian in the modern world, must
know from what point of vantage to speak in a bourgeois society, must in fact be a genius who could create a new form and
a new standard to judge it by. One man who did these things is
Bernard Shaw. I have already described his Romantic genius
and his invention of naturalistic comedy. It remains to examine
some of his plays as individual works of art, that is, as satisfying
wholes.

The thesis that Shaw and modern high comedy are one and
the same thing, as Molière and classical high comedy are one
and the same thing, would not be absurd. It would be a more
intelligent thesis than many of those that have found their way
into print. Nonetheless, it would be wrong. Courtly comedy
may, as we are told, belong to a homogeneous group which, perhaps, a single genius can in his life work sum up for us. Modern
comedy—if we are certain of little else we can be certain of this
—belongs to no homogeneous group. The modern satirist rests

on no rock of generally granted assumptions. He clings to whatever life belt comes his way in a tumultuous ocean. Such a time yields no keys of the kingdom (except in best sellers). It offers no *summa* of established truths. If a man claims to have discovered *the* mythos of the twentieth century we know he is a charlatan and we suspect he is well paid for it. Not "the one true religion" but "the varieties of religious experience" is the phrase of the times. For the word *religious* one might make any substitution according to the subject under discussion. And so: the varieties of comic experience.

Others besides Shaw should be discussed in a chapter on modern comedy, and since this book so far has abounded in generalization it will be well to discuss particular works. Two works of Shaw, shall we say, and two other plays. In recent years we have been learning to read lyrics more accurately, more richly, and with more attention to structure. Whether we are actors, directors, theatergoers, or armchair students we need to learn to read plays well too. The possibilities are rich. There are the delightful folk comedies of Garcia Lorca and J. M. Synge. Or one might jump back to the early nineteenth century to the proto-modern German Grabbe, whose untranslated *Scherz Satire Ironie und tiefere Bedeutung*—"Jest, Satire, Irony, and Deeper Significance"—is one of the gems of fantastic comedy, an ancestor of E. E. Cummings' uproarious play *Him.* Ibsen's *Comedy of Love* needs only a good verse translation to reveal it as one of the remarkable comedies of the century. Strindberg's comedies need to be recovered from beneath the blanket of ignorance or solemnity that at present hides their author and his work from view. Akin to Strindberg in their acidity are two of the greatest comic talents of the past hundred years: Carl Sternheim and, before him, Henry Becque. The latter is known, if at all, for his diabolically clever yet forbidding *Les Corbeaux,* a naturalistic slice of life such as the talkers of the movement, like Zola, could never have created. Becque's masterpiece, however, is *La Parisienne,* a great comedy which ought to have given the *coup de*

*grâce* to the French light comedy of adultery and to the class of
people it treats of. Unhappily plays are not so influential. Like
Shaw, Sternheim manfully tried to put the bourgeois back into
his classic place as the butt of high comedy. His cycle entitled
"From the Heroic Life of the Bourgeoisie" is a masterpiece
*manqué*. Unlike Shaw, Sternheim cannot find a vantage point
for his judgments. There is much brilliant satire. But since it is
no longer possible to laugh at the bourgeois from above as our
Restoration playwrights did, he can find only one place to
laugh from—Bohemia, and very likely from its sea coast, that is,
from nowhere at all.

As one thinks of all the comic talent of our modern stage, one
is impressed with the fact that most of it has gone into noncomic plays such as Sean O'Casey's *Juno and the Paycock*. In
this class Chekhov and Schnitzler seem to me pre-eminent.
Chekhov wrote nothing better than *The Cherry Orchard* and
Schnitzler nothing better than *Intermezzo*. Both plays are described by their authors as comedies, but in neither case can one
accept the description as anything but an ironical comment on
the play. To be sure there are comic elements in both plays. To
be sure we can, if we wish, reshape our notions of comedy to fit
them. Short of this, though, we shall have to admit that both
are of a new middle genre, both are highly original *drames*.
How confusing the term comedy has grown may be gauged by
the title of one of Schnitzler's most tragic pieces: *The Comedy
of Seduction*.

If our choice of plays for analysis is to be governed by their
individual significance, their difference from each other, their
difference from Shaw, and the likelihood of their being known
to the reader, a wise choice might be Oscar Wilde and Luigi
Pirandello, two of the best and best-known modern comedians,
one of whom keeps close to the upper boundary of comedy,
which is farce, the other of whom borders the lower boundary,
which is tragedy. Since Bernard Shaw, though he ranges over

the whole comic territory, is customarily in its middle regions, let us begin with him.

## II

Shaw's *Candida* (1895), one of the best liked of his plays, is about a trite situation. A young man enters the home of a married couple and falls in love with the wife. In the commodity drama of Shaw's day—the Parisian drama of Emile Augier, Dumas *fils,* and Victorien Sardou—there are two ways of dealing with such a situation. The young man can be the hero, the husband can be either a tyrant or a bore or both, and the play can be a protest against bourgeois marriage: an idea for Dumas *fils.* Alternatively the husband can be a genuine pillar of society, the lover a fool or a scoundrel, and the play can end with a vindication of hearth and home and with the discomfiture of the intruder: an idea for Augier.

In the opinion of his audiences Shaw wrote the Augier play. That is why it is so popular. On the surface the titillations of modernity, underneath an utter conventionality: that is what the literati have made out Shaw to be; that is what the public accepts him as. And the Augier play is actually contained within Shaw's. Shaw does show an attractive modern couple upholding the dignity of marriage. The husband of the triangle is such a socialist as everyone can imagine hobnobbing with Shaw himself at meetings of the Fabian society. Against the talented and generous character of this man, the effeminacy of the lover is calculated to excite the contemptuous laughter of any audience. *Candida* audiences go home fairly glowing with the feeling that after all Shaw did the decent thing in the end.

But did he? A moment's thought tells us that the Reverend James Mavor Morell is not what we thought he was. He has been the victim of a life-illusion of Ibsenite proportions: he has thoroughly misunderstood the marriage on which all his boasted confidence and happiness were based. The aesthetic lover, however, whom audiences, congratulating each other on their normality, invariably laugh at, turns out to be stronger than the famous strong man Morell. That, as it proves, is not saying much. Eugene Marchbanks is strong by any standard. He is all the time acquiring that last ability of noble mind, the ability to live without illusions, and at the end he has acquired it. A look through the play will convince the skeptic that Shaw invariably puts the truth in Eugene's mouth and seldom in anybody else's. Even the things that arouse most derision are truths which nobody in the play—or perhaps in the playhouse—shares with Eugene. Shaw, then, pretends to weight the scales in favor of the husband, when actually the lover is the bigger man. Do we then have the Dumas play? Is Eugene the hero, Morell a millstone round his wife's neck? Obviously not. Eugene's superiority leads not to adultery but to his voluntary departure. This aspect of the play preaches, with Schiller and Ibsen, that the strongest man is he who can stand alone.

All this is to judge by the relative weight given to the male rivals in the triangle. It is to reckon without the eponymous heroine. And, since she is indeed an expression of the feminine enigma, she is best left to the last. On the surface Candida seems to be everything to this play: title, leading role, master of the situation. Her charm is so great that no audience would wish to look behind it. Her mastery of people seems so sure that we are not inclined to pry into its nature and its motivation. On the stage psychological backgrounds are obscured by the corporeal presence of actresses.

Ponder Candida's words and actions, however, for two minutes, and the drama of sentiment falls down like a pack of cards. She is expert at keeping the women away from her husband, yet, aware as she is of her own charms, she does not hesitate to flaunt them before an obviously susceptible young man. She denies all suspicion that he is in love with her long after the fact has become evident, and even if she is sincere in this, one cannot find her the more admirable for possessing so large a capacity for self-deception. A feline cruelty drives her to taunt her husband by declaring that she would give herself to Eugene if necessary, while taunting Eugene by pointing to him and histrionically demanding: Do you call *that* a man? She caps her cruelty by a fake climax in which she portentously pretends to choose between the two men. Obviously she could not do anything else with Morell but keep him, especially since her own chief pleasure in life is bossing him around; and by this time it is doubtful whether Eugene would take her anyway. He has learned better. Eugene, however, has the good grace to be sad about it all. Candida, by way of a parting thrust, admits she would not fancy being permanently linked to a man fifteen years her junior.

The play is not Augier, for marriage is not vindicated. On the contrary, now that the scales have fallen from Morell's eyes, this marriage can never be the same again. It is not easy to be reillusioned. When the play is seen in this light, Morell is the protagonist, and the climax is a typically Shavian stripping-off of illusion. At last we have a possible theme for a Shavian play: The Reverend James's Unconversion. Yet we have seen that in another aspect Eugene is the protagonist, indeed the hero, and that Shaw might have named after him a play: The She-Devil's Disciple. This title leads us back to Shaw's secret. Candida, who is not the heroine that she seems, whose problems are not the main subject of the play as the title of it might suggest, is indeed master of the situation, not, as she thinks, in controlling and understanding all that goes on, but in unintentionally, perhaps inadvisedly, curing both men of their illusions about her and their relation to her. It is by her means that the popular parson is unconverted. It is by her means that the poet learns to live without happiness—that is, without women. The subject of the play is the destiny of the two men. Candida, who alone is unchanged at the end, is the link between them.

Is she, then, the villain of the play? To push the argument so far, simply to invert the more obvious interpretations of the play is to be no nearer to the truth than they. Although we have always been told that Shaw is so much a propagandist that all his characters are merely trumpets of Shavian good or anti-Shavian evil, in actual fact Shaw attains to an astonishing, many-sided objectivity. As skillfully as any other dramatic dialectician who has ever written, he can do full justice to thesis and antithesis alike. That is why people find him contradictory and seldom look for a Shavian synthesis. In *Candida* Shaw shows all the truth there is in the Augier philosophy and all the truth there is in the Dumas philosophy. He himself surpasses both—but not with a third dogma, nor even with a new formula—The Heroine as Villain. He surpasses both by the all-roundness of his vision. If Shaw has on occasion praised partisanship, he has also said: "My plays have only one subject: life; and only one attitude: interest in life." Certainly *Candida* is evidence for this claim.

Candida is not simply a bad woman. The sweetness which she pours over the whole play is not the suspect and poisonous sweetness of a she-devil. It is genuine. But it is combined with other, less amiable qualities. Indeed if the whole play has a sweetness and charm such as James Barrie courted all his life without ever fully achieving, it is because sweetness can be relished only in conjunction with a contrary tartness. Barrie, being wholly saccharine, is emetic. *Candida* is the sweeter for not being all sugar. The *Candida* atmosphere—bland yet delicate, graceful yet gay, tender yet ironical—is an emanation of the *Candida* dialectic.

### III

*Captain Brassbound's Conversion,* which Shaw (vainly) wrote for Ellen Terry and Henry Irving in the last year or so of the nineteenth century, features a modern version of a pirate king. Brassbound roams the seas plotting vengeance on the wicked uncle who has caused his mother's imprisonment and death. But when he has lured the wicked uncle into the Moroccan mountains and is about to hand him over to the tender mercies of a sheikh, there arrives a superior sheikh whose head will be demanded by the British government if Englishmen are kidnaped in his territories. Brassbound is handed over to the American navy, though he is finally set free through the intercession of the uncle's kindly sister-in-law. Naturally, the pirate king would like to marry the lady after this, and the lady herself is not hostile; but in the end they agree to part.

This is the simple air on which Shaw plays variations. What is his method? A silent moving picture of a performance would record scene after scene of what the Germans call *kitsch* and what Americans call *corn*. In a corny Moroccan setting—all taken, Shaw informs us, from a book by Cunninghame Graham —are enacted corny scenes of pursuit and rescue, spiced with love interest. And there are other conventional ingredients of a graver sort. The plot is unfolded in resolutely Ibsenite fashion, that is by conversation and innuendo referring to buried crime about which we only gradually become clear. The play is subtitled: An Adventure.

Only subtitled. The main title is *Captain Brassbound's Conversion,* and of the conversion which is the subject of the play, a plot summary gives no inkling. At this point we hit upon Shaw's method of inversion, which in such a play as this is not the simple inversion of *Arms and the Man.* According to the pattern, an Englishman and his sister-in-law are rescued by civilization from the clutches of a pirate-villain. According, however, to the interpretation imposed upon the pattern, Brassbound is the hero and protagonist. Yet—and it is such double twists which are the making of Shavian drama—Brassbound is no hero in Douglas Fairbanks style. He is disreputable and down at heel. He is also no villain, since the person he chiefly imposes upon is himself. He has something of the manner of a Byronic sort of hero; but then the Byronic hero is himself an ambivalent figure, compounded equally of strength and weakness. How are we to take Brassbound? In view of the conversion at the end, shall we say that he is a villain converted to virtue as summarily as Edmund in *King Lear?* All possible interpretations are suggested by the play itself, and the method of their suggestion is Shaw's dramatic dialectic. The primary meaning of Brassbound's character appears in the upshot. The real man has been hiding behind the mask of a villain-hero. Degenerating further and further into a shabby tourists' escort, Brassbound, true to his name, shored up the heroic purpose of vengeance against his ruins. He hoarded photographs and newspaper cuttings for purposes of mournful and vengeful contemplation. Then a woman lays bare his soul, and he is converted to realism.

Shaw's technique is not, as has been alleged, to render a serious problem palatable by a silly story. The silly story functions as an integral part of a whole. It is the basis of dozens of ironies, of which the central irony is the contrast between romance and reality, illusion and actuality, silly stories and flinty facts. This irony pervades the whole work. When, for instance, we are told a *kitsch* story of crime in the West Indies, and the question is raised why a solicitor was not sent from England, the prosaic but simple explanation is that the value of the estate was less than it would have cost to make it worth a lawyer's while to leave his practice in London. When we are confronted with fighting sheikhs out of pulp fiction, we find that their actions are determined by the prosaic but significant fact of British imperialism. It may be recalled that Shaw had condemned the staging of fights and crimes as mistakes. This, however, does not mean that he eschews such things. He uses them, but ironically, not naïvely. They are always ridiculous in Shaw, and their ridiculousness always has a point.

Like the plot, the characters are given ironical meaning. Even the American captain, primarily a tool of the plot, is given a touch of significance as "a curious ethnological specimen, with all the nations of the old world at war in his veins." Every minor character enforces an irony. Hallam, the wicked uncle, is a judge and a pillar of society; conservatism shows its other face in Rankin, the defeatist missionary whose only convert in Morocco is a London slum boy named Drinkwater. Drinkwater is Brassbound on a lower level of culture. Like Brassbound he feasts upon romance—in the pages of the pulps. Brassbound's great theme is his innocent mother punished by Hallam; Drinkwater has been acquitted by Hallam when actually guilty. This contrast shows Hallam as at once ruthless and incompetent.

In this framework of fictions, the problem of romance and realism is thrashed out by violent juxtapositions and confrontations. Rudolph Valentino is, as it were, confronted with Henry Ford. There is irony within irony. If Brassbound does not support his role of villain, Hallam does not support his role of hero. The initial irony of his character is one that Ibsen had rendered familiar: the pillar of society is a scoundrel. Hallam has played a tricky game in the West Indies and Brassbound's mother was driven to her death. The law, moreover, which Hallam administers in England is interpreted by Shaw to be crude vengeance wreaked by a class of crooks masquerading as churchgoers. Yet Hallam is not a villain, for he is more a victim than a free agent. He only does what his class does and what he has been brought up to do. He means well and is privately harmless. Far from battening on his ill-gotten gains, he is finding the West Indian estate more a liability than an asset. Brassbound for his part is no avenging angel. His interpretation of the facts is quite as incomplete and primitive as Hallam's. In fact, his standards are the same: like Hallam, he believes above all in revenge. Pillar of society and piratical hero are equally guilty because identically guilty.

The conversion of Brassbound is effected by Lady Cicely Waynefleet. The last page of the play, in which the two agree to part, is one of the best illustrations of the achievement of Shavian comedy. It is neither glib nor ponderous, neither flippant nor sentimental. It is a taut, terse, and true ending in which the dialogue, so far from being an independent stream rippling over the stones of a plot, is fused with theme, story, and characterization. Brassbound presses Lady Cicely to marry him to the point where she is about to consent. At that point he withdraws the offer. We infer that Brassbound has found himself anew in the experience of dominating Lady Cicely. "You can do no more for me now," he says, "I have blundered somehow on the secret of command at last." When Brassbound leaves, Lady Cicely says: "How glorious! How glorious! And what an escape!" It is one of the splendid and expressive endings of comedy. It reveals that Lady Cicely herself found the escape from the real to the romantic entirely glorious. The conversion of Brassbound almost caused the apostasy of his savior. That is the ultimate irony. But since Brassbound *was* converted, he could not allow it. The title of the piece is quite inevitable, and it is the only thing in the whole play that is not ironical.

## IV

Such is Shavianism, the most unmixed triumph of high comedy on the modern stage. To turn back to Shaw's early creations of the nineties is to be reminded of the only other writer, so to speak, in the field: Oscar Wilde.

*The Importance of Being Earnest* (1895) is a variant, not of domestic drama like *Candida* or of melodrama like *Brassbound,* but of farce, a genre which, being the antithesis of serious, is not easily put to serious uses. In fact nothing is easier than to handle this play without noticing what it contains. It is so consistently farcical in tone, characterization, and plot that very few care to root out any more serious content. The general conclusion has been that Wilde merely decorates a silly play with a flippant wit. Like Shaw he is dismissed as "not really a dramatist at all." Unlike Shaw he does not have any such dramatic structure to offer in refutation of his critics as underlies a *Major Barbara* or a *Candida.* We cannot turn to him for the dialectical steel frame of a Molière or a Shaw. Yet we shall only display our own insensitivity if we dismiss him.

Insensitivity to slight and delicate things is insensitivity *tout court.* That is what Wilde meant when he declared that the man who despises superficiality is himself superficial. His best play is connected with this idea. As its title confesses, it is about *earnestness*, that is, Victorian solemnity, that kind of false seriousness which means priggishness, hypocrisy, and lack of irony. Wilde proclaims that earnestness is less praiseworthy than the ironic attitude to life which is regarded as superficial. His own art, and the comic spirit which Congreve embodied and which Meredith had described, were thereby vindicated. Wilde calls *The Importance of Being Earnest* "a trivial comedy for serious people" meaning, in the first place, a comedy which will be thought negligible by the earnest and, in the second, a *comedy of surface* for connoisseurs. The latter will perceive that Wilde is as much of a moralist as Bernard Shaw but that, instead of presenting the problems of modern society directly, he flits around them, teasing them, declining to grapple with them. His wit is no searchlight into the darkness of modern life. It is a flickering, a coruscation, intermittently revealing the upper class of England in a harsh bizarre light. This upper class could feel about Shaw that at least he took them seriously, no one more so. But the outrageous Oscar (whom they took care to get rid of as they had got rid of Byron) refused to see the importance of being earnest.

One does not find Wilde's satire embedded in plot and character as in traditional high comedy. It is a running accompaniment to the play, and this fact, far from indicating immaturity, is the making of a new sort of comedy. The plot is one of those Gilbertian absurdities of lost infants and recovered brothers which can only be thought of to be laughed at. Yet the dialogue which sustains the plot, or is sustained by it, is an unbroken stream of comment on all the themes of life which the plot is so far from broaching. Perhaps *comment* is too flat and downright a conception. Wildean "comment" is a pseudo-irresponsible jabbing at all the great problems, and we would be justified in removing the prefix "pseudo" if the Wildean satire, for all its naughtiness, had not a cumulative effect and a paradoxical one.

Flippancies repeated, developed, and, so to say, elaborated almost into a system amount to something in the end—and thereby cease to be flippant. What begins as a prank ends as a criticism of life. What begins as intellectual high-kicking ends as intellectual sharp-shooting.

The margins of an annotated copy of *The Importance* would show such headings as: death; money and marriage; the nature of style; ideology and economics; beauty and truth; the psychology of philanthropy; the decline of aristocracy; nineteenth-century morals; the class system. The possibility of such notations in itself means little. But if we bear in mind that Wilde is skimming steadily over mere topics all through *The Importance,* we can usefully turn to a particular page to see precisely how this works. To choose the opening page is not to load the dice in a dramatist's favor, since that page is usually either heavy-going exposition or mere patter which allows the audience to get seated. Here is Wilde's first page:

ALGERNON. Did you hear what I was playing, Lane?

LANE. I didn't think it polite to listen, sir.

ALGERNON. I'm sorry for that, for your sake. I don't play accurately—anyone can play accurately—but I play with wonderful expression. As far as the piano is concerned sentiment is my forte. I keep science for life.

LANE. Yes, sir.

ALGERNON. And, speaking of the science of Life, have you got the cucumber sandwiches cut for Lady Bracknell?

LANE. Yes, sir.

ALGERNON. Oh! . . . by the way, Lane, I see from your book that on Thursday night, when Lord Sherman and Mr. Worthing were dining with me, eight bottles of champagne are entered as having been consumed.

LANE. Yes, sir; eight bottles and a pint.

ALGERNON. Why is it that at a bachelor's establishment
the servants invariably drink the champagne? I
ask merely for information.

LANE. I attribute it to the superior quality of the wine,
sir. I have often observed that in married house-
holds the champagne is rarely of a first-rate brand.

ALGERNON. Good heavens! Is marriage so demoralizing as that?

LANE. I believe it *is* a very pleasant state, sir. I have
had very little experience of it myself up to the
present. I have only been married once. That was
in consequence of a misunderstanding between
myself and a young person.

ALGERNON. I don't know that I am much interested.
in your family life, Lane.

LANE. No, sir. It is not a very interesting subject. I
never think of it myself.

ALGERNON. Very natural, I am sure. That will do,
Lane, thank you.

LANE. Thank you, sir. *(He goes out)*

ALGERNON. Lane's views on marriage seem somewhat
lax. Really, if the lower orders don't set us a good
example, what on earth is the use of them? They
seem, as a class, to have absolutely no sense of
moral responsibility.

This passage is enough to show the way in which Wilde at-
taches a serious and satirical allusion to every remark. The
butler's "I didn't think it polite to listen, sir" is a prelude to
the jokes against class society which run through the play.
Algernon's first little speech touches on the foolish opposition
of life and sentiment, science and art. Talk of science and life
leads by Wildean transition back to the action and the cucumber sandwiches. Champagne takes the action to speculation on
servants and masters, and thence to marriage and morals. A
little dialectical climax is reached with the answer to the ques-

tion: "Is marriage so demoralizing as that?" when Lane coolly replies: "I believe it *is* a very pleasant state, sir," and adds, by way of an explanation no less disconcerting by Victorian standards, "I have had very little experience of it myself up to the present. I have only been married once." Which is followed by the explanation of the explanation: "That was in consequence of a misunderstanding. . . ." It cannot be said that marriage in this passage receives the "staggering blows" which the ardent reformer is wont to administer. But does it not receive poisoned pin pricks that are just as effective? Are not the inversions and double inversions of standards managed with dexterous delicacy? "No, sir. It is not a very interesting subject." A delicious turn in the argument! And then the little moralistic summing-up of Algernon's: "Lane's views on marriage seem somewhat lax. Really, if the lower orders don't set us a good example . . ." And so it ripples on.

We are accustomed to plays in which a serious plot and theme are enlivened—"dramatized," as we say—by comic incident and witticism. Such plays are at best sweetened pills. "Entertainment value" is added as an afterthought, reminding one of the man who, having watched for weeks the construction of a modern Gothic building, cried one day: "Oh, look, they're putting the architecture on now!" Oscar Wilde's procedure is the opposite of all this. He has no serious plot, no credible characters. His witticisms are, not comic, but serious relief. They are in ironic counterpoint with the absurdities of the action. This counterpoint is Wilde's method. It is what gives him his peculiar voice and his peculiar triumph. It is what makes him hard to catch: the fish's tail flicks, flashes, and disappears. Perhaps *The Importance* should be defined as "almost a satire." As the conversations in *Alice in Wonderland* hover on the frontier of sense without ever quite crossing it, so the dialogue in *The Importance* is forever on the frontier of satire, forever on the point of breaking into bitter criticism. It never breaks. The ridiculous action constantly steps in to prevent the break. That is its function. Before the enemy can denounce Wilde the agile outburst is over and we are back among the cucumber sandwiches.

The counterpoint or irony of Wilde's play expresses itself theatrically in the contrast between the elegance and *savoir-faire* of the actors and the absurdity of what they actually do. This contrast too can be dismissed as mere Oscarism and frivolity. Actually it is integral to an uncommonly rich play. The contrast between smooth, assured appearances and inner emptiness is, moreover, nothing more nor less than a fact of sociology and history. Wilde knew his England. He knew her so well that he could scarcely be surprised when she laughed off his truisms as paradoxes and fastened a humorless and baleful eye on all his flights of fancy. Wilde had his own solution to the problem stated by Meredith, the problem of finding a vantage point for satire in an unaristocratic age. It was the solution of Bohemianism. For Wilde the Bohemian attitude was far from being a philosophy in itself—a point which most of his friends and enemies, beginning at the Wilde trial, seem to have missed. Bohemianism was for Wilde a mask. To wear masks was Wilde's personal adjustment to modern life, as it was Nietzsche's. Hence we are right in talking of his pose as we are right in talking of Nietzsche's vanity. The mistake is in believing that these men deceived themselves. If we patronize them the joke is on us. If Wilde seems shallow when we want depth, if he seems a liar when we want truth, we should recall his words: "A Truth in Art is that whose contradictory is also true. The Truths of metaphysics are the Truths of masks." These words lead us to Pirandello.

## V

Since Shaw and Wilde no dramatist has written first-rate drawing-room comedies. The best have been by our Maughams and Behrmans and Bernsteins. Writers have been turning from the formality of the drawing room toward a grotesqueness which, in its nearness to *commedia dell' arte* or to Aristophanes, may seem more primitive, yet which, in its psychological depth and intricacy, may well be more sophisticated. Strindberg himself, as we have seen, sometimes achieved comedy by giving a quick twist to one of his own tragic themes. Wedekind aimed at tragedy, but by the novel method of using almost exclusively comic materials, thus reversing the technique of Strindberg's comedies. In Italy a whole school of dramaturgy, *"teatro del grottesco,"* arose under the leadership of Luigi Chiarelli, who said: "It was impossible [in the years immediately preceding 1914] to go to the theater without meeting languid, loquacious granddaughters of Marguerite Gautier or Rosa Bernd, or some tardy follower of Oswald or Cyrano. The public dropped sentimental tears and left the playhouse weighed down in spirit. The next evening, however, it rushed in numbers to acclaim a naughty skit like *The Pills of Hercules,* in order to re-establish its moral and social equilibrium." From Chiarelli's scorn for the New Drama, already old, of Dumas and Hauptmann, Ibsen and Rostand, came his own play, *The Mask and the Face,* which was the starting point of a petty literary movement and of a great dramatist, Luigi Pirandello.

*Right You Are (if you care to think so!)* (1916) has often been regarded as the quintessential Pirandello. Let us look into it. The basis of the play is some sort of "bourgeois tragedy," something that would have stirred the audiences of the old-new drama which Chiarelli had laughed at. The domestic unhappiness of a husband, a wife, and a mother makes up the tragic triangle. A commentator named Laudisi is the *raisonneur* à la Dumas.

The peculiar thing about the tragic situation in this domestic tragedy is that we do not know what it is: a fact that is as much second nature to Pirandellians as it is disconcerting to others. The peculiar thing about the *raisonneur* is that instead of giving us the correct view of the tragedy he tells us that all views are equally correct. But then, according to Pirandello, this is the correct view.

A man lives with his wife on the top floor of a tenement while the mother lives at his expense in a lavish apartment. The wife never leaves the tenement, and her mother never goes nearer the daughter than the street below from which she shouts up to the daughter. This state of affairs not unnaturally sets tongues wagging. Asked for an explanation, the husband says the mother is deluded. She thinks the wife is her daughter, though actually she is the husband's second wife. Her daughter, his first wife, died, though the mother dare not believe it. . . . We are settling down to believe this version of the story when we hear from the mother an equally convincing version. The son is deluded. He never recovered from the delusion that his wife died, and they had to let him marry her again under the impression that she was another person.

Neither mother nor husband seems to have an axe to grind. Each is solicitous for the other's good. Each has a good reason for strange conduct. The mother needs to see her daughter often and must pay her visits. The husband must keep her in the street so that she shall not discover her error. Pirandello is at great pains to balance the two interpretations exactly, to tug our feelings now this way, now that, now up, now down, on the alarming switchback of his thinking. We may think ourselves on the right track, for example, when the husband, untrue to his story, is furiously angry with the old lady and tries to convince her that his wife is not her daughter. But, as soon as she leaves, his rage subsides. He was just play-acting, he tells us, to confirm her impression—so necessary to her peace of mind— that he is mad.

In the end the wife herself is summoned to unravel the mystery. She says: "I am the daughter of Signora Frola [the mother], and I am the second wife of Signor Ponza [the husband]." The *raisonneur*, who already has told us that there is no one true version of the story but that all versions are equally true, steps forward, and his peals of laughter end the play. Whereupon one school of critics praises Pirandello for his profound "phi-

losophy of relativity," and another condemns him as "too cerebral"—only "mentally dramatic," as George Jean Nathan has
it, *Right You Are* being "written for intelligent blind men."
The critical boxing ring would seem to be set for a bout concerning the drama of ideas.

Like Shaw, Pirandello has not been averse to the report that
his drama is all intellect—no man minds being thought a mighty
brain—and here are some of his words: "People say that my
drama is obscure and they call it cerebral drama. The new
drama possesses a distinct character from the old: whereas the
latter had as its basis passion, the former is the expression of
the intellect. . . . The public formerly were carried away only
by plays of passion, whereas now they rush to see intellectual
works."

Such is the Pirandello legend. Around every great man there
grows a legend which, whether fostered by himself or not, is
always a distortion, sometimes a gross distortion of his real
nature—if we may assume the existence of so un-Pirandellian
an entity. The omission which I disingenuously made in the
above quotation from Pirandello is a casual remark that happens to be more revealing than the pontificality of the rest. It
is this sentence: "One of the novelties that I have given to the
modern drama consists in converting the intellect into passion." Let us discount here the claim to originality. Strindberg
had already perfected the art referred to. A succession of dramatists from Vigny on had announced a new drama of thought
and intellect. The essence of Pirandello is not his intellectual-
ity. It is his conversion of the intellect into passion. Perhaps
Strindberg had done that too; it is the theory behind his naturalistic tragedies; yet in Strindberg passion summons intellect
to work its will, while in Pirandello passion and intellect tor-
ture each other and join in a mutual failure. The quintessence
of Pirandellism is this peculiar relation of intellect to feeling.

Ostensibly Pirandello's plays and novels are about the relativity of truth, multiple personality, and the different levels

of reality. But it is neither these subjects nor—precisely—his treatment of them that constitutes Pirandello's individuality. The themes grow tiresome after a time, and those who find nothing else in Pirandello give him up as a bad job. The novelist Franz Kafka was long neglected because his work also gave the impression of philosophic obsession and willful eccentricity. Then another and deeper Kafka was discovered. Another and deeper Pirandello awaits discovery.

Before he can be discovered the perpetual "cerebration" concerning truth, reality, and relativity will have to be dismissed as the hocus-pocus that it is. At face value the argument of *Right You Are* is that, since both the mother and husband give a contradictory but equally plausible account of the same events, and since the daughter jumbles the two incomprehensibly, therefore there is no objectively true version of the story. This is a complete *non sequitur*. All events can be reported in different ways. This might only mean that some reports must be wrong, not that there is no right view. There is actually nothing in the plot of *Right You Are* to indicate that there can be no correct version of the story. The unusual thing is that we do not know what it is. This is very Pirandellian—not only, however, in that it is used to bolster a rather confusing, if not confused, discussion of truth, but also because it leads us to what we might venture to think is the real Pirandello.

The wife's longest speech—of three sentences—is as follows: "And what can you want of me now, after all this, ladies and gentlemen? In our lives as you see there is something which must remain concealed. Otherwise the remedy which our love for each other has found cannot avail." The concealment which leads on the superficial, pseudo-metaphysical level to a discussion of truth is here very differently associated. There *is* a true version of the story but it must not be known lest the lives of three people concerned be shattered. But, someone will protest, could not Pirandello use the prerogative of the omniscient author and tell *us* without telling the characters what the remedy

is which their love has found? He could. But his refusal to do
so is more to his purpose. The truth, Pirandello wants to tell
us again and again, is concealed, *concealed,* CONCEALED! It
is not his business to uncover the problem and solve it for us
as in a French *pièce à thèse.* The solution of the problem, the
cure for these sick human beings, is to leave their problem
unsolved and unrevealed. The unmasker of illusions is at best
a Gregers Werle, at worst one of the gossips of *Right You Are.*
On the superficial level Pirandello is protesting against the
spurious helpfulness of the scandalmonger, the prying reporter,
and the amateur psychoanalyst; at a deeper level he is asking
that the human soul be left a little territory of its own—which
also, perhaps, was one of the themes of Kafka.

As for dramaturgy, if the "remedy" were explained, the play
would inevitably be built around this key to the whole problem. Pirandello could not afford—whatever the inducements—
to have the emphasis so distributed. He wants to accent the
refusal to search for a key. So he has his *raisonneur* argue that
there is no key—an argument which sticks in people's minds
as if it were the substance of the play. Actually the play is not
about thinking but about suffering, a suffering that is only
increased by those who give understanding and enquiry prece-
dence over sympathy and help. Pirandello took from the *teatro del grottesco* the antithesis of mask and face, the mask
being the outward form, the face being the suffering creature.
At its crudest this is the theme of the clown with a tender heart.
Already in Chiarelli the mask and the face had, however, the
broader meaning of the social form, identified with tyranny,
and the individual soul which it sought to crush. In his best-
known plays Pirandello elaborates on this antithesis. We see a
central group of people who are "real." They suffer, and need
help, not analysis. Around these are grouped unreal busybodies
who can only look on, criticize, and hinder. In *Naked,* which
is the first Pirandello play to read since it does not lead one off
on the false trail of relativity and truth, the mystery *is* dissolved,

as in *Right You Are* it is not, and the result is the destruction of the protagonist. Note that this mystery, constituted by the illusions without which the heroine could not live, is not the Mask. The Mask is the social and antihuman tyranny of, for example, a novelist for whom the heroine's unhappy lot is grist to the mill. The Mask is the interference of the mechanical, the external, the static, the philosophical, with our lives. Thus not only the smug novelist of *Naked* and not only the disingenuous truth seekers of *Right You Are* are the Mask. Pirandello himself—and every novelist and playwright—is the Mask. His material is the flux of suffering; his art stops the flow; its stasis is at once its glory—in immortalizing the moment—and its limitation, since life, being essentially fluid, is inevitably misrepresented by art. In drama, life wears a double mask: the mask imposed by the dramatist and that imposed by stage production. Three plays are devoted to this fact. In the best of them —*Six Characters in Search of an Author*—the three levels of reality are played off against one another throughout, and a fourth level is implied when we find one character judging another by what he happened to be doing on one shameful occasion, in other words by one isolated fact, which, wrongly taken as typical, becomes a Mask on the face of the real man. What if all our characterizations are like this? Just as we found, Pirandello argues, that there is no objective truth, so we find also that there are no individuals. In the one case we have only a number of versions or opinions. In the other we have only a succession of states.

Exactly as in the matter of truth, so in the analysis of character the extreme conclusion is a *reductio ad absurdum* too barren to be the real motive force of such powerful works as Pirandello's. His characters in fact are effective not in direct relation to these conceptions, but because these conceptions enable him to suggest beneath the Mask of the physical presence the steady ache of suffering humanity. What a pessimist Pirandello is! says someone. Certainly. But again the point of

Pirandello is not his philosophy—of relativity, personality, or pessimism—it is his power to conceal behind the intellectual artillery barrage the great armies of fighters and the yet greater armies of noncombatants and refugees. Pirandello is a pessimist. So also must many of the people of Europe be, people who have lived through the extraordinary vicissitudes of the twentieth century, uncomprehending, passively suffering. Modern people are of course no more passive and uncomprehending than their ancestors. It is simply that they are more aware of their helplessness. Even as Proust speaks for the passive semiaristocrats whom our new order has swept out of existence, so Pirandello, like Kafka, like Chaplin, speaks not for the aware and class-conscious proletarian but for the unaware, in-between, black-coated scapegoat.

All this is in *Right You Are*. In a note to the director of the play one might write as follows:

"Make a marked distinction between the enquirers into the story, who are a sort of chorus representing what Pirandello regards as the Mask and the three 'real people' involved in the domestic tragedy. The Three are typical people of a middle-class tragedy in that they express grief and arouse pity without terror. Note how Pirandello's initial descriptions of the characters and his subsequent stage directions stress alike the genuineness and acuteness of their sufferings.

"Now the odd thing is that the wholly sad theme is placed in a satiric frame. Since this contrast, already familiar to you in the *teatro del grottesco, is* the play, you had best be careful to secure the exact balance that is needed. The Three must act with unmitigated and uninterrupted pathetic force. But the Chorus—as we may call the other characters—must never enter into their sufferings. They must be as detached as a callous doctor at a deathbed. They must not, out of consideration of their Three colleagues, play down their own frivolity any more than the Three must soften their agony in order to come closer —as there is a natural tendency to do—to the mood of the

Chorus. Only if the contrast between the two groups is kept sharp will you find that the effect of the grotesque is attained. Otherwise the effect will be of blurred incongruity.

"You already understand how and why this bourgeois tragedy differs from tradition in not revealing its true nature. That is a primary irony which your production can point up by making the alternation of explanations go snip-snap so that the brilliance is its own justification. Otherwise your audience will regard all this as the lumbering preparation for a denouement which, after all, never takes place. An almost equally important irony is that between the celebrated 'cerebral' dialogue of Pirandello and the deep agony which—as your Three must make clear —is the core of the action. This irony is more than the contrast between the Three and the others. The Three actually join in the intricate analysis of cause and effect, motive and act, which is the constant subject of discussion. The point is that these analyses are not 'coldly intellectual.' They are positively maniacal. (You might look up Pirandello's essay on humor where he maintains that the humorist takes a wild pleasure in tearing things to pieces by analysis.) By its maniacal quality the 'cerebration' enters into relationship with the agony, a relationship at once logical and psychological.

"You recall how in *Cyrano de Bergerac* Rostand rendered Hugoesque tragedy palatable by making it over into a tough-jointed tragi-comedy. The grotesque contrasts of *Right You Are* might be regarded as Pirandello's way of making 'bourgeois tragedy' work—by making it over into a tough-textured comedy. Perhaps comedy is not the best word for such a play, but then you as a practical man are less interested in that question than in the correct interpretation of the play whatever its generic name. For you the significance of Pirandello's version of bourgeois tragedy is that it sets the audience at a distance, preserving them both from tears and from boredom. Do not be shocked when they laugh *with* your Chorus *against* the Three or when they are amused with Laudisi when perhaps weeping would seem more in order. Their laughter is significant. For one thing it is what enables them to stomach the unmixed horror of Pirandellian diet. It is not stupid laughter exactly. Pirandello has 'comedified' his tale. If the laughter he arouses prompts an unflattering interpretation of human nature, that is intended. The old theatrical business, at which you are adept, of mingling laughter and tears was never more calculated, more intricate, more meaningful, or more depressing than here.

"Accentuate then—do not soften—the clashes of sound and color of which the play is composed. If you let it work, you will find the whole thing ultra-theatrical. I should say: if you let *them* work, for a Pirandello play is made up of actors, not of scenery. That must be why our friend Mr. Nathan thought it was written for blind men. But remember that actors—especially the actors of the *commedia dell' arte* whose skill Pirandello wished to revive—once were, and can be again, the main part of the show. Let them throw their arms and legs about, let them swagger—in a word, let them act and talk instead of strolling and muttering like mannequins with a pin loose. If they perform their roles from outside instead of pretending to *be* the people who are not people, Pirandello would be better pleased. As you know he called all his plays Naked Masks—not naked faces. Let your actors remember that. Naked Masks—a violent oxymoron indeed! Is not such a figure of speech a pointer, for you and the rest of us, to the strange genius of its author?"

## VI

Shaw—Wilde—Pirandello: they are the three great wits of the modern stage. All three in their different ways have achieved great comedy by playing an ironic counterpoint against one of the stock tunes of commodity theater or commodity literature. In their hands domestic tragedy, domestic comedy, adventure story, and farce are transmuted into an uncompromising critique of modern civilization. The old comic (and realistic) contrast between appearance and reality, between pretensions and actions, ideals and facts, finds—in different ways—a restatement and thereby a new form and a new meaning. If the splendid, forthright dialectic of Shaw, the witty arabesque of Wilde, and the tortured, syncopated rhythms of Pirandello are, in a sense, new molds for old themes, the themes cannot themselves remain unaffected. Form and meaning are not independent. New form implies new meaning too.

What is new, what is modern, about modern comedy? Writers on earlier schools, in their *obiter dicta,* let us know that the early form that they are discussing no longer exists. All they have to tell us about such comedy as does exist is that it can't hold a candle to the old stuff. Just as writers on Shakespeare seek to add to his glory by comparing him with Ibsen, whom they believe to be a sociologist, so writers on Restoration Comedy try to flatter their subject with a disparagement of Wilde or Shaw, whom they believe to be mere phrasemakers. Edmund Wilson was making a much more serious attempt to state a difference between Restoration Comedy and Shaw when he suggested that, where Restoration Comedy depended for its effect on the contrast between elaborate etiquette of expression and naked sensuality of motive, Shavian comedy depends on the contrast between expressed ideals and economic motives. Though Mr. Wilson's antithesis is too neat—the supposedly Shavian contrast existed, for instance, in Farquhar around 1700 —it springs from a correct awareness that modern comedy reflects not only the surface but the structure of modern society. The Marxist analysis and the Shavian analysis of this society are identical not because Shaw is a follower of Marx but because both seek and find the dramatic contradictions of this revolutionary period. Our clever craftsmen of today, journalists or playwrights, perform an operation known as "dramatizing" their material, which is evidently regarded as *per se* undramatic. The real dramatist, as Hebbel knew, as our Shakespeare scholars are beginning to teach, finds in the society around him the dramatic elements. In *Major Barbara* Marxian and Shavian dialectic are one because the contradiction in Shaw's fable is the contradiction in capitalist society. Wilde and Pirandello, who make fewer pretensions to sociology, are not less socio-analytic. To re-read Wilde's collected works is to realize that Wilde was as angry and righteous as Carlyle, only that he chose the mask of a Bohemian rather than that of a curmudgeon. As much as Schnitzler or Chekhov he is the agonized witness of aristocratic decay. Pirandello's comedy is also distinctively modern. His subject is what might be called Twentieth-Century Blues, by which I mean not any particular, localized disillusionment such as that of the lost generation of the twenties or that of ex-communists today. I mean the disillusionment that is common to all these: disillusionment over the failure, not so much of socialism or liberalism, as of humanness itself in our time. In Pirandello's world there is only littleness and suffering. Perhaps it was the realization that littleness and passive suffering are untragic that impelled Pirandello to make comedies out of them. As comedies they are more moving!

The material in this chapter—or in this book—is certainly insufficient to enable us to say: Modern comedy is thus and thus. One aspect of it that has already been touched upon, however, will be enough to clinch the point that modern comedy is modern. The master of a new comedy, I said, must know from what point of vantage to speak in our very unclassical society. I instanced Sternheim as one who did not know, and Shaw as one who did know. Shaw speaks not, as Meredith thought the comedian should, on behalf of society as it is but on behalf of society as it should and perhaps could be. He speaks as a rebel, as a Voltairean or Nietzschean "free spirit," and, as we have noted, sets up between himself and his audience the relation of antagonism. Shaw's audiences simply *have* to laugh him off as a joker; their only alternative would be to shoot themselves. All this—and all important modern comedy— is contrary to comedy according to Meredith, which is unzealous, unsatiric, and very amenable. Of Byron, Meredith wrote: "He had no strong comic sense, or he would not have taken an antisocial position, which is directly opposed to the Comic. . . . Comedy, on the other hand, is an interpretation of the general mind, and is for that reason of necessity kept in restraint." If what Meredith says is true, comedy would be impossible except when there is a coherent "general mind" and when therefore society seems wiser than the individual. He cannot see that comedy might also be the individual's protest against the general mind. We should not be surprised that he cannot see it. If what Meredith could not see is manifest to our eyes we owe that chiefly to the life work of Shaw.

Byron's stand, though it offended Meredith, lays down a precedent for the position which a writer of comedy must take up when he feels that society is rotten and the general mind corrupt. If Shaw is most evidently the comedian of a revolutionary period, Wilde, the Bohemian, is but a different sort of rebel, a rebel in a mask, a rebel dressed up for a fancy dress ball. And Pirandello? Neither rebel nor Bohemian, he declared that his home was a hotel room with a typewriter in it in any metropolis in the world. Something of a fascist in the head, Pirandello was at heart—a refugee. His point of vantage—it is a Pirandellian paradox—was that of an outcast. Even as he wrote his comedies his mad wife was beating on the door. Anything further from the elegant socialite of Meredith's image would be hard to imagine. As modern tragedy reached a kind of terminus in Wedekind, modern comedy seems to reach a kind of terminus in Pirandello.

Discussion of Shaw, Wilde, and Pirandello can go on indefinitely. Would it help us nearer to a definition of comedy than we were at the beginning of the chapter? If one cannot say *a priori* what comedy is, if it is hard to reach more than platitudinous definitions by generalizing about all known schools of comedy, we might doubt whether the exact study of particular comedies is of much assistance either. Obviously such a study cannot enable one to characterize *other* works. The question is rather what it reveals in particular comedies that superficial acquaintance would not reveal. In the present instance our four analyses—correlated with other knowledge— have suggested some notions about modern comedy, notions which might plausibly be considered either too tentative or too general to be of any use. Detailed study of particular works naturally calls attention from generic to individual qualities, which is pleasant since the good things in art are essentially individual. Very well then. In the teeth of logicians and lexicographers one is content to read comedies without knowing exactly what comedy is.

Ich bin der reiche bin der bare
Ich bin das zeichen bin der sinn
Ich bin der schatten bin der wahre
Ich bin ein end und ein beginn.

STEFAN GEORGE

# 7. AUGUST

# STRINDBERG

## I

EVEN IF WE ARE NOT ABSOLUTELY SURE WHAT COMEDY IS, OR tragedy either, we have nevertheless been able to discuss modern drama chiefly in terms of tragedy and comedy. Admitting that tragedy and comedy *might* be so defined as to exclude all drama since 1800, I yet preferred to name the traditions in which Ibsen and Shaw wrote Tragic and Comic respectively. On this interpretation the creation of a middle genre in the eighteenth century did not mean the end of tragedy and comedy but a change in the nature of tragedy and comedy.

What happened after the rise and fall of "bourgeois tragedy"? We have seen how the nineteenth-century forms of tragedy in their turn split and sundered, how another period of dissolution set in. We have seen that Pirandello wrote a kind of comedy which might almost as easily be called tragedy and how Wedekind wrote a kind of tragedy that might almost as easily be called comedy. In other words: As Lillo and Lessing had abandoned the firm norms of Racine and Molière for their "middle genre," so Wedekind and Pirandello abandoned the norms of Ibsen and Shaw for *their* middle genre. The French experimentalist Guillaume Apollinaire wrote: "According to the particular case the tragic will outweigh the comic or vice versa. But I do not think that henceforward one can endure without impatience a theatrical work in which these elements do not confront each other. . . ." The German experimentalist Bertolt Brecht wrote in approval of the painter Breughel: "Neither is there in him a separation of tragic from comic; his tragic contains his comic and his comic his tragic."

Now there is one playwright whose life work seems to embody the transition in drama from the nineteenth to the twentieth century. So far I have chiefly mentioned him as one who came *after* Ibsen, as the representative of the close of an era. But the close of one era is the opening of another. August Strindberg looks both ways. And it is now high time to examine more closely this pivotal and still largely unknown figure.

If it be asked how a major modern writer can be so little known, I can only reply that I do not know, but that it certainly is the case. The distribution of fame is capricious, not only among the masses and in an author's lifetime but also among the intellectuals and after the author's death. It is true that in recent years a number of writers who have the disadvantage of being dead, foreign, or esoteric have been sold to a large minority public in America. Among them are E. M. Forster, Franz Kafka, Baudelaire, and Kierkegaard. Among those who have been tried with rather less success are Rimbaud, Lautréamont, Stefan George, and Charles Péguy. That all these writers have been promoted partly by appeals to snobbery is, however, not their fault. All of them are important, and in their rediscovery there is more than modishness. They all stand in near relation to our deeper as well as to our tea-party interests. What is regrettable is only that so many others, equally deserving, are overlooked, that the choice of proto-moderns is left to the accident of commercial enterprise, so that, as Mr. Philip Rahv once put it, we bury as many classics as we exhume. No such burial would be more surprising, were we not aware of the ways of the world, than that of August Strindberg.

That Strindberg is well known to readers of Swedish literature is of course of little import: each Scandinavian country cherishes a hundred authors whom we need not be overanxious to read. But Strindberg is more than an outstanding Swede. He is *the* outstanding Swede. He is the one Swede who rightly belongs in the main European tradition, as those great cultural internationalists, the Germans, have from the first acknowledged. There have been two other such Scandinavians in modern times: Ibsen and Kierkegaard. The one, as we have seen, received the kind of fame which ruins a man's serious reputation. The other has had a serious reputation only in Scandinavia and, inevitably, Germany. The American discovery of Kierkegaard is certainly welcome. But why was there not a rediscovery of Ibsen and a discovery of the playwright whose portrait hung on Ibsen's wall—August Strindberg, of whom Ibsen said: "I am an enemy of his—but I cannot write a line except when this bold man with his mad eyes looks down on me"?

A generation ago it looked as though the same people who championed Ibsen in America—such as James Huneker, Archibald Henderson, and a little later H. L. Mencken—might do the same for Strindberg. Two series of plays, seven volumes in all, were issued; also most of the autobiographies and single volumes of plays and stories. In 1924 Eugene O'Neill wrote: "Strindberg was the precursor of all modernity in our present theater. . . . Strindberg still remains among the most modern of moderns, the greatest interpreter in the theater of the characteristic spiritual conflicts which constitute the drama—the blood—of our lives today." But Strindberg did not make his mark in America. He lay in the cold storage of college Scandinavian departments or tucked away in the littlest of little theaters. *Miss Julia* or *The Father* turns up here and there in an anthology and the name of Strindberg has perhaps no associations in the public mind, unless it be the dim recollection of another lunatic genius who perhaps never left off beating his wife.

The intelligentsia in England and America are always predominantly radical and advanced, and Strindberg could not easily be take under the wing of any advanced fowl. He was "morbid," antifeminist, reactionary, religious. He was too pious for the radicals and too unruly for the respectable. Except in Germany, where a large section of the intelligentsia is always fascinated by the daemonic, Strindberg was an unwelcome guest. Ousting Wagner, the favorite of his youth, an older Bernard Shaw spoke of "the giants of the theater of our time, Ibsen and Strindberg" and gave his Nobel prize money for better translations of the Swedish genius whom he had long considered "the only genuinely Shakespearean modern dramatist"; but the number of people interested in artistic merit for its own sake is almost negligibly small. The "outer" public is interested in entertainment and reads what the outer critics tell it to read; the "inner" public is interested in being in the swim and reads what the more high-flying critics have just discovered to be the solution for the world's ills. Strindberg was not one of the discoveries. The Modern Library dropped him. Soon not one of his fifty-five Swedish volumes was available in English. He might have come in with the revulsion against Marxism of the late thirties and early forties, had someone left one of his books on the desk of an Arthur Koestler or a W. H. Auden. Nobody did, and now he will have to wait till another generation is disillusioned, which may not be long.

Meanwhile let historians and our Negligible Few note the existence of this clever, contradictory, perplexing, exasperating,

almost contemptible yet wholly astonishing genius. We are here
interested in him as dramatist, but Strindbergian drama has to
be approached indirectly and with circumspection, for what do
they know of drama who only drama know?

## II

August Strindberg (1849-1912) is a remarkable and representative man. He represents "the plight of modern man"—by
which I suppose we mean the plight of some modern men or
part of the plight of all modern men—as richly as Stendhal,
Kierkegaard, Dostoevski, Nietzsche, or Tolstoy. He is by no
means the greatest of these men, but his is a peculiar contribution: he is, for example, more explicit about themes which some
or all of them raise. That may of course be one reason why he
is not as great, say as Kierkegaard or Nietzsche. Explicitness may
be the manifestation of a less finely ironic mind. Yet Strindberg's is not the flat explicitness of the extrovert. The completeness with which he reveals himself implies not only love of
confession and mastery of naturalistic technique but ruthless
introspection and psychological genius. Nietzsche and Freud, if
no one else, should have convinced us that psychological genius
*means* ruthless introspection and is more an heroic daring than
a preternatural gift of knowing. This genius Strindberg has.
That is one reason why his autobiographies are great documents, great as confessions, great as the record of a major mind.
Here, if anywhere, our understanding of Strindberg must begin.

Influenced by Kierkegaard's vogue, some have been talking
of "existential" and "nonexistential" writers. Nonexistential
writers, we gather, are those who are but names attached to self-
explanatory masterpieces. Existential writers are those whose
significance is disclosed in their life and work and in the inter-
dependent development of both. Life and work with them are
one. They write themselves through life in one long autobiography. Kierkegaard, Nietzsche, and Strindberg are existential.

Alone among them, however, Strindberg wrote overt autobiography in a completely frank way and at length. The nineteenth century produced several Dionysian geniuses, several
great men who sought to live out in their own lives the tragedy
they saw about them, but none charted the process so exactly
nor so passionately as Strindberg. His autobiography is perhaps
the greatest direct expression of the subjectivism which has
been one of the leading tendencies of European literature since
the Romantic Movement.

Strindberg looks back to the Romanticists. When he was not
a conscious disciple of Rousseau, he was an unconscious disciple.
He is Romantic in the vulgar sense of expressing passion quite
openly, quite toweringly, and of pushing it to an extreme or to
an eccentricity. He is Romantic also in the deeper sense of trying not only to recognize the magnitude of the passions but also
to discover their proper status. He is both an intense lover and
a precise analyst of his love. In himself he recognizes two kinds
of love, the two kinds which Western tradition has called *eros*
and *agape,* human and divine, sexual and sacred. Contrary to
current assumption, the Romantic idea has not been an unam-
biguous endorsement of either. The Romanticists rediscovered
*eros* and *agape* precisely by rediscovering their ambivalence. It
is the ambivalence of *eros* in Goethe's *Werther* that made the
book a scandal and a great event. Any eighteenth-century hack
might have rhapsodized about passion; it was the closeness of
passion and death, of creative love and its contrary, that Goethe
put his finger on. What we call the Freudian approach, the
stress on ambivalence, the sense of the subterranean, and the
intellectual analysis of these, is pure Romanticism, and if Freud
has given us the most systematic documentation of this approach, Strindberg has given us not only the most circumstantial case history but the ultimate Romantic self-analysis along
Freudian lines. "Daring frankness" is something that publishers
attribute to every gossip and every pornographer. Strindberg's
frankness is unique. The frankness of others is modified by a

modesty which stops short or by an immodesty which goes too far, by inhibition or by exhibition. Freud's is a modest autobiography; Rousseau's and Frank Harris' are exhibitionist. Almost alone among autobiographers Strindberg told everything without telling more than everything. He was a great descriptive artist, and if he alternately loved himself to the point of narcissism and despised himself to the point of indignity, he somehow contrived to make these tendencies his servants. Though in the plays and novels self-dramatization plays an inordinate role, the autobiography is surprisingly literal. It should be taken as, among other things, the historical foundation upon which the fiction and the drama are an imaginative superstructure. Art was a sort of sublime self-indulgence for Strindberg, autobiography and history a self-discipline. The discipline consisted in a compulsion to get rid of his past by exactly recording it. He was not loath to publish confessions which incriminated half a dozen identifiable people. . . .

If the autobiography establishes Strindberg's Romanticist affiliation it also proves him one of the founders of Modernism. This is no paradox. In the perspective of today Romantic and Modern do not indeed seem antithetical. Modernism is a development from Romanticism, a development partly by revulsion but just as much by continuation. Freud is a Romanticist; he is also correctly regarded as a Modernist. He gave a new concrete embodiment to Romantic principles, thus fulfilling one of the deepest urges of Modernism. This is the sense in which Ibsen and Shaw are Modernists. This is the sense in which Strindberg is a Modernist.

"Modern" is the word which would occur to any reader of those parts of Strindberg's autobiography which, before Freud, though after Stendhal, describe very fully the author's mother fixation. Strindberg's account of his childhood is already so analytic that the work of the psychoanalyst is supererogatory. Though, after a long "illicit" union, his father married his mother, Strindberg was conceived outside wedlock, and the sense of stigma, coupled with a sense of his mother's lowly origin, followed him through life. He rebelled against his mother. On the other hand, with true Freudian ambivalence, he was violently attached to her. "Her image," says the auto-biography, written in the third person, "seems glorified, and draws him with unbreakable cords of longing. This feeling of loneliness and longing after his mother followed him all through his life . . . he never became himself, never a complete individuality." When the mother died, Strindberg "was not to be comforted. He shrieked like one drowning." Then arose a variant of the Hamlet situation. Strindberg "criticized his father for becoming engaged before the expiration of the year of mourning. He conjured up his mother's shade, prophesied misery and ruin, and let himself go to unreasonable lengths." He proved unable to kiss the stepmother at the wedding, and later when the father beat his brother, he cried: "If Mother had lived . . ." He sees a performance of *Hamlet* and applies it to himself: ". . . it is fine to lament one's destiny and to see it lamented. At first Hamlet was only the stepson; later on he becomes the introspective brooder, and lastly the son, the sacrifice to family tyranny." In the child Strindberg we see all the attitudes of the adult: the alternation of madonna worship and misogyny, the deep and incessant spiritual unrest—connected in the first volumes of the autobiography with masturbation anxiety—and, on top of all, masochistic enjoyment of pain. Fine indeed to lament one's destiny and to see it lamented! Strindberg did both to the extent of over fifty volumes. And not in volumes only. Strindberg's love of theater is his narcissism. He insisted on *seeing* his destiny lamented. Is not this very Romantic? Is it not also very Modern?

One need not follow Strindberg through his marriage with Siri von Essen and his less sensational though no less symptomatic later marriages, in order to have some impression of his personality. Strindberg's intellectual development is just as important as that sexual history which has been the basis of his

limited notoriety. Strindberg's home was pietist. Like many
another he rebelled against domestic piety under the influence
of David Strauss and Ernest Renan and joined the ranks of the
cockahoop midcentury positivism which was the *avant-garde* of
contemporary Europe. Subsequently he went through a number of phases embracing nearly all attitudes which modern
intellectuals have taken up: juvenile radicalism; political disen-
chantment; hero worship and a fascistic contempt for the herd;
preoccupation with science; insanity (if that is an attitude); a
literary Catholicism à la Huysmans; and finally one of those
Higher Syntheses uniting science and occultism under the ban-
ner of Swedenborg. Strindberg lived out all the phases of modern militancy and modern defeatism, political and antipolitical,
religious and antireligious. His discovery of the English mate-
rialist Buckle was like a later generation's discovery of Marx;
his discovery of Swedenborg was like a later generation's discovery of Kierkegaard.

## III

The life work of Strindberg may be arranged in three concentric circles. Tangential to the outermost circle are his occasional
works, translations, essays, and treatises; within it are the autobiographies which are the raw material for Strindberg's art
works; within the second circle are the novels, a rough attempt
to impose form upon the chaos of his experience; within the
inmost circle as Strindberg's central achievement are his plays.
The latter may be variously grouped. Some of them have been
discussed in Chapters II and III as attempts to recreate high
tragedy. Taking the whole body of plays together we find two
extreme types, both Swedish in inspiration: at one end the
chronicle history play, at the other the fairy play. Strindberg
modified both these forms. After Büchner, and at the same time
as Shaw, he helped to shape an informal and intimate type of
chronicle play. After the German Romanticists, and at the same
time as Maeterlinck and W. B. Yeats, he made out of fairy tales

a delicate and sophisticated theater. More important than these extreme forms are Strindberg's deviations from the rival simplicities, namely his own quasi-tragic naturalism and his own kind of fantasy, deviations which were both intensely personal and intensely European.

Although Strindberg never succeeded, either posthumously or in his lifetime, in making contact with British or American culture, he was from the first more successful in France and Germany. And his best plays fall into two groups: the "naturalistic" plays which we can associate with the French director André Antoine; the "late" plays which we can associate with the German director Max Reinhardt. Let us look at the first group.

In the Paris of the eighties and nineties Strindberg was very much in the swim. He read Desprez' important treatise on Naturalism and learned from it that drama should abandon Scribean intrigue in favor of a forceful simplicity of form and the psychological analysis of a *"sentiment aigu."* He praised Zola. He visited Antoine's Théâtre Libre and was much impressed by the *quarts d'heures* or brief one-act plays of the French dramatists. The French had long advocated the concise and concentrated type of play. Strindberg was to go even further. The popular, pompous French critic Brunetière was soon to argue that drama consists of a conflict of wills. Strindberg resolved to reduce the conflict to its directest manifestation: one person mentally struggling with another. He liked to think that such a play as *Othello* provided a precedent. It does not. Iago's assault upon the nervous system of Othello is neither resisted nor suspected. The conflict of which Brunetière spoke had almost always been veiled. The Strindbergian idea is to bring it quite openly upon the stage. His naturalistic tragedies are nervous and intellectual duels to the death. Of the first of them he wrote:

> *The Father* is the realization of modern drama and as such is something very curious. Very curious because

the struggle takes place between souls. It is a battle of brains, not a dagger fight or poisoning with raspberry juice as in *Die Räuber*. The French of today are still seeking the formula, but I have found it.

In structure *The Father* (1887) was not revolutionary; Strindberg's next plays—*Miss Julia* and *Creditors*—were. Francisque Sarcey, perhaps the most influential theater critic of nineteenth-century Paris, and therefore of nineteenth-century Europe, had talked of the *scene à faire,* the climactic scene of a plot which it was the dramatist's duty not to narrate but to present on the stage. Strindberg went further than Sarcey and asked: Why present anything else? Four acts of a five-act play, he reasoned, are but scaffolding. Remove them and the essential drama will be all the more striking. If Ibsen's four- or five-act pieces could be described as "one long catastrophe" would it not be out-Ibsening Ibsen to accomplish the same thing in one act, in one *short* catastrophe? French concentration could never be carried further than this. Strindberg himself did not approach it often. In *The Father* the division into acts is retained, and there are several characters in addition to the dueling couple. *Miss Julia* is more compact, but there·remain decorative elements such as the ballet. The shorter one-act plays are built pretty much to the formula but their scope is hardly tragic. Perhaps only one play fully represents the theory in practice: *Creditors*. Strindberg writes: *"Miss Julia* still made concessions to romanticism and *décor* but *Creditors* is a really modern piece, human, amiable, with three sympathetic characters, interesting from one end to the other." Though our ideas of amiability may differ from his we are bound to accept Strindberg's verdict that *Creditors* is the ultimate reach of his naturalism. And it is a superb play.

We often find that the inventors of "new" forms in modern literature carry a formula as far as it can go. Having reached the North Pole they can go north no longer. That is true of Strind-

berg. Having invented his new naturalistic form Strindberg did
not proceed to use it. He abandoned it, and in his next great
period of dramatic productivity—the last dozen years or so of his
life—he writes on another pattern. If the earlier formula had
been the duet in a naturalistic setting, the later formula was the
solo in an Expressionistic setting. If the earlier pattern had been
Strindberg's conflict with Siri von Essen, the later was that of a
solitary old man looking back over his buried hopes and past
opportunities. If the form of the earlier plays was Antoine's
Naturalism, the form of the later plays is a new sort of intimate
theater which Strindberg himself requires us to associate with
Max Reinhardt, who opened his Chamber Playhouse in Berlin
in 1906. In a memoir written for the actors in his little Stockholm theater, Strindberg wrote: "Reinhardt brings the idea of
chamber music into drama: intimate nature of spectacle, em-
phatic statement of the theme, care given to the execution."
The theory of Chamber Drama, as further expounded in the
memoir, is not of course a retraction of the theory of theater
expounded in Strindberg's naturalistic days (in the preface of
*Miss Julia* for instance). At both times Strindberg stresses the
prime need of a single powerful motif, at both times he outlines
a scheme for an intimate theater with a small auditorium and
its attendant effects upon dramatic style. The Memoir goes on
to deplore calculated effects, passages written for applause, brilliant acting roles, tirades and display: in fact the whole bag of
professional tricks, most of which the earlier Strindberg had
resorted to and some of which the most austere later Strindberg
did not actually eliminate.

Perhaps the most challenging thing in the Memoir is what
Strindberg says about dramatic form. Dramatic criticism had
been a battle of centuries as to the correct or the best form of
drama—whether Greek, Shakespearean, neo-classic, or "well-
made." Strindberg's declaration that form must be left fluid so
that a theme may be allowed to find whatever form suits it best
is perhaps the obvious retort to all this sort of squabbling. But

it is the kind of obviousness which apparently only a genius is equipped to discover at the right moment. Fluid form! Certainly Strindberg lived up to his own injunction—always feeling his way, always trying to discover organic and expressive shapes for chaotic experience. Nowhere is this clearer than in the plays of the last period. Let us look at a couple of them: *The Ghost Sonata* (1907) and *There Are Crimes and Crimes* (1899).

## IV

*The Ghost Sonata* is perhaps the most interesting of the dream plays since it combines the out-and-out fantasy of *The Dream Play* with the eery realism of the nonfantastic Chamber Plays such as *After the Storm*. Nor is it unintelligible except to those who think it more polite not to enquire into poetic mysteries in general. For all the heterodoxy of style and the fantasy of the action, the play is simple in structure and straightforward in its symbolism.

The three compact scenes constitute a statement, a counterstatement, and a conclusion. In Scene I an Old Man, Strindberg *alias* Hummel, tells a youthful Student about the long series of events which has brought him at last to a wheelchair, a spectator on the scene of life. We are prepared to view Hummel sympathetically throughout Scene I and part way through Scene II, for he is an effective advocate of his own cause, but when, after he strips another character, the Colonel, morally naked, he is himself arraigned on the same charges, we are not surprised or disappointed that he hangs himself. Scene III is a dialogue between the Student and a beautiful Young Lady. Will youth succeed where age failed? At first it seems as if this might be Strindberg's meaning. But the young couple soon realize that evil is much the same today as it was yesterday. Indeed the Young Lady dies as a tribute to this fact. The Student recommends religious resignation, and the play ends.

Such is the outline. It is filled in by Strindberg with enough matter for several plays. There are two "eternal triangles," and an illegitimate daughter from each is among the characters. Strindberg links his personages by these—and several other— amorous episodes of a past which is dead but not at rest. As a character in another Strindberg play has it, "Everything is dug up! Everything comes back!" Ghosts appear on the stage, and more formidable than the ghosts are the still living old people who are but ghosts of their former selves. The lover of Hummel is now a crazed old mummy who lives in a closet and thinks she is a parrot except when, with the lucid license of nightmare, she becomes sane in order to denounce her man. She is mocked by the presence of a statue of herself as she was in the days of her youth. Hummel's former fiancée is a white-haired old lady but, lest we form too ideal a conception of her, we learn that she was seduced by the Colonel whom Hummel had cuckolded. The knots of legitimate and illegitimate relationship are tied and retied until we have a group of persons resembling a European royal family. The mummy comments: "Crime and guilt bind us together."

The themes and situations are old Strindbergian *idées fixes*. People have gone off on various journeys through life, yet they are tied to their past, to their actions, to the house where they were born. "We have broken our bonds," the mummy continues, "and gone apart innumerable times but we are always drawn together again." Guilt hangs in the air, and the crimes that lie behind it are—as ever—crimes of tyrannous possession, which Strindberg always represented in two metaphors: the vampire sucking the blood of his victim or the creditor using his power over the debtor. This sounds like a leftist critique of capitalism, but for Strindberg capitalism is the symbol of human possessiveness in general. "You killed the Consul," says the mummy to Hummel, "strangling him with debts. You have now stolen the Student, binding him with an imaginary claim against his father, who never owed you a halfpenny. . . ." Or, as another character describes Hummel: ". . . he also drank the soup stock and we had to fill it up with water—he sat out there like a vampire and sucked the juice out of the house. . . . Later I met this man in Hamburg under another name, he was a money lender then, a bloodsucker." The metaphor shifts and shifts back again.

Scene III might have been an idyll had it not been interrupted by a Cook, no less alarming than the Cook in *Alice in Wonderland,* who shrieks: "You take the sap out of us and we out of you." The Young Lady explains: "We get the grounds when she has had the coffee. . . . She belongs to the Hummel family of vampires. She is eating us." An editor-translator protests at Strindberg's unfair attitude to servants in this passage (!) but the point is that servant and master are linked in one universal guilt. The symbol of the Cook is an instance of the way in which Strindberg can convert one of his neurotic obsessions—the suspicion that servants take the best of the food for themselves—into a potent and objective symbol. He who knows something of madness is well equipped to portray society as a madhouse.

The dubious part of Scene III and of *The Ghost Sonata* as a whole is the ending. In order not to end on the negative note sounded by the spontaneous death of the Young Lady, Strindber appeals in rapid succession to Buddha, some Christian verses from the Poetic Edda, soft music, and a picture by Arnold Boecklin: "The whole room disappears, and in its place appears 'The Island of the Dead' as background. Soft music, very quiet and pleasantly sad, is heard from the distant island." Such is the final curtain. It is not surprising that at least one critic—Bernhard Diebold—accuses Strindberg of fumbling—of appealing to color and sound when he cannot find the right conclusion for his play. At this point one must admit that there is an element of Wagnerian hocus-pocus in Strindberg. I have said that his autobiography is scrupulously genuine. And that is true, for Strindberg is honest even to the point of revealing his own dishonesty; there is a lack of pose in the writing of the auto-

biography precisely because pose is one of the qualities it em-
phasizes in its subject. "It is fine to lament one's destiny. . . ."
Strindberg had his photograph taken in tragic postures. He
posed as the Sufferer, and has been rewarded by books on
Strindberg, "the bedeviled viking," "the battling and suffering
soul," and so forth, all couched in terms of elephantine earnestness. It is the pose in Strindberg, the pretentious, arty, and spectacular in him, that explains the way he fascinates some and dis-
gusts others. We need not be either fascinated or disgusted.
Strindberg's self-dramatization, like Rousseau's, like Nietzsche's,
is a fact but not in itself a refutation of all his views or a condemnation of all his achievements. Strindberg, moreover, differs
from these men not, it is true, in being a neurotic or in being a
genius, but in being a man whose genius itself is neurotic. In
most neurotic geniuses the genius, I should think, is the healthy
part of them. In Strindberg this is probably not always so. His
visions are themselves mad. If they are of value—and I think
they are—it is because morbid symptoms are but exaggerations
of "normal" symptoms. The gigantic pictures of insanity and
nightmare are but enlargements of the images and dreams of
the sane. They too are human and universal.

Strindberg, says Diebold, resorts to stage tricks when he cannot work out his artistic problem. That is how he comes to be
linked with Reinhardt and later with Expressionism. His fantasies, says the critic, lack all inner dialectic once the sex duel
of the naturalistic tragedies is dropped. Drama should be dialogue, but they are monologue. They are amorphous, rambling,
and meaningless. Since they can proceed to no conclusion
Strindberg abruptly ends them with the Gothic window of a
church, the transformation—using the latest stage machinery—
of a castle into a chrysanthemum, or a picture by Boecklin accompanied by "pleasantly sad" music. Being a theatrical genius,
Strindberg evolves a technique of evasion of which the formula
is to use visual and musical elements to conceal weak spots in
the drama. Such is the argument of Bernhard Diebold.

It is an intelligent and a necessary argument, necessary because there are always those who will defend the use of music and spectacle as the real arts of the theater as opposed to the mere words of the "literary" dramatist. Strindberg, with his carefully chosen sonatas by Beethoven and pictures by Boecklin, seems to give "high-brow" sanction to this "low-brow" prejudice. He consequently has a powerful appeal to the more highbrow type of low-brow, to lovers of the arty and the extraordinary, to cultural charlatans. Diebold's argument was certainly a wholesome antidote to the cult of Strindberg prevalent in the Germany of his day. In America it is gratuitous. Moreover in his legitimate dislike of current Expressionism, Diebold read back into Strindberg the shortcomings of his callowest followers. As Ibsen unjustly got the blame for Ibsenism, as every original genius gets the blame for the doctrines of his inferior admirers, so Strindberg is blamed for Expressionism.

No more than many other plays which appear under such rubrics is *The Ghost Sonata* one of the "world's greatest plays." But it is a brilliant and complex piece such as none but Strindberg would have dreamed of attempting. Perhaps its best qualities are its superficial qualities: color, rhythm, shifting tempi, *élan*, cleverness, atmosphere, and theatricality. Nevertheless it has a core. The ending does indeed indicate Strindberg's failure to find a meaning in life which he could confirm from inner experience. His religion is always pasted on. But this very fact is what makes the religious plays—except for their forced conclusions—much richer than the religious drama of most other moderns. The latter tend to write self-conscious religious propaganda. Strindberg represents the modern would-be religionist much more explicitly when he so patently fails in simple, positive faith. And it is his undignified maneuvering, his vacillation, his passionate insincerity, his wriggling to and fro, that make his spiritual escapades interesting and almost amusing. Most of our more recent neo-religious poets are solemn and sour, and exact from us an almost funereal deference. They are consequently tiresome and unconvincing. Strindberg we begin by taking with a pinch of salt. But the salt does not lose its savor, and we end by taking him seriously if not *au pied de la lettre*.

## V

Perhaps the Strindberg we come to respect is neither the dazzling lunatic of the naturalistic "tragedies" nor the melo-dramatic mystic of the dream plays. It is the less unequivocal, more ironic Strindberg of what he calls his "comedies." *Comrades* contains the essential teaching of Strindberg on women. It is also sane—which means that in it Strindberg evinces some appreciation of the thick, ambiguous texture of life itself, and of the consequent need for some sort of moral as well as dramatic irony, of the need for not taking tragedy too tragically. The point is perhaps more deliberately advanced in another "comedy"—*There Are Crimes and Crimes*—as the title best implies.

The play is about a Parisian playwright who deserts his child and her mother for another woman. The child dies. The father feels guilty and at the end of the next to the last act prepares to die with his new lover:

> HENRIETTE. But we'll go into the river now, won't we?
> MAURICE. (*Takes Henriette by the hand as they walk out together*) Into the river—yes!
>
> CURTAIN

Strindberg has, however, prepared the way for a different ending by the early introduction of an Abbé who says: "*O crux! Ave spes unica!*" which means: "Salvation is the alternative to suicide." Since the playwright Maurice himself remarks that "it is quite simple to figure out a fourth act when you have three known ones to start from," we expect to find Strindberg again proposing a religious solution, this time a solution that is painstakingly prepared. The interesting thing is that he does not do so. Maurice has rejected the world and given himself up to prayer and asceticism; but the curtain does not go down on this touching scene. On the contrary, a friend arrives (*"enter a messenger"*) and announces that Maurice is not such a failure in worldly respects as he has been supposing. His reputation has been cleared. His play is on again at the theater. He is popular and will soon be rich. If Strindberg intends a religious play, this clearly is the moment for the rich young ruler to give up all and follow Swedenborg. Maurice, however, immediately starts rearranging things with the Abbé. He is of course too clever to throw him over completely. "Tonight," he tells the Abbé, "I will meet you at the church to have a reckoning with myself; tomorrow evening I go to the theater." Everyone, including the Abbé, is pleased by the compromise, and the protagonist accepts both God and Mammon, like the religionists of Butler's *Erewhon*.

Modifying Pascal's advice, Strindberg resolves to bet on the next world—and on this world too. It is not an uncommon resolve. The unusual thing is to find anyone openly subscribing to it and—still more unusual—using it as the denouement of a quasi-religious work. Two perfectly good endings lay to hand: suicide or retirement to a cloister. Strindberg prefers to bring in a messenger announcing a change of outward fortunes that releases the protagonist from both obligations. This kind of trick we associate with melodrama; yet in this instance it is less sensational than would be either of the other alternatives.

Strindberg calls the play a comedy. Yet, like other comedies of his, such as *First Warning* and *Comrades,* it reads like a tragedy till you reach the final nontragic solution. I say *reads* because in production it would be the director's task to enforce a comic interpretation upon the play from the opening curtain on. Nor would this be directorial distortion. Correctly staged, or reread, *There Are Crimes and Crimes* is a sort of comedy, an encounter with life in a quizzical and unheroic yet undefeatist and unabashed spirit. The irony of the ending is precisely that

such "fake melodrama" is truer to human nature than the "logical" suicide or the "logical" monasticism. This is not necessarily
cynicism. The proposal to combine a little religion with a little
fun is appalling alike to the apostles of consistent devotion and
to the apostles of consistent hedonism. Nevertheless it is what
many have wanted without knowing it and what even more
have taken without admitting it. It is, that is to say, profoundly
human, and therefore acceptable to the comic spirit. *There Are
Crimes and Crimes* shows us how close the comic spirit may lie
to the tragic spirit. Whole scenes of the play could be included
in either a comic or a tragic version. Does everything depend
on the ending after all? In this case, yes. Not, however, upon
the question of the happiness or unhappiness of the ending.
The comic ending will not be particularly happy. There is no
reason to suppose that Maurice will be happier in future than
he has been in the past. It is a *true* ending, comic in its acceptance of ordinary human nature, in its refusal to look to an
heroic solution. Apart from Strindberg perhaps only Samuel
Butler could have devised such a tragi-comedy of compromise.
Ibsen, for all his self-questionings, would never have permitted
himself so "unserious" a solution.

While Ibsen is known as a negative skeptic but was really a
positive believer, Strindberg, known as a dogmatist, was above
all a skeptic. That is clear from *There Are Crimes and Crimes*.
Perhaps all the Chamber Plays, intentionally or not, bear witness to it. In them we see his inability to believe not only the
materialism of his youth, which he now openly abhorred, but
also the religion which he pretended to have discovered later
and which he was to go on parading till the day when he asked
that the bible should solemnly be laid upon his corpse. Lytton
Strachey said of an English poet that he lost his faith as a young
man and spent the rest of his life looking for it. This loss and
this search constitute one of the major themes of our era, a
theme on which there are many variations. I recently read, for
instance, of an artist who "goes precisely to religion to find a

pretext and justification for venting his abhorrence, not only of the epoch, but of humanity and himself. Perhaps," the writer added, "this hatred and this desire to suffer lie profoundly at the heart of our epoch." In the end Strindberg did not hate mankind, but his religiousness is related to the psychology here described. He certainly desired to suffer. He certainly vented much abhorrence. He certainly brandished the Absolute like a club.

If Strindberg's mental development differs from that of other modern seekers after the Absolute, it is because of its inconclusiveness. Kierkegaard also sought, and his search is one of the most far-reaching. But surely his findings were too much of a foregone conclusion. Tolstoy's search also offends by its shocking conclusiveness and the absurdity of the conclusions. Nietzsche's search was probably the most rigorous of all. He searched heaven and hell, which is more than a mortal can stand; he emerged from his campaigns neither a Dionysus nor a Christ but an imbecile and a paralytic. Strindberg alone fought unremittingly. He championed first this absolute, then that, then the other. His frequent changes, his perpetual misgivings, kept him in a state of tension—and high vitality—to the end. His failure to be saved was his salvation. And the final irony was that in some strange fashion he seemed to know it. The Absolute was for him a flag to wave and a goal that must never be reached. The Absolute for him was relative.


# VI

What is Strindberg's place in the history of drama?

This question has already been answered in part by my remarks on his Romanticism and his Modernism, and by the discussion in earlier chapters of his place in the tradition of tragedy. We have seen that Strindberg was a man of the nineteenth century—indeed almost a synopsis of the century's beliefs, illusions, and attitudes. His dramaturgy is of the epoch in that he remains in the peep-show theater of illusion, suspense, individual psychology, and domestic tragedy. What he tried to do was to intensify, not destroy, all these. The intimate theater is a device to that end. And too many imitators of Strindberg have drawn upon this "bourgeois" Strindberg—upon the wild sexual emotion of the naturalistic "tragedies," upon the unconvincing religiosity of the dream plays, upon the shrill egoism, the false horticultural denouements, and the like. I am thinking again of the Expressionists. In Strindberg and in all these there is a great deal of the world weariness of "decadence" and much less, perhaps, of the promise of a future.

Yet we have seen that there are other Strindbergs besides the misogynist daemon and the Swedenborgian sage. His readers have noticed this, I believe, and have expressed it in various ways. The historian Erich Kahler, for instance, having written of Ibsen that he wove the nineteenth century's "struggles of conscience into a ghostly cloud that continually broods over the scene," added: "In the plays of the other great Scandinavian, Strindberg, especially in the Chamber Plays, ethical problems have been dissolved in the stagnant mire of a forced life together. Guilt can no longer be fixed. . . . Individual relations and characters have lost their individual values and flow apart in a general mist of psychic decay. Even the spook of the abysses is no longer embodied—it is omnipresent." In other words Strindberg's dramas reflect a later phase in cultural history than Ibsen's. He is of the twentieth century as well as the nineteenth. A living seismograph, Strindberg can feel the twentieth century coming, can feel a gathering in the air of all the hate and ferocity of renewed barbarism.

Is he the starting point of twentieth-century drama? Postponing that question to the next chapter, we should remind ourselves that, since Strindberg was a great artist, many of his great qualities belong, not to the nineteenth nor to the twentieth century, but to himself alone. Since he was an artist he was not wholly an imitator. Since he was an artist he cannot wholly be imitated.

Another caution: the question whether Strindberg helped twentieth-century drama into the world is not yet completely answerable because the twentieth century still has plenty of time to discredit any attempted answer. If the twentieth century ever possesses a large body of great drama, playwrights may look back with gratitude to the man who both fulfilled and destroyed, in Christlike ambiguity, the laws of the nineteenth-century prophets of the drama. If on the other hand the twentieth century proves to be deficient in great drama, Strindberg will seem more of an undertaker than a midwife, a very unusual undertaker of course, a moody, philosophical, exhibitionistic undertaker, and what is still more disconcerting, an undertaker with a twinkle—is it sympathy or derision?—in his eye.

The higher fantasy has a greater reality than this actuality. These banal accidents of existence are not essential life. My whole life is a dream.

AUGUST STRINDBERG

# 8. FROM STRINDBERG

# TO JEAN-PAUL SARTRE

## I

IN THIS BOOK THE PERIOD OF "MODERN" DRAMA HAS BEEN TAKEN
several different ways. It has been taken to mean "postclassi-
cal," that is, beginning in the eighteenth century with the
decay of the aristocratic *ancien régime* and the decline of the
older tragedy and comedy. This is the sense in which the "bourgeois tragedy" of Lillo and Lessing is modern. In the second
place it has meant "postindustrial," that is, beginning in the
nineteenth century after the effects of the industrial revolution
and the democratic movement had made themselves felt. This
is the sense in which the music drama of Wagner is modern.
Finally it has referred to the New Theater movement, beginning in the eighteen-eighties, which includes Ibsen, Shaw,

Wilde, Hauptmann, Becque, Chekhov, Schnitzler, Synge, and Gorky.

The period of "modern" drama, then, may be said to begin around 1730, or around 1830, or around 1880. Up to now it has been chiefly with these three fresh starts that I have been concerned. But already a fourth has intruded. Although August Strindberg emerged with the New Theater movement, his work looks forward to much later developments, to the time, in fact, when Chiarelli and Pirandello would find the New Theater old-fashioned, to the time of the Expressionists and O'Neill— and, perhaps, beyond that time. Somewhere between 1900 and 1925 arose a "fourth modernism," whose roots one must dig a little to discover.

In earlier chapters we have seen how the "bourgeois tragedy" gradually took shape like clay under the hands of a sculptor, grew firm and beautiful in the modern drama of Ibsen, and subsequently fell apart again. The falling-apart is evident in the last play of Ibsen himself—*When We Dead Awaken*—where there are odd contradictions in the plot and where, therefore, the taut, logical consistency which had been, as it were, the ground floor of Ibsen's edifices is lost. That was in 1899. Much earlier than this had occurred a large-scale attack on the forms of nineteenth-century drama—and apparently on all form—in the extreme Naturalism of Zola and Jean Jullien, with their doctrine of the "slice of life." This attack and this doctrine were not, however, as subversive as they sounded. The Naturalistic masterpieces of the New Theater movement—Tolstoy's *Power of Darkness,* Becque's *Les Corbeaux,* Gorky's *Lower Depths*— had form enough in their own way. For the better playwrights, an apparent inconsequentiality of incident soon became a mere mask concealing their real face.

Chekhov is one of the clearest examples of this. A play of his may seem to be a "slice of life" to the casual first-nighter who misses the usual unilinear development of a plot, for Chekhov does *pretend* to be an extreme Naturalist. And, since a new form always seems formless to the conservative mind, his actual method can pass unnoticed. If the usual progression of a story is termed "linear," the Chekhov pattern might be termed spatial. Chekhov's method is to arrange a natural sequence of social gatherings around his key subject and situation. The progression of a Chekhov play is therefore the gradual uncovering of the subject and the situation—by accidents, if you will, but by accidents which have to be carefully planned by the playwright on dramatic and rhythmical—one could almost say musical—principles. The purpose of Chekhov's pretense to Naturalism resembles the purpose of Ibsen's pretenses: Chekhov wishes to establish an ironic relation, a tension, between the surface and the substratum of his art.

In theory ruling out all form—unless the pure chronicle and document are forms—the formula of the "slice of life" did not give the *coup de grâce* to nineteenth-century drama. Unable to contribute a form of its own, it operated as a partial dissolvent of other forms—but only a *partial* dissolvent. Thus the more gifted artists benefited from Naturalism in that they found to hand a more malleable medium than their fathers had found. Without needing to begin all over again, they could achieve a certain originality of form, they could bring back to the theater rich and raw hunks of life that had been excluded from it. But the men of the New Theater movement did not go much further than this. They did not—with solitary exceptions—become founders of the fourth modernism although, wise after the event, we may now read into their plays intimations of changes to follow.

The great exception was Strindberg. Already in 1888 his *Miss Julia* had provided—in preface and play alike—a theory of character that anticipates Pirandello (and Proust) and that was the death of "bourgeois tragedy." "Bourgeois tragedy" implied a moral standard, a high bourgeois sense of right, comparable to the high aristocratic sense of right in the older aristocratic tragedies. In *Miss Julia* character has fallen to bits. The broken

pieces are in our hands. Instead of a kind of middle-class tragedy we have a bitter jest against all tragedy. Instead of adopting
the Ibsenite architectonic Strindberg prides himself on the re-
introduction of the monologue, the pantomime, and the dance.
It is true that in the preface he insists that these items must be
strictly subordinate to the drama; they were nevertheless a
Trojan horse within the gates of the nineteenth-century citadel.
With the insurgence of the Dream and Chamber Plays the citadel fell. Such, as we have seen, is the story of Strindberg's in-
vasion of the drama.

What influence did Strindberg have on the future of the
drama? Admitting that cultural influence is never exactly
measurable, one can say at least that more than any other single
man he destroyed nineteenth-century drama. He enabled his
successors to begin with an almost clean slate. So much for his
negative influence. On the positive side, his influence has been
openly acknowledged by a number of genuine talents such as
his Swedish disciple Pär Lagerkvist and more widely-known
playwrights as O'Neill, O'Casey, and Denis Johnston. Along
with the great director himself, Strindberg inaugurated the era
of Reinhardt in European theater. In central Europe he was
*the* dramatist of the new staging with its electric lights, its artistic settings, and its mechanical miracles.

This is not all. It seems to me that Strindberg is a turning-
point in a more important way. If it is true that after Ibsen the
"bourgeois tragedy" disintegrates, if it is true that Strindberg's
"tragedies" are grim jests and that his "comedies" overlap tragedy, are we not reminded of the "first modernism" in the eighteenth century, when an older tragedy and comedy gave place to
an intermediate genre? With Strindberg tragedy and comedy
are in the melting pot once more. The tragic and comic elements come together again in different combinations. In some
measure, of course, *every* good playwright brings together these
elements in different combinations. Yet from time to time—not
often—there is a major regrouping that implies deep cultural

changes and the galvanic energy of a revolutionary genius. Admittedly it is too early to say with finality what twentieth-century drama is; but, judging by the generation that has passed since his death, we may at least wonder if Strindberg is not such a revolutionary genius.

The role of such a genius is not only to break with the past, but also to salvage those traditions that are still living and hand them on filled with new life. Strindberg broke with many traditions, but two—the two we have already found most important in the nineteenth century—he handed on, renewed,, to the twentieth. These are the traditions of naturalism and non-naturalism, the theaters of the outer and of the inner eye, of objectivity and subjectivity, realism and fantasy. Strindberg excelled in both directions. His "tragedies," his "comedies," and his chronicle histories were a new naturalism. His fairy and dream plays were something new in fantasy and subjectivity. On the boulevards, which live on a dilution of yesterday's culture, the drama after Strindberg might continue to be precisely what it was before. The artistic theater could never be the same again.

"The drama after Strindberg" is a serviceable phrase. Strindberg stands at the threshold of our century. What new paths has dramatic art traveled since? That is the question I now turn to. Naturalism has moved far. Its furthest reach, probably, is the Epic Drama of Bertolt Brecht, which will be described in the next chapter. Nor has the antinaturalistic animus subsided. It too has an interesting record—into which we can proceed to look without delay.

## II

If I have made the fourth modernism seem more heavily indebted to Strindberg than it really is, if I have used his name as a *symbol* of changes which were not actually effected by him alone, it may be well to cite a very different account of the subject, or rather of its non-naturalistic side which is now our topic. Strindberg was a mighty force. But doubtless it is only convenience that entices one to speak as if he had changed history unaided. Mr. Francis Fergusson, a teacher, director, and critic of rare taste and knowledge in these matters, accounts for the fourth modernism without reference to Strindberg at all:

> The most interesting writers for the stage between 1918 and 1939—among whom I should include Yeats, Eliot, Cocteau, Obey, Lorca—start completely afresh. The influences of the Moscow Art Theater, the Ballet, and the Music Hall, combine to produce a new conception of the theatrical medium. Not only nineteenth-century naturalism, but most European drama back through the seventeenth century, is explicitly rejected in favor of medieval farce, Greek tragedy, peasant rituals and entertainments.
>
> —From *The Kenyon Review* (Autumn 1943).

The important thing is that Mr. Fergusson's diagnosis of the change corroborates mine: around the time of the First World War begins a new modernism in which the antinaturalistic impulse is strong. For what is it that medieval farce, Greek tragedy, peasant rituals and entertainments have in common? Perhaps only one thing: remoteness from the nineteenth-century naturalistic play. What is it that Yeats, Eliot, Cocteau, Obey, and Lorca have in common? Perhaps only one thing: hostility to the nineteenth-century naturalistic play.

In reaction from naturalism the poets of modernism have renewed the now old and familiar campaign to bring verse back in the theater. Generally the crusade for verse drama gets little further than high-minded sentiment in talks to earnest, low-heeled ladies. Three of the names mentioned by Mr. Fergusson, however, are those of first-rate poets who have also been passionately interested in drama: Garcia Lorca, T. S. Eliot, and W. B. Yeats. If their work—though it is too early to be certain

about it—does not strike me as central to the development of
the drama, I had better explain why not.

Garcia Lorca's might have become so; he was probably the
most gifted playwright of his generation; but the Falangists
killed him before his art emerged from the experimental stage.
(Even so his "experiments" are riper than the "masterpieces"
of our acknowledged and anthologized dramatists.) T. S. Eliot,
might yet become a first-rate dramatist. His *Sweeney Agonistes*
is probably the best theatrical verse written in English during
this century; *Murder in the Cathedral* and *The Rock* contain
excellent things and are almost ostentatiously stageworthy; *The
Family Reunion* is a brilliant attempt to unite the drawing-
room play with Greek tragedy. Yet *Sweeney* remains a fragment; *Murder* and *The Rock* are something less than ordered
wholes; *The Family Reunion* is an attempt that is hardly a triumph. (Incidentally, its success and failure are exactly opposite
to those of *Mourning Becomes Electra*. Eliot's "conception" is
clear, noble, and mature, his "communication" uncertain, irreg-
ular, and incomplete. O'Neill's "communication" is rapid,
strong, almost overwhelming, his "conception" is rude, simple-
minded, gaga.) Eliot's essays on drama show how finely he ap-
preciates the drama of the Elizabethans (if not of the moderns)
and his practice shows him the possessor of a superb histrionic
gift. Why is he not an important playwright?

Perhaps the career of W. B. Yeats will help us to understand.
W. B. Yeats is another dramatist *manqué,* whose insufficiency
cannot be explained by the fact that he was a poet. He was not
the pure lyrist of popular imagination, who divides his time between the woods and the library. He was one of the founders of
the Abbey Theater, Dublin, and for many years a director of
its policies. Nonetheless his dramatic output is disappointing.
The early plays, among which *Cathleen ni Houlihan* is characteristic and famous, suffer from all the limitations of his early
poems: they depend on the cult of the peasant, on belief in
fairies, on softness of texture and poeticism of mood and

phrase, on the atmosphere of Celtic twilight. (The misty and mythic *Plays for an Irish Theater,* 1911, contained even more misty and mythic designs by Gordon Craig himself.) When Yeats became a much better poet, as he did at the onset of the fourth modernism, he became a somewhat better playwright. His little prose play about Swift—*Words upon the Window Pane*—shows how much more crisp and concrete his art had become. One of his very last plays—*Purgatory*—has the terrible beauty of his best poems. And it is a play, not a closet drama. Only a fool could read the later plays and dismiss Yeats as "a poet, not a playwright." If he never wrote a major play it was not for lack of native endowment. Why then—it is the question I have asked about Eliot—did he stop short?

It is not a question one can confidently answer. What I surmise is that Yeats did not submit himself to the discipline of the theater as he did to the discipline of the book. Perhaps, though he was fascinated by the idea of drama, he did not really like the actual theater. There is evidence for this in such lines as these, written by Yeats already in 1916:

> Being sensitive, or not knowing how to escape the chance of sitting behind the wrong people, I have begun to shrink from sending my muses where they are but half welcomed; and even in Dublin, where the pit has an ear for verse, I have no longer the appetite to carry me through the daily rehearsals. Yet I need a theater; I believe myself to be a dramatist. . . . My blunder has been that I did not discover in my youth that my theater must be the ancient theater that can be made by unrolling a carpet or marking out a place with a stick, or setting a screen against the wall. Cerainly those who care for my kind of poetry must be numerous enough, if I can bring them together, to pay half-a-dozen players who can bring all their properties in a cab and perform in their leisure moments.

These are revealing words. Yeats was a dramatist. He needed a
theater. But he could not bear to sit "behind the wrong people." He does not know what to do with the drama in our mass
civilization unless it be to limit it to imitations of the ancient
Japanese Noh plays performed in a friend's drawing room. A
new type of drawing-room play indeed! Yeats was entitled, if he
wished, to reject Ibsen (especially since he ignorantly believed
him to be dull and chiefly sociological). But what an alternative
he provides! Parlor games á la japonaise! One can sympathize
with an artist's rejection of the commercial theater. In fact that
is nowadays the least one can expect from him. But Yeats
wanted to break with the art theater too. He felt lured to it,
but he had not the appetite for rehearsals, and the wrong people were always in the auditorium.

Of course Yeats was right, right in some respects, right in
those respects which touched him most nearly. The Abbey
Theater could nourish a quaint and naturalistic wit like Synge
or a naturalistic and hard-hitting satirist like O'Casey. It provided the soil for *some* kinds of drama, but not for Yeats's kind
—a drama which uses the idiom of modern poetry. Yeats tried to
enliven his poetic drama with dance and music. Had he lived
in Paris or Vienna he might have come up against composers
and choreographers who would have been colleagues in a great
enterprise. The fact that he lived in Great Britain was a limitation. It was probably the ultimate limitation. Drama is a social
art. Although it does not require the support of the masses or of
any large class, it does require a tradition that lives in some
group homogeneous enough to make a crowd in the theater.
The poetic drama can exist today only where there is a very
lively intelligentsia that is interested in such things. Neither
London nor Dublin is such a place. For that we have to go to
the continent. In Paris Yeats could have found not only good
composers and good choreographers. He could have found an
audience. Not that his "purer" verse plays could have succeeded
even there. Yeats would have had to learn that (in Cocteau's

figure) theatrical poetry is not tenuous like gossamer but thick like the rigging of a ship and visible at a distance. . . . Yet he would have found soil to grow in and he would have grown.

Because the opportunities in English—and even Irish—theater were so limited, Yeats and Eliot have had to seek their fulfillment largely in nontheatrical verse. That is perhaps about the only definite statement one can make in answer to the query about their shortcomings as playwrights. It forces upon one the further query, however: what of the places—the very few places —which offered greater opportunities? If the work of great artists like Lorca and Eliot and Yeats is not in the main stream of dramatic evolution, is not even in the main stream of nonnaturalism, what is?

### III

In the twenties there were three major attempts to wean the modern artistic theater from naturalism. The Germans tried Expressionism (on which I have already commented). The Russians tried brilliant new styles of acting, staging, and directing (and since none of these could engender a new *drama,* comment is hardly needed). The French had a third way of doing things —a way which perhaps has no name, though lovers of the theater will perhaps think of it as the tradition of the Vieux-Colombier. Here comment is certainly called for.

Mr. Fergusson places the fresh start around 1919, but that was only the date when already accomplished changes won public recognition. We have seen that Expressionism began before the First World War and that the modernist, antinaturalist theater in Russia is of prerevolutionary origin. So also with the new movement in French antinaturalism. I do not refer to the plays of the symbolist poets in the nineties. Even in Paris the poetic theater of the symbolist poets had not been a success despite the efforts of Paul Fort with his Théâtre de l'Art and Lugné Poë with his Théâtre de l'Oeuvre. This theater had been too much akin to the early plays of Yeats. No, in France as elsewhere the strong opposition to naturalism came not from poetic drama but from the advocates of dancing, music, and design, and new techniques—from the Strindbergians, one might say, or, taking a longer view, from the Wagnerians.

The beginnings of the fourth modernism might be seen in such a piece of brilliant, Bohemian theater as Alfred Jarry's *Ubu Roi* before 1900. After Jarry came Guillaume Apollinaire, whose antinaturalism is much more highly developed.

In 1903 Apollinaire wrote most of a play, *Les Mamelles de Tirésias*, which was not to be completed and produced for fourteen years. In a preface he protests against stage illusion. Calling his play *un drame surréaliste* (and thus coining the word surrealism), Apollinaire asks demurely why inanimate objects should not speak, why the techniques of popular entertainment such as the circus should not be used, why propaganda—his play is propaganda for an increased birth rate (!)—should not be gay, why burlesque should not be mixed with pathos. Free fantasy is to succeed the realistic *pièce á thèse,* which only gave the public the illusion that it could think. In Apollinaire's play the wife who refuses to have children coolly removes her breasts on the stage—and they are found to be balloons on strings. A single character represents the whole people of Zanzibar and is accordingly armed with *"revolver, musette, grosse caisse, tambour, tonnerre, grelots, castagnettes, trompette d'enfant, vaisselle cassée."* Characters speak through a megaphone when addressing the audience. They are dressed in the fanciful garb of a cubistic carnival. Since it sums up the attempts of so many non-naturalistic experimenters of the period, the Prologue is worth citing:

> On tente ici d'infuser un esprit nouveau au théâtre
> Une joie une volupté une vertu
> Pour remplacer ce pessimisme vieux de plus d'un siècle
> Ce qui est bien ancien pour une chose si ennuyeuse
> La pièce a été faite pour une scène ancienne
> Car on ne nous aurait pas construit de théâtre nouveau

*Un théâtre rond à deux scènes*
*Une au centre l'autre formant comme un anneau*
*Autour des spectateurs et qui permettra*
*Le grand déploiement de notre art moderne*
*Mariant souvent sans lien apparent comme dans la vie*
*Les sons les gestes les couleurs les cris les bruits*
*La musique la danse l'acrobatie la poésie la peinture*
*Les choeurs les actions et les décors multiples. . . .* \*

The Wagnerian *gesamtkunstwerk,* at Bayreuth so portentous a religion, has in Paris become a sport. Although Apollinaire was less frivolous than, say, Marinetti with his Italian
Futurist Theater (which was sheer hokum) he was still a jester
and therefore a breaker more than a maker of forms. His ideas
had to be followed up by other people. As Jean Cocteau's translator put it:

> This search for the poetry of the theater, which is a
> further attempt to find the correct material and ad-
> just the proportions, and which went of necessity hand
> in hand with the reaction to realism, has been con-
> ducted vigorously during the quarter of a century
> under consideration (1909-1934) by three men of
> whose importance we become increasingly aware:
> Serge Diaghileff, Jacques Copeau, and Jean Cocteau.
> Diaghileff, organizing, encouraging, and giving the
> direction to a large company of dancers, painters, and
> musicians; Copeau, forming his men culturally, pre-
> paring artists in the multiple activities of the dramatic
> stage; Cocteau, an artist himself engaged in all these

\* We hereby try to bring a new spirit into the theater, a joy, a voluptuous-
ness, a virtue to replace that pessimism over a century old, which is quite an
age for a thing so tiresome. The play was made for an old-fashioned stage,
since they wouldn't have built us a new theater, a circular theater with two
stages, one in the middle, the other like a ring around the spectators, permitting
a grand deployment of our modern art, marrying—often without apparent links,
as in life—sounds, gestures, colors, shouts, noises, music, dancing, acrobatics,
poetry, painting, choruses, actions, and multiple *décor.*

activities, and also discovering the formulae to express
the needs of the ballet and dramatic stage alike.

It is impossible not to be attracted by this sort of thing. Who
would not like to have seen *Parade* in 1917—text by Cocteau,
*décor* by Picasso, music by Erik Satie, choreography by Leonide
Massine? The glittering names bear witness to a real theatrical
culture such as might well be the envy of our Eliots and Yeatses.
Copeau's Théâtre du Vieux Colombier, founded in 1913, is
almost unique among modern theatrical ventures in its closeness to the highest culture of its time and place. Whereas even
"high-brow" American playwrights like Maxwell Anderson
write at an appreciably lower level than the best American
poets, novelists, and critics, Copeau and his troop belonged to
the circle of André Gide and his colleagues on the newly
founded organ the *Nouvelle Revue Française*. In their hands
the *gesamtkunstwerk* grew sober and austere. For the first time,
perhaps, it was delicate and altogether in good taste.

"In leaving reality behind," Gide had announced in 1904,
"the theater is today weighing anchor." Jean Cocteau was the
outstanding playwright of the new spirit, at least after his dramatic talent first fully revealed itself in *Orphée* (1926), a retelling of the Orpheus story in fantastic, whimsical, hilarious,
grotesque, and somehow moving terms. His theory of the
drama solves many problems that had proved too much for the
fancy-dress tragedians and the poetic dramatists. First, he clari-
fies—as we have noted in passing—the nature of theatrical as
opposed to lyric poetry. His watchword is not poetry *in* the
theater but the proper poetry *of* the theater. Second, he calls
for a "cooling off" of the drama, which had indeed reached rare
temperatures in the nineteenth century—not excluding the New
Theater movement of the eighties and nineties. This cooling is
most triumphantly manifested in *The Infernal Machine,* where
Cocteau minimizes suspense by having a chorus tell the whole
story beforehand. He amply makes up for sweaty excitement

and cheap thrills by richness of texture. Thirdly, Cocteau follows Apollinaire (instead of the symbolists and neo-romanticists) in requiring gaiety, fancy, and extravagance in the theater.

The crowning dramatic achievement of Cocteau (if we except the movie *The Blood of a Poet*) is his version of the Oedipus story *The Infernal Machine*. This deliberate, quasi-naïve, adroit series of pictures "flooded in the livid mythical light of quicksilver" is one of the legitimate triumphs of the antinaturalistic theater. It does not, however, dispel all doubts about Cocteau's view of drama or about the future of his dramatic practice. The weakness of Cocteau's theater is what might be called his aestheticism. Here, for example, is how he introduces his play *The Human Voice*, which is a little melodrama with a single character speaking over the phone and finally strangling herself with the wire:

> It would be a mistake to believe that the author seeks the solution of some psychological problem. All that's needed is to solve problems of a purely theatrical nature, the mixture of theater, preaching, the platform, the book, being the evil against which something had to be done. Pure theater would be the fashionable phrase, if pure theater and pure poetry were not pleonasms—pure poetry meaning poetry, and pure theater, theater. There oughtn't to exist any others.

Cocteau protests against the mixing of theater with literature, homily, and propaganda. But this mixture, if it is a mixture at all, is not artificial. The theater was not born free of literature, homily, and propaganda. They are a natural unity from which Cocteau wishes to abstract one element and call it "pure." Yet he is happy enough to do some mixing himself in other ways. He is willing to mix music, dance, painting, and speech, which surely do not make a very "pure" concoction. From the Wagnerites he seems to inherit also the view that the arts all "aspire to the condition of music" and that literature can be purified of nonmusical elements. Only on this assumption could there be "pure" theater. And it is an erroneous assumption.

The fate of the Parisian experiments with ballet and mime and the like is strangely similar to the fate of German Expressionism. Both movements were adventurous, challenging, importantly symptomatic. Both were genuine attempts to grapple with real and cruelly difficult theatrical problems. Both presented an imposing front. Yet both suffered from hollowness. Like Georg Kaiser, the prince of the Expressionists, Jean Cocteau has shown brilliant qualities and shown them in a genuinely theatrical way; but the center of his drama—as of Kaiser's—is a vacuum. If Kaiser tried to seize the essence of life without its content, Cocteau has tried to seize its content without its essence; and the result is equally unsatisfying. It is partly due to Kaiser and Cocteau—though much more to their hangers-on —that the term Experimental Theater came to suggest the merely brilliant, the technically clever, the assiduously heterodox, the forever incomplete.

I would like to apply to Cocteau some words which Mrs. Diana Trilling wrote about someone else: "His intellect and fantasy are put at the service of a playful destructiveness; they are the instruments of neither an understanding nor an ordering of his world. That is, whatever his apparent ease, he is far too disconcerted by the complicated society which has educated him, and to which he has access at so many points, to be able to face up to its literary challenge." One should think of this analysis when reading the apologias of Cocteau's unqualified admirers. "The play *Orphée*," writes one of them, "works on people like music, leaving the mind free to think its own thoughts. Those who wish to understand, instead of believe, stand outside Cocteau's world looking for a door that is not there." Surely this is nonsense. Music does not leave the mind to think its own thoughts unless that mind is thoroughly unmusical (like Walt Disney's, to judge by *Fantasia*). The mind thinks its own thoughts in sleep and daydream, not in experiencing works of art. As for believing and not understanding, how can one decide *what* to believe except by understanding the rather various and mutually incompatible possibilities? And this request that we believe in Cocteau's rightness—apparently in a religious or quasi-religious fashion—is it not rather odd, coming as it does from opponents of didacticism? When antididacticism comes full circle, as it does here, it may be to the point to cite, as an antidote, some words of the didactic naturalist Bertolt Brecht, in which he explains the purpose of the chorus in a play of his: "To prevent the spectator from 'swooning away,' to combat 'free' association, small choruses can be placed in the auditorium to show him the right attitude, to invite him to form his opinions, to summon his experience to his aid, to exercise control. . . ." I quote this in order to illuminate Cocteau's world by contrast. Brecht's words also show a much stronger determination to cool the drama off and accurately to adapt the means to the end.

## IV

The question for some years has been: can the non-naturalistic drama of Paris, for all its charms, grow into something more mature? If Cocteau is the prophet, the Zola of this anti-Zolaist school of drama, and *The Infernal Machine* is his *Thérèse Raquin,* where is the master, the Henry Becque? Without such a man the first-rank importance of French non-naturalism would not be apparent. During the late thirties the man did not appear. Then came 1940. Wiseacres whispered that, far from being fruitful, sophistication had caused the fall of France. It was not till 1945 that news came out of a liberated France that she had again a serious theater and that it was again a non-naturalistic theater, a theater of the inner eye, a subjectivist theater—nay, so one reporter announced, an "existential theater."

Under the influence of so-called existential philosophy,

which is particularly concerned with the individual, his inner nature, and his fate, two men, Albert Camus and Jean-Paul Sartre, had written plays that brought new hope for the French theater. Since my readers may have had no opportunity of acquainting themselves with any of these plays, I will report on two of them more explicitly than I have been reporting on known plays. Whether or not Jean-Paul Sartre is the Henry Becque of non-naturalist modernism, his two dramatic works—*Huis Clos* ["Behind Closed Doors"] and *Les Mouches* ["The Flies"]—do seem to represent a new stage, a newly acquired maturity in this tradition. And it should be of more than passing interest to note that *Behind Closed Doors* was produced by the Théâtre du Vieux Colombier about a month before D-day, 1944, and that *The Flies* had already been produced by Charles Dullin, upon whom Copeau's mantle had fallen, in the darkest days of the German occupation.

*Behind Closed Doors* presents a strong situation. Three people who have recently died are in hell. Though in this life they were not acquainted, they are condemned to spend eternity together in one room. Each tries to work out plans for his own happiness with one of the others; but there is no scheme by which all three can be happy. Even the one who is left out of the dual happiness of sex can ruin that happiness in the other two by her (or his) perpetual presence. In the end all three realize that the apparently innocuous arrangement of locating three very different people in one room—where, furthermore, neither sleep nor tears may ever break the tension—creates as horrible a hell as adamantine chains and penal fire.

There is nothing in all this, of course, to astonish us. The British *Outward Bound* and the American *Hotel Universe* have for long pleased Philistine audiences with their judicious mixture of boulevard theater and supposedly deep dealings with the next world. Boulevard playwrights like H. R. Lenormand and J. B. Priestley have impressed theatergoers with the proposition that time is not real. And it is not only the subject matter

of Sartre's play that will have a familiar ring. Its technique has
no secrets from those who know their Ibsen and Strindberg. It
is a highly concentrated one-act play of steadily increasing emotion; even some of the eeriness may seem Strindbergian. The
craftsmanship might more properly be termed Ibsenite, since it
chiefly consists of keeping the audience from knowing the facts
too early, that is, to describe it more positively, of letting discoveries explode like carefully adjusted time bombs all through
the action. It is a well-made drawing-room play that releases its
secrets with all the finesse and aplomb that Parisian audiences—
of the boulevards rather than of the Vieux Colombier—have
long expected and received. The dialogue is the smoothly filed,
urbane prose of the French naturalistic tradition. The story has
plenty of the kind of good poignant sex about it that one associates with run-of-the-mill French plays and novels and with
French movies good and bad. Adultery, infanticide, Lesbianism, a traffic accident, double suicide in bed, refusal to fight
for France, death before a firing squad—what more could a
French movie director desire? The setting—to cap everything—
is a Second Empire drawing room; and it is pleasant to note
that the dramatic unities are scrupulously observed even in
hell.

Having assembled all the elements of a bad and deeply conventional play, Sartre has gone on to make a good play out of
them. Like so many of the playwrights discussed in this book he
uses commodity literature as the raw material of his art. If *Behind Closed Doors* is a drawing-room play, that is hell's crowning irony. The Second Empire scenery which had graced the
plays of Sardou, Dumas, and Augier is transferred to the nether
regions—or rather, more terrible still, the nether regions are
transferred to it. Evidently this playwright has serious designs
on us.

Yes: *Behind Closed Doors* is a moral play. It is a play of character according to Aristotle's definition: "Character is that which
reveals moral purpose, showing what kind of things a man

chooses or avoids." It shows what kind of things three people chose and avoided to earn for themselves eternal damnation. It shows what kind of things they continue to choose and avoid even in hell. What is hell? It is to be a botched character and to be forever imprisoned with other botched characters. When one of Sartre's people complains that the eternal penal colony lacks a hangman, another replies: "They've done it to economize on personnel, that's all. It's the customers who serve themselves as in cafeterias . . . each one of us is the hangman for the two others." Sartre solves his triangular problem with great skill. The action speeds up, slows down, turns, twists back on itself, as each of the three plots anxiously in his own interest. A joins B against C, then B deserts to C in order to fight A, then . . . the psychological and histrionic possibilities of this formula are fully exploited. If, of course, Sartre gave equal prominence to A, B, and C, the play would lack concentration and sharp focus which he obviously seeks. A man is therefore placed in the center; two women are peripheral. A neat, old-fashioned Parisian pattern. But Sartre has new-fashioned intentions. His three people are three mirrors of one action; they are there to give form, variety, and meaning to what else might easily be another Bohemian play. Speaking of the fourth modernism of the twenties, Mr. Fergusson writes. ". . . We see now some of the dangers in the new line. One needs, I think, to place against Cocteau's theatrical virtuosity, and Eliot's abstract theological framework, and Lorca's luxuriant popular imagery, the [Henry] Jamesian and classic conception of an Action, seen in the round, seen from many angles." Sartre is trying to satisfy Mr. Fergusson's wish.

The three people of *Behind Closed Doors* are Garcin, a pacifistic journalist who has been shot attempting to avoid military service; Inès, a Lesbian employee of the post office who seduced her cousin's wife Florence and, when the cousin was killed in a streetcar accident, goaded Florence to suicide; and Estelle, a narcissistic society lady who married for money, had a child by an adulterous union, killed the baby, and by so doing drove her lover to suicide. Of the three, Garcin seems by far the least guilty; he has indeed always posed as a hero and for a time he continues to do so even in hell; but there are a few facts, at first concealed from us, that continue to haunt him. The moralist and hero had consistently ill-treated his wife. He let her bring his breakfast into his bedroom after having installed a mulatto mistress in the bed. His heroism is dubious. He did not face his punishment but tried to escape to Mexico. When he defends himself with the question: "Can one judge a life by a single action?" Inès forces certain home truths upon him:

> GARCIN. Can one judge a life by a single deed?
>
> INÈS. Why not? You have dreamed for thirty years that you have courage; and you allowed yourself a thousand weaknesses because everything is permitted to heroes. How convenient it was! And then, in the hour of danger, they put you on the spot . . . you took the train for Mexico.
>
> GARCIN. I didn't dream the heroism. I chose it. One is what one wishes to be.
>
> INÈS. Prove it. Prove that it was not a dream. Deeds also decide what one has wished.
>
> GARCIN. I died too soon. I wasn't left time to perform *my* deeds.
>
> INÈS. One always dies too soon—or too late. And yet there is one's life—finished; the shot is fired, you must foot the bill. You *are* your life and nothing else.

I had almost said that this passage is the climax both of the plot and of the argument. That is not quite true. It is the climax of the argument and not of the plot. It is an apparent climax that gives way—in high dramatic fashion—to a yet greater climax, after which there is a sudden drop and the play ends in hideous quiet. This is the action: deprived by Inès' words of his last illusions, Garcin decides at last to gratify Estelle's wish to sleep with a man, though under Inès' very eyes. He throws himself upon her. But Inès pursues the couple with her eyes and tongue, shouting "Coward! Coward!" for Garcin now knows that he had been *afraid* to be a soldier. He releases Estelle. "Hell," he concludes, "is other people." Infuriated, Estelle stabs Inès with the paper knife. Vain anger. "That has been done already, don't you understand?" Inès screams, "and we are together forever." Hysterical laughter shakes them all. Then sudden silence. All inwardly take stock of the situation. *"Eh bien, continuons,"* Garcin says, "very well, let's continue."

Such is Sartre's almost Gothic tale. It is melodrama of course. Even if the haunted house be called hell, even if the Kafkaesque attendant be some minor devil, even if the bell that fails to ring at crucial moments (or the door that opens magically or not at all) is interpreted with allegorical pomp, we need not try to be wholly solemn in our acceptance of the play. No more than in the case of Strindberg—whose long one-act structure and moral imagery Sartre here emulates—is it an insult to interpret the author a little whimsically. The question: is he serious? is highly ambiguous. All works of art are serious. Sartre has written a play with ideas in it which he is in deadly earnest about, and since these ideas are carefully integrated with the action we are bound to take them "seriously." Nevertheless, and intending no slur, I would call *Behind Closed Doors* philosophic melodrama. It is certainly not tragedy—there is no tragic dignity, no tragic protagonist, no tragic anything—unless one wishes to spout oracularly about the tragedy of human life as a whole. It is not comedy—there is no laughter or acceptance in this unqualified and almost demoniac assault upon human nature. If Strindberg broke up again the forms of comedy and tragedy, there is here no indication that Sartre is trying to put Humpty Dumpty together again. *Behind Closed Doors,* like so much of the best post-Strindbergian work, belongs to a new intermediate genre. And if this designation is too vague I am offering the description "philosophic melodrama" to characterize this combination of

histrionics and serious thought, this latest experiment of the
French antinaturalistic drama, this latest analysis of the soul
under the secret scrutiny of the inner eye.

*The Flies* is a "drama in three acts" about Orestes, his sister
Electra, and the god Jupiter. The situation is explained to us
in the first act. Having been brought up abroad, Orestes has
just returned, as a young man accompanied by his tutor, to
Argos, where he finds the town still doing penance for the murder of his father Agamemnon by his mother Clytemnestra and
her lover. The latter, now King Aegisthus, seeks to place himself in a good light by leading the ceremonies. Act I prepares
us for the rites of the anniversary of the murder. Two antag-
onisms are intimated, one—that between Electra and the monarchs—already old and bitter, the other—that between Jupiter
and Orestes—still in germ. The young Orestes of this act is no
avenger; he no longer feels that the affairs of Argos are much
concern of his; rational, mild, and detached, he is inclined to
let the dead bury their dead.

Act II consists of two imposing tableaux. The first is the anniversary rite. Aegisthus is to release the spirits of the dead from
the underworld; for one night they will return to their former
haunts. In defiance of him and his rites Electra arrives clad in
white and dances a joyous dance before the people. Only, she
declares, if the gods give a sign of disapproval will she desist.
Now Jupiter is in the crowd. He gives a sign, and Electra's gesture fails. Yet she has stirred the depths of Orestes' soul. After
the ceremony he for the first time declares his identity to her.
Very soon they are planning the murder of the king and queen.

The second tableau is a scene in the palace. Jupiter, who has
listened to the conversation of Orestes and Electra, comes to
warn Aegisthus. But the king is weary of guilt, weary of re-
pentance, weary of living. He will not bother to defend himself.
And so when Jupiter leaves Aegisthus is at once slain by
Orestes. So is Clytemnestra.

When Act III opens, Orestes and Electra are asleep in a temple beneath the protective statue of Apollo. Around them, waiting for their latest prey, the Eumenides wait in a ring. Jupiter arrives. He offers to protect Orestes and Electra from the mob that is already howling at the doors and to ensure to them their parents' throne. Electra, badly shaken already by the murder of her mother, succumbs to his blandishments and polemics. Orestes resists. Jupiter makes the walls of the temple disappear, displays to Orestes the kingdoms of the world and his power over them; but it makes no difference. Orestes faces and outfaces the mob without Jupiter's help. He tells the people they are released from their penitentiary obligations. Declining the throne, he leaves the dwellings of men. The Eumenides slink off like whipped dogs. The flies, which throughout behave as minor Eumenides, leave too.

In these days, when classic stories reappear chiefly in burlesque (the Lunts in *Amphitryon 38;* Ray Bolger in *By Jupiter!*) it may seem strange to find a myth altered but neither travestied nor prettified. *The Flies* is a decidedly unusual sort of alteration. It is not merely the retelling of the classic story in sensitive modern language and with the aid of modernist techniques, like André Obey's charming *Viol de Lucrèce*. It is not a retelling of the story in a modern setting and with the aid of modern psychology, like the lugubrious *Mourning Becomes Electra*. It is not a modern story into which the Eumenides are injected, like the suggestive but strained *Family Reunion*. It is not a transposition into a surrealistic key, like *Orphée* . . . .

Yet in mentioning a work of Cocteau's we do come close to discovering a significant parallel and a significant contrast, namely, that between *The Flies* and *The Infernal Machine*. Sartre follows Cocteau in relating the myth in colloquial modern speech, but not in modern dress, and in imposing upon it his own, very un-Greek interpretation. He follows Cocteau in his command of splendid, non-naturalistic scenic effects, which, though grandiose in appearance, can be achieved with the columns, steps, and other statuesque and architectural effects that

one associates with the Vieux Colombier. There is even some
call, in *The Flies*, for a choreographic treatment—of the Eumenides and the crowd for example—which would help to give
a production the same well-considered beauty and stylization
that Cocteau had long demanded.

The *contrast* between *The Infernal Machine* and *The Flies*
is most clearly marked in the total meaning of the two plays.
Consider *The Infernal Machine*. To reinterpret a Greek myth
is no small task for one who believes in "pure" theater and
who is determined at all costs to avoid not only pedantry and
political propaganda but also all didacticism. Cocteau accordingly adopts the formula which can be operated with least fuss:
he simply inverts the Greek idea. In Greek tragedy the gods—
that is, the laws of the universe—are just; tragedy, so far from
casting an aspersion on their wisdom, confirms it. In Cocteau's
play the gods are malicious. They plot against unoffending mor-
tals. Their "infernal machine" engineers disaster. The protagonist is almost the opposite of a Greek hero until—and this is the
conclusion of Cocteau's play as stated in advance by his chorus
—"after delusive good fortune the king is to know true misfortune and supreme consecration, which, in the hands of the cruel
gods, makes of their playing-card king, in the end, a man."

Now some of those who regard modern drama as a body of
dull problem-plays and wish for the resuscitation of "real tragedy" may be inclined to view Cocteau's solution with favor. Unlike the neo-romanticists, he has not merely copied a Greek or
Elizabethan tragic pattern; he has sought a genuinely modern
pattern; yet, avoiding "ideas" and controversies, he has sought
the "purely human," the purely tragic. To me this seems to be
precisely his limitation. The purely human is as unreal an abstraction as the purely poetic and the purely theatrical. To leave
out the intellect, the element of thought, is to deprive oneself
of a great part of human awareness. In drama it is to deprive
oneself of the awareness exemplified in modern drama since
Hebbel and Ibsen, it is to remove oneself from what we might

paradoxically call the modern tradition, and, in however brave and brilliant a manner, to be an antiquarian and a theorist. No wonder one feels a certain emptiness in Cocteau! The difference between him and Sartre, if I am not mistaken, is the difference between Experimental Theater and a maturely modern theater. *The Infernal Machine* might be dignified with the name of Tragedy, *The Flies* degraded with that of Problem Play or Propaganda, but the latter—whether or not it is a better work of art (and I think it is)—seems an altogether more satisfactory solution of the problem of modern drama. Perhaps we have come to a stage when the nontragic drama may better represent us than tragedy; for our outlook is not tragic; and there is no adequate reason, I think, why it should be.

It is one of the clichés of dramatic theory that tragedy is deep and courageous and that the nontragic drama falls short of tragedy through being shallow and cowardly. Nontragic drama tends—it is said—to the easy solution, to extreme optimism for example. It has the happy ending of melodrama, not the unhappy ending of tragedy. Yet that Sartre's philosophic melodramas cut deeper than any twentieth-century "tragedy" has done or is likely to do should be clear after further analysis.

While Cocteau repeats the old Oedipus story in a modern way, Sartre's reinterpretation is so thoroughgoing that he has to reconstruct the narrative at many points. From the start he brings Jupiter into it. The first thing seen when the curtain goes up is a "statue of Jupiter, god of the flies and of death, eyes white, face daubed with blood." The play is a duel between god and man. As Cocteau shows Oedipus grow human under the stress of the gods' inhuman treatment, so Sartre shows Orestes acquire humanity through violence and in opposition to the divine will. Cocteau leaves the transformation to the end, and that is tactful of him since it is a rather pointless process: of what comfort is it that a man grows human in a world run by omnipotent fiends? This is neither the Greek philosophy nor the modern. The transformation of Sartre's Orestes, on the other hand, has a point; in fact it is the subject of the play.

At the outset Orestes is an intellectual, and very much above the battle. His attitude is finely suggested in the line *"et quelle superbe absence que mon âme"*—"what a superb absence is my soul." He observes that "there are men born with a commitment [*engagé*]: they have no choice, they are thrown along a certain path, at the end of the path there is a deed waiting for them, *their* deed." But he is glad that he is not of their number. The crisis of his life is therefore the moment after Electra's dance when he resolves after all to carry out the murder. He has to do it, not because of any doom on the house of Atreus, not because he must bring about what is already fated, but for the opposite reason, because he must free the house of Atreus and the people of Argos, because the act will be for him as well as others an emancipation, a justification by works. "Can one judge a life by a single deed?" Garcin had asked, and Inès had replied: "Why not? . . . Deeds alone decide what one has wished. . . . You *are* your life and nothing else." Where Garcin fails, Orestes succeeds. The two men are obverse and reverse of the same coin. *Behind Closed Doors* is damnation; *The Flies* is redemption. Gradually Orestes turns from sophisticated aloofness to passionate participation. He kills the tyrant. He kills his own mother. Unhumbled by any sort of guilt, he cries: "Liberty has swooped down on me like a thunderbolt . . . I have done *my* deed!"

*The Flies,* like Goethe's *Egmont* and Schiller's *Wilhelm Tell,* is a political drama of resistance to tyranny, of belief in freedom. One can imagine what force some of the lines must have had in occupied France: the arguments for action, for tyrannicide, the recurrence of the word *"liberté,"* the fascistic ugliness of all the symbols of authority, the libertarian audacity of Orestes. Yet the political meaning of the piece is strictly secondary; for political freedom is portrayed as the product of a prior freedom of a kind more difficult both to conceive and to realize.

This is the freedom which Ibsen long ago placed above all other freedoms but which many latter-day collectivists have often pooh-poohed as a bourgeois illusion: the freedom that comes of finding and realizing the self. Collectivists often assume that to pursue the goal of self-realization is to be an anti-social egoist. For Sartre, however, self-fulfillment and altruism are complementary. Let us see how this can be.

When Jupiter warns Aegisthus he explains that the two of them are natural allies, since they occupy corresponding places in earth and heaven respectively. Both are monarchs. Both love Order. Both share the secret which, if generally shared, would mean the end of Order, *viz.* that men are free. Orestes is dangerous to both of them not only because he has learned the secret but because his doing so renders him immune to divine influence. Now this liberty of Orestes—"I *am* my liberty," he says—consists of an inner self-possession and self-knowledge *as a result of which* he will also demand political freedom in the shape of freedom from tyrannical government. Inviting Electra to go with him to a far country, he says:

> ORESTES. You will give me your hand and we shall go . . .
> ELECTRA. Where?
> ORESTES. I don't know; toward ourselves. On the other side of the rivers and the mountains there is an Orestes and an Electra waiting for us. We must seek them patiently.

If Orestes' former unfree state of mind was described as a "superb absence," his new state of liberty is admitted to be "an exile." The distinction is subtle. The difference between the "absent" youth and the "exiled" free man is that the exile is nevertheless *engagé,* committed to human society.

Orestes' liberty is a paradox. Precisely where we learn that it is an exile, we learn also that it involves social responsibility.

JUPITER. What do you expect to do?

ORESTES. The men of Argos are my men. I have to open their eyes. . . . Why should I refuse them the despair that is in me, since it is their lot?

JUPITER. What will they do with it?

ORESTES. What they wish; they are free, and human life begins on the other side of despair. . . .

Having freed himself from within, Orestes can help to free his people from without. Having found his freedom, and having confirmed it by tyrannicide, Orestes can liberate the people. "Your faults," he tells them, "your faults and your regrets, your nocturnal agonies, the crime of Aegisthus—all are mine, I take them all upon me. Fear your dead no longer, they are *my* dead." Reminding them of the piper whose playing lured the rats from a rat-infested city, he leaves Argos, another pied piper of Hamelin, followed by the cringing Eumenides and their flies.

Is this a Christian solution? Is Orestes a Christ expiating the sins of others? Electra had asked him about this question:

ELECTRA. You wish to expiate our sins?

ORESTES. Expiate? I said I would install within myself all your repentancies but I did not say what I will do with them. They're screeching hens: perhaps I'll wring their necks.

ELECTRA. And how could you take charge of our ills?

ORESTES. You are anxious to be rid of them. The king and queen alone keep them in force in your hearts.

There is more humanism in this attitude of Orestes, more positivism, than there is theology. Sartre's play can certainly not be accused of appealing to Rome; what might be more disconcerting is that favorite American question: is it democratic? The doctrine of redemption by the one free spirit who does not

shrink from murder beforehand, nor apologize for it after-
wards, has a Nietzschean ring. An Orestes who knows that his
freedom is an exile and that human life begins on the other
side of despair is something of a Zarathustra. What then? Is this
undemocratic? Not unless democracy is committed to the extrovert psychology and cheery optimism of cheap liberal journalism, not unless democracy is committed to belief in purely
external change, not unless democracy is committed to the belief that the people can do all the governing themselves without
leadership, without greatness. If it is so committed, so much the
worse for democracy.

Is *The Flies* absolutely coherent? As yet I have not known it
long enough to be quite sure. I do not know whether the vagueness that exists in my mind concerning certain relationships is
my own vagueness or Sartre's. When, for instance, must the hero
Orestes be in exile and when among men? What is the moral
difference between his murdering Aegisthus and his murdering
his mother? What kind of power is Jupiter meant to have?
What is this god to whom we owe our being, yet to whom we
owe no allegiance? This god who has power over nature but not
over free men? To answer these questions one would have to
live with the play for a time; and one would like to see it performed and to read more of Sartre's other work.

At present we are entitled to say that Sartre *may* be the man
whom the theater of the French *avant-garde*—particularly the
Vieux Colombier—has long awaited. If he continues to write for
the stage, and if fate is favorable, there is no knowing how good
he might not become. On the lowest estimate he is the literary
man of the hour; and his plays are among the best of the hour.
By exhibiting, in one play, the "dead souls" of the modern
age and, in the other, a modern savior (who has to kill his
mother in order to find himself and be one with people), Sartre
projects our spiritual conflicts as movingly as any playwright

since Strindberg. I say *projects*. Even Strindberg did not *resolve* them.

"From Strindberg to Sartre": this is not a journey to a goal. I pick out Sartre only as an outstandingly interesting example of a playwright of the nineteen-forties who has developed the antinaturalistic drama a little further.

One fact about his Existential Theater is of very curious interest: that, although it is in the tradition of the Vieux Colombier, although it is inspired by an extreme concern with the inner world, it nevertheless approaches naturalism at many points. It eschews verse and favors sharp naturalistic dialogue. It opens the windows of the soul upon the outer world of social and political relationships. In this respect it has moved almost as far from Cocteau as from Maeterlinck. So has it in its didacticism. Can it be that the antinaturalists are prepared to learn from the naturalists? Might the naturalistic and antinaturalistic streams flow into one river? These are questions to bear in mind as we turn to Sartre's rival doctrinaire in the drama of the forties—Bertolt Brecht.

... misunderstood naturalism ... believed that art consists in repro-
ducing a piece of nature in a natural way. But ... the greater naturalism ... seeks out the points where great battles take place.

AUGUST STRINDBERG

# 9. FROM STRINDBERG

# TO BERTOLT BRECHT

## I

WHEN ONE OF THE BEST JUDGES OF DRAMA SAID THAT THE
more original playwrights of the twenties "start completely
afresh," he listed only antinaturalists. The antinaturalists always
get the credit for originality. Actually the naturalists were just
as much in revolt. In a sense they were twice as much in revolt,
since they rejected not only the antinaturalistic styles—such as
Expressionism—but the established Naturalistic styles of the
nineties. They wanted to be more naturalistic still.

Of all the attempts to bring onto the stage even more of life,
even less embellished by histrionics, Epic Theater is probably
the most far-reaching. And though the ideas of Epic Theater
may be known in America, if at all, by way of certain productions of the Federal Theater, by way of certain particular ideas

such as the Living Newspapers in which Arthur Arent presented the current news by means of actors, by way of certain
things in Marc Blitzstein, Paul Green, Thornton Wilder, it is
still necessary to go back to some of the main sources of these
phenomena, not because they are the sources but because they
are the purest and often the best examples of the genre. It is
necessary, in short, to investigate the work and habitat of Bertolt Brecht, the unacknowledged fountainhead of so much in
the theater of the past twenty years. For even the best imitations
of Brecht—such as the rather sketchy extravaganzas of W. H.
Auden and Christopher Isherwood—are no index to the
original.

The seedbed of Epic drama was that strange, exciting, im-
permanent state of affairs—the culture of the Weimar Republic.
Although Epic did not make such a noise in the world as did
Expressionism, it nevertheless began with the first flush of the
fourth modernism immediately after the First World War.
Even before that critics had spoken of the *Episierung des Dramas*
—the making-over of drama into epic—when Gerhart Hauptmann
wrote his episodic *Die Weber* ["The Weavers"]. The Naturalism
of the nineties was a first step toward Epic, for the general
loosening of form brought many dramas into existence that
were narrative rather than "well-made plays." The three-vol-
ume play *Die letzten Tage der Menschheit* ["The Last Days of
Mankind"], written by the great Viennese satirist Karl Kraus
during the First World War, is a giant Epic Drama of war and
peace. When the early twenties are thoroughly chronicled many
kindred phenomena will be found.

One therefore takes with a pinch of salt the assumption made
by Mr. Erwin Piscator in his book *Das politische Theater* ["The
Political Theater"] that Epic Theater was invented by him. But
I do not mean to belittle his services to the theater. His work
illustrates better than anything else the "starting completely
afresh" which the naturalistic theater, the theater of the outer
world, undertook at the same time as the theater of the inner

world. To comprehend just how far the repudiation of the play, the unified drama, could go in favor of Epic slices of life one must follow Mr. Piscator's own account.

According to *Das politische Theater,* the first Epic Drama was a production of Piscator's in 1924 at which he used (in addition to actors) films and placards. There is a record in the book of another 1924 production entitled *Revue Roter Rummel* ["The Rowdy Red Revue"] which Piscator composed and executed with one Gasbarra "whom," he writes, "the Party had sent me." An eye-witness account is provided:

> It was a pilgrimage for the masses. As we approached, hundreds were standing in the street and vainly trying to get in. Workers exchanged blows to get seats. In the hall everything full and jam-packed. The air enough to make you faint. But faces beamed—on fire for the start of the production. Music. The lights go out. Silence. In the audience two men are quarreling. People are shocked. The dispute continues in the gangway. The footlights are switched on and the disputants appear before the curtain. They are two workmen talking about their situation. A Gentleman in a top hat steps up. Bourgeois. He has his own *Weltanschauung* and invites the disputants to spend an evening with him. Up with the curtain! First scene. Now it goes snip-snap. Ackerstrasse—Kurfuerstendamm. Tenements—cocktail bars. Porter resplendent in blue and gold—a begging war cripple. Fat paunch and thick watch chain. Match vendors and collectors of cigaret stubs. Swastika—Vehm murders—*Was machst du mit dem Knie—Heil dir im Siegerkranz* [popular song and patriotic anthem]. Between the scenes: Screen, movie, statistical figures, pictures! More scenes. The begging war veteran is thrown out by the porter. A crowd gathers in front of the place. Workmen rush

in and destroy the cocktail bar. The audience co-
operates. What a whistling, shouting, milling . . .
unforgettable!

Pretty crude stuff! But there is method in Piscator's callowness.
Let us look at the program of *Trotz Alledem* ["For All That"]
1925, when "the Communist Party told us to arrange a production in the Grosses Schauspielhaus on the Berlin Party Day."
This production was a historical review in twenty-four scenes
with films in between:

> Scene I: Berlin expecting war. Potsdam Square.
> Scene II: Meeting of the Social Democratic Section
> of the Reichstag, July 25, 1914.
> Scene III: In the Kaiser's Castle, Berlin, August 1,
> 1914. . . .

After the final scene comes "the rising of the proletariat: Lieb-
knecht lives!" and a chorus in which the audience joins. Although the whole thing is more of a demonstration than a
drama, the temper and the method of a new realism—narrative
realism—is here suggested. This is one of Brecht's starting
points. Others are indicated in Piscator's perhaps rather bump-
tious remarks, directed against both Expressionism and its contrary: "Not man's relation to himself, not his relation to God,
but his relation to society is the main issue." And again: "No
longer the individual with his private, personal destiny, but the
age itself, the destiny of the masses is the heroic factor of the
new dramaturgy." Above all: "Authors must learn to grasp the
material in all its factuality, the drama of the great simple
phenomena of life. The theater demands naïve, direct, uncom-
plicated, unpsychological effects."

One should acknowledge that Piscator failed, as much as
Reinhardt, to make headway beyond a certain point. He continued the unhappy tradition of making the director—himself—
the central figure in the theater. While at one moment he

pleads that this is because he cannot find any good dramatists, at another he registers a determination not to accept completed scripts, but to hand out material to authors and have them dramatize it along with him in the theater. This sounds chummy, but it would be really mischievous if the dramatist happened to be good. Piscator's book closes with the avowal that the theater has to be remodeled in its outlook, its dramaturgy, its architecture, and its technique, but that this cannot be done before the revolution. The masses under capitalism evidently do not wish to pay for a Piscator theater, and he is on the rocks just as if he had frankly addressed himself to the intelligentsia.

## II

Today Piscator's work is interesting as a prelude to Brecht. The root idea of Brecht's Epic Drama is expressed in the name. Of the three types of literature—epic, dramatic, and lyric—the first two are to be fused, and Brecht has no objection to admitting the lyrical element too. This is against all the laws of the elders. Most older critics insisted on keeping the three types separate just as college-educated movie critics today believe that the movies should be epic and that the drama should be—dramatic. There have long been those who favor separation of the genres; there have also been those who favor mingling. (In all spheres racial purity and cross-fertilization are rival allegiances.) There have long been two types of dramatic structure too: the open, diffuse play which starts early in the narrative and proceeds through it in many scenes and, on the other hand, the closed, concentrated play which has a late point of attack and lets us look back on the story from its climax—which is the play. In modern times we have been so schooled to respect the latter method—the method of Scribe, Dumas, and Ibsen—that it is regarded as "dramatic method" *pur sang*. Teachers of playwriting teach it as such. Critics of the novel have it in mind when they write of the dramatic type of novel. Indeed when we hear people saying that it was impudent of Shakespeare not to adopt the method, it is time to call a halt. Shakespeare's predecessors shared the impudence, and if the Greeks used the late point of attack they certainly had little else of the "dramatic method" which is found in its entirety only in the modern "well-made play" and—perhaps—in French classical tragedy. Most dramatic masterpieces are therefore, by this criterion, undramatic. The Greeks and the French use long Epic narrations. Shakespeare's open structure is copied by all his imitators from Goethe to Hugo. Brecht's Epic procedure is this open structure.

But the Epic Drama is more than a particular style of architecture. It drops other features of the Ibsenite play. The latter was built around a center, a crisis. Its unfolding was a gathering of clouds, its climax a thunder clap. With this pattern goes identification of the spectator with a protagonist, which presupposes a high degree of *illusion* as to his reality and a high degree of *suspense* in the telling of the tale. We have seen how the process of ever greater and greater concentration proceeded as far as Strindberg's *Creditors* and *Miss Julia,* of which latter Strindberg wrote that he had eliminated all act and scene divisions because: ". . . I have come to fear that our decreasing capacity for illusion might be unfavorably affected by intermissions during which the spectator would have time to reflect and to get away from the suggestive influence of the author-hypnotist." This pattern has not been much affected by modern experiments prior to Brecht. Expressionism abandons natural appearances but attempts to elicit an even more compelling drive of sympathetic emotion. It is obvious that dream and nightmare plays intensify the emotional participation of the audience in the play. We can best see the contrast between Epic Theater and earlier experimentalism by keeping the theory of Epic in mind while reading Nicolas Evreinov's account of his monodrama, an experimental form often regarded as the furthest departure from orthodoxy. In monodrama there is only one character to a play:

> The task of monodrama is to carry the spectator to the very stage so that he will feel that he is acting himself. . . . The "I," the acting character, is a bridge from the auditorium to the stage. . . . The spectator must know from the program with whom the author invites him to have a common life, in whose image he himself must appear. . . . Monodrama forces every one of the spectators to enter the situation of the acting character, to live his life, that is to say, to feel as he does and through illusion to think as he does . . . in the end it must be clear to the dramatist that if he wishes to represent the life of the spirit, he must deal not with external realities but with the internal reflections of the real objects, because for the psychology of a given person his subjective perception of the real object is important but not the object in a relation indifferent to him. . . .

Evreinov's monodrama is the furthest possible reach of the drama of individual psychology, the spirit, the subjective element, and it is coupled with a higher degree of identification than had ever before been demanded. If this "theater of myself" is at one extreme, Brecht is at the other. The following chart, made by Brecht himself, lets us see this more clearly:

| *The "Dramatic" Theater:* | *The Epic Theater:* |
|---|---|
| the stage embodies a sequence of events | the stage narrates the sequence |
| involves the spectator in an action and | makes him an observer but |
| uses up his energy, his will to action | awakes his energy |

| | |
|---|---|
| allows him feelings | demands decisions |
| communicates experiences | communicates pieces of knowledge |
| spectator is brought into an action | is placed in front of an action |
| is plied with suggestion | with arguments |
| sensations are preserved | till they become insights |
| man is given as a known quantity | man an object of investigation |
| man unalterable | alterable and altering |
| tense interest in the outcome | tense interest in what happens |
| one scene exists for another | each scene exists for itself |
| linear course of events | curved course of events |
| *natura non facit saltus* | *facit saltus* |
| the world is what it is | the world is what it is becoming |
| what man should | what man must |
| his instincts | his reasons |
| thought determines reality | social reality determines thought |

The facts before us already are sufficient to indicate that Epic Theater is naturalistic in a broad sense and is also a radical departure from most familiar types of drama. If Wagnerism is behind the antinaturalistic dramaturgies, as we have found it to be, it is interesting to find that Brecht protests against the *Schmelzprozess* by which Wagnerism merges one art with another, thus forfeiting the individuality of each. He demands singers who will act and narrate the piece and not pour forth their souls "which," he says, "are a private matter." For the Brechtian Epic Opera the orchestra will be small and disciplined. It is distinguished from Wagnerian opera as follows:

| *Wagnerism:* | *Epic Opera:* |
|---|---|
| the music enlivens | the music communicates |
| music heightening the text | music expounding the text |
| music asserting the text | music taking the text for granted |
| music illustrating | music taking a stand |
| music painting the psychic situation | music indicating behavior |

The fact that Brecht is not a Wagnerite does not of course make him a Zolaist. Zola had been known for his emphasis on determinism by heredity and environment and, secondarily, for a theory of presentation which in the theater was the highest degree of realism ever attained. Indeed dramatic critics often mean by the term Naturalism nothing more than a highly realistic staging in which everything is done to create the illusion that "a play is a slice of life." Real furniture and real beer replaced canvas and empty glasses. On the stage actors imitated the speech and deportment of men in the street. Playwrights co-operated by eliminating soliloquies, asides, songs, and other "interruptions."

By these tests Brecht is not a Naturalist at all. Epic staging and acting are not realistic in the manner of Antoine. They seek to destroy precisely the *illusion* of actuality which was the latter's chief aim. The Epic stage, accordingly, is artificial. Instead of assembling on the stage real rooms, buildings, and their furniture, it uses slides, charts, film projections, simultaneous scenes, and tableaux rolled across the stage on treadmills. Brechtian acting, like Pirandellian acting, is also anti-illusory. The actor must not pretend to *be* the character. He must play the role from the outside, not—as the Expressionists demanded— in a stylized and unindividual manner, but with as much finesse as Stanislavsky himself could have wished. The playwright for his part brings back choric commentary by introducing narrators, songs, soliloquies, and other "interruptive" devices.

Brecht is not a Naturalist; but he is a naturalist. He wishes to be as faithful as possible to objective facts. Precisely because he has abandoned the fourth wall theory of presentation, which contrary to the conscious intention of its upholders tended to make a dream world of reality, Brecht is able to be more, not less, of a naturalist than the Zola of *Thérèse Raquin*. Zola's Naturalistic theater, dedicated to actuality, was a theater of illusion, phantasmagoria, and—it might even be maintained— escape. It differed from its ostensible opposite Neo-Romanticism in that one escaped to an ugly not to a beautiful island. Now the "unrealistic" elements in Epic staging are all devoted to imparting a greater sense of the actual world. They say to the audience: "The actual world exists and it is our subject. But this play and this stage are not it." Zolaism, by saying: "The action on the stage is not a play at all but real life," created what an Epic dramatist would consider a sophisticated form of illusionism, unnaturalness, and theatricality.

The genus naturalism is a much broader thing than the species of the nineties. Negatively in its repudiation of the realm of dream and subjectivity, positively in its primary concern with the external, social world and the forces that move it, Epic Drama is in the broad tradition that I have called naturalism. If Expressionism and Neo-Romanticism were a rebound from the earlier Naturalism, Epic Drama was a rebound from the New Romanticism and Expressionism. If the earlier Naturalism came in with the discovery of the "true meaning of life" in Darwinist science, the later Epic Drama came in with the discovery of the "true meaning of life" in Marxist science. "Today," says Brecht, "when the human being must be grasped as the totality of social relationships, only the Epic form can enable the dramatist to find a comprehensive image of the world. The individual, precisely the flesh and blood individual, can be understood only by way of the processes wherein and whereby he exists. The new dramaturgy must acquire a form which will not make use of throbbing suspense, but will have a suspense in the relationship of its scenes which will charge each other with tension. This form will therefore be anything but a stringing together of scenes such as we find in revues."

*Only* the Epic form will do! Like his opposite number Cocteau, who says that "pure" theater should be the only kind, Brecht mars his highly interesting suggestions with dogmatism and oversimplification. His defense of the theater of objectivity, for instance, is as ingenuous as Piscator's. In one essay he goes so far as to complain of the fact that "until now the theater has been a medium for the self-expression of the artist." Unlike the language of the scientist, he continues, "dramatic imagery has sought rather to construct an independent world of emotion—to organize subjective sensations." Brecht assumes that the drama of subjectivity is very easy to manage: "for this purpose neither accuracy nor responsibility is required." Luckily, after all these centuries of inaccuracy and irresponsibility, salvation is at hand:

> In recent decades, however, a new kind of theater has developed—one which sets itself the goal of an accurate picture of the world. . . . The artist who belongs to this theater no longer attempts to create his world. . . . His purpose is to create images informative of the [external] world rather than of himself. . . . The artist must refashion his whole method to suit a new purpose.
>
> The visionary ignores discoveries made by others; the desire for experiment is not among the mental traits of the seer. Unlike the visionary and the seer, the artist in pursuit of a new goal finds no subliminal apparatus ready to serve him. The inner eye has never needed microscope or telescope. The outer eye needs both.

Brecht assumes here that the individual self is only a repulsive "subliminal apparatus," a source of foolish visions and dangerous illusions. Even if it were, that would be no reason for ignoring it; if the artist's mind is so strange a beast it should be put under close observation. Obviously Brecht is either parroting the clap-trap of scientism or giving vent to that hatred of the self which is the root of all too much of the altruism and social conscience of our time. Even more than Bernard Shaw, Brecht habitually overstates any proposition that is serviceable to his art. Such a passage as I have just quoted should in itself be proof that Epic theory cannot always be taken literally. It does not even square with Brecht's practice. He does not eliminate stage-illusion and suspense; he only reduces their importance. Sympathy and identification with the characters are not eliminated; they are counterpoised by deliberate distancing.

"The effect of genius," said Longinus, two thousand years ago, "is not to persuade or convince the audience, but rather to transport them out of themselves. . . . The object of poetry is to enthrall." Brecht says: "I do not like plays to contain pathetic overtones, they must be convincing like court pleas. The main thing is to teach the spectator to reach a verdict." Well: it is legitimate that some of the purposes of poetry should change in two thousand years, but one doubts if they have really changed as much as Brecht suggests. Certainly the modern drama—as we have amply seen—has been much more inclined to persuade and convince than was premodern drama, nor am I one of those who regret it. But there is no need to exaggerate. Like Shaw's criticism of Shakespeare, Brecht's denunciation of pathetic overtones has more significance as an attack on contemporary sentimentalism than it has literal truth. But it is not really necessary to pulverize Euripides, Shakespeare, and Racine —the masters of pathetic overtones—in order to scold Sudermann and Barrie.

The disproof of Brecht's theory is Brecht's practice. His art makes up for his criticism. In his art there is stage-illusion, suspense, sympathy, identification. The audience is enthralled and —most important of all—the highly personal genius of Brecht finds expression. The apparently "objective" presentation of facts is for Brecht, as it was for Zola, an opportunity for individual and "subjective" expression. I do not mean that Brecht and Zola are in the end as subjective as Sartre and Evreinov. That would be to replace overstatement with overstatement. I mean that no work of art is wholly "objective" or "subjective." It is a matter of emphasis. In his theoretic pronouncements Brecht carries the naturalistic emphasis to an impossible extreme—impossible, that is, in practice. It follows that his practice must be either a catalogue of failures or inconsistent with the theory. The latter is the truth. Brecht is a naturalist but non-naturalistic elements are of more and more importance as his art develops.

The dramatic art of Brecht has so far gone through four phases. In the first, his apprenticeship, he took up the problems of the theater where Strindberg and Wedekind left them, that is to say, he had to think through the whole question of form almost from scratch. To help himself in this task he studied, and made adaptations from, Chinese, Elizabethan, and Spanish plays; and before the end of the twenties he had written four outstanding original works. Two were plays in a style of highly personal naturalism, two were operettas equally idiosyncratic. Only the last of all these to be written—his version of the *Beggar's Opera*—is fully developed Epic Theater. Hence it is the culmination of Brecht's first period.

If the first phase is cynical and brilliant and very much of the twenties, the second is stark and solemn and very much of the thirties. If the works of the twenties permitted hostile critics to dismiss Brecht as a cabaret wit, the works of the thirties permitted them to dismiss him an "artist in uniform," a "minstrel of the GPU." Though Brecht's bleakest, barrenest works belong to this period, so also does his *Saint Joan of the Stockyards,* a rich satire, and a kind of prelude to the third phase, the first years of exile from Germany, during which Brecht wrote two full-scale dramatic fantasies about the Nazi movement. But probably the major works of the middle thirties are *Mother Courage and Her Sons* and *Fear and Misery of the Third Reich*. In the first Brecht withdrew from the current struggle to compose another Epic play in verse and prose, in song and monosyllabic conversation, a sardonic and circumstantial record, based on the seventeenth-century writer Grimmelshausen, of the process of war. In *Fear and Misery* Brecht and the Third Reich are for the first time face to face. The title is a parody of Balzac's *Glory and Misery of the Courtesans,* and the work itself —a portrait of one cell after another in the social organism—is a twentieth-century *comédie humaine* in miniature. In a series of over twenty scenes, unconnected by characters or plot, connected only by theme, the people of Hitler's Germany are revealed. Between the scenes a choric voice is heard, and (in the shorter stage version) a group of Nazi soldiers sings Brecht's words to the tune of their party hymn at the beginning and end of each act.

Though the narrative structure, the interruptions, and many other technical devices are Epic, one of Brecht's most friendly critics has suggested that in general the play need not be taken as Epic but can be interpreted as good drama with no theoretical strings attached. Certainly the more mature experimentalism of this play is able to draw on established methods much more than could the severe Epic plays in which Brecht first tried out his ideas. Such a scene as "The Jewish Wife" is in the nineteenth-century tradition and would have been accepted by Antoine for the Théâtre Libre. *Fear and Misery* is the *fullest* of the plays of the thirties. Its new use of realism, of strong situation, tableau, innuendo, charade, should prove to those who feared the contrary that Brecht is willing not only to exclude established forms and ideas from his theater but also to bring them back again in new ways.

But enough cataloguing. When we come to Brecht's latest phase, the phase of the nineteen-forties, I have to assume, as with Sartre, that my readers have not seen or read the plays. I accordingly propose to round out this chapter with two more rather detailed exegeses.

## III

Like the two plays of Sartre, the two most interesting plays of Brecht's latest manner—*The Good Woman of Sezuan* and *The Caucasian Circle of Chalk*—are moralities "showing what kind of things a man chooses or avoids." They are both parables in Eastern settings and somewhat in the manner of Chinese theater. Both are Epic in their dramaturgy: the main story is framed, in one play by a singer and a chorus who act as narrators, in the other by alternate scenes in which the gods discuss the action. From time to time characters talk directly to the audience. There is suspense, but it is minimized. Each scene is interesting for itself and not as preparation. . . .

*Der gute Mensch von Sezuan* ("The Good Woman of Sezuan") tells how three of the gods come down to earth to learn if there is any goodness in human beings. They begin by looking for someone hospitable enough to offer them a night's lodging, and find nobody but the little Chinese prostitute Shen Te. She proves indeed to be the only human being who is thoroughly good, and the rest of the story is that of her life after the gods set her up in a little store with money of her own.

Very soon Shen Te finds herself imposed upon by the unscrupulous poor. A family of eight dumps itself on her doorstep. She finds that the store is in a bad location, that the rent is too high, that the tradesmen swindle her. Who is to pay her bills? Shen Te is hustled by her housemates into inventing a cousin named Shui Ta who is to settle her debts. Our surprise when a Shui Ta arrives and does so is mitigated by the discovery (made by the audience only) that he is Shen Te wearing a mask. At first Shui Ta is intended to be only a temporary helper. When he arranges for the marriage of Shen Te to the wealthy banker Shu Fu it seems that his services can be dispensed with. But no. The young flier Yang Sun, too poor to pursue the art of flying, unable to get a job, is about to hang himself from a willow tree when Shen Te sees him and falls in love. They agree to marry. Although Shui Ta discovers that Yang is marrying chiefly for money, Shen Te does not seem able to resist him. Only at the last moment, when she is certain that Yang Sun will prevent her paying her debts in order to satisfy his ambitions with her money, does she draw back.

Returning to meet her monetary needs alone, and finding herself pregnant, Shen Te again calls upon Shui Ta, who rapidly becomes a Tobacco King, a successful capitalist paying starvation wages and overcrowding the living quarters of his workers. Beginning at the bottom, Yang Sun works his way up in Shui Ta's factory until he is a manager. Meanwhile Shen Te's time grows near. The waistline of Shui Ta is seen to expand. Yang Sun hears a woman's sobbing in Shui Ta's room and feels sure that Shen Te is imprisoned there. Shui Ta is brought before a court of justice to account for his cousin's disappearance.

In the final scene of the play the three gods act as Shui Ta's judges. Shen Te recognizes them. Asking for the court to be cleared, she removes her mask and confesses all. But the judges are not angry. They are glad to find their one good human being again:

> THE FIRST GOD. Say no more, unhappy woman! What are we to think, we who are so glad to have found you again!
>
> SHEN TE. But I must tell you that I am the bad man whose misdeeds have been reported to you by everybody here!
>
> THE FIRST GOD. The good man whose good deeds have been reported by everybody!
>
> SHEN TE. No, the bad man too!

Shen Te is desperate. How is she to go on living? What about her baby? The gods are not worried. "Only be good and all will be well," is their parting counsel. Hymning the praises of the good woman of Sezuan, they ascend into heaven on a pink cloud.

In other words it is impossible to be good, in the traditional sense of altruistic, gentle, loving, in a world that lives by egoism, rapacity, and hate. A Christian might argue: "You can't change the world. All you can do is to exercise the Christian virtues in your own small circle." Brecht replies: "This is topsy-turvy reasoning. Your small circle is no circle but a segment of a large circle. The segment has no independence. It can move only when the whole circle moves. *Only* by altering the world can goodness become practical." Shen Te wished to be kind. But on one occasion she finds herself allowing an old couple to be ruined because she does not pay her debt to them. On another occasion she will not help a poor man to find redress for an injury willfully inflicted by the Barber Shu Fu because at the time she is trying to win Shu Fu's lucrative hand. In order to survive, the good girl needs the assistance of the brutal exploiter. And when she appeals to the gods she receives as answer: "Are we to confess that our laws are lethal? Are we to repudiate our laws? Never! Is the world to be changed? How? By whom? No: everything is all right."

The theme of *The Good Woman of Sezuan* is not, and is not meant to be, hard to grasp. Clarity is the first requisite of didacticism. The surprising thing is the way Brecht makes his lessons into works of art. Obviously there were many ways of bungling the treatment of the Sezuan story. It could lose force through being too quaint and charming. It could fall short of art if the allegory were too earnest and ponderous or if the propaganda were too eager and importunate. Brecht manages to escape these pitfalls, and the result is something entirely new in didactic theater. Although the message is firm and sharp, it is not coaxed into us by pathos or thrown at us in anger. It is worked out by craftsmanship, that is, by Epic procedure and Brechtian characterization. The dialogue, delicate but not quaint, strong but not heavy, poetic but not decorative, is diversified with songs such as only Brecht could write, using a manner which has ripened down the years since his *Beggar's Opera*. The mock naïveté, the speeches to the audience, the witty exchanges, the Chinese conventions, go to make a rich texture and a rapid tempo. The big scenes in the grand manner—such as the wedding (which never takes place) of Shen Te and the final trial scene—give the piece a dignity and a spaciousness that Brecht has perhaps only once before achieved—in his biographical play *Galileo*.

## IV

*Der kaukasische Kreidekreis* ("The Caucasian Circle of Chalk") opens with a discussion of the rights to a piece of land between two groups of Russians who return to it after the Nazis have been driven out. The question is: upon what principle should the question be settled? The main action of the play is an answer to the question.

During a civil war the governor's baby is abandoned by its mother (who is more interested in saving her fine clothes) and brought up by the servant girl Grusche. Like Shen Te, Grusche is driven into wrong actions by sheer necessity. To guarantee the child a respectable home and a decent upbringing, above all to free the child from being thought her bastard, she consents to marry. After all, she can say to herself, the prospective husband is ostensibly dying. Unfortunately the latter turns out to be very much alive, and when Grusche's sweetheart returns from the wars he finds her married and—apparently—a mother. Without giving her a chance to tell him the whole story he leaves in despair. Her "bad" marriage, entered upon with "good" motives, is having mixed results: bad for herself, bad for her lover, good for the child. There are five acts, and this is the end of the third.

The fourth act is the story of an eccentric low character named Azdak. The vicissitudes of civil war make this almost Shakespearian rogue into a judge. He passes the most unusual judgments—in a case of rape he holds the woman responsible on account of her alluring buttocks—but they always favor simple folk and not their exploiters. Act V is the comedy of Azdak in his capacity of judge under the rebel government. Later the original government is restored and, since Azdak has by chance saved the life of one of its high officials, he is reappointed judge under the restored regime. One of the cases before him is that of Grusche, charged with having stolen the late governor's child. Azdak places the governor's wife and Grusche in a chalk circle with the child; they are both to take hold of it; the one who pulls hardest and gets the child out of the circle wins the lawsuit. The mother pulls violently and wins. Whereupon Azdak reverses the decision and gives the child to Grusche, who loves the child too much to do it harm. He also gives her a divorce so that she can marry her sweetheart and all can end happily. The chorus states the principle

> that what there is
> shall belong to those who are good for it, thus
> the children to the maternal that they thrive
> the carriages to good drivers that they are driven well
> and the valley to the waterers that it shall bear fruit.

In general what I said in praise of *The Good Woman of Sezuan* applies also to *The Caucasian Circle of Chalk*, which belongs next on the shelf to it. If there is an additional reason to praise the latter, it is that it contains one of Brecht's best-drawn characters—the inimitable Azdak. Now Brecht has often been accused of a lack of interest in the individual, and no doubt many a flippancy can be quoted from his essays, notes, or conversation to this effect. We have seen that the theorist Brecht professes that the individual is unreal except as the sum of social relations. All the same the best characters in his plays are individuals in a perfectly conventional sense. They have the same quality as the characters in "bourgeois" and prebourgeois literature. Whatever his intentions or his rationalizations,

Brecht is not an out-and-out collectivist who cannot see the individual trees for the social wood.

There is a Brecht below the political level, a Brecht whose traits gradually become clear to those who absorb his works. (I use the pompous phrase "absorb his works" to underline the necessity of taking Brecht seriously and reading him attentively, which very few of his critics have done.) Henry James said: "When vigorous writers have reached maturity, we are at liberty to gather from their works some expression of a total view of the world they have been so actively observing. This is the most interesting thing their works offer us." And since some such assumption has underlain my investigation of our greatest modern playwrights Ibsen, Shaw, and Strindberg, I think it applicable also to Brecht. The political Brecht is a socialist. Beneath the socialist is what we might call the Confucian—by which I mean that Brecht's economic interpretation of human life, his materialism, is at the service of a finely humane, ironic, salty appreciation of normal experience. When he defends the normal, the ordinary, and the common, he is not therefore championing vulgarity and mediocrity; he is championing human nature. It is this that makes the average socialist writing appear bourgeois by comparison, for the average socialist writing is socialist only, so to speak, in terms of party policy. It is this that makes Brecht a poet of democracy in a sense deeper than that applied to the zealous supporters of particular causes. Today his is an uncommon sort of belief in the common man.

It was complained against some of Brecht's early plays that the people in them were unheroic and unsaintly, unsatanic also and therefore "undramatic." Their life had none of the memories or the high purposes of life in Shakespeare or Ibsen. There may have been justice in the complaint. Yet the point is that Brecht does not find "vegetative" life, that is, common, happy-go-lucky experience as disgusting as did the elegant critics of the conservative journals during the Weimar Republic. I do not mean that he loves the suburbs or that he worships the workman. Consider this little piece of his entitled "The Mask of Evil":

> *An meiner Wand hängt ein japanisches Holzwerk*
> *Maske eines bösen Dämons, bemalt mit Goldlack.*
> *Mitfühlend sehe ich*
> *Die geschwollenen Stirnadern, andeutend*
> *Wie anstrengend es ist, böse zu sein.**

This is a human and moral study. It is hard to be bad. Evil is a mask. The corollary of this is that it is natural to be good. Although within a framework of injustice and error, it is not easy to be natural—in fact it is impossible, as we learn in *The Good Woman of Sezuan*—that is no disproof of the original proposition. Before we can be natural again, before we can be good, there will be much struggle, and we ourselves will have swollen veins; that is the political problem. Its presupposition is a Rousseauistic belief in the natural, an almost Chinese willingness to rejoice in vegetative life.

Not that satisfaction in the processes of life is enough. Brecht represents goodness also as dynamic. "Great is the temptation of goodness," sings the chorus in *The Circle of Chalk* as Grusche makes up her mind to save the governor's child whatever the cost to herself. Temptation indeed! An almost futile temptation in a society where justice can be done only through flukes and eccentricities, only through the canny, queer horse sense of the wise fool Azdak. Yet despite the fact that "goodness is impossible" the Grusches and the Shen Tes exist and from time to time succumb to the fatal "temptation of goodness."

---

* On my wall hangs a Japanese woodcarving
  Mask of an evil demon, painted over with gold.
  Pityingly I see
  The swollen veins of his brow intimating
  How great a strain it is to be evil.

## V

The real character of Brecht might be illuminated by comparison with Jean-Paul Sartre, a comparison of Epic Theater, the theater of the outer eye, with Existential Theater, the theater of the inner eye. There is a basis for comparison in that, of the plays analyzed here, one by each playwright gives a picture of things as they are and should not be *(Behind Closed Doors* and *The Good Woman of Sezuan)*, and one by each playwright *(The Flies* and *The Caucasian Circle of Chalk)* shows the working out of positive and right moral principles. The differences are obvious. The starting point is different, the atmosphere is different, the philosophical background is different, the style is different, the emphasis is different. Brecht, I imagine, might easily think of Sartre as—in Arthur Koestler's terminology—a yogi, a believer in change purely from within, and Sartre might easily think of Brecht as a commissar, a believer in change purely from without.

Both would be wrong. We saw that Sartre's Zarathustrian exile is no escape, that Orestes is, on the contrary, utterly *engagé,* that self-fulfillment is for him a moral and social as well as a personal and spiritual thing. We can see too that Brecht does not set up society as an abstraction against the individual. His aim is to change the world so that the goodness of a Shen Te can come into effective existence. His preoccupation is the amiable common humanity of a water-carrier, the unsung heroism of a member of the underground who has to accept ostracism with a good grace after he returns from the concentration camp, the enlarging of the area of human knowledge and control at the hands of a Galileo.

"Neither the saint nor the revolutionary can save us," says Mr. Koestler, "only the synthesis of the two." If he means that both the inner and the outer eye are necessary to men, then nobody will disagree. Certainly these four plays of Sartre and Brecht call for some combination of the two. Sartre is no yogi.

The yogi is an exile without being *engagé*. He could say with the immature Orestes "what a superb absence is my soul." Brecht is no commissar. The commissar wants to have the world changed—as in the end Shen Te does—but he has not Shen Te's kindness as his motive, he is no victim to the "temptation of goodness." Both Brecht and Sartre are attempting a synthesis of the individual and the social. They differ in coming at it from opposite directions. Brecht reaches the individual via the collectivity, Sartre reaches the collectivity via the individual.

They are rival revolutionaries. Brecht's revolution is Marx's. It is "from without," for man is not independent of "externals." Sartre's revolution is—shall we say Nietzsche's? the Existentialists'? Christ's? It is "from within," for man is not simply a piece of the landscape. Yet Sartre's "inner" revolution leads to the liberation of Argos, and Brecht's "outer" revolution would bring "inner" peace to Shen Te. Sartre's hell is personal, yet a vote of censure against a society is inferred. Brecht's hell—Sezuan—is social, yet it is its meaning in individual lives that is measured. Perhaps Sartre's argument starts from a metaphysic, but its significance spreads out over the natural life of man. Perhaps Brecht's argument is simply socialism, but its significance is seen much more concretely, dramatically, poetically than in so-called "proletarian literature". . . .

If the ideas in these Epic and Existential plays are not incompatible, their dramaturgy makes one think that the naturalistic and antinaturalistic traditions may also be coming closer together. We found in the last chapter that Sartre was appreciably closer to naturalism than were his predecessors in the tradition of the Vieux Colombier. Brecht, for his part, has learned more from the modern antinaturalist theater than perhaps any other playwright who aims at an accurate picture of the outer world. When, to secure a more faithful version of the external world, Brecht gave up more and more of the methods of stage realism in favor of Chinese and other conventions he was using nonnaturalistic techniques for naturalistic ends. He was mixing the two primary elements of art—nature and convention—in a new way. When his plays took the form of operettas and fantasies, parables and abstract moralities, he was approaching a synthesis of what the naturalists and their antagonists had intended.

"X," writes one of our critics, "brings to his form of didacticism a creative and critical skill that has made ample use of the three most vitalizing tendencies in contemporary writing: the revolt against realism, the widening of the content of poetry, and the return to myth." X could be Sartre. It happens to be Brecht. The work of both encourages one to look forward to a future for drama. What kind of a future? It may be one in which older concepts of tragedy and comedy have little meaning. Even the dominance of naturalism, and the concomitant insurgency of antinaturalism, may be at an end. Who knows? Whatever the future for tragedy and comedy, for naturalism and non-naturalism, the work of Sartre and Brecht—in ways that are often different and sometimes the same—is a fairly adequate apologia for the playwright as thinker.

So that the Fault lies not in the Audience's desiring Absurdities but in those who know not how to give 'em anything else.

CERVANTES

I do not know whether the university will some day turn out playwrights; for the present, in all theatrical matters, the university is certainly the place to look to.

HENRY BECQUE

# 10. BROADWAY—

# AND THE ALTERNATIVE

### I

PROBABLY NOT MANY WOULD JOIN MR. BENNETT CERF IN DENY-
ing that the situation of the theater is today very problematic.
Most discussions of the problem, however, go wrong—not in
denying its existence but in regarding it as new and peculiar
to our generation, and thus in attributing it to some localized
cause, such as the rise of movies or the high Manhattan rents.
It should be recognized that the theater is almost always a problem. Over a century ago Carlyle wrote: "Nay, do not we English
hear daily for the last twenty years, that the Drama is dead,
or in a state of suspended animation: and are not medical men
sitting on the case, and propounding their remedial appliances,
weekly, monthly, quarterly, to no manner of purpose?" Such
statements are to be found not only in times of dramatic

drought but also in the harvest seasons. Looking back on the
eighteen-nineties today, we regard them as years of considerable
dramatic achievement; Bernard Shaw's *Dramatic Opinions,*
written at the time, tell another story. We think of the Restoration as the age of Congreve, yet the great comedian was very
inconspicuous in his own day, and his now acknowledged masterpiece was a total failure on the stage. Shakespeare, the most
read and the most performed of all dramatists, was probably
best known in his lifetime for his cheapest and rawest plays,
and a contemporary editor boasts that one of his best plays was
"never clapper-clawed by the hands of the vulgar."

The theater is always in trouble because its success depends
upon too rare a set of coincidences. A poem needs only an author
and a reader. A sonata needs a composer, a performer, and a
listener. Closer to the drama is the symphony, which requires
teamwork, co-ordination at the hands of a conductor, a large
audience, and a heap of money. The drama, however, boasting
of being a meeting place of all the arts, requires a too rare conjunction of economic, social, and artistic elements. Especially in
its synthetic manifestations, which include everything in musi-
cal-choreographic-spectacular-mimetic-rhetorical theater from
the Greeks to *Tannhäuser* and beyond, drama is the most impossible of the arts.

Yet the very citation of titles reminds us of its possibility. The
fact is that, while high theater has a harder time than any other
high art, the popular theater, dedicated to entertainment, and
today functioning chiefly on the screen and over the air, is perpetually the most flourishing of the arts. It is the art which most
excites children, savages, and all who are least conscious of
artistic leanings. It seems to be an inextinguishable and indis-
pensable art, an addiction more universal than smoking. It followed the doughboys to foxholes on tropical islands. It followed
the dehumanized, doubly "mechanized" divisions of the Third
Reich. It lures the schoolboy twice a week to the movies; it

entices the student to turn on the radio while supposedly studying.

Entertainment means the redemption of leisure time by a pleasing titillation of the senses and of that small part of the brain which the simplest jokes call into play. Entertainment is an infinitely complex industry devoted to the evocation of the crudest responses. In its modern form it presupposes an audience that is already tired, inclined to be bored, probably not educated and certainly not cultured, yet not totally illiterate, but acquainted with that segment of knowledge and sensibility provided by the radio and the press. The power of entertainment in modern life is shown by the fact that even the knowledge presupposed in entertainment is acquired through entertainment, for what is modern reporting and propaganda if not a cunning use of histrionic method in the commercial, political, and educational spheres? All information is nowadays supposed to be "entertainingly" presented, and the results are evident in radio news reports and radio advertising, in the screen popularization of musical and literary classics, and in schools where the pupils expect to be entertained by the teacher. The founders of democracy hoped and expected that universal suffrage would mean a sober presentation of issues to a people which would soberly weigh them. A recent development, however, is the setting of political slogans to hot jazz choral music and the staging of vast political pageants that would be the envy of a Roman emperor. At the center of these entertainments is the very symbol of entertainment itself, the man-god, hero, and totem animal of modern civilization, the film star.

The techniques of the theater, run wild, have taken over every other branch of public communication, especially in countries where industrialism and mechanization have gone furthest. The Salvation Army began the application of the methods of mass entertainment to religion, and visitors to Aimee Semple MacPherson's Los Angeles Temple know how far the idea has been carried since the days of General Booth. Northcliffe and

Hearst pursued the same art in politics, and Goebbels turned their skill into an industry. A Nazi rally, where masses of soldiers saluted and applauded and sang at given signals, where music, spectacle, and oratory combined in a macabre *gesamtkunstwerk,* and where the master tragi-comedian himself played systematically upon every group prejudice and stock response—this was at once the apotheosis and the nemesis of entertainment.

Entertainment has almost been the death of all the arts. How could music hope to survive the onslaughts of the popularizers? What room is there for Beethoven in a world where a hundred hacks make his music "more entertaining" by removing his individuality? How could literature survive the *Saturday Evening Post?* Recently a writer in that journal defended himself with the argument that Shakespeare also was a popular writer, not afraid to use as material the cliché absurdities of current convention. Great writers, he argued, come out of the hard school of commercial writing, not out of coteries. The hardheadedness of the remark and its one per cent of truth give it the color of plausibility, and while criticism remains unhistorical the argument is not easily disposed of. But history supplies the answers, and they are germane to our theme. To be popular in an aristocratic culture, like ancient Greece or Elizabethan England, is quite a different matter from being popular in a middle-class culture. Like Dr. Johnson, our critic is suspicious of those who do not write for money. And there is nothing wrong with money. It all depends on what is demanded of you in return. To earn his living Shakespeare had, for example, to acquire a highly complex literary language, far above the usage of his native Stratford; to earn his, the modern *Post* writer has to unlearn anything he might have learned from acknowledged classics, or from the depths of personal experience, and acquire the crude, vacuum-concealing lingo which titillates the miseducated sensibility.

That is only one factor among many, but it permits us to

glimpse the difference between Elizabethan and modern culture. Industrialism, capitalism, and the democratic movement created an unprecedented cultural situation; its problems are the subject of all the anti-industrialist, anti-capitalist, and anti-democratic literature which lovers of the arts have written in the past hundred and fifty years. The essence of the matter is that the extension of literacy to the previously illiterate majority created, not a nation of philosophers, but a nation of newspaper readers. In this context popularity takes on a new meaning.

Popularity is a very flexible term and an impossible criterion. Medieval and Chinese drama are "popular" in that they appeal to a totally illiterate populace; the "popular" *Post* is read by many college graduates and, perhaps, hardly at all by the least educated classes for whom the funnies and the pulps suffice. The pulps are "popular"; so is Somerset Maugham. The difference can be appreciated only by those who recognize the cultural stratification which has taken place in recent generations. While changes in the mechanics of communication and the promotion of democratic and religious ideas have in modern times brought men closer together, other forces have wrenched them apart. One need hardly mention nationalist politics, imperialist economics, and racial ideology. The same technology which brought men closer through mechanized transport and telegraphy kept them apart by the method of their manufacture, mass production. The kind of man they created was portrayed by Charlie Chaplin in *Modern Times*.

There is no need to linger over the general matter of middle-class culture. The point is that if the new conditions have significance for the culture as a whole, they have all the more significance for the drama, which has had the closest link with the people, possibly, of all the arts. In the days before general literacy, the drama was, with the sermon, the great bond between verbal culture and the people; in books on the drama one constantly reads that drama is the least esoteric, the most democratic of the arts. Drama critics are indeed never tired of asserting that great drama belongs to the people, and that obscurity and "rareness" are out of place on the stage; theorists of the drama insist on the communal character of theatrical experience and cite LeBon on the psychology of the crowd. Well and good. But what becomes of the drama in an age like ours when popular taste is debauched, when "entertainment" has a monopoly of public attention, when greedy capital controls production and consumption alike? Low-brow writers will repeat their argument that art, particularly dramatic art, is always an adjustment of an artist's purpose to public demand. But, as I have said, it all depends on what is demanded: if the public's demands, or the plutocrat's demands, are degrading, we shall not have dramatic art at all; which is the situation on Broadway today. To be sure, drama depends on an audience, upon common human experience, upon crowd psychology; but there are crowds and crowds. There is a difference between an audience of Athenians at a time when the Athenian citizenry represented, so we are told, one of the peaks of human and social development, an audience for whom a play was also an important rite, and a crowd of oddly miseducated twentieth-century folk who for years have been subjected to half-baked ideas and cheap sensations.

At this point someone will say that, at times when drama flourished, audiences were not always Periclean. They were often illiterate or frivolous or both. When Stanislavsky's audiences changed from the sophisticated upper classes of Tsarism to the ignorant peasantry and proletariat of the early Soviet years, this very aristocratic director was, after initial apprehension, delighted by the spontaneity and keenness of the latter, even when the play performed was *The Cherry Orchard*. Such facts prove that an ignorant audience can enjoy a great play. They do not prove that all ignorant audiences would enjoy that play or that even the same ignorant audience would enjoy every great play. They do not reveal how far such an audience understands the play, nor do they help us to settle what for us is the great problem, the problem not of the ignorant and illiterate but that of the half-literate, the possessors of the little knowledge which is a dangerous thing, the readers of the pulps and the Hearst press, and even the comparative high-brows who read *Collier's* and the *Saturday Evening Post*. Today it is almost inconceivable that any drama could satisfy the canons of the most exacting criticism and also be popular. Already in the nineteenth century, Matthew Arnold wondered whether drama had become an impossibility. The vulgarization and consequent social stratification of culture had gone too far, he seems to have thought, and modern British society in particular lacked the homogeneity which drama requires. Some critics have met the situation by lowering their standards. They consider the exacting critics *too* exacting, and erupt occasionally in jibes against high-brows, aesthetes, sophisticates, and coteries. More disconcerting are the arguments of those who are distressed by mediocrity yet who are reluctant to draw revolutionary conclusions.

*Theatre Arts,* the only theatrical magazine of repute in the English-speaking world, frequently publishes such arguments. One of its most intelligent writers, Mr. George Beiswanger, has gone so far as to discourage us from even *trying* to make a home for drama in America. The drama, he observes, has little past and little present here, and there is no reason to suppose that it will have a future—"which may or may not be too bad," he adds; "after all, there is no moral compulsion, is there, for any one type or branch of art to continue in existence?" Mr. Beiswanger thinks that vaudeville will do instead of drama. "Such a masterpiece" as *Oklahoma!* possesses a "perfection" which has "deep subconscious roots." At last the Composite Art Work has triumphed:

> There is one stage today on which all the theater
> arts unite in happy combination to produce theater
> that is sheer, ample, and without inner tension or

quarrel. I refer again to the musical stage, to such natural triumphs of the American theater imagination as
*Lady in the Dark* and *Oklahoma!* Grant that these are
not Shakespeare nor Euripides nor Dante. But they
come close to being Aristophanes or Molière. Increasingly they approach opera. And they are our own, genuine outpourings of American temperament, honest
mirrorings of what we are. An age cannot fight itself.
It has to make what theater it can. . . .

Here is a revived and jazzified Wagnerism which does not omit
Wagner's nationalism and praise of the soil nor his belief in
the historical inevitability of his success. One is tempted to
meet assertion with assertion by retorting bluntly: *Oklahoma!*
is *not* in the same class as *Tartuffe,* commercial musical comedy
does *not* approach great opera. . . . And what can an age do
except fight itself? The great minds of the modern age are the
great fighters against the modern age. An age can and must fight
itself.

But the point in Mr. Beiswanger's argument which most concerns us here is less fundamental. Mr. Beiswanger rejoices in
song and dance and *décor,* in the *élan* of stage performance
which, though indescribable, may yet be stronger in one's experience than many a playwright's mere words. The playwright's
work Mr. Beiswanger, following professional usage, calls a
"script," and it is, he tells us, the mere shadow of the theatrical
reality. Mr. Beiswanger's way of looking at things is symptomatic. His remarks remind us of the fact that popularized Wagnerism is probably the most widespread dramatic theory—or the
most widely held preconception—of our day. The assumption
is that theater is primarily a musico-visual art, an art of spectacle,
movement, and melody. It is ballet, it is opera. But it is not
drama. The actor is never at more than one remove from the
dancer. Unity and character are imposed upon this composite
art work by an artist-director.

Since the decline of Zolaist Naturalism some such theory has underlain much of the most adventurous theatrical endeavor. So as not to place all the responsibility of it on Mr. Beiswanger— who does not subscribe to every article of the doctrine—we can call the theory *theatricalism*. It goes back to Max Reinhardt, who made the theatrical director the artistic dictator in the world of drama (though like dictators in politics he was subject to approval by the men of money). Max Reinhardt began as an actor, and when he turned to dramatic dictatorship he at first produced those plays which his actor's good instincts led him to approve: he introduced Wilde, Maeterlinck, Wedekind, and Strindberg to a large public. Theatricalism, however, led him astray, and he introduced a yet wider public to *The Miracle* and a Shakespeare with elephantiasis. The name of Gordon Craig should also come in again here. Where Reinhardt elevated the director, Craig elevated the stage-designer above the dramatist, and in one of his most vigorous flights of theatricalism he succeeded in subordinating the twin genius of Ibsen and Duse to the megalomania of Craig. The final refutation of Craig was that so many of his designs could not be executed at all; they were pretentious fantasies. Reinhardt's theatricalism ended by his losing contact with the drama, Craig's by his losing contact with the theater itself. The wheel had come full circle.

The theatricalist view is even more suspect in its relation to the actor. It is of course refreshing to realize anew that the art of acting is akin to dancing, yet the devotion of actors to psychological analyses should not be interpreted as a passing fancy of nineteenth-century realism. From the Greeks to Ibsen the actor has represented, by elocution as well as by movement, human character and human destiny. There is no apparent reason why he should forfeit the riches of his heritage even for a dancer's birthright. When drama takes on the abstract character of pure music or pure dance it ceases to be drama; when, as a compromise, it tries to combine the abstract with the concrete it is invariably the drama, the words, that suffer. The words are the weakest element in *Oklahoma!* They are the weakest ingredient in the Wagnerian brew, though Wagner guarded against the weakening by projecting as much as possible of the drama into the music.

The theatricalists try to make drama without the help of a dramatist. Even where the high theater has had 'most scope—in Soviet Russia and Weimar Germany—there has been more theatrical and technical than dramatic and creative talent. Such dramatists as Georg Kaiser scarcely exist without the boon of a modernistic staging; it is the poverty of such an imagination that does indeed justify the critic in speaking of scripts and libretti. Twenty years ago dozens of books announced a theatrical renaissance which had either just begun in Russia or Germany or was about to flower in America or England. The evidence of the renaissance was chiefly drawn from stage-design and directing; ten years later it was found in the rightness (*i.e.* leftness) of the author's social philosophy. Now many productions in these decades equaled or surpassed *Oklahoma!* and retained also a certain seriousness—at least of intention. *Oklahoma!* insofar as it is unorthodox at all, represents the experimentalism of the earlier decades degraded, now that the faiths and affirmations of those years are out of favor, into "middlebrow" terms. Lacking the seriousness of purpose, the sternness of outlook, the originality of yesterday's experiments, *Oklahoma!* proclaims the bankruptcy of theatricalism.

I have already formulated the truth that few have cared to assert, as follows: *a drama not verbalized is a drama not dramatized.* The dramatist not only charts out a plan of procedure, he conceives and realizes a work of art which is already complete —except for technical reproduction—in his head, and which expresses by verbal image and concept a certain attitude to life. He is a writer, a poet, before he is a musician or a choreographer. Wagner of course showed that many dramatic elements can be embodied in orchestral music; silent movies showed how much can be done with the visual element alone; but if you add Wagner to Eisenstein and multiply by ten you still do not have a Shakespeare or an Ibsen. This is not to say that drama is *better* than music, dancing, or the visual arts. It is different.

The comparison of a script to a musical score is apt insofar as performance is the proper mode of presentation for both; and it is true that the director's function is properly that of the conductor, namely, to be utterly faithful and subordinate to the composer. Yet if the comparison be submitted to the crude test of common experience it is manifestly inexact. Even the professional musician does not read scores with ease or relish; but from our childhood we have innocently cherished the "scripts," however shadowy, of Shakespeare. Are we to forfeit that pleasure at the bidding of even very unacademic theorists?

Here we abut upon the old and vexed theme of the reading of plays as opposed to seeing them in the theater. The spokesmen of "theater arts" have rendered good service in insisting that good drama is always good theater and should therefore be performed; but Mr. Beiswanger gives the show away (almost literally) when he argues that good theater is always good drama or that, if it is not, drama does not matter anyway. The defenders of the arts of the theater are infected by the commodities of the theater once they forget that all the arts of the theater are means to one end: the correct presentation of a poem. It goes without saying that a dramatic poem is a particular kind of poem; that the dramatic poet must visualize stage action in all its intricacy; and that there is undramatic poetry as the theatricalists always remind us; I am reminding them—since they end by throwing out poetry altogether—that there is also *dramatic* poetry. Now poetry which is dramatic, being shaped to the human throat, and directed at the human heart and head, cannot but be readable. What are the great theatrical pieces which make boring reading? Is *Oklahoma!* an instance? If so, it is comforting to know that the plays of Shakespeare, Congreve, Molière, Ibsen, and Shaw are not. Even O'Neill, the prince of melodramatists, is highly readable. It seems that the dichotomy of theatrical and dramatic is questionable. Closet dramas, the dramas which supremely are offered to us as dramatic reading matter, are seldom good poems of any kind and therefore are seldom good reading; yet—to confuse us further—one classic instance of this genre, Tennyson's *Becket,* was a stage favorite of that most theatrical and theatricalist genuis, Henry Irving.

What is behind theatricalism? The dichotomy of theater and drama existed as early as the eighteenth century. As the public was stratified into what we now call high- and low-brows, the theater was similarly split. While Iffland and Kotzebue found it easy to amuse the public with their cheap wares Goethe learned to look upon the theater, well as he served it, with a certain disdain, and when the duke's mistress insisted on staging a play featuring a performing dog Goethe left the theater for good. The younger generation of German writers (and I pick out Germany because it was at that time theatrically the most flourishing country) made of literature an antithesis to drama. They followed Goethe in writing plays that were too cumbersome for production; but they did not inherit any of his genius, and the literary play earned at this early date a name for dullness and pedantry. In this situation, as in ours today, the one thing needful was a reaffirmation of dramatic essentials. Two more Germans, Otto Ludwig and Friedrich Hebbel, provided it in the forties and fifties. Though these two proficient playwrights and superb dramatic theorists were antagonists, they had a common goal: to appeal from the drama of artifice to an as yet unborn drama of substance. Since then every serious dramatist has had to run the gantlet between those who feared that he was too theatrical to be poetic and those who feared that he was too poetic to be theatrical. In our own time T. S. Eliot was provoked by the antipoetic William Archer into reaffirming that poetry is not necessarily undramatic. Bertolt Brecht goes yet further in denying that lyric and narrative verse are necessarily out of place on the stage.

In the arts, as in religion, no single, double, or triple reaffirmation is ever enough, and today we need reminding of the essentials as much as ever. I have been arguing that the part of the devil has in our time been played by theatricalism, which has now penetrated as far from Broadway as the literary quarterlies. Of course a play is a play, but this simple axiom—which is the only truth behind theatricalism—should not need so much promotion. Studies, such as Stark Young's, of the artistic values in the subsidiary arts of the theater are useful if you have also Mr. Young's literary sense. Today we see the results of placing the emphasis on the arts of the theater—on each separate instrument, or on the conductor, but not on the composition. After a moving performance of *Rosmersholm* at the Yale Drama School, I heard the drama students comment on everything except Ibsen's lines and Ibsen's meaning. The young men and women could lecture you on lighting, costumes, *décor,* acting, direction, but it seemed not to matter what was being lit, costumed, decorated, acted, and directed. Textbooks on drama remain bad. Such criticism as exists is impressionistic or inspirational, and one reads such evasive sentimentalities as: "The best criticism of a play is a production of it." Criticism is not a substitute for a production; it ought to be a prerequisite for all participants in a production. Drama is now relegated to the colleges, but our modern professors are often more antiacademic than Broadway itself. Campus producers, who have the opportunity of presenting any play irrespective of the box office, voluntarily produce pure box-office commodities, lukewarm from Broadway, in the pathetic belief that this is real theater and not mere literature.

What are the simple essentials to which we should return and what are the revolutionary conclusions to which we are impelled? I have said that drama is the most exacting of the arts, and if we think on the usual scale and on the usual lines this is undeniable. Yet there is point too in recalling Goethe's remark to the effect that the essentials of theater are two boards, four barrels, and a handful of actors. In some ways the theater is incredibly complex and will remain so; in others it is simple to the point of crudity, and the theatricalists have dressed up a wide-eyed lass in the garb of a courtesan. Otto Ludwig put Goethe's thought slightly less simply when he said that the drama consists of uniting the two arts of poetry and acting. Two arts; and they do not include the arts of directing and stage-design. *The dramatist is a poet*—that is, an imaginative writer of verse or prose—*who transmits his work through gesturing elocutionists.* Keep close to these simple elements and you will be able to maintain an essential distinction between drama and the pure spectacle of silent movies. The sound movie is different. There might be drama on the talking screen, though the attempted elimination of acting in current movies is one of the nondramatic elements which distinguish them from drama proper. There is of course character acting in most movies, but the "normal" parts are just stars presenting themselves in different costumes. On the stage the "straight part" is also transmitted through the actor's own personality, but the interest of his performance consists in the compromise he makes between himself and his role (synthesis might be a better metaphor) in the practice of a craft which we are aware of as such. Eventually the screen may unlearn its illusionism, yet the stage will retain immense advantages in nonillusionistic performance, advantages arising from the "psychic" contact between the living actor and his audience.

Hollywood has been expert in many ways, but it has never attended to the two basic requirements of drama: it is against poetic imagination and it will not let actors act. (Such an achievement as Victor McLaglen's performance in *The Informer* is a rare event indeed.) But should the screen be dramatic? We all know the party line of the Higher Critics of the movie: plays should not be transferred to the screen, so runs the tale, for the screen will develop its own art forms according to its own potentialities. There can be no objection to this line of thought even though we suspect that the antiliterary prejudice—which is a prejudice against culture itself—is again at work. Only what *are* the potentialities of the talking screen? They differ from those of the silent screen in adding the dimension of dialogue—which, potentially, is poetry. Actually the screen has suffered not by being literary but by being theatricalist. Every MGM movie is a Reinhardt show.

To obtain the simple essentials—trained acting and a real dramatic "script"—one revolutionary conclusion is needed: the repudiation of the theater as it is now financed and organized, which means, positively stated, the acceptance of a special, limited audience. This is not a snobbish plan, for the special, limited audience may consist of trade-unionists or of college students or of unemployed. It may well be a more earthy audience than that of Broadway where the cheapest seat is usually $1.20. The audience at a "popular" Broadway play is not popular. It consists of a fairly well-to-do class of citizens who insist on their usual diet; if they enjoy an unusual dish (as I noticed at a performance of *The Skin of Our Teeth*) it is for the wrong reasons. Nor is the provincial audience much better. Many amateur groups that began with good intentions soon submitted to pressure and started giving Broadway plays. At this point theatricalism is seen in its true colors: it is a "high-brow" rationalization of "low-brow" taste in drama. Since the pundits are all theatricalists now, there is no one to give a lead. You may study drama for years in drama departments and still be unable to tell a good play from a bad. To prefer Wedekind to Maxwell Anderson would be thought outrageous snobbery by many professors (if they had heard of Wedekind at all). Of course the problems of a college drama department are peculiar. The kind of student who "takes" drama is seldom concerned with the imagination of a Shakespeare or a Sophocles. He is more often an exhibitionist and an aspiring movie star. Nevertheless I shall quite deliberately harp on the college in this discussion of the present plight of drama because I am convinced that the campus is one of the few places where something might be done about it. On some campuses much has been done already. Not on many. I spent some time at one of the most artistic and experimental colleges in the country, and saw for my pains Sutton Vane's *Outward Bound,* Barrie's *Twelve Pound Look,* and worse. Alas!

In another chapter I tried to show that Henrik Ibsen, the so-called father of modern drama, was never more a poet than in his last prose plays, which are highly subjective and obscure. If we follow the history of high drama since Ibsen we shall find that most of it is minority drama, written for small theaters, demanding from its audience considerable sophistication, knowledgeability, and refinement, if not also such a command of politics, economics, philosophy, or religion, as the readers of popular magazines would not care to be cumbered with. After Ibsen came Strindberg, who founded his Intimate Theater at Stockholm and, taking a tip from Reinhardt, invented the Chamber Play on the analogy of chamber music; his preface to *Miss Julia,* a document as rewarding to the student of modern theater as Aristotle's *Poetics,* and his *Dramaturgy* lay down the principles of the new art. The great organizations through which we have a modern drama at all—the Théâtre Libre, Freie Bühne, Independent Theater, the Abbey Theater, the Moscow Art Theater, the Provincetown Players, were all minority organizations, and most of them not very "successful" at that. In performing the modern masterpieces in improvised conditions before a handful of enthusiasts in a Little Theater one is fully in the spirit of the modern dramatists. One is succeeding. It is those who go to the academy to study Broadway who fail.

## II

Having as our aim the production of good plays, and recognizing the present economy of the theater for what it is, we are led to the Little Theater as to a home. The term includes every kind of small theater which by choosing good plays declines competition with the commercial houses. It may be a busy, year-round repertory theater run professionally. It may limit itself to a few productions organized by professionals in their spare time. It may be the hobby of amateurs. It may be part of a college curriculum. In protest against the commercial theaters, all these forms of noncommercial theater have been formed in growing numbers over the past sixty years. In England and America the virtual elimination of provincial theaters by the cinema was the greatest challenge that the noncommercial theater had ever received. The challenge was taken up in hundreds of towns.

Although in many places the results were encouraging, at least for a time, in the end few of the Little Theaters were governed by uncompromising devotion to drama. We live in a society where money rules the minds as well as the bodies of men. Those whom Broadway and Hollywood do not control economically they lure and dominate spiritually. Many Little Theaters have succumbed. Some, with more or less sincerity, blame it on their audiences. Others work out far-fetched arguments for what they are doing. The Little Theaters have become links in a chain store which has its headquarters in New York City. One Little Theater manager of my acquaintance refused to read the manuscript of an unperformed play on the grounds that if it were good it would have been done on Broadway. Compare the programs of any Little Theater you know with those of the same theater twenty years ago and you will, nine times out of ten, notice a deterioration.

It is discouraging. So many things in the theater are discouraging that any man of sense would give up. But the theater is a *femme fatale,* and for those who feel her fascination the question: what is to be done? has perpetually to be asked and perpetually to be answered affirmatively.

If the problem is to make a small theater with solely artistic aims, then one of the best places to apply the pressure today is the college or the university. Not—as I have acknowledged—that all is well there. But the university's problems are *less* insoluble than those of the commercial world. A township may fail to support a Little Theater from sheer lack of funds or from sheer lack of interest in "high-brow" art. In the township the economic problem will always be acute in one way or another. Forgetting that Christ and the Provincetown Players were born in a stable, people build too lavish a theater and then complain that their minority public is too small to keep it going. With few exceptions local Little Theaters either go bankrupt or they go Broadway. The same is true of the *avant-garde* theaters of New York. The college theater, on the other hand, can be independent of moneyed interests and of the general public. Of course it can fail through stupidity or fear. What human enterprise cannot? May we not assume that there might be less stupidity and fear on the campus than elsewhere? One of the best presumptive factors in favor of a college theater is, surely, that colleges exist for the promotion of taste and intelligence.

The prescription for the ideal Department of Drama is that the college or university appoint as its director a man who respects and understands old and new dramatic art and that it give him absolute power. After a given term it can dismiss him if it does not approve; while the term is still on he should be in full control, limited neither by local nor student taste. What kind of programs would our ideal campus director sponsor? Ideas of a perfect repertory vary, and there is no need to lay down a scheme in a vacuum. We might indeed venture the opposite kind of generalization and declare that *no* rigid scheme is desirable. A college theater should not be, for example, wholly given over to Shakespeare production, as the Oxford University Dramatic Society has been. Nor should it limit itself to new plays as the Théâtre Libre did. The chief function of the Théâtre Libre was to help along young authors who might later succeed on the commercial stage. It was lucky enough to fall in with a new and significant movement in the history of the drama. A college theater that tried to emulate it would undoubtedly find itself producing student plays that would do little good either to the actors or the audience. Having the students write plays should not be forbidden; but at least we should not have to see them too often on the stage.

The college theater should beware of totally excluding on principle anything but the current commodities of Broadway and the hopeful efforts of our friend who has written a play. Taking a vast area of dramatic literature for our province we might demarcate four particular sections: first, masterpieces from the Oriental and ancient Greek drama to the eighteenth century; second, productions of such new plays as are of evident merit or of possible importance as experiments; third, productions from the modern repertoire since Büchner, which, though not necessarily new, is still largely untried and unknown, the great body of drama which this book has done something toward describing; the fourth—the only part where merit is not a major consideration—might consist of plays of historical interest, for the college theater is the only place where we can see plays of the remoter past which are not masterpieces. Within the four fields the choice of plays will obviously be governed by many practical considerations such as the possibilities of the available stage and the number, quality, and nature of the actors on hand. Beyond such dictates of necessity or common sense I have only one general recommendation: that plays be chosen which we would otherwise have little chance of seeing. This means avoiding the guidance of old programs and of school anthologies of the drama, which have not only repelled generations of students by their double columns, but have established a deadening kind of critical orthodoxy by endlessly reprinting the same plays. The adaptation of a novel will be strictly taboo unless by transmogrification the novel has become a play in its own right. . . .

It would be a pleasure to elaborate a plan for a campus theater. But the material is sufficient for my present purpose if I have made it clear what kind of minority theater can exist here

and now without our having to wait for a social revolution or
the second coming of the Lord. It remains to consider how the
minority theater fits into the broader scheme of things.

I know from experience what the objection to my plan will
be: it is "undemocratic." It is for the superior few. Is the theater
as an art to have no general and popular function? A first retort
to this is Oscar Wilde's pronouncement: "Art should never try
to be popular. The public should try to make themselves artistic." Or, as Chekhov put it in one of those delightful letters
of his: "You must not lower Gogol to the people, but raise the
people to the level of Gogol." In the popularizations of the
classics as perpetrated by Hollywood we seen the consequence
of art's trying to be popular, the consequences of lowering Gogol
to the people. But I can imagine an objector saying: "What
are you doing to raise the people to the level of Gogol? You
seem chiefly occupied with Gogol himself and with those who
are *already* on that level. What of the others?" One answer to
this is that culture cannot be imposed on people any more than
democracy can. Democracy cannot be imposed by a master since
democracy means that a people has no master. It possesses itself.
Culture means that the individual possesses himself; culture is
made part of a man by training and habit and will. That is why
Wilde said: "The public should try to make themselves artistic,"
and not: "The public has to be made artistic."

There are other difficulties. Many people who talk of raising
others to the level of Gogol are not at the level of Gogol themselves, or, if they are, they proceed to lower themselves to the
level of those whom they are trying to raise. Consequently no
raising takes place. You cannot raise others above your own
level. If therefore there are those who champion the level
of excellence it behooves them to stand as near that level as
possible. No compromise can be permitted. Talk of raising the
masses is mere demagogy in the mouth of a man who does not
claim—in stated respects at least—to be superior. Without the
prior existence of standards of excellence, without the prior

existence of minority culture, no general development is possible. Without aristocracy, no democracy.

If we have already a small theater with the highest artistic standards it is time to talk of a People's Theater too. The latter should follow in the wake of the former. In the same letter in which Chekhov ridicules the idea of lowering Gogol to the people, he writes: "Apropos of the popular theaters and popular literature—all that is foolishness, sugar candy for the people." How true this is our "popular" arts on stage, screen, and on the air can today bear witness. On the other hand, when Chekhov wrote about the theaters of Moscow he said: "There are theaters enough for the intelligentsia and the middle-class public in Moscow, and if there is a need for an additional theater it is for a People's Theater." The gist of this is not that slaves deserve their circuses when the *aristoi* have their temples of enlightenment, but that a People's Theater will be a fraud if it is not guided by taste and intelligence.

Let us not be half-hearted in support of the idea of a People's Theater which, like the Little Theaters, will exist outside the orbit of commercial theater. If we look forward to any sort of democratic future we must wish not only to eliminate Philistine opposition to minority culture, but at the same time to help the people raise themselves to the level of Gogol. To raise them, I have said, is impossible. The function of education is to help men to raise themselves. In addressing itself to this end the People's Theater is fundamentally different from the Little Theater. While the Little Theater aims at maintaining the highest standards, the People's Theater aims at the raising of low standards in a manner that is pleasant, unpatronizing, and unobtrusive. In this enterprise the Federal Theater in the thirties was a fine piece of pioneering. Its record shows that it neither surrendered to Broadway—as, perhaps, the Theater Guild has done—nor was unpopular. The People's Theater is a unique democratic adventure which can only be understood as a quite different institution from both "high-brow" and "low-brow" institutions.

"The first requisite of the People's Theater," Romain Rolland wrote in his classic manifesto *Le Théâtre du Peuple,* "is that it must be a recreation." Not all plays suited to a Little Theater will be in place here. That popular art has degenerated into a "show business" for the tired businessman is not to say that it could ever be the diametrical opposite of this, as is the *théâtre intime* of the dramatic expert. Even if we could wipe off overnight the cultural margarine which middle-class rule has smeared over the masses, there would still be little concern among people whose prime business in life is nonartistic for the plays of a modernist *avant-garde*. Art must necessarily be one thing to the intellectual who gives his professional attention to it and quite another to the rest of mankind. For the nonprofessional art is at best a recreation and a hobby; it cannot therefore be too exacting. To recognize this fact one need not follow those who conclude that undemanding art with wider appeal is also *superior* to other work. The less exacting is after all only the less exacting. Yet there is this to be said on the other side. Although in these days we have to be on our guard against the slippery smoothness and false simplicity of our *Oklahoma!*'s, we should also recall the possibility of an acceptable and proper crudity. Indeed it is the rawest bits of our movies and Broadway plays that usually are the best. In the low comedian a fresher and richer popular art survives. Such a feature should not be unnoticed by the director of a People's Theater. A People's Theater cannot be solemn or sedate. It should throw its weight about. Its comedy can be coarse without prurience and light without slickness. It can ignore subtle psychological plays about the neuroses of the intelligentsia such, let us say, as Schnitzler's admirable *Intermezzo*. It does not need to be told that the poor are very poor indeed in Naturalistic plays of compassion addressed to the lachrymal glands of the rich.

No. The People's Theater differs from commercial theater in conforming to Romain Rolland's second demand: "the theater ought to be a source of energy." Today men spend tremendous energy upon sports and gadgets and resort to a book or a "show" only when they are too tired for anything else. Over a century ago Schiller complained that in the theater the muse "takes to her broad bosom the dull-witted scholar and the tired business man and lulls the spirit into a magnetic sleep by warming up the numb senses and rocking the imagination with a gentle motion." The radio and the movies have increased this passivity a hundredfold. It can be broken down by a People's Theater. Those who saw certain productions of the Federal Theater saw that even a modern mass audience can be roused from the somnolescence which has become the traditional tribute paid by the public to art.

The third and last of Rolland's requisites for a People's Theater has much to do with the *means* by which energy is aroused. "The theater," he says, "ought to be a guiding light to the intelligence." Didacticism in the theater! The very notion is enough to set some people aggressively snoring. Nevertheless it is chiefly through drama with a *Tendenz*—or axe to grind—that energy has been infused into modern audiences. One might cite Reinhardt again. He was no propagandist. He sought for aesthetic reasons to break down the separateness of actor and audience by using a circus ring instead of a peep-show stage with a proscenium. The possibilities of this experiment became clear through his productions of *Danton* by Rolland and *Danton's Death* by Büchner in which the experience of his massed actors merged with that of his mass audience in the gigantic Theater of the Five Thousand. Perhaps inadvertently, the power of political drama was revealed. Reinhardt is a great founder of Little and of People's Theater.

Of yore the theater was a violent place where vegetables were hurled at the actors. In France a play could be the occasion of riots and political crises. Passing over plays like *A Doll's House*

and Galsworthy's *Justice,* which allegedly hastened social legis-
lation, it was not perhaps till the Bolshevik Revolution that
the theater—in several parts of the world—became again a center
of social excitement. The books on Soviet Theater are one long
testimony to this fact. Outside Russia echoes have been heard.
At the Piscator production of Ernst Toller's *Hoppla! wir leben!*
in Berlin, 1927, when the mother said, "There's only one thing
to do—either hang oneself or change the world," the youthful
audience burst spontaneously into the "Internationale" and kept
it up (an ambiguous compliment to the performance!) till the
end of the play. Aesthetically very limited, the leftist theater of
America in the thirties managed sometimes so to chime in with
the convictions of the audience as to awaken a similar militant
exultation. In the extraordinary social dynamics of the large
theater we have a factor that little concerns the art theater but
that is very much the concern of a People's Theater.

The political theater is not solely of political interest. It is
through politics that the modern drama occasionally becomes
a People's Theater. The political shade of the message is a matter for a political discussion. What is of more interest here is
the fact that political theater can by touching the spectator's
everyday interests rouse him from his torpor till he becomes
alert, inquisitive, and then pleased, angry, contemptuous, or
whatever, according to plan. This at least the social theater of
America in the thirties did show. In the twenties it was more
in making lively contact with the audience's daily experience
than in stating political dogmas that Piscator's Epic Theater
made an—in many ways—auspicious beginning. Bertolt Brecht's
Epic Drama hopes to make a big contribution to the People's
Theater of the future. Its unorthodox interpretation of theatrical psychology is an attempt to replace the theater of trance
and thrill with a rational theater. But if Brecht talks of ration-
ality he is far from having in mind the "sophisticated," difficult
kind of play which is necessarily limited to the art theater (let
us say such a piece as Denis Johnston's *The Old Lady Says No!*).

He has in mind the kind of rational question which might mean more to the average spectator than does the "unintellectual" sob stuff which the movies provide.

"I do not like plays to contain pathetic overtones"—to cite Brecht's dictum again—"they must be convincing like court pleas. The main thing is to teach the spectator to reach a verdict." This is an overstated repudiation of modern entertainment (including its most pretentious products with their spurious sublimities) which also hints at some of the possibilities of a People's Theater. Brecht is one of the few serious playwrights who have thought much of People's Theater as a new art which is not to be created by the vulgarization of older art but by means proper to itself. He agrees with our newspaper critics that the play should not be written for literary men who will discuss its artistic merits but for ordinary men who will discuss its subject matter. The correct prolongation of a Brecht play is a discussion of the matter involved. The audience does not ask: is it good? or even: what does it mean? but: is it true? does it work?

Epic Theater is at present an affair for the Little Theater; in the long run its place is likely to be in a People's Theater. The two types of noncommercial theater, though importantly distinct, are not absolutely unconnected. If the nature of each is respected there can and should be give and take between them. Up to the present both have suffered through being confused with each other. Enterprises which ought to have been People's Theaters have suffered from the "high-brow" policies of managers who took them for Little Theaters or just did not understand any sort of distinction between the two. On the other hand, organizations that seemed cut out for Little Theater work have prated of taking drama to Middle-Western farmers or some other victims of their philanthropic lust. There is need here for clarity on the cultural structure of modern society.

The body of this book is about playwrights and what they have to say. In the Foreword and in this concluding chapter

I have sketched the living context of modern drama. Through-out all sections of the book a pedagogic—I hope not an ob-jectionably academic—attitude is present and unabashed. I sympathize with the reader's probable prejudice against didacti-cism. None of us likes to fall into the hands of doctrinaires. If in the twenties men had a grudge against writers for their non-partisan "irresponsibility," today we are getting our fill of pious advocacy. A decade or more of intense propaganda—red, pink, or merely religious—has made us very suspicious of uplift. All of which is to say that didacticism has been so degraded and perverted that we have come to hate didacticism itself. Because poison has been found in our medicine bottles we have come to view medicine with suspicion. Or, if we do not doubt the medicine, we doubt that the theater is an adequate dispensary. As a teacher, it may be felt, the playwright is in a very weak position. The pamphleteer and the novelist certainly seem to have the better of him. The trouble is—so this argument runs—that the theater is a place people go to to be amused. Their serious moods they keep for the study. When they go to the theater it will either be to a piece of nonsense frankly regarded as such or to a classic like *Hamlet* (complete with Maurice Evans) which also will leave them unmolested. Indeed, it is felt, one might go to the theater for almost any reason save to clear up one's ideas or to acquire new ones.

There is wholesome sense and too much truth in this argu-ment. Yet I think it can have decisive force only if the drama has no future at all. For although the "theater of ideas" has de-veloped chiefly since Hebbel, in a broader sense the playwright has always been a thinker, a teacher, or, in modern jargon, a propagandist. Born out of Greek religion, reborn out of medi-eval catholicism, Occidental drama has almost never rid itself of its admonitory tone and its salvationist spirit. We have seen how middle-class drama arose from the high moral intentions of the eighteenth century. Rousseau's two theatrical ideas—pop-ular festivals and education through the theater—were taken up by the revolutionaries of 1789, who laid down a precedent for the Bolsheviks by their belief in the propagandist power of the theater. Belief in the strength of the artistic theater is not confined to ambitious playwrights. It is confirmed by realistic statesmen bad and good. Hitler was just as convinced of it as Lenin. The feeling that the theater is necessarily impotent is mainly due to a sense of the current heart failure of the Little Theaters and the prostitution of the big. It need not be so. Looking at the theater of the moment, one is bound to conclude that dramatic art is dead. I have not advocated trying to revive the dead theater, but rather setting up Little Theaters and People's Theaters independently of the theatrical industry. Little Theaters can best be established on the campuses. People's Theaters can be established only with government subsidy; but that, surely, is not to put them permanently outside the realm of possibility.

As for the playwright, life will be hard for him. Yet he will persevere. "The silkworm," as Hebbel put it, "does not stop spinning because woolen stuff is the fashion, and the dramatic spirit does not stop creating because the theater is closed to it." Even if Broadway, like an isle of Laputa, continues to exert its lethal pressure, even if governments continue to tax rather than subsidize the serious theater, from the fastnesses of our Little Theaters let us shout: THE THEATER IS DEAD, LONG LIVE THE DRAMA!

# NOTES

**—TO THE FOREWORD.**

**PAGE 10** "ANNA LUCASTA" . . . ENDS ON THE CUS-
TOMARY NOTE OF HOPE. Or doesn't it? The *New York
Times,* May 6, 1945, tells us:

> In the published version Philip Yordan has seen fit to bring
> down his curtain with Anna marching into the snow and
> the audience trying to figure out what happens to her.
> When the matter was put up to Harry Wagstaff Gribble,
> who directed *Anna* up in Harlem and also for Broadway
> (and found Hilda Simms), he tossed his hands into the air

and informed us that ending *Anna* was one of its severest headaches. For example, when Mr. Yordan first wrote his play . . . Anna, at the end, was just an ungrateful wench who refused to be uplifted by Rudolf. When Harlem first saw it, Anna went out into the snow and was found dead. A later version had her in the snow castigating herself for her meanness, and in still another ending she embraced Rudolf and the curtain came down on a spiritual note.

The best idea would be to stop the action five minutes before the end and let the audience play a guessing game.

**PAGE 14**       THORNTON WILDER, CLIFFORD ODETS, AND EUGENE O'NEILL . . . CHIEFLY PROMISING. The reader who wishes to take these playwrights more seriously than I is referred to their most intelligent champions. Wilder is praised in "Expressionism—Twenty Years After," by A. R. Fulton, *Sewanee Review*, Summer 1944, and in "Thornton Wilder's Theater," by H. Adler, *Horizon*, August 1945. Odets is discussed in deadly earnest by Kenneth Burke in an essay "By Ice, Fire, or Decay?" included in his book *The Philosophy of Literary Form* (Baton Rouge, La., 1941) and by Harry Slochower in a section of his *No Voice Is Wholly Lost* (New York, 1945) entitled "Through the Lower Depths." As to O'Neill, I would defend the apparent impudence of calling him merely "promising" with this statement which O'Neill made to Barrett H. Clark a few years ago: "All the most dramatic episodes of my life I have so far kept out of my plays, and the majority of the things I have seen happen to other people. I've hardly begun to work up all this material, but I'm saving up a lot of it for one thing in particular, a cycle of plays I hope to do some day."

O'Neill goes on to indicate that this cycle will dwarf everything that he—or perhaps anybody else?—has done before: "There'll be nine separate plays, to be acted on nine successive nights; together they will form a sort of dramatic autobiography, something in the style of *War and Peace* or *Jean-Christophe*." And again: "There will be many plays in it and it will have greater scope than any novel I know of. Its form will be altogether its own—a lineal descendant of *Strange Interlude* in a way, but beside it *Interlude* will seem like a shallow episode."

For a further note on O'Neill, and on the literature about O'Neill, see page 318ff. below.

**PAGE 17**                    Since Georg Brandes most Scandinavian writers have classed IBSEN AND BJÖRNSON together. In one of the better books on modern drama (*The Modern Drama,* New York, 1915) Ludwig Lewisohn says of Shaw: "This remarkable writer is not, in the stricter sense, a creative artist at all." Lewisohn names Galsworthy as the leading English dramatist, claiming that his "dialogue is the best dramatic dialogue in the language." The foolish self-conceit of HENRY ARTHUR JONES is best known in his controversies with Shaw and Wells. It is equally evident in *The Renascence of English Drama* and *The Foundations of a National Drama*. As for WILLIAM ARCHER, if he helped to make Ibsen famous in England, he also shackled the master with his own horrible, heavy English and thus delayed the real understanding of Ibsen's genius. Consistently belittling SHAW ("a born meliorist and wit instead of a born dramatist," "an imperfect ventriloquist," "he had not much innate dramatic instinct") he championed the egregious PINERO as "the regenerator of the English drama" and "the brilliant and even daring pioneer of a great movement." His book *The Old Drama and the New* (London, 1922) hindered the recognition of legitimate modernity in drama by basing the defense of Ibsenite realism on sheer Philistinism. Although he dared not attack Shakespeare, Archer vented his spleen against all the rest of Elizabethan drama in such classic howlers as this:

"Of course I am not blaming the Elizabethans for living in an uncivilized and unsanitated age: I am only saying that it was, even artistically, their misfortune and not their merit." As for us of the twentieth century: "we are living not in a period of decadence, but of almost miraculous renascence." Praising *Hindle Wakes* because a character in it weeps instead of speaking poetry, Archer lamented that even "Shakespeare had to fall back on words." Archer himself was known to the public as the author of a cheap melodrama, *The Green Goddess.*

**PAGE 18**        GEORGE JEAN NATHAN in *Art of the Night:*

> The perfect play, after all, offers small ground for interesting critical exploration . . . for all the things that may be said of perfect plays have already been said a hundred times and said better. . . . The point is simply that, since we know what absolute worth is . . . the business of criticism has become the business not so much of arguing that what is excellent is excellent as of arguing that what is not excellent should be excellent. . . .

In other words, Nathan's aesthetic is the female schoolteacher's belief that great art should leave you gasping not talking. He has no belief in the criticism of art, he says, but only in the criticism of criticism. Art is all "warmth" and "emotion," "heart" and "pulse"—to cite Nathan's own terms. To understand drama we need "the mind of a gentleman" and "the emotions of a bum." What do we need to understand George Jean Nathan? A considerable knowledge of the American intellectual scene with its peculiar brands of stuffiness and antistuffiness, preciosity and antipreciosity, real tough-guyism and pseudo tough-guyism, all emanating from the same excessive self-consciousness and *malaise.* Recommended reading: *The Smart Set,* the literary cradle of Nathan and his friend H. L. Mencken, and *The American Mercury,* which they founded.

Nathan's aesthetic is a rationalization of his own talent which is for *(a)* advertising and *(b)* debunking. A critic on Broadway could have done no greater service than to have advertised Sean O'Casey (or even Eugene O'Neill, if we remember what the alternative to O'Neill is on Broadway). To have debunked Pinero, Brieux, Maxwell Anderson, Clifford Odets is something; to have summed up Sir James Barrie as "the triumph of sugar over diabetes" is almost everything. If Nathan is not a great critic of drama, indeed not, as he boasts, a critic of good drama at all, he has been a great fighter against all kinds of nonsense. He consistently puts all his critical colleagues to shame with his superior taste and brains. He tilts also against unacademic academicians like the late Brander Matthews. He believes in testing the bad by the standards of the good; and he usually knows what *is* good too.

**—TO CHAPTER 1.**

**PAGE 22**    KAREL CAPEK (1890-1939), Ernst Toller (1893-1939), and Georg Kaiser (1878-1945) are probably the most famous experimental playwrights of this century. The fact that none of them ever wrote a great play has not enhanced the reputation of experiment. Alike in their passionate, nervous, hedging philosophies and in their bold, loose, unfinished, messy Expressionistic forms, they will represent to history (that journalistic goddess) the nineteen-twenties. Such plays as the *Gas* trilogy, *Masse-Mensch,* and *R.U.R.* are already museum pieces; they were valuable in their day in that they helped to break the ascendancy—for the intelligentsia at least—of the Broadway play.

**PAGE 25**    BALZAC, FLAUBERT, AND THE BROTHERS GONCOURT. All of whom, incidentally, wanted to be great dramatists—as did the British novelists of the day from Dickens to Meredith. They succeeded by proxy. Turgenev made his magnificent *Month in the Country* out of Balzac's play *La Marâtre*. Sternheim made his admirable *Der Kandidat* out of Flaubert's play *Le Candidat*. Strindberg cited the short novels of the Goncourt brothers as an inspiration for his short naturalistic plays.

**PAGE 26**       THÉRÈSE RAQUIN . . . SUCCESSFUL NEITHER ARTISTICALLY NOR COMMERCIALLY was nevertheless a highly significant play. In the preface to the earlier novel-version Zola had written:

> In *Thérèse Raquin* I wanted to study temperaments and not characters. That's the book in a single phrase. I chose people supremely dominated by their nerves and their blood, devoid of free will, dragged along in each action of their lives by the fatalities of their flesh. Thérèse and Laurent are human brutes, nothing more. In these brutes I tried to follow step by step the soundless working of the passions, the thrusts of instinct, the cerebral derangements consequent upon a nervous crisis. The *amours* of my two heroes are the satisfaction of a need; the murder they commit is a result of their adultery, a result which they accept as wolves accept the killing of sheep; finally, what I was obliged to call their remorse consists of a simple organic disorder, in a rebellion of the nervous system stretched to breaking point.

Omit the title and the name of the author, and one would guess these lines to be about one of the Naturalistic plays of Strindberg, who, however, did not absorb French Naturalism till well into the following decade. *Thérèse Raquin* (1873) anticipates his *Miss Julia* (1888) as surely as another French play—*La Révolte* (1870) by Villiers de l'Isle Adam—anticipates Ibsen's

*Doll's House* (1879). Anticipation is perhaps not the best word. Ibsen and Strindberg first went to school to the French Naturalists and then excelled their masters. For the correspondence between Strindberg and Zola see page 316 below. Ibsen's attitude to Zola is expressed in a remark he made to someone who compared him with the French novelist: "Only with this difference, that Zola descends into the cesspool to take a bath, I to cleanse it."

**PAGE 28**    SAXE-MEININGEN. The Duke is a hero of Lee Simonson's *The Stage Is Set* (New York, 1932). Since he immediately preceded Antoine in time, since indeed Antoine saw his troupe in Brussels, he is sometimes regarded as the founder of modern staging. Sometimes he is laughed at for his very demonstrative realism—he even used a real dead horse on the stage—and *Meiningerei* became a jocular term of reproach. Between 1874 and 1890 the Meininger company gave 41 plays and 2,591 performances.

**PAGE 33**    ...WE GO TO THE MOVIES, that is, in America, about fifty-five million of us go weekly. All fifty-five million should read *Hollywood, the Movie Colony, the Movie Makers* by Leo C. Rosten (New York, 1941). The odd five million should also try *The Hollywood Hallucination* by Parker Tyler (New York, 1944), perhaps the only book that begins to ask what kind of experience we have at the movies.

**PAGE 37**    ADOLPHE APPIA. Another of Lee Simonson's heroes, Adolphe Appia (1862-1928) can be represented as the founder of all post-Naturalist design. One director said: "All that has been accomplished since 1900 in the renovation of our dramatic art—from Reinhardt stairways to Russian constructivism—is due to Appia." Appia designed the fancy dress of modern tragedy. Starting with Wagnerism, the great landmark in the history of Tragedy in Fancy Dress, Appia found the pictorial setting which Wagner's operas had needed but, under the maestro's own regime, had not found. As the naturalistic plays of Ibsen's middle period did not find their *inszenierung* till Antoine and others arrived, so Wagner did not have a Wagnerian setting till Appia arrived. Even then Appia's settings were not accepted by Bayreuth, which like all shrines was loyal rather to the letter than to the spirit of the founder's teaching. Few of Appia's designs ever reached the stage at all. The influence was indirect. And even if Lee Simonson has exaggerated that influence, Appia remains a *locus classicus* for the theory of the modern stage. Appia's place then is not only with the "fancy" tragedians, even great ones like Wagner, but also among the founders of a modern theater which need not be tied to one school of dramaturgy. Appia's initial inspiration was Wagner. But as he grew older his style developed away from pure Wagnerism. It tended toward elimination of everything but lines and masses. Let us hope it was an historical accident that we associate this later style with his setting of Claudel's not very satisfactory play—all too prelusive of Werfel's *Song of Berna-dette—The Tidings Brought to Mary*. Appia has laid down the principles for Art Theaters yet unborn.


PAGES 38-39    CRAIG, STANISLAVSKY, MEYERHOLD, TAIROV, REINHARDT, BRAHM. You need look up but one of these names in any good library catalogue to find that a whole literature has grown up around the modern directors and designers. Let me mention one or two volumes of special interest. Again there is Lee Simonson's book. A sound survey of Western theater, especially since Antoine, is given in Mordecai Gorelik's *New Theaters for Old* (New York, 1940). Craig's books (one is as good or bad as another) are the give-away on Craig for anyone who can find the man in the style. The Russian theater is amply chronicled both by its own leaders and by enthusiastic visitors to the USSR. Most of the books deal with earlier, more experimental Soviet theater. A later phase is reverently described in *The New Soviet Theater* by Joseph MacLeod (London, 1943). The files of *Theatre Arts* are probably the richest store of pictures of modernist design.

**—TO CHAPTER 2.**

**PAGE 46**        ... CRITICS AND HISTORIANS. The handiest books in the field, though they are chiefly concerned with English drama, are *The Drama of Sensibility* by Ernest Bernbaum (Cambridge, Mass., 1925) and *The Early Middle-Class Drama* by Fred O. Nolte (Lancaster, Pa., 1935). The three quotations from eighteenth-century advocates of a middle genre are by Fréron, Mercier, and Beaumarchais respectively.

**PAGE 47**        "TRAGEDIES" AND "COMEDIES."

1722 Steele's *The Conscious Lovers.*
1731 Lillo's *George Barnwell.*
1741 La Chaussée's *Mélanide.*
1753 Moore's *The Gamester.*

**PAGE 48**        OTTO LUDWIG (1813-1865), famous in Germany for his rather stupid play *Der Erbförster,* ought to be famous everywhere for his *Shakespearestudien*—"Shakespeare Studies"—not because they tell us anything about Shakespeare that we could not easily find elsewhere, but because they probe into drama, and especially modern drama and its problems,

with skill and even genius. All Ludwig quotations in the text
are from this collection of jottings.

**PAGE 49**        EGON FRIEDELL's *Cultural History of the
Modern Age* (New York, 1932) may not be very highly regarded
by political historians, but its three volumes are worth buying
for Friedell's drama criticism alone. Friedell was a Viennese
actor. His book contains some of the best commentary ever
written on the plays of Goethe, Schiller, Ibsen, and others.

**PAGE 49**        EUGÈNE SCRIBE (1791-1861), unacknowledged patron saint of Broadway, is listed in textbooks as the in-
ventor of the *pièce bien faite* (and as the remaker of opera in
virtue of libretti he wrote of the *comic* and also the *grand* variety). One of the most prolific and influential playwrights of all
time, he has been praised by the critical historians. Petit de
Julleville said that Scribe wrote the best comedies of the period
1800-1850. Following Emile Faguet, Scribe's American biographer N. C. Arvin wrote (in *Eugène Scribe and the French
Theater 1815-1860*, Cambridge, Mass., 1924): "Practically every
innovation, every reform, every novelty found in the drama of the
nineteenth century originated with Scribe, and the highest
point in the development of the main genres of dramatic literature was reached in his plays." This ambitious overstatement
lets us know how unacademic our historians of the theater can
try to be. Against it I would like to place three other exhibits:

1. You go to the theater, not for instruction or correction,
   but for relaxation and amusement. Now what amuses
   you most is not truth but fiction.

2. As for us, four or five years of *feuilletons* etc. led us to
   this idea, confirmed by the success of M. Scribe: that the
   theater had nothing literary about it and that thought
   there amounted to very little.

3. He made of dramatic art an empty form. After Scribe progress has consisted solely in bringing back to the theater all that Scribe excluded from it.

The first of these three remarks is Scribe himself addressing the French Academy—a symptomatic and symbolic event! Here is a "betrayal of the clerks" if you wish!

The second statement—made by Théophile Gautier—shows the demoralizing effect which entertainment—that is, Scribism—has on real writers. The playwright as thinker? He is the *infâme* which the Scribean theater sets out to crush.

The third statement, by the sober René Doumic *(De Scribe à Ibsen,* Paris, 1893), discloses a truth which is a summary of the present book and of the history of drama since Scribe.

**PAGE 49**   KOTZEBUE (1761-1819) was, with Iffland, the leading commodity playwright of the age of Goethe; in the arts of theatrical vulgarity he anticipated Scribe. His popularity was prodigious. The author of *The School for Scandal* capped his career as a playwright by translating Kotzebue's *Pizarro. Menschenhass und Reue,* under the more modest title of *The Stranger,* was one of the most popular plays of contemporary England. The German Romanticist and dramatic theorist A. W. Schlegel represented Iffland and Kotzebue as parasitic upon Goethe and Schiller:

> Stella, Clavigo, Kabale, Fiesco,
> Räuber gemahlt in dem krudesten Fresco
> Brüteten Iffland und Kotzebue aus.

In his *Das bürgerliche Drama* (Berlin, 1898) Arthur Eloesser correlates the success of Kotzebue with the growth of modern entertainment, the physical expansion of the theaters in his time, the rise of theatrical journalism, and the ascendancy of star actors.

PAGE 50 HEBBEL DESCRIBED A DRAMA . . . I agree with Friedell in finding the Journals distinctly the most interesting of all Hebbel's works. But this opinion is heretical. The standard sources for Hebbel's views of drama—and the sources of the views cited in this chapter—are two articles belonging to a controversy with a Danish professor, *"Mein Wort über das Drama"* and *"Ein Wort über das Drama,"* plus the *Vorwort* to his play *Maria Magdalena*. Unhappily these profound pieces are written in ugly, sprawling German. The partial translations —in T. M. Campbell's *Hebbel, Ibsen, and the Analytic Exposition* (Heidelberg, 1922)—are considerably simplified.

Why is Hebbel unknown except to specialists in German literature? He is unconvincing in all the translations so far made, witness the *Three Plays* in Everyman's Library. His mind is austere, involved, even awkward, hardly attractive, very "German" in the sense of solemn and ostentatiously philosophical. All the same he should certainly be represented in Barrett H. Clark's anthology *European Theories of the Drama* (Cincinnati, 1918). He should certainly be read by those who wish to know European literature and drama.

Those who do read Hebbel will be able to correct the impression given in this chapter that *Maria Magdalena* is characteristic of Hebbel's work as a whole. Actually it is the only "Ibsenite" play he wrote. Elsewhere he deals with ancient history and legend.

PAGE 58 In America the chief obstacle to the recognition of "PEER GYNT" as a masterpiece and a delight is the prose version published in the Modern Library *Eleven Plays of Ibsen*. But for this volume Ibsen would not be very widely known in America; nor would he be widely misunderstood. The Oxford Press published a good, low-priced translation in rhymed verse by R. Ellis Roberts in the World's Classics series. It is a pity that Mr. Roberts slights his own work by encouraging us in his preface not to take *Peer Gynt* seriously. The symbolism bothers him and so he tells us to ignore it and just enjoy the "poetry." "It cannot be said too often that the poetic value of *Peer Gynt* is primary; the satirical, symbolic, and religious values subsidiary." Such a conception of "poetry" as external to the symbolism which it bodies forth is an insult to the imagination of Ibsen. No wonder Mr. Roberts does not think so highly of Goethe's *Faust*—there isn't enough "poetry" in it. No wonder he places Browning above both Goethe and Ibsen. *Peer Gynt* remains to be interpreted. The commentaries—including the longest, by Henri Logeman—are but scholarly annotations. A little taste, a little sympathy, and a little common sense would go further in the analysis of the poem than any critic has yet chosen to go.

**PAGE 59** GERHART HAUPTMANN. Thirty years ago it would have seemed worse than high-handed to pass over Hauptmann in a single sentence. He was often considered the greatest playwright of the age. His works were translated into English for a collected edition—a rare honor for a foreign playwright who is barely middle-aged. Today he is hardly a name except to professional students of German literature. Hauptmann is still alive, but, unlike his contemporary Thomas Mann, he has not had an artistic development commensurate with his early promise. Unlike Thomas Mann he declined into the role of a patron of Nazi Kultur. Kindly overlooking the ignominy of Hauptmann's later career, we should think of him as belonging to the twenty-five years that followed his sensational *Before Dawn*, the play which touched off the Naturalist movement in the German theater in 1889. What is popularly expected of a Naturalist is provided in Hauptmann's play—and in *The Weavers, Lonely Lives, Rosa Bernd,* and others—much more than in the plays of Zola, Becque, or Ibsen. The ostentatious sordidness of Hauptmann's plays' content, however, is no more disturbing than the uneasy state of mind that they seem to reflect. They are certainly unhealthy, not, as their early critics felt, because they mention sex, poverty, and disease, but because they dwell upon sex, poverty, and disease without interpreting them. I do not mean merely without propagandizing about them. What Hauptmann lacks is the moral and intellectual stature of a great artist. He is without organic development because his genius is not an organism; it is a machine. Hauptmann is the outstanding Naturalist *and* the outstanding Neo-Romanticist of contemporary Germany. Later he was both Christian-mystical *and* wildly neo-pagan.

It was in vain that Hauptmann encouraged us to compare his many-sidedness—or two-facedness—with that of great writers. Nietzsche is ambiguous, Hauptmann is equivocal. Nietzsche is martyred by the internal conflict; Hauptmann manufactures it for the benefit of the public. Versatility is to the great a cruel burden; to Hauptmann it is the commodity he has to sell. We have to admire a work of his not because it is what it is but because it is not what Hauptmann's other works are. Advertised as a pure artist (as against a thinker) Hauptmann only illustrates again the impossibility of pure art in that sense. The virtuoso does not achieve great art. Great art implies more than facility, versatility, technique, talent, brilliance. It implies moral caliber in a sense puritans will never understand and mental strength to an extent not yet recognized by psychoanalysts. The playwright must be a thinker not only if he wishes to be a propagandist. He must be a thinker if he wishes to be a great playwright.

**PAGE 60**      STRINDBERG AND ZOLA. Zola's letter, acknowledging the receipt of *The Father,* December 14, 1887, reads in part:

> Your play interests me very much. The philosophical idea is very daring, and the characters are boldly drawn.

You have traced the doubt of paternity with a powerful and disquieting effect. Finally, your Laura is the true woman in the unconsciousness and the mystery of her qualities and faults. She will remain buried in my memory. In all, you have written a very curious and interesting work, in which there are, especially at the end, some very beautiful things. To be frank, however, the recourse to analysis there troubles me a little. You know that I am not much for abstraction. I like my characters to have a complete social setting that we may elbow them and feel that they are soaked in our air. And your captain who has not even a name, your other characters who are almost creatures of reason, do not give me the complete sense of life which I require. But the question between you and me here is really one of race. Such as it is, I repeat, your piece is one of the few dramatic works which have moved me profoundly.

Some months later Strindberg sent *The Father* to Friedrich Nietzsche, telling him what Zola's response had been. Nietzsche replied:

I read your tragedy twice over with deep emotion; it has astonished me beyond all measure to come to know a work in which my own conception of love—with war as its means and the deathly hate of the sexes as its fundamental law— is expressed in such a splendid fashion. But this work is really destined to be presented by M. Antoine in Paris at the Théâtre Libre! Simply demand this of Zola. At the moment he prizes it very highly when he attracts attention to himself.

I cannot but deplore, of course, the preface he has contributed, although I should have been sorry to miss it, for it contains countless naïvetés. That Zola disapproves of "abstraction" puts me in mind of a German translator of one of Dostoevski's novels, who also cared nothing for "abstraction"—he simply left out recourses to analyses—they annoyed him! How odd, too, that Zola is unable to distinguish between types and creatures of reason! And that he should demand a complete social setting for your tragedy! And when he finally tried to make a question of race of the whole matter, I almost shook with laughter! As long as taste really existed in France, the whole instinct of the race showed itself opposed to all that he represented—it is precisely the Latin race which protests against Zola. In the final analysis he is a modern Italian—he worships the *verismo*. . . . With expressions of my highest esteem, Yours, Nietzsche.

**PAGE 64**        WEDEKIND AND O'NEILL. Frank Wedekind (1864-1918) is a playwright of Strindbergian power. That he is unknown in England and America must either be because there is so much sex in his plays or because his world is a Continental, a central European, perhaps even a peculiarly German world. The latter reason, however, will only satisfy cultural nationalists and champions of the folksy. We do not shut out Chekhov because he is peculiarly Russian. Wedekind has simply been unlucky. If we had a good minority theater he would be staged there.

Wedekind's realm is an extraordinary one, and few have really tried to pass its frontiers. The monster *Sex* stands in the way. The mere presence of sex establishes responses which are likely to be irrelevant in a serious work of art. It attracts the young and iconoclastic who greet it in the name of Frankness. It repels the old and conservative who complain of Dirt. Neither young nor old bother much about what an artist says of sex. A D. H. Lawrence who regards sex as a sacred mystery and a Bertrand Russell who wants to bring it into the open are both alike in the eyes of the public: they are both "sexy." Wedekind is "sexy." The only collection of his plays in English is entitled:

*Tragedies of Sex* (translated with an introduction by Samuel Eliot, New York 1923). But what is Wedekind's view of sex? That is a question the public would not ask. The answer is this. Wedekind began by championing the body as against the spirit which we have overprized and overpraised. His *Awakening of Spring* demonstrates the innocence of life itself and the guilt of life haters. "The flesh," Wedekind announced, "has its own spirit." But he did not stop there. The tragedy of *Damnation* (as Eliot calls *Tod und Teufel*) is the discovery that devotion to bodily joy is in the end joyless. This subtler analysis underlies Wedekind's finest play *Der Marquis von Keith* in which the epicure ("*Genussmensch*") is portrayed as a martyr. This is the conclusion of the man who is hailed as one of the founders of nudism, the inspirer of Jacques Dalcroze, the misunderstood genius-reformer self-portrayed in *Such Is Life*.

It is, of course, not by his ideas that Wedekind lives, but by his discovery of amazing forms to express the ideas. His ideas recur like maddening obsessions: genius is slighted, nakedness is noble, society is a circus, man is a beast—these notions are certainly no more than an "ideological superstructure." What is perpetually astonishing in Wedekind is his imagination and his dialectic. The flesh is presented to us through the intellect and through the nerves. If the flesh has its own spirit, the spirit has its own flesh. Wedekind's circus, Diebold said, is full of tragic clowns. Wedekind criticizes the bourgeois world by revealing its *under*world, which the bourgeois world is antithetic to, yet which it implies. The bourgeois is shocked by the underworld because it is a caricature of his own overworld. Such an underworld is Wedekind's gallery of whores, swindlers, procurers, perverts, and epicures. Macheath in Bertolt Brecht's *Dreigroschenoper* goes further than Wedekind and suggests that the bourgeois is worse than the *untermensch*: "What is the burgling of a bank to the founding of a bank?"

In English there is no literature about Wedekind worth considering. In German Diebold is his acutest, but not his most

friendly, critic. A disciple has written of him to the extent of
three volumes: *Frank Wedekind, sein Leben und seine Werke*
(Munich, 1922-1931) by Arthur Kutscher. This work is full of
good information. The trouble with Wedekind's followers is
that they regard him as God. They follow him with sympathetic
credulity into the extravagances of his last plays, of which
*Franziska*—"Wedekind's *Faust*" (!)—is the most pretentious and
the most preposterous.

If Wedekind is grossly underrated and ignored, almost the
opposite could be said of Eugene O'Neill. Discovered some
thirty years ago by the brightest theater critic America has ever
had—George Jean Nathan—O'Neill has been well promoted by
him and others ever since. Where Wedekind seems silly and
turns out on further inspection to be profound, O'Neill seems
profound and turns out on further inspection to be silly. This
is true at least of his most ambitious and late plays, *Mourning
Becomes Electra* (1931) and *Days without End* (1933). Even the
relatively convincing and certainly powerful *Desire under the
Elms* is blemished by O'Neill's telepathic touch: at the moment
when words could do most he dispenses with them altogether;
he did not dare to introduce the eloquent soliloquy here though
elsewhere he reintroduces the rather ignoble device of the
aside. As a theatrical craftsman O'Neill is tremendously talented. He therefore appeals to the critics. He is no thinker.
And therefore he appeals to them even more. Now every great
writer is a thinker—not necessarily a great metaphysician but
necessarily a great mind. Among the recognized great playwrights of the past there are no exceptions to this rule. O'Neill,
however, has yet to show us he has a mind. So far he has only
been earnest after the fashion of the popular pulpit or of professors who write on the romance of reality. Precisely because
he pretends to too much, he attains too little. He is false, and he
is false in a particularly unpleasant way. His art is *faux-bon*.
The "good clean fun" of a Hitchcock movie is better. . . . Well,

we shall see. For the past ten years O'Neill has been hatching plays on the quiet. They have fruity titles like *The Long Day's Journey into Night* and *The Iceman Cometh*. If they are good, good. If they are anything like *Days without End,* we need not trouble to discuss whether O'Neill is a great dramatist any more.

There is a growing O'Neill literature. In 1929 Barrett H. Clark wrote a full-length book about him; Professor S. K. Winter followed in 1934; and in 1935 he was almost canonized by a Catholic critic, Richard Dana Skinner. Against O'Neill the most eloquent protestant was Virgil Geddes in his *The Melodramadness of Eugene O'Neill* (Brookfield, Conn., 1934). The essay by Joseph Wood Krutch cited in the text is the introduction to *Nine Plays of Eugene O'Neill* in the Modern Library. And of course O'Neill is the No. 1 exhibit in any history of American Drama. This is the misfortune of American drama.

**PAGE 68**   STRINDBERG KNEW THE SECRET, his disciple O'Neill did not. This is admitted by O'Neill's advertising manager, George Jean Nathan, in a very perceptive passage. (Is Nathan a critic after all, profiting by his own dictum "the best critics are the inconsistent critics"?) Here is the passage (from *Materia Critica*):

> Whenever, as in the case of such of his plays as *Welded* and *The First Man,* Eugene O'Neill tries on the whiskers of Strindberg, the results are singularly unfortunate. Following the technic of Strindberg, O'Neill sets himself so to intensify and even hyperbolize a theme as to evoke the dramatic effect from its overtones rather than, as in the more general manner, from its undertones. His attempt, in a word, is to duplicate the technic of such a drama as *The Father,* the power of which is derived not by suggestion and implication but from the sparks that fly upward from a prodigious and deafening pounding on the anvil. The at-

tempt, as I have said, is a failure, for all one gets in O'Neill's case is the prodigious and deafening pounding. The sparks simply will not come out. Now and again one discerns something that looks vaguely like a spark, but on closer inspection it turns out to be only an imitation lightning-bug that has been cunningly concealed in the actors' sleeves. O'Neill, in such instances, always goes aground on the rocks of exaggeration and overemphasis. His philosophical melodrama is so full of psychological revolver shots, jumps off the Brooklyn Bridge, incendiary Chinamen, galloping hose carts, forest fires, wild locomotives, sawmills, dynamite kegs, time fuses, mechanical infernal machines, battles under the sea, mine explosions, Italian black-handers, last-minute pardons, sinking ocean liners and fights to the death on rafts, that the effect is akin to trying to read a treatise on the theme of bump-the-bumps. He rolls up his sleeves and piles on the agony with the assiduity of a coalheaver. He misjudges, it seems to me completely, the Strindberg method. That method is the intensification of a theme from within. O'Neill intensifies his theme from without. He piles psychological and physical situation on situation until the structure topples over with a burlesque clatter. Strindberg magnified the psyche of his characters. O'Neill magnifies their action.

A magnificent analysis and unluckily not limited in validity to *Welded* and *The First Man*. Mr. Nathan has successfully prosecuted his own client.

**—TO CHAPTER 3.**

**PAGE 74**      KLEIST. Heinrich von Kleist (1777-1811) is another marvelous genius who somehow is left to academicians to admire. As with Hebbel, the difficulty is in translating him.

Nobody in England or America has come along to do for the great German playwrights what Schlegel and Tieck did for Shakespeare.

Of late there has been much searching for modernity among older writers, with the result that Hölderlin, Büchner, Kierkegaard, and many others have been rediscovered. Not so Kleist. Within Germany Kleist was revived by the Stefan George Circle and has even been regarded as the greatest German playwright; elsewhere he remains unknown. Yet his psychological subtlety and macabre brilliance are what people call modern, and in the words of a sound historian we can infer a tradition from Lessing, through Kleist, to Hebbel. I quote R. F. Arnold in his compilation *Das deutsche Drama* (Munich, 1925):

> Rupert, Jeronimo, and Sylvester Schroffenstein, the old Norman in *Guiscardo*, Amphitryon, Achill, and Penthesilea, the Great Elector—all have something about them of the examining magistrate. *Käthchen* starts out with a criminal investigation, and in *Der zerbrochene Krug* the scene in general is a tribunal. The whole drama is a long series of more or less unerring questions, true and untrue depositions, correct and incorrect conclusions—a game of chess in which every move alters the total situation until in the end the comical king is checkmated. If the direct ancestor of this dramatic dialectic is Lessing, its immediate heir is unmistakably the Hebbel of *Der Diamant*, of *Herodes*, and *Gyges*.

A full-length, rather pedestrian account of Kleist in English is given in *The Dramas of Heinrich von Kleist* by J. C. Blankenagel (Chapel Hill, N. C., 1931).

**PAGE 80**     VIGNY. Perhaps second only to *Hernani* in notoriety during the decade of Romanticism in the French theater (1830-1840), Vigny's *Chatterton*—a tiresome enough play in itself—has an interesting preface in which Vigny calls for a drama of thought. In summing up his subject as "the spiritual man stifled by a materialistic society" he sums up by anticipation a great deal of modern drama down to the days of Zolaist Naturalism and, later, Expressionism.

**PAGE 84**          BEKKER. Paul Bekker's *Richard Wagner, His Life and Work* (New York, 1931) is probably the best sympathetic account of Wagner's theory and practice of music drama. We may not wish, with Bekker, to abstain from criticism of Wagnerism or to fall in so often with Wagner's own nebulous terminology; but it is right that every important artist should sometime be expounded by an ardent admirer.

**PAGE 89**          . . . WHAT OPERA CAN DO. I do not mean that nobody has ever considered these problems, but that our judgments of opera are for the most part made without consideration of them. Of course there are exceptions. Without invading the forbidding field of academic musicology, I might mention among books which contain interesting remarks about the relation between opera and drama: *Eurydice, or the Nature of Opera* by Dyneley Hussey (London, 1929), and *Aspects of Modern Opera* by Lawrence Gilman (London, 1924). Hans Pfitzner, in his *Vom musikalischen Drama* (Munich, 1915), is a more searching analyst, but the Wagnerism which spurs him on operates also as a pair of blinkers. More modern views are found in essays of the Schoenberg circle, such as *A Guide to Alban Berg's Opera "Wozzeck"* by Willi Reich (New York, 1931). Perhaps the most original and thoroughgoing thinker in this sphere is the Danish philosopher Søren Kierkegaard, who devotes a section of his *Either/Or* to music and particularly to Mozart's *Don Giovanni*. Postulating that "music is the demoniac," that "in the erotic sensual genius, music has its absolute object," Kierkegaard goes on to argue the supreme musical, dramatic, and human importance of Don Giovanni, who, he says, "is the absolutely musical idea." It is impossible fully to show what Kierkegaard is driving at without explaining the context of this theory, which I must not do here. My present point is that Kierkegaard's analysis—made for far other reasons—contains superb passages of technical dramatic criticism, superb insights into the question of "music drama." If he cannot quite prove his point that *Don Giovanni* is and must remain the only completely satisfactory opera, Kierkegaard does, I think, prove his more modest point that "Don Juan can only be expressed musically," and he proves it empirically by demonstrating the differences between Mozart's version of the legend and (among others) Molière's. Perhaps no other critic has so brilliantly shown how dramatic music must be interpreted dramatically, and not as pure music, yet how opera is quite distinct in its method from spoken drama. See *Either/Or,* Vol. I, pp. 35-110 (Princeton, N.J., 1944).

PAGE 94      STRINDBERG, MAETERLINCK, HUYS-MANS, PELADAN. Strindberg's enthusiasm for Maeterlinck is recorded in his *Dramaturgy* (available in Emil Schering's German version) and reported in A. Jolivet's *Le Théâtre de Strindberg* (Paris, 1931). Biographers also report his closeness to Huysmans, whose *rapprochement* with the Church was one of the literary events of the time, and to the strange Péladan whose penchant was for the occult.

PAGE 96      C. E. VAUGHAN'S *Types of Tragic Drama* (London, 1908, reprinted 1936) already cited above, page 93, is an amiable introduction to the subject, though distinctly weak on modern drama. The whole history of the drama is represented as a development "from exclusion to inclusion, from a less to a more complete idealization of the material offered by human life, from a narrower to a wider rendering of all that the heart of man presents to our observation." Vaughan's view that drama culminates in Maeterlinckism receives confirmation in Allardyce Nicoll's *The Theory of Drama* (London, 1931). Quoting "The Tragical in Daily Life," Professor Nicoll comments:

> This probably is the most important piece of creative criticism on the drama that has appeared for the last century. We see it expressed in the theater itself, not only in *Pelléas et Mélisande,* but in many of the domestic dramas of Ibsen. There is an attempt in both to pass from the Shakespearean conception of tragedy to another conception more fitting to the modern age. *There is an endeavor to move from the tragedy of blood and of apparent greatness to the tragedy where death is not a tragic fact and where apparent greatness is dimmed by an inner greatness. Shakespeare found the world of character, of inner tragedy; the modern age has found the world of the subconscious,* adapting it, as every age has adapted the desires and the moods of its time, to the requirements of the theater. It is for this reason that we may regard this and similar pronouncements of Maeterlinck as among the greatest contributions to the development of the drama since the end of the sixteenth century. It is a proof that the creative instinct in the theater is still vital and pulsating.

The last sentence quoted might have been excused in 1903; it would have seemed less plausible in 1913; it was actually published in 1923, and not modified in the rewriting of 1931. The passage which I have italicized is presumably the core of the matter. Either it is verbiage, or it is the beginning of an argument that is not followed up. It would have been a very interesting argument, one can't help feeling; but it does not exist. Would it be churlish to suggest that whenever it stumbles on something interesting the academic mind is embarrassed and in a hurry to get back to safety?

**PAGE 97**     MAETERLINCK AND CLARE BOOTHE LUCE.

Both the Maeterlincks agree that the great American play is *Mourning Becomes Electra*. They speak with authority, having kept abreast of our stage through Burns Mantle's yearly anthologies [which contain only extracts and synopses]. Somewhat unexpectedly they both turn out to be Clare Boothe Luce fans. "She pinches things like *that*," Maeterlinck exclaimed. . . .—*The New Yorker*, July 24, 1943.

For other Maeterlinck items of recent date see: *Reader's Digest*, August 1941; *The Rotarian*, July 1942; *The American Magazine*, July 1943; *Good Housekeeping*, August 1943.

**PAGE 97**     MAETERLINCK, CRAIG, AND MARIONETTES. Craig's case was for what he called Über-marionettes instead of actors. Maeterlinck called his first play "a play for marionettes," and later published several plays under the title *"Trois petits drames pour marionettes."* Maeterlinck's British biographer declares that these labels are ironic and that Maeterlinck undoubtedly intended all his plays for human actors: "The characters are described as marionettes, it is likely, because the scene is spiritualized by distance. We look down on the movements of the puppets as from a higher world. . . ." This hardly militates against my argument that Maeterlinck wished to by-pass the actor. On the same page Mr. Bithell paraphrases Maeterlinck as saying "the actor is become an automaton through which the soul speaks more than words can say." The actor as automaton, the wordless play—Maeterlinck is not so far from Craig after all. See *Life and Writings of Maurice Maeterlinck* by Jethro Bithell (London, 1913) p. 69.

**PAGE 98**      EXPRESSIONISM. Probably the best general introduction is *Expressionism in German Life, Literature, and the Theater* (1910-1924) by Richard Samuel and R. Hinton Thomas (Cambridge, England, 1939). The Six Points are taken from C. E. W. L. Dahlstrom's *Strindberg's Dramatic Expressionism* (Ann Arbor, Mich., 1930) which is ultra-academic in procedure but highly informative. The liveliest, most intelligent book in the field is Diebold, *op. cit.* The nearest thing to an Expressionist Manifesto is Kasimir Edschmid's *Über den Expressionismus in der Literatur und die neue Dichtung* (Berlin, 1919). Noting Edschmid's addiction to words like enthusiasm, soul, and ecstasy, one can also note particular doctrines, such as:

1. The doctrine of essences: "The sick man is not only the cripple who suffers. He becomes sickness itself. . . ."
2. The doctrine of internationalism: "This kind of expression is not German, not French. It is supernational."
3. The doctrine of divinity: The Expressionist poet "sees the human element in whores, the divine element in factories. . . . Everything acquires a relation to eternity."

In regard to Expressionist theater it is important to note that it included other things besides modernist stage designs. One one of the most interesting little documents of Expressionism is an "Afterword to the Actor" in Paul Kornfeld's play, *Die Verführung*, (Berlin, 1918). Kornfeld challenges the naturalistic school of acting, which after its own victories over classical acting in the nineties, had been supreme. If an actor is to die on the stage, says Kornfeld, let him *not* visit hospitals to see how men really die, let him act the *idea* of dying, let him realize that the operatic tenor who dies with a high C on his lips gives a better impression of death than an actor who wriggles and squirms. On the positive side, however, the theory of Expressionist acting is limited; all stylization is more of a demonstration against an earlier mode than a style in its own right. Bertolt Brecht's Epic Theater has richer ideas for a renovation of acting, and such artists as Peter Lorre, Oscar Homolka, and Helene Weigel were beginning to make of them a school of practice when Hitler came to power. Perhaps, then, we owe it partly to the late Führer that naturalistic acting of the school of Brahm and Stanislavsky is still unchallenged on our stages.

**PAGE 100**     LOVELY PICTURE BOOKS mentioned here (and on pp. 17, 40, 284) include:

1919 *The Theater Advancing,* by Gordon Craig.
1921 *The Theater of Tomorrow,* by Kenneth MacGowan.
1922 *Continental Stagecraft,* by Kenneth MacGowan and Robert Edmond Jones.
1925 *The New Spirit in the European Theater,* by Huntly Carter, author of *The New Spirit in Drama and Art, The New Spirit in the Cinema, The New Theater in Russia, The Theater of Max Reinhardt.*
1928 *Stage Decoration,* by Sheldon Cheney, author of *The New Movement in the Theater, The Open Air Theater, The Art Theater.*

**—TO CHAPTER 4.**

**PAGE 104**     D. H. LAWRENCE wrote three plays, none of them without interest. In one he tries vainly to put to theatrical use some of the *Sons and Lovers* material; in a second he attempts what in the preface he calls Tragedy by way of a picture, still of course very topical, of relations between capital and labor; in a third he essays poetic prose and a biblical sublimity by way of a play about David. JAMES JOYCE'S one play *Exiles* is important and exciting for students of Joyce, but I cannot go all the way with Mr. Francis Fergusson in finding it a fine play in its own right. All the same Mr. Fergusson's essay (announced as the preface to a 1946 reprint of the play) is very persuasive. And it brings out very fully the deep debt of Joyce to Ibsen. HENRY JAMES made a much more persistent and successful attempt to master the dramatic medium than either Lawrence or Joyce—witness his two volumes of unperformed *Theatricals* and two or three unpublished (though not unperformed) plays, *e.g., Guy Domville, The American,* and *Owen Wingrave.* We learn something of the nature of the theater in modern society from James's various failures. When James wrote the ambitious *Guy Domville* the play was over the heads of the public and almost nobody but Bernard Shaw liked it. When James decided that drama could not be serious and wrote that the playwright has to throw the cargo overboard in order to save the ship, he wrote four farces which were never produced at all. To those who are less interested in the theater than in Henry James, the years of dramatic experiment are chiefly important as a technical preparation for the master's last great novels. See Léon Edel's *Henry James: les années dramatiques* (Paris, 1931).

In our own time W. H. AUDEN has written poetic plays—*Paid on Both Sides, The Dog beneath the Skin, The Ascent of F6, On the Frontier*—but despite his own comedic and poetic brilliance, his borrowings from Eliot and Brecht, and his collaboration with Christopher Isherwood, he has not made a dramatist of himself. Much less have his ex-comrades in arms Stephen Spender (whose greatest service to the stage is his translation, with Goronwy Rees, of Büchner's *Death of Danton*) and Louis MacNeice.

PAGE 106 THE STAGE IS A TRIBUNAL. This image has haunted many playwrights, for the stage seeks procedures in real life which offer ready-made histrionic patterns. The court of law presents conflict verbalized and concentrated. It presents intelligent talk but not the free, disinterested talk of the philosophic symposium: its talk is directed at a decision. Naturally therefore "the stage as tribunal" is particularly characteristic of the modern stage. After Kleist and Hebbel, Ibsen and Strindberg gave the pattern a twist towards subjectivism. Ibsen wrote:

> To live is to fight with fiends
> That infest the head and heart.
> To write is to summon oneself
> And play the judge's part.

And Strindberg wrote: "To write plays is the most interesting thing in the world. Like a little god one probes hearts and loins . . . one judges . . . one punishes . . . one absolves or one rewards." In our own time Bertolt Brecht has posed his problems in many courtroom scenes—two of which are mentioned in Chapter IX above. To Brecht the courtroom—this archetypal pattern of human argument, action, and responsibility—is of extra use because it is an antidote to the excessively private and expansive emotions of the popular art which he combats. The court scene in the conventional twentieth-century play is but an incident in a story which takes place chiefly in bedrooms, drawing rooms, and night clubs—a public incident in private lives. In Brecht the court is the very center. The public incident is more important than the private life. Out of such considerations once grew a plan of his to use the theater as a courtroom for many acted trials: that of Socrates, a witches' trial, the trial of Karl Marx's *Neue Rheinische Zeitung,* "an eviction trial against an unemployed worker in Germany and alongside it a Soviet trial where a working woman wins a title to space in an apartment."

PAGE 115     FLAWS AND INCONSISTENCIES OF "THE
RING." See Ernest Newman's *Life of Wagner*, Vol. II, Chapter
17, where Newman describes the different and inconsistent
drafts which Wagner jumbled together. In *The Perfect Wagnerite*, Bernard Shaw long ago found many inconsistencies on
mainly internal evidence. My own attempt to interpret these
psychologically is to be found in *A Century of Hero-Worship*,
Part Three, Chapter I.


PAGE 115          The juxtaposition of "MEISTERSINGER"
AND "TRISTAN" is not capricious. The one is the comple-
ment of the other not only in the general—and, it may appear—
fanciful ways described in the text but in many particulars. In
*Meistersinger* Hans Sachs sings;

> *Von Tristan und Isolde*
> *Kenn ich ein traurig Stück,*
> *Hans Sachs war klug, und wollte*
> *Nichts von Herrn Markes Glück.*

"Of Tristan and Isolde I know a sad drama, Hans Sachs was
intelligent and desired nothing of Herr Marke's fate": this interesting statement gives a hint of the relationship between
Wagner's two most accomplished "music dramas." Sachs parallels King Marke, Eva parallels Isolde, Walther parallels Tristan,
and Beckmesser parallels Melot. Each piece, that is, has a hero
and heroine, a villain, and a fourth character who has a claim
to the heroine which he magnanimously surrenders. *Tristan*
is the "tragic" working of the material, *Meistersinger* the
"comic."

The two operas are similar in their dramaturgy as well as in
their substance. This more mature Wagnerian dramaturgy pre-
cludes the high jinks of spectacular opera. The three acts constitute the exposition, complication, and culmination respectively, that is to say, the drama moves in three deliberate and

simply demarcated stages. Those who judge by the standards of spoken drama find both operas too slow, for in simplifying his action Wagner is trying to let the music do his dramatic work. Where in naturalistic drama there could be nothing but silence and in poetic drama there could be only the discreet under-statements of love poetry, Wagner has his music embody the emotion fully and with emphasis. His climaxes in both operas are therefore musical climaxes created·out of what in spoken drama might be pauses or transitions. The first act sets the pace and creates the atmosphere; the second presents the major con-flict and the dominant passions; the third is the full climax, a feast of finality.

I conclude that whoever is concerned with the relations be-tween music and drama must study Wagner's theory—or, better, his practice. Whatever our objections to Wagnerism, and most of us have strong objections, we still have much to learn from this monster who was also a world-genius.

PAGE 116     "TRISTAN" AS DECADENT POEM. Lest this characterization seem abstract or pretentious, the following quotation from a letter of Wagner's addressed to his Isolde, Mathilde Wesendonck, may say something: "Child! This Tris-tan will be something *frightful!* This last act!!! I'm afraid the opera will be banned—if the whole thing is not travestied by a bad performance—only mediocre performances can save me! Perfectly good ones would certainly send people crazy. . . ." Kurt Hildebrandt adds the following information on the re-hearsals for the premiere of *Tristan:* "The performers were in despair. Even von Bülow calls the opera impossible. The chorus master in Munich is driven into a madhouse—in von Bülow's opinion by the excitement at rehearsals. The performer of Tris-tan died shortly after the first performance"; see Hildebrandt's *Wagner und Nietzsche* (Breslau, 1924), which is the most dra-matic presentation of the relations between the two men. Of course the prime documents on this subject are Nietzsche's works on Wagner—*Richard Wagner in Bayreuth, Der Fall Wagner,* and *Nietzsche contra Wagner*—and the Nietzsche-Wagner correspondence.

**PAGE 118**        BOURGEOIS TRAGEDY—the subject of Chapter II above. A rudimentary chronicle of the genre might read somewhat as follows:

1731 *The London Merchant, or the History of George Barnwell,* by George Lillo.

1755 *Miss Sarah Sampson,* by Lessing.

1784 *Kabale und Liebe* ("Love and Intrigue"), by Schiller.

1844 *Maria Magdalena,* by Hebbel.

1879-1890 Ibsen's "modern" plays.

1887-1890 Strindberg's "naturalistic" plays.

1890-1910 Main period of Wedekind's work.

1931 *Mourning Becomes Electra,* by Eugene O'Neill.

**PAGE 119**        IBSEN'S REPUDIATION OF VERSE. See *The Letters of Henrik Ibsen* (New York, 1905), p. 367. In addition to this volume there are two other collections of Ibsen's opinions in English: *Speeches and New Letters* (Boston, 1910), and *From Ibsen's Workshop,* a selection from his notes and first drafts, published as Volume XII in William Archer's *The Works of Henrik Ibsen* (New York, 1912). Those who cannot read Norwegian may read the complete posthumous work of Ibsen in German: *Nachgelassene Schriften* (Berlin, 1909), four volumes.

**PAGE 122**        REPRESENTATIVE CRITICS OF THE LAST GENERATION. The first is W. T. Price, *The Technique of the Drama* (New York, 1892), p. 166. The second is Richard Burton, *How to See a Play* (New York, 1914), p. 153.

Cf. the opinion of the great playwright Henry Becque: "A dramatist may have two ends in view: one, to please the public, the other to satisfy only himself. I have chosen to satisfy myself." Or, as Oscar Wilde phrased it: "The work of art is to dominate the spectator; the spectator is not to dominate the work of art."

**PAGE 123**        "LITTLE EYOLF." As far as I know no really plausible exegesis of the play was given until Hermann J. Weigand published his article in the *Journal of English and Germanic Philology,* January 1923. It was later reprinted in his important book *The Modern Ibsen* (New York, 1924). Henry James sensed the peculiarity of the play without really being able to say what it was. See *Theater and Friendship, Some Henry James Letters* (New York, 1932), Chapter VIII. In his essay "Henrik Ibsen" in *Essays in London and Elsewhere* (New York, 1893) James shows a fuller comprehension than anyone else of his generation of Ibsen's subtlety—"his independence, his perversity, his intensity, his vividness, the hard compulsion of his strangely inscrutable art." Phrases throughout the essay show James's discrimination and puzzlement: "angular irony," "conscious supersubtlety," "superficially simple," "such aesthetic density," "obscurities and ironies." So it is that James proceeds to a partial condemnation of Ibsen who "asks the average moral man to see too many things at once." He complains of "the absence of humor, the absence of free imagination, and the absence of style." One might suggest that James missed the grim humor of Ibsen's portraits of Manders and Tesman, that he did not know *Peer Gynt,* and that the apparent absence of free imagination is due to the circumstance that—in James's own words—Ibsen dealt "essentially with the individual caught in the fact." If even James did not fully understand Ibsen it was because his own aims and attitudes were so different. He complained that Ibsen's plays end where the real interest begins. Bernard Shaw had the same idea when he protested that the one flaw in Ibsen is his retention of the "tragic" ending. The real tragedy of the Hedda Gablers, Shaw says, is that they *don't* shoot themselves. Francis Fergusson writes: "And I think one can see that if Rosmer and Rebecca, for example, had married under the eyes of a group of interested and intelligent friends instead of jumping into the millrace together, a truly 'bristling' Jamesian subject would have resulted." As things are, James declares that in Ibsen's plays "the lamp of the spirit burns as in tasteless parlors with the flame practically exposed." Without invalidating the mind or method of either artist, this fine sentence—from *Notes on Novelists*—indicates how far apart Ibsen and James were.

**PAGE 126**          A BALLAD as follows:

> The two lived in a cosy house
> In autumn and winter weather,
> The fire came and the house was gone
> They must search in the ashes together
>
> For down in the ashes a jewel is hid
> Its brightness the flames could not smother
> And if they search faithfully he and she
> 'Twill be found by the one or the other
>
> But even if they find it, the gem they lost,
> The enduring jewel they cherished
> She never will recover her vanished faith
> Nor he the joy that has perished.

**PAGE 130**          BERNARD SHAW AND JAMES JOYCE. It is hard for us to see that only by *not* being in the swim could one champion Ibsen in the early days. In 1905 Shaw wrote to his biographer Archibald Henderson: "The critics of the nineteenth century had two first-rate chances—Ibsen and Wagner. For the most part they missed both. Second best they could recognize; but best was beyond them." Hence the importance and significance of *The Quintessence of Ibsenism* and *The Perfect Wagnerite*. When Joyce reviewed Ibsen's *When We Dead Awaken* in the *Fortnightly Review* he was a lonely lad of eighteen; the young Joyce championed Ibsenism against the fashionable Celticism of the Irish Literary Theater; from some of the phrases of a letter he sent to Ibsen on the latter's seventy-third birthday, as well as from his love of *When We Dead Awaken,* we have the impression that Joyce saw the subtler and deeper things in Ibsen. He speaks of the master's "lofty impersonal power," his "willful resolution to wrest the secret from life," and his "absolute indifference to public canons of art, friends, and shibboleths."

Incidentally, one should add to the list of eminent colleagues who appreciated the later and more complex Ibsen—Bernard Shaw, James Joyce, Henry James, Rainer Maria Rilke—the name of Thomas Mann. Mann's views, however, are considerably at variance with my present chapter since, speaking of *Parsifal* and *When We Dead Awaken,* he finds in Wagner and Ibsen not contrast but similarity. He regards them as kindred giants of the decadence: "What we used to call *fin de siècle,* what was it but a miserable satyr-play of a smaller time, compared with the true and awe-inspiring dying-away of the epoch whose swan-song was the last word of these two great musicians?"—*Freud, Goethe, Wagner* (New York, 1937).

**PAGE 131**     "AXEL'S CASTLE" is mentioned advisedly. The best book so far written about the "aesthetic withdrawal" of so many writers at the end of the last and the beginning of the present century, it gives the setting of Ibsen's final period. Though Ibsen continued to be known as the forerunner of Galsworthy he had actually been recognized as a poetic symbolist by *(e.g.)* Jeannette Lee in *The Ibsen Secret* (New York, 1907), a pioneer work marred only by the fact that Miss Lee was as heavy and prosaic in her symbolist analysis as her predecessors had been in their sociological emphasis.

**PAGE 131**     VAN WYCK BROOKS, *The Opinions of Oliver Allston* (New York, 1941), Chapters XVIII and XIX. Brooks includes Ibsen among his Primary authors who are forward-looking and cheerful, while he relegates the bulk of modernist literature to the rank of Secondary because it is backward-looking and cheerless.

**—TO CHAPTER 5.**

**PAGE 143**     EUGÈNE BRIEUX (1858-1932) was called by Shaw "incomparably the greatest writer France has produced since Molière." A fantastic appraisal, why did Shaw make it? Shaw's favorable judgments, like his condemnations, are all *arrière-pensée*. Precisely because Paris was the center of Occidental theater it has been all the more a stumbling block for the drama. Henry Becque, who might in other circumstances have written plays in profusion, wrote but two mature, full-length plays and spent years in spiritual paralysis over his always unfinished *Les Polichinelles*. It is not surprising that Shaw, who as critic and playwright had been fighting the theater of Scribe and Sardou for years, should bubble over with joy when Brieux came along and gave off at least a spark or two of dramatic genius in the direction of what we might call Shavian or pedagogical naturalism. In championing a Brieux and damning a Shakespeare, Shaw may remind us at first of poor William Archer; if we understand both his ulterior motive and his passion for Shakespeare we shall, however, qualify our first impression.

**PAGE 147**     SHAW AND ACTUAL PRODUCTION.
Shaw's capability in the arts of the theater is known to all the actors and theater men who have been associated with him. It is proved in print by such a pamphlet as his *The Art of Rehearsal*. His contact with great actors and actresses is a subject in itself. In England and America there is already a long tradition of Shavian acting in the grand manner—from Richard Mansfield to Katharine Cornell, from Mrs. Patrick Campbell to Robert Morley. *Ellen Terry and Bernard Shaw, A Correspondence* (New York, 1931), whatever its standing for students of *erotica,* is a theatrical document of the first rank. It represents the strivings of the great British dramatist of the age to coax into better drama the great British actress of the age and, through her, the great British actor of the age, Henry Irving. Irving, however, preferred Sardou's Napoleon to Shaw's and the twin stars of the Lyceum never appeared in *The Man of Destiny,* which was written for them (complete with Irving's mannerisms written into the leading part). Shaw writes: "As nobody nowadays has the least notion what the old stock companies were like, and as my own plays are written largely for the feats of acting they aimed at, and as moreover both Ellen Terry and Irving were rooted like myself in that phase of the evolution of the theater, I may as well say a word or two about them." Whoever would get the full point of Shaw's plays on Napoleon, Caesar, and Joan should read the French and English historical plays which he and his fellows saw in the seventies, eighties, and nineties. The Lyceum alone offered plays about Dante, Richelieu, Catherine de Medici, Napoleon, and Becket.

**PAGE 147**   HESKETH PEARSON'S BIOGRAPHY—*G. B. S., A Full-Length Portrait* (New York, 1942)—perpetuates popular fallacies about Shaw, such as those already cited in Archer and Lewisohn. Most critics since 1930 have seen more in Shaw. In his *British Drama* (revised edition, 1933), Professor Allardyce Nicoll argued that Shaw was a playwright, not a philosopher, and this line, directly contrary to that of the older critics, was followed by Edmund Wilson in the essay mentioned in my text, "Bernard Shaw at Eighty" in *Triple Thinkers* (New York, 1938). A larger view than that of Archer, Lewisohn, Nicoll, or Wilson is taken by Jacques Barzun in his essay, "G. B. S. in Twilight" in the *Kenyon Review*, Summer 1943.

**PAGE 151**   MAX BEERBOHM AND G. K. CHESTERTON. Among weekly critics of theater, Max Beerbohm is second only—at least among British and American critics—to Bernard Shaw, whom he succeeded on the staff of the *Saturday Review* in 1898. Shaw's articles reappeared in two volumes as *Dramatic Opinions* (New York, 1907), Beerbohm's—including several pieces on Shaw—in *Around Theaters*, also two volumes (New York, 1930).

As for Chesterton, even those of us who cannot rate him nearly so high as Shaw must admit that his *George Bernard Shaw* (New York, 1909) remains the best book on Shaw after more than thirty-five years.

**PAGE 156**   WILLIAM JAMES. When in *A Century of Hero-Worship*, Part Five, Chapter 2, I joined the names of James and Shaw, Mr. Sidney Hook commented in the *Nation*, October 7, 1944: "To link together, as he does, the social philosophies of William James and Shaw is an intellectual outrage." The letter in which James expressed great sympathy with the Shavian spirit is printed in Archibald Henderson's

*Bernard Shaw, Playboy and Prophet* (New York, 1932), pp. 326-327.

**—TO CHAPTER 6.**

**PAGE 159**     QUASI-FINAL DEFINITIONS OF COMEDY and tragedy. Since the mind of the pedant is always and forever the same (hence the justification, no doubt, of our neo-classical and neo-medieval schemes of education) it is just as relevant to quote an old theorist as a new. According to Scaliger's *Poetics* (1561), tragedy and comedy can be exactly differentiated by action, character, ending, style, and historicity. Here is how Scaliger goes to work:

> In comedy, Chremetes, Davi, Thaides of humble rank are chosen from rural districts; the beginning is turbulent; the ending, happy; ordinary language is employed. In tragedy, kings and chieftains are chosen from cities, fortified towns and camps; the beginning is calm; the ending, horrible; the language is dignified, refined, and differentiated from vulgar speech; the whole impression is one of apprehensions, fears, threats, exiles, and deaths.

Today our terminology is different; but our readiness to provide formulas is unabated. In *The Cutting of an Agate* W. B. Yeats defines tragedy so as to exclude Shakespeare who, we are told, always wrote "tragi-comedies." This theory would not offend Bernard Shaw who, for his part, has maintained that "Ibsen . . . firmly established tragi-comedy as a much deeper and grimmer entertainment than tragedy" ("Tolstoy: Tragedian or Comedian?" in *Pen Portraits and Reviews*). Writing of the class struggle in the preface to his play *Touch and Go*, D. H. Lawrence offers another view: "If we really could know what we were fighting for, if we could deeply believe in what we were

fighting for, then the struggle might have dignity, beauty, satisfaction for us. If it were a profound struggle for something that
was coming to life in us, a struggle that we were convinced
would bring us to a new freedom, a new life, then it would be a
creative activity, a creative activity in which death is a climax
in the progression towards new being. And this is tragedy."
Still more recently W. H. Auden has dichotomized tragedy
thus: "Greek tragedy is the tragedy of necessity; i.e., the feeling
aroused in the spectator is 'What a pity it had to be this way';
Christian tragedy is the tragedy of possibility, 'What a pity it
was this way when it might have been otherwise'; the *hubris*
which is the flaw in the Greek hero's character is the illusion of
a man who knows himself strong and believes that nothing can
shake that strength, while the corresponding Christian sin of
Pride is the illusion of a man who knows himself weak but believes he can by his own efforts transcend that weakness and
become strong"—*New York Times Book Review*, December 16,
1945. Amid the welter of hunches, *aperçus*, axes-to-grind, and
incomplete theories, the opportunity for a philosopher-critic to
reconsider the whole history and range of tragedy and comedy
is great. In this book, however, we can only skirt the subject
and raise the question.

**PAGE 161**      GEORGE MEREDITH's *Essay on the Idea of
Comedy and of the Uses of the Comic Spirit*. Among the serious deficiencies of the essay is a definition of a spirit of comedy
which excludes satire, irony, and humor. Meredith equates his
idea of comedy with his idea of amiability: "You may estimate
your capacity for Comic perception by being able to detect
the ridicule of them you love without loving them less" etc.,
etc. Sometimes he is downright silly, as when he coolly observes: "Those who detect irony in Comedy do so because they
choose to see it in life." Looking through the essay today I have
difficulty in discovering what could have impressed me about it

once. Perhaps it was some of the following observations which bear on the social aspect of comedy:

1. "The Comic poet is in the narrow field, or enclosed square, of the society he depicts; and he addresses the still narrower enclosure of men's intellects, with reference to the operation of the social world upon their characters."

2. For Comedy "a society of cultivated men and women is required, wherein ideas are current and the perceptions quick, that he may be supplied with matter and an audience."

3. "A perception of the comic spirit gives high fellowship. You become a citizen of the selecter world, the highest we know of in connection with our old world, which is not supermundane. Look there for your unchallengeable upper class!"

4. Meredith is too wise to think Molière the poet of the aristocracy alone: "For the amusement of the Court the ballets and farces were written, which are dearer to the rabble upper, as to the rabble lower, class than intellectual comedy. The French bourgeoisie of Paris were sufficiently quick-witted and enlightened by education to welcome great works like *Le Tartuffe, Les Femmes Savantes,* and *Le Misanthrope. . . .*" There follows such a hymn of praise to the middle class as would have warmed the heart of James Mill or Lord Macaulay: "In all countries the middle class presents the public which, fighting the world, and with a good footing in the fight, knows the world best. . . . Cultivated men and women, who do not skim the cream of life, and are attached to the duties, yet escape the harsher blows, make acute and balanced observers. Molière is their poet."

PAGE 163    LORCA AND SYNGE. Synge's folk comedies— *The Playboy of the Western World, The Tinker's Wedding, In the Shadow of a Glen*—have long been famous. It was Edwin Honig, in his valuable book *Garcia Lorca* (New York, 1944), who pointed out that Lorca was a second Synge both in folk tragedies like *Blood Wedding* (Norfolk, Conn., 1939) and folk comedies like *The Shoemaker's Prodigious Wife* (in *From Lorca's Theater, Five Plays of Federico Garcia Lorca*, New York, 1941).

**PAGE 163**        GRABBE (1801-1836) a brilliant, freakish dramatic talent. not really discovered until the twentieth century, and then only in Germany. Like Büchner he is a good instance of the fact that a play need not succeed at once to succeed in the end. Before the titles of his chief works I give the date of composition (which is usually also the date of publication) and after them the date of the first production:

| | |
|---|---|
| 1827 *Herzog Theodor von Gothland* | 1892. |
| 1827 *Nanette und Maria* | 1914. |
| 1827 *Scherz, Satire, Ironie, und tiefere Bedeutung* | 1876. |
| 1829 *Don Juan und Faust* | 1829. |
| 1829 *Die Hohenstaufen* | 1875. |
| 1831 *Napoleon* | 1868. |
| 1838 *Hannibal* | 1918. |

**PAGE 163**        STERNHEIM (1878-    ) is associated both with Expressionism and with the anti-Expressionist trend known as *die neue Sachlichkeit*—"the new factuality." *Aus dem bürgerlichen Heldenleben* (1908-1922) includes his best comedies: *Bürger Schippel, Die Hose, Der Snob, Die Marquise von Arcis*. The last-named has been published and performed in an excellent adaptation by Ashley Dukes, entitled *The Mask of Virtue*. A translation of *Der Snob* under the title of *A Place in the World* is to be found in *Eight European Plays*, ed. W. Katzin (New York, 1927).

PAGE 163     HENRY BECQUE (1837-1899), whose genius was paralyzed by Sarcey and the Parisian theater, had as great a natural gift as any modern playwright outside our Big Four. In the histories he is listed as the head of an undistinguished school of French dramatists who wrote what is called *comédie rosse*—a type of acrid, raw, naturalistic comedy not long ago popularized in America by *The Little Foxes*. Rather than vainly trying to revive Henry Céard, Romain Coolus, Georges Ancey, *et al.*, I prefer to call attention to a little genealogy of more distinction. Whether each of these authors actually influenced the other I do not know; legitimate or illegitimate, here is the family tree:

1885  *La Parisienne,* by Becque.
1887  *Comrades.* Perhaps Strindberg's best *comédie rosse.*
1897  *Der Kammersänger* ("The Tenor"). Wedekind's amazing one-act satire.
1908-1922  *Aus dem bürgerlichen Heldenleben.* Sternheim's *comédie rosse* cycle.

Another of Ashley Dukes's admirable English versions—*Parisienne*—was performed and published in London in 1943.


PAGE 164     CHEKHOV (1860-1904) and SCHNITZLER (1862-1931) might each have had a full chapter in this book had it aimed at being a comprehensive history of the best modern drama. The former has probably a high enough reputation, at least among connoisseurs, though even they have tended to praise in Chekhov the one element that borders on the meretricious: his wistfulness. This is so overstressed by modern actresses that the light-foot Chekhov can be as elephantine on the stage as Sudermann or Philip Barry. Those who know best—Maxim Gorky and Stanislavsky, not to mention the tart comments in Chekhov's own *Letters on Literature* (London, 1924)—emphasize the demure concreteness of Chekhov, his highly artistic, Jane

Austen-like naturalism on the one hand and, on the other, his affirmative attitude to life. Chekhov's peculiar aroma results, indeed, not from adolescent posturing and guttural murmurings about going to Moscow, not from mannered lifelessness and actressy affectation, but from the interplay between the facts of provincial Russia in 1900, so painstakingly reproduced, and Chekhov's impulses and ideals. It is precisely because Chekhov is so positive a person, such a lover of life, that his Russia is so sorry a place. It is a cage for wild birds. It is a mantelpiece for stuffed seagulls.

Brushing aside spurious Chekhovism (Greta Garbo will do instead), we are free to analyze the symphonic structures which are Chekhov's plays. That this has seldom been done as yet is proved by the ugly slashes in the text of even the most imposing Chekhov productions. Cuts in Chekhov—as in Shakespeare—are like vandalism in an art gallery. It is as if you cut every tenth bar out of a Beethoven trio. Chekhov did not talk pretentiously about new form. He did not talk; he acted. In his achievement we see the real possibilities of the "slice of life" theory, of the naturalistic rejection of the "well-made play." Chekhov gives the *illusion* of a slice of life by being not less but more skillful in construction than the playwrights of the boulevards. His naturalism means abandoning recourse to the easy symmetry of plot and building a graceful edifice out of the trickier material of rhythm, leitmotiv, tempo, and panorama. As Chekhov put it himself in words that to the present-day reader suggest Henry James: "When a man spends the least possible number of movements over some definite action, that is grace."

To the kind of critic who appeals to "the decline of the ruling class" or "the rising bourgeoisie," Arthur Schnitzler is Chekhov all over again. The twilight mood, the elegant setting, the refined naturalism of the technique are common to both playwrights. In both the central conflict is between the outgoing, loving impulses and circumstances which thwart them.

Yet the two are utterly different. In technique Schnitzler stays closer to the orthodox French play. He is not averse to using sentimental tricks such as letting the heroine of *Intermezzo* sing a song which in overtheatrical irony refers to her own case. And he often stretches the long arm of coincidence in his plots. The catch is that though there is much improbability of event—especially too neatly timed exits and entrances—there is no improbability in psychology. Schnitzler sets up an interplay between his "artificial" framework and his "real" people. The effect is characteristic and wonderful. It is as if a play of Sardou suddenly were to come alive. Like Pirandello, Schnitzler plays one level of reality against another. But he does it quite differently. Pirandello starts from the human reality and "distances" it with the aid of an artificial frame; Schnitzler starts from the frame and lets his characters walk out of it into real life. Pirandello uses the trick to make reality comic and thus bearable. Schnitzler uses it for the shock which the spectator experiences when the frame is ruptured. If Pirandello is belittled when we exclusively look at his intellectual problems, Schnitzler is belittled when we exclusively look at his moral and practical problems. Schnitzler was once known as the playwright who attacked dueling, who advocated the New Morality, who was Dangerously Frank, who asked: should a doctor tell?, who wrote on the Jewish problem. All these things are secondary in his art, which is the scene of a much more primordial conflict, that which Freud has called the conflict of Love and Death, a conflict within which most others can be subsumed.

The relation of Schnitzler's work to the ideas of Comedy and Tragedy is more complex than I indicate in the text. *Der Ruf des Lebens* ("The Call of Life"), for instance, has a somewhat tragic form, yet in substance is almost the exact opposite of tragic. (There is no name for the opposite of tragic; *comic* is certainly not the word.) Tragedy has perhaps always implied a study of *responsibility;* often it has shown the retribution that follows *irresponsibility.* The pseudo-tragic ending of *Der Ruf des Lebens* is antitragic, though calamitous, in that the idea of responsibility is explicitly turned down. The good doctor tells the protagonist Marie, who has killed her father under provocation, not to be worried with the thought of guilt. Not that he justifies the action. Rather he finds the idea of justification meaningless. "You are good," says Marie. "Good?" Schnitzler's spokesman replies, "I?—Yes. In the same way as you are a criminal . . . Words!—On you the sun still shines and on me—and on them (*he points to the children who run across the meadow*). On her (*pointing to Marie's dead sister*) it does not. That's all I could be certain about on this earth." Thus a new kind of tragedy—or, better, a nameless something that is not tragedy—is made out of modern skepticism.

Some would proceed to damn Schnitzler as a nihilist and a decadent. Words are cheap. Politically defeatist, no doubt, Schnitzler yet stands for the truth as he sees it, which is the artist's basic position. Schnitzler stands for conscience, and against illusions, especially the illusion that irresponsible pleasure makes men happy. All through his life he said the same things and painted the same picture with different emphases. The public has liked his early work best, the delicate "comedy" of *Anatol* or the delicate "tragedy" of *Liebelei*. Inveterate Schnitzlerians champion the late *novellen* and such late plays as his haunting, dim *Der Gang zum Weiher* ("Road to the Fish Pond"). Personally I most admire the middle period of *Der Einsame Weg, Der Ruf des Lebens, Zwischenspiel,* and the great "comedy" of sexual promiscuity *Reigen*.

Perhaps the two best books in English on Chekhov and Schnitzler are, respectively: William Gerhardi's *Anton Chekhov* (New York, 1923) and Sol Liptzin's *Arthur Schnitzler* (New York, 1932).


**PAGE 167**        IS CANDIDA THE VILLAIN? An author's interpretation of his own work can never be regarded as authori-

tative, but, for what it is worth, here is Shaw's opinion on the
question as conveyed in a letter to James Huneker:

Don't ask me conundrums about that very immoral female,
Candida. Observe the entry of W. Burgess: "You're the
lady as hused to typewrite for him." "No." "Naaow: *she*
was younger." And therefore Candida sacked her. Prossy is
a very highly selected young person indeed, devoted to
Morell to the extent of helping in the kitchen but to him
the merest pet rabbit, unable to get the slightest hold on
him. Candida is as unscrupulous as Siegfried: Morell himself sees that "no law will bind her." She seduces Eugene
just exactly as far as it is worth her while to seduce him.
She is a woman without "character" in the conventional
sense. Without brains and strength of mind she would be a
wretched slattern or voluptuary. She is straight for natural
reasons, not for conventional ethical ones. Nothing can be
more cold-bloodedly reasonable than her farewell to Eugene: "All very well, my lad; but I don't quite see myself
at fifty with a husband at thirty-five." It is just this freedom
from emotional slop, this unerring wisdom on the domestic
plane, that makes her so completely mistress of the situation. Then consider the poet. She makes a man of him
finally by showing him his own strength—that David must
do without poor Uriah's wife. And then she pitches in her
picture of the home, the onions, and the tradesmen, and
the cossetting of big baby Morell. The New York *hausfrau*
thinks it a little paradise; but the poet rises up and says,
"Out then, into the night with me"—Tristan's holy night.
If this greasy fool's paradise is happiness, then I give it to
you with both hands, "life is nobler than that." That is the
"poet's secret." The young things in front weep to see the
poor boy going out lonely and brokenhearted in the cold
night to save the proprieties of New England Puritanism;
but he is really a god going back to his heaven, proud,

unspeakably contemptuous of the "happiness" he envied in the days of his blindness, clearly seeing that he has higher business on hand than Candida. She has a little quaint intuition of the completeness of his cure; she says, "he has learnt to do without happiness."

This analysis is at many points in accord with mine, at some point not.

Shaw told Huneker: "I should certainly be lynched by the infuriated Candidamaniacs if this view of the case were made known." He added, in words that help us to understand him as an artist:

> I tell it to you because it is an interesting sample of the way in which a scene, which should be conceived and written only by transcending the ordinary notion of the relations between the persons, nevertheless stirs the ordinary emotions to a very high degree, all the more because the language of the poet, to those who have not the clew to it, is mysterious and bewildering and therefore worshipful. I divined it myself before I found out the whole truth about it.—*Iconoclasts: A Book of Dramatists* (New York, 1908), pp. 254-256.

These suggestive, rather cryptic comments deserve to be capped by another. In a letter to his daughter, published in *The Crack-Up* (New York, 1945) F. Scott Fitzgerald wrote: "*Strange Interlude* is good. It was good the first time, when Shaw wrote it and called it *Candida*."

PAGE 183        THREE PLAYS of Pirandello and three levels of reality:

1921 *Six Characters in Search of an Author.*
1924 *Each in His Own Way.*
1930 *Tonight We Improvise.*

**—TO CHAPTER 7.**

**PAGE 195**          EACH SCANDINAVIAN COUNTRY . . . See
any history of any Scandinavian literature. A cross-section of
the best Scandinavian drama since Strindberg has been published in *Scandinavian Plays of the Twentieth Century* (Princeton, 1944), 2 vols. They are not bad plays; but they do not whet
the appetite.

**PAGE 195**          SHAW, IBSEN, O'NEILL, AND STRIND-
BERG. The story of Ibsen and the picture is told in V. J.
McGill's *August Strindberg*, p. 11. It is also said that Ibsen
thought Strindberg his superior. (If so he was wrong.) O'Neill's
testimonial is quoted from a Provincetown Players program.
Shaw's tributes are taken from the prefaces to *Back to Methuselah* and *Three Plays for Puritans,* respectively. Henderson tells
us that Strindberg's portrait has hung in Shaw's workroom
alongside Nietzsche, Descartes, and Einstein. Pearson adds this
anecdote about Shaw:

> Taking advantage of a visit to Stockholm, he called on
> Strindberg to advise him to appoint William Archer as his
> English translator. "Archer is not in sympathy with me,"
> objected Strindberg. "Archer wasn't in sympathy with Ib-
> sen either," returned Shaw. . . . Having reported this con-
> versation verbatim to Archer on a post card, Shaw contin-
> ued: "After some further conversation, consisting mainly
> of embarrassed silences and a pale smile or two by A.S.,
> and floods of energetic eloquence in a fearful lingo, half-
> French, half-German, by G.B.S., Strindberg took out his
> watch and said in German, 'At two o'clock I am going to
> be sick.' The visitors accepted this delicate intimation and
> withdrew."

PAGE 197          STRINDBERG'S AUTOBIOGRAPHIES. English versions and the years they cover are as follows:

1. *The Son of a Servant,* 1849-1867.
2. *The Growth of a Soul,* 1867-1872.
3. *The Author,* 1872-1886.
4. *The Confession of a Fool,* 1875ff.
5. *Fairhaven and Foulstrand,* 1892-1894.
6. *Inferno,* 1894-1897.
7. *Legends,* 1897-1898.

(The eighth volume—*Alone*—has not been translated.) The
break between 4 and 5 indicates not only a break in time but
also in style. The first four books are in the "naturalistic" vein
like the plays with which they are so closely related—*The
Father, Miss Julia, Creditors.* The last four belong to the
"spiritual" realm of the dream plays.


PAGE 200          SIRI VON ESSEN, whose stormy marriage with
Strindberg is recorded in *The Confession of a Fool* and, less
literally, in *The Father* and *The Link* and other "naturalistic"
plays was accused by her husband of everything from Lesbianism to feeding the dog better than she fed August Strindberg.
The marriage with Frida Uhl (1893-1894) was not quite so tempestuous, and the marriage with Harriet Bosse (1901-1904) was
almost calm. Like many of our "high-brow" prophets of simple
womanhood, Strindberg married complex intellectuals. Two of
the three wives were actresses, the other was a writer.


PAGE 201          SWEDENBORG. The name to many of us suggests only a drab, queer sect. To the historian of culture, however, Swedenborg is a major influence on imaginative writers
such as Blake, Balzac, Flaubert, Baudelaire, Yeats, and Strindberg.

**PAGE 201** . . . THREE CONCENTRIC CIRCLES—an idea of A. Jolivet's. Not the least of the merits of his book *Le Théâtre de Strindberg* is that it makes available to those who have no Swedish a great deal of the research of the leading Strindberg scholar, Martin Lamm. The two chief studies of Strindberg in English—*August Strindberg, the Bedeviled Viking* by V. J. McGill (New York, 1930) and *August Strindberg* by G. A. Campbell (London, 1933)—are decidedly limited both as to scholarship and criticism.

**PAGE 201** BÜCHNER AND THE GERMAN ROMANTICISTS. Even more than Grabbe, Georg Büchner (1813-1837) is a standing disproof of the view that no playwright succeeds after his death who does not succeed during his lifetime. Büchner's success was postponed until the generation of 1910-1920, when Max Reinhardt produced his *Death of Danton* and Alban Berg made an opera out of his *Wozzeck*. Antedating not only Zola but also Turgenev and Ostrovski, he is an illustration of the fact that dramatic naturalism was not an invention of the eighties. Regarded by many as a twentieth-century playwright born too early, I prefer to suggest that our notion of what is typically "nineteenth-century" is invidious and arbitrary. The nineteenth century produced Büchner!

Because the German Romanticists wrote many bad plays and contributed from the "high-brow" side to the divorce of theater and drama we tend to forget their positive services. We do not read Ludwig Tieck's *Dramaturgische Blätter,* highly as they were esteemed by Goethe, Heine, and Hebbel. We fondly believe that nobody tried to produce Shakespeare in an Elizabethan manner on an Elizabethan stage before 1900. Early in the nineteenth century, however, Tieck denounced the *Illusionsbühne* and called for a *Raumbühne,* by which he meant a stage of platforms and staircases in the approved modern manner. Producing *A Midsummer Night's Dream* at Potsdam in 1843, Tieck used (instead of scenery) stairways, draperies, pillars, and balconies, on a three-tier stage. Long before Shaw, Tieck assaulted the popular Parisian theater as the octopus that it was. In his demand for a more intimate theater and a more experimental leadership, in his demand for a realistic middle-class drama, in his demand for more natural acting and careful enunciation, he is a great pioneer of modern theater. We would not think Thornton Wilder's *The Skin of Our Teeth* so audacious if we had read *Die verkehrte Welt* and *Der gestiefelte Kater* by Tieck.

**PAGE 202**  DESPREZ AND ANTOINE. *L'Evolution naturaliste* by the young Louis Desprez was one of the many books which helped to create a Zolaist climate of opinion. Allusions to André Antoine, who gave the Zolaists their chance in the theater by founding the Théâtre Libre in 1887, are intermittent throughout this book. One of the two plays which were done at the Théâtre Libre under the common title of *Les quarts d'heure—Entre frères* by Henri Lavedan and Gustave Guiches—was regarded by Strindberg as a model of the genre.

**PAGES 202-203**  BRUNETIÈRE AND SARCEY. Ferdinand Brunetière (1849-1906) was the leading academic critic of drama in France when Francisque Sarcey (1828-1899) was the leading journalistic critic. The former fluttered the academic dovecots in America with his "law of the theater," a not very enterprising rehash of the idea "drama is conflict" in terms of volition. What a fascination this kind of question exercised in the years before the First World War can be judged by readers of Henry Arthur Jones's introduction to the English translation, or of Brander Matthews' *The Development of the Drama* (1903),

Clayton Hamilton's *The Theory of the Theater* (1910), and
William Archer's *Playmaking* (1912).

Contrary to appearances, Sarcey is a more complex and controversial figure. He liked Dumas *fils*, Sardou, and Augier, the
best theater of his youth and middle age, and he was a die-hard
opponent of the Naturalism and Symbolism of his later years.
Since the latter schools have stood the test of time much better
than the former, since we naturally think harshly of a theater
critic who could find little but hocus-pocus in Ibsen or Becque,
we neglect to note that Sarcey, for all the smug Philistinism that
blemished his work, was often right and his opponents wrong.
Although he did not seek out the grain of genius in Maeterlinck, he pounced on the nonsense which is just as certainly
there. He not only recognized Strindberg's talent and declared
that he had more sense of theater than any other playwright of
the Scandinavian school, he also disengaged some of the essentials of Strindberg's art: his clarity of exposition, his assured
logic, his skillful preparations, his kinship with *"nos faiseurs de
mélodrames ou de nos vaudevillistes."* Above all in the essays
under the title *"Les lois du théâtre,"* in the first of the eight
imposing volumes of his *Quarante Ans de Théâtre* (Paris, 1900-
1902), Sarcey makes one of the most intelligent of all attempts
to describe the craft of the theater. The art of theater, he
argues, is a system of conventions which give an illusion of
reality to an audience. A play, therefore, is *not* "a slice of life
artistically put on the boards" as the Zolaist Jean Jullien had
put it, not, at any rate, unless the word *artistically* cancels out
the rest of the remark. We shall understand theater, says Sarcey,
by studying the peculiar conditions of theater: the psychology
of crowds, their expectations and predilections as mirrored in
dramatic conventions. It is necessary, he insists, to accommodate the facts and sentiments of life to the particular disposi-
tions of spectators. "It is impossible to separate the art from its
conditions, as it lives only through and by them, as it is not a
subtle inspiration wafted from heaven or emanating from the

depth of the human mind, but something wholly concrete and definite which, like all living things, cannot exist except in the environment to which it is adapted. . . ." Here Sarcey is a pioneer of much modern scholarship which has dug up the facts of ancient and Elizabethan theater and has proved to the hilt that they are essential to the complete understanding of the drama. So much in Sarcey's favor. The way in which he could contrive to be so right in theory and so wrong in specific allegiances might at first be puzzling. It arises from the single circumstance that Sarcey's analysis of modern culture was deficient. He quoted Molière's dictum: "There is no other rule of the theater than that of pleasing the public" and failed to differentiate between Molière's public and Sardou's. The point comes up again in Chapter X above.

**PAGE 207**     BERNHARD DIEBOLD's book *Anarchie Im Drama* (Frankfurt, 1925) is one of the best books in the whole field of modern drama. Its main subject is German Expressionism, of which the analysis is magistral, and Diebold writes the best things obtainable on the art of Strindberg, Wedekind, and Sternheim, not to mention the lesser men of Expressionism proper.

Having mentioned the outstanding English and French critics of our period, I should add that Germany produced no less outstanding talents. During the Weimar Republic, Diebold, Alfred Kerr, Julius Bab, and Herbert Ihering kept up a marvelously high standard.

**PAGE 214**     ERICH KAHLER'S *Man the Measure* (New York, 1943) is a general history of civilization that, like Egon Friedell's, is particularly good for its criticism of certain authors. Kahler has the *feel* of modern European literature. Very few people have.

## —TO CHAPTER 8.

**PAGE 220**     O'NEILL, O'CASEY, AND DENIS JOHN-
STON. O'Neill's admiration of Strindberg was most eloquently
expressed in the program of the Provincetown Players quoted
above, p. 195. *The Flying Wasp* (London, 1937), O'Casey's one
book of criticism—a splendid attack on the London theater,
even if Mr. O'Casey suffers from the illusion that New York is
better, a "romantic" illusion of distance—contains respectful
allusions to Strindberg. The influence of the dream plays is
written all over Denis Johnston's *The Old Lady Says No!*, an
Expressionist retort to W. B. Yeats' too slight play *Cathleen ni
Houlihan*.

**PAGE 224**     YEATS' later plays are spread over four volumes:

1. *Four Plays for Dancers,* 1921.
2. *Wheels and Butterflies,* 1934.
3. *The Herne's Egg and Other Plays,* 1935.
4. *Last Poems and Plays,* 1940.

It is from the very interesting notes in the first of these volumes
that my quotation is taken.

**PAGE 229**     Several of COCTEAU's plays have been trans-
lated without being published. The only translation in print is
Carl Wildman's version of *La Machine Infernale* (Oxford,
1936) from the introduction to which I have quoted on p. 228.
Readers of French might be able to find Cocteau's libretti:
*Oedipus Rex* (for Stravinsky), *Antigone* (for Honegger), *Le
Pauvre Matelot* (for Milhaud). Other Cocteau titles (not men-

tioned in the text) are: *Le Boeuf sur le Toit, Les Mariés de la Tour Eiffel, Roméo et Juliette.*


PAGE 232          EXISTENTIAL THEATER. The news of the new theater came to America via the English monthly magazine *Horizon*, May 1945. In what does the existentialism of the plays consist? Sartre has almost answered this question in one sentence of an essay in which he wrote: *"L'existence n'est pas une délectation morose, mais une philosophie humaniste de l'action, de l'effort, du combat, de la solidarité."*

A somewhat longer quotation will reinforce the point:

> Every object has a being and an existence. A being—that is to say a constant sum of attributes. An existence—that is to say a certain effective presence in the world . . . The existentialist holds . . . that in man—and only in man—existence precedes being.
>
> That means quite simply that man primarily *is* and only secondarily is he this or that. In a word man has to create his own being. It is in throwing himself into the world, in suffering there, in wrestling there, that he bit by bit defines himself. And the definition remains forever open. You cannot say what this particular man is before his death nor what humanity is after it has disappeared.

Does existentialism lend itself to dramatic art? Or is it an embarrassment? "It is evident," says John Russell in *Horizon*, "that existentialism, based as it is largely upon the inner rhetoric of temperament, is very well suited to the theater." H. A. Mason, however, maintains in *Scrutiny* that "in *Les Mouches* the philosophical theses remain outside the play, which thus lacks inner coherence. . . . The author is illegitimately pulling the strings and intervening like his own Jupiter to bring off firework effects." Now it seems that I had the advantage over these critics in that I read Sartre's play before I knew anything of Sartre's philosophy. From this experience I can uncategorically report that the philosophy of the Sartre plays is so far from being obtrusive that they can painlessly be assimilated by audiences who have never heard of Kierkegaard or Heidegger.

**PAGE 237**          "HUIS CLOS" AND GARCIN'S COWARDICE. A supplement to some of my sentences is provided by Alexandre Astruc in his essay "Jean-Paul Sartre and *Huis Clos*" in John Lehmann's yearbook *New Writing and Daylight* (1945):

> Actually, Garcin's crime is not that of being a coward—is he one anyway? No one will ever know, he died before he could prove his courage: he died too soon (but one always dies too soon). Nor that of Estelle in being an infanticide, nor naturally that of Inès in being Lesbian. Their real sin is having made others suffer during their existence, of having wanted to live through the tortured conscience of another. Garcin has made his wife suffer, Inès her girl friend, Estelle her lover: they will be punished in that wherein they sinned: through others. Thus, in the end, Garcin's cowardice, likes Inès' sexuality, are their *punishment,* rather than their sin. Garcin will suffer through his cowardice (or his impossibility of showing his courage: which comes to the same): Inès through her inversion and Estelle through her sensuality. The punishment, if it comes from others, is nevertheless rooted in the conscience of each of the characters. They themselves are their own torturers,

## —TO CHAPTER 9.

**PAGE 250**    PISCATOR AND BRECHT. Piscator's book, *Das politische Theater* (Berlin, 1929), from which all the quotations are taken, is a very interesting and unintentionally revealing bit of social and personal history. Piscator was something of a youthful prodigy; and unfortunately he still is. A more objective account of some of his doings is to be found in Herbert Ihering's *Reinhardt-Jessner-Piscator oder Klassikertod?* (Berlin, 1929).

Ihering comments on the influence of Piscator and Brecht: "It is astonishing that the poet should have more influenced the theater and the director than the drama. Most attempts to come to an understanding with the political and social present go back to Piscator, most attempts to create a new form to Brecht."

Some of Ihering's further comments on Brecht's Epic Drama might be worth adding here:

> Brecht replaced greatness with distance. That is his historic achievement in the theater. He did not make people smaller. He did not atomize characters. He put them at a distance. He took away the actor's obtrusive *gemütlichkeit*. He demanded a reckoning with the events. He insisted on simple gestures. He had to have clear, cool speech. No emotional chicanery was permitted. The result was the objective, Epic style.

My first long quotation from Brecht (p. 259) is taken from an unpublished Prospectus of the Diderot Society. The charts (pp. 255, 257) are from the notes to *Mahagonny* in the *Gesammelte Werke* (London, 1938). Neither *Der gute Mensch von Sezuan* nor *Der kaukasische Kreidekreis* is as yet published in any language, though a translation of the latter—which I quote —has been prepared by W. H. Auden and James Stern. For further particulars see the bibliographical note in my version of *Furcht und Elend des dritten Reiches* ("The Private Life of the Master Race") (New York, 1944).

**PAGE 254**    EVREINOV'S MONODRAMA. The quotation from Evreinov is taken from Oliver M. Sayler's *The Russian Theater under the Revolution* (Boston, 1920), Chapter XIV. See also *The Theater in Life* by Nicolas Evreinoff (New York, 1927). His little monodrama *The Theater of the Soul* has been published more than once in English—*e.g.* in *Chief Contemporary Dramatists,* Third Series, ed. T. H. Dickinson.

**—TO CHAPTER 10.**

**PAGE 275**    THEATER ALWAYS A PROBLEM. In the first volume of his *Quarante Ans de Théâtre,* Sarcey wittily mentions a collection of dramatic brochures which he had recently come across. Among the titles were:

1768 *Causes de la décadence du théâtre.*
1771 *Du théâtre et des causes de sa décadence.*
1807 *Les causes de la décadence du théâtre.*
1828 *Considérations sur . . . les causes de la décadence des théâtres.*
1841 *Recherches sur les causes de la décadence des théâtres . . .*
1842 *A quelles causes attribuer la décadence de la tragédie . . . ?*
1849 *De la décadence de l'art dramatique.*
1860 *De la décadence des théâtres.*
1866 *Rapport au Sénat sur la décadence de l'art dramatique.*
1871 *De la décadence des théâtres et les moyens de les régénerer.*
1876 *Cri d'alarme sur la situation de l'art dramatique.*
1880 *Du théâtre à sauver.*

**PAGE 276**        ENTERTAINMENT . . . ON THE SCREEN.
Rosten's *Hollywood,* already cited, contains a remark germane
to the theme of my chapter: "The people who read the *Atlantic
Monthly* also see the Marx brothers' pictures; but how many of
the people who see the Marx brothers read anything above the
level of *True Confessions?*" Since, however, Mr. Rosten does
not know what conclusion to draw from any of his data (except
to excuse Hollywood's offenses as juvenile delinquency which
the industry will later grow out of) it is necessary to go elsewhere for enlightenment—for instance, to James T. Farrell's
*The League of Frightened Philistines* (New York, 1945) which
contains two admirable essays on Hollywood in which Darryl
Zanuck, Walter Wanger, and other spokesmen for the present
state of affairs are put where they belong.

**PAGE 278**        THE "SATURDAY EVENING POST," see
"On High-brow Writing," by Maurice Zolotow in the monthly
*Politics,* August 1944. The argument that "Shakespeare was also
a popular writer" is a regular gambit even in academic criti-
cism. Professor Allardyce Nicoll devotes the first chapter,
"Shakespeare and the Cinema," of his *Film and Theatre* (New
York, 1936) to it. The uneasiness and resentment that motivates
this elaborate Justification by Shakespeare is revealed when
Mr. Nicoll turned with relief from minority art to the mass-
produced movie:

> We are not dealing here with fond theories spun from the
> brains of idealistic visionaries desirous of making the film
> a toy for aesthetes and superior intellectuals; we are watch-
> ing something much more significant—the sure develop-
> ment of an art out of conditions which have made many
> regard it only as an industry (p. 107. cf. p. 29, p. 49).

This low-brow academicism is the real "treason of the clerks."
When we realize that this particular "traitor" is perhaps the

greatest living scholar in the field of theater, the only comment
is *"et tu, Brute?"*

**PAGE 280** THE PSYCHOLOGY OF THE CROWD. Cf.
Mr. Nicoll's phrase: "the sure development of an art out of
conditions." In a splendid onslaught against what he called this
"cheap materialism," J. E. Spingarn traced its history from
Castelvetro in the Renaissance to the present. Spingarn spoke of
"all this pedantry of 'dramatic technique,' of 'dramaturgic
skill,' of *scènes à faire,* of the conditions of the theater, the influence of the audience, and the conformation of the stage" and
concluded:

> If we wish to understand dramatic literature itself, we must
> seek understanding in the great plays and not in the dead
> materials out of which plays are made. . . . For the true
> dramatic critic will transfer his interest from the drama
> itself to the "laws of the theater" or the "conditions of the
> theater" only when the lover studies the "laws of love" and
> the "conditions of love" instead of his lady's beauty and his
> own soul.—From "Dramatic Criticism and the Theater,"
> 1913, reprinted in *Creative Criticism* (New York, 1917).

**PAGE 281** THE CRITIC AND "OKLAHOMA!" See Mr.
George Beiswanger's Broadway Letter in the *Kenyon Review*
(Spring 1944) and his article "Theater Today" in *Journal of
Aesthetics and Art Criticism,* Vol. III, Numbers 9-10. The idea
that *Oklahoma!* is *echt amerikanisch* and has "deep subconscious roots"—"the roots run . . . to vaudeville . . . dance of
every kind, and much that comes straight from the folk"—is on
all fours with the cultural nationalism recently advertised by
Van Wyck Brooks and others. It is not new. Twenty years ago

Waldo Frank rejoiced over the death of high theater in America as follows:

> The drama-culturists seem to have gone and may it be for-
> ever—such simple and fundamental artists as Chaplin,
> Brice, Jolson, Fields, Whiteman, Savoy, with a host of other
> gorgeous jazzers and apocalyptic dancers have come into
> their own: shamelessly they hold the stage and win the
> plaudits which went once to the dim drama of discus-
> sion . . . This is all to the good, for of such folk-stuffs shall
> be built our indigenous theater.

As for the European drama: "These spirits of revolt—Andreyev, Wedekind, Maeterlinck, Romains—are not true for us. . . . Absorption in them is a natural growth for their countrymen; for the American it is a dangerous trick."—*Salvos* (New York, 1924).

**PAGE 285**     THE READING OF PLAYS. Aristotle said: "Tragedy like epic poetry produces its true effect even without action; it reveals its power by mere reading." Lessing said: "A masterpiece is seldom as well represented as it is written; mediocrity always fares better with the actors." In the antiliterary tradition, however, Spingarn names Castelvetro, Diderot, Voltaire, Schlegel, Sarcey, and Brander Matthews. Perhaps the most uncompromising remark is that of the Victorian man of letters H. D. Traill:

> Of every drama, as we moderns understand the term, it
> may, I hold, be affirmed that, though some of them may,
> and do, contain great literature, they are, to the extent to
> which they are literary, undramatic, and, to the extent to
> which they are dramatic, unliterary.

This tradition lies behind the following comments of living men of the theater:

The unliterary theater is the only genuine form of theatrical art.—Theodore Komisarjevsky.

This book is concerned with the theater and not with drama—a distinction in terms which I think is clear to all. I understand drama to be a branch of literature.—Norris Houghton.

**PAGE 287**    STARK YOUNG, in several small books, very modest in appearance compared with the LOVELY PICTURE BOOKS mentioned above (p. 329), made one of the best contributions to the understanding of theater arts:

1923  *The Flower in Drama.*
1925  *Glamour.*
1926  *Theater Practice.*
1927  *The Theater.*

**PAGE 287**    TEXTBOOKS ON DRAMA REMAIN BAD. An exception is *Understanding Drama* by Cleanth Brooks and Robert Heilman (New York, 1945). Here at last plays are given rigorous analysis by critics who believe that great drama means something. Everybody should read their analyses of *Henry IV*, Part I, *The Way of the World*, and *The School for Scandal*. Messrs. Brooks and Heilman write: "There can be no question that the legitimate drama is primarily an auditory art, and that the dialogue is its primary element. For drama, therefore, costumes, setting, and even acting itself are, finally, secondary. It is the word which is primary here; and this fact may explain why a good play retains so much of its dramatic power even when merely read in the study or the classroom." Which is excellent; and this book is an endorsement of the Brooks and Heilman position. Unfortunately, in the course of their book their indifference to the arts of the theater comes to seem excessive; one ought to know something of what Richard Boleslavsky called the "music of action" and one can fully study this music only in the theater. A certain academicism limits *Understanding Drama*. I do not refer here primarily to the staid and stolid tone of the editors' writing, or even to the fact that they sometimes seem more interested in *defining* tragedy than in experiencing it, but to the shabby treatment accorded to modern drama in their book. After their scholarly and intelligent report on Shakespeare and Congreve, their account of Ibsen seems amateurish and jejune. It was surely unnecessary to publish so naïve an analysis of *Rosmersholm* after the work done on this play by Bernard Shaw, Lou Andreas Salome, Roman Woerner, and Hermann Weigand. Brooks and Heilman think that Ibsen is trying, or ought to have been trying, to be Shakespeare, and that he is not doing well at it. They even suggest that *Rosmersholm* ought to be in verse. Having been told that Ibsen wrote Problem Plays, but finding him really not so bad after all, our modern editors suggest that *Rosmersholm* is a Problem Play unsuccessfully trying to be a Shakespearian tragedy. A strange formulation of Ibsenism! Obviously our Shakespeare scholars— one could give many more examples—have not yet begun to understand that an Ibsen or a Shaw has his own purposes and methods in drama, purposes and methods different from those of earlier tragedy and comedy. Is it not the classic error of academicism to classify first-rate examples of a new genre as second-rate examples of an old genre? And of all old genres has not Shakespearian drama been the greatest hindrance to all new departures? "It is when you are not able to write *Macbeth* that you write *Thérèse Raquin*," said Robert Louis Stevenson. If he meant that you write a second-rate work when you are not able to write a first-rate work he is right but not very profound. If he meant that you only write a modern play when you can't write an Elizabethan play he was talking the kind of nonsense that makes one understand, and to a large extent support, Bernard Shaw's assault on Shakespeare.

PAGE 287       CAMPUS PRODUCERS AND BROADWAY.
One of the few campus theaters that has uncompromisingly
broken with Broadway consequently receives this treatment in a
book ostensibly devoted to the improvement of the noncommercial theater:

> The criticism most readily leveled at Bennington Theater
> by those who have come into close contact with it or with
> its students or its faculty is that it has an unrealistic ap-
> proach to the stage of today, that it leads an ivory tower
> existence, out of touch with the theater of the market place
> and the crossroads, that its mountain retreat is shrouded in
> a kind of haze.

I like "the market place and the crossroads"! Just where both
are located is disclosed by the same author in another lyrical
passage:
"Broadway will not disappear; at least not until New York
blows away. It will beckon; it will be a mecca; it will remain
the standard of reference; its nod of approval will set the
stamp. . . ."—From *Advance from Broadway* by Norris Houghton (New York, 1941).

PAGE 289       ONE REVOLUTIONARY CONCLUSION,
which received its most eloquent statement by the founder of a
great French Little Theater, Jacques Copeau, director of the
Théâtre du Vieux Colombier, writing in the *Nouvelle Revue
Française*, 1913. The proposal to start an art theater is preceded
by a magnificent burst of indignation:

> A mad industrialism which from day to day more cynically
> degrades our French stage and repels from it the cultured
> public; the monopoly of the greater part of our theater by

a handful of entertainers in the hire of shameless merchants; everywhere, even in high places, whose authority should bring with it a certain sense of pride, the same spirit of show and speculation, the same lack of taste; everywhere the spectacle of an art that is dying, and of which there may even be no question any longer, in the parasitic toils of bluff, of auction methods, of exhibitionism; everywhere shallowness, disorder, indiscipline, ignorance, and folly; contempt for the artist, hatred of beauty; an overproduction becoming ever more foolish and more futile, a body of criticism becoming ever more complacent, a public taste wandering farther and farther astray:—these are what anger us and now drive us to revolt.

I shall not try to state all other opinions on this question, but the editorial views of *Theatre Arts* might here be noted. The first number of the magazine (1916) contained a statement of purpose in which an offensive was declared against the "established theater, organized as a business." The result of this and other concomitant offensives was to be the "ultimate conquest of the 'regular' theater." And how, in the end, would the theatrical businessmen give up? The little manifesto looks forward to "the day when the speculators would step out of the established playhouse and let the artists come in."

Twenty-eight years later this view of things is modified. In an editorial of October, 1944, the businessmen are no longer expected to walk out. Their help is requested for the furtherance of artistic theater. If the show *This Is the Army* could earn ten million dollars for war relief why, it is asked, could not similar shows earn a little money for the artistic theater? John Golden is giving money for a Shakespeare repertory company. Could not this be a precedent?

Now whether waiting for men of power to abdicate or asking them to share their wealth is a better strategy was not discussed in *Theatre Arts* and need not be discussed here. Neither proposal is very convincing to me, and a sentence from the *Theatre Arts* editorial hints at some of the reasons why: "The end of World War I heralded a rebirth of the American theater— Where are the rebels now? . . . the theater of 1944 has a power which it did not have in 1919—the power to stifle adventure, to quash initiative."

Another illustration. Two of the mainstays of *Theatre Arts* a generation ago were Kenneth MacGowan and Robert Edmond Jones. In 1933 Professor Allardyce Nicoll wrote in praise of new tendencies in Hollywood as follows: "The summoning of men such as MacGowan and Edmond Jones to Hollywood indicates, too, the beginning of a new policy." Where are the rebels now?

**PAGE 290**    MINORITY ORGANIZATIONS. The "FREIE BUEHNE" for instance secured seven hundred members in its first year. In its second year only five performances were given, in its third only one, then finis. The history of minority theaters in America can be pieced together by readers of:

1917 *The Art Theater,* by Sheldon Cheney.
1929 *Footlights across America,* by Kenneth MacGowan.
1941 *Advance from Broadway,* by Norris Houghton.

**PAGE 294**    THEATER AND DEMOCRACY. To this day the most telling statements on this subject (to which the rest of my chapter might be regarded as a rejoinder) are those of the great critic of *Democracy in America,* Alexis de Tocqueville, Vol. II, Book 1, Chapter 19: "Some Observations on the Drama amongst Democratic Nations." Here are seven of his dicta:

1. If you would judge beforehand of the literature of a people which is lapsing into democracy, study its dramatic productions.

2. At the theater men of cultivation and of literary attainments have always had more difficulty than elsewhere in making their taste prevail over that of the people, and in preventing themselves from being carried away by the latter.

3. In democracies dramatic pieces are listened to but not read. Most of those who frequent the amusements of the stage do not go there to seek the pleasures of the mind but the keen emotions of the heart.

4. If the effect of democracy is generally to question the authority of all literary rules and conventions, on the stage it abolishes them altogether and puts in their place nothing but the whim of each author and of each public.

5. In written productions the literary canons of aristocracy will be gently, gradually, and, so to speak, legally modified; at the theater they will be riotously overthrown.

6. People who spend every day in the week in making money, and the Sunday in going to church, have nothing to invite the muse of comedy.

7. The dramatic authors of the past live only in books. The traditional taste of certain individuals, vanity, fashion, or the genius of an actor may sustain or resuscitate for a time the aristocratic drama among a democracy; but it will speedily fall away of itself—not overthrown but abandoned.

Lest I seem to claim any originality for my rejoinder let me quote the great pre-Shavian dramatic critic of Victorian England, George Eliot's "husband," G. H. Lewes:

The Drama is everywhere in Europe and America rapidly passing from an Art into an Amusement; just as of old it passed from a religious ceremony into Art. Those who love the Drama cannot but regret the change, but all must fear that it is inevitable when they reflect that the stage is no longer the amusement of the cultured few, but the amusement of the uncultured and miscultured masses, and has to provide larger and lower appetites with food . . . the mass, easily pleased and liberally paying for the pleasure, rules the hour.

Unless a frank recognition of this inevitable tendency cause a decided separation of the drama which aims at Art from those theatrical performances which only aim at Amusement of a lower kind (just as classical music keeps aloof from all contact and all rivalry with comic songs and sentimental ballads), and unless this separation take place in a decisive restriction of one or more theaters to the special performances of comedy and the poetic drama, the final disappearance of the art is near at hand. . . . It is only by a rigid adherence to the principle of specialization that such a scheme can have a chance. The theater must be mounted with the sole purpose of performing works of art for an art-loving public.—*On Actors and the Art of Acting* (London, 1875).

**PAGES 294-295**    WILDE AND CHEKHOV both had a full understanding of the plight of the theater in modern society. The quotation from Wilde is from "The Soul of Man under Socialism," which with the essays in *Intentions,* helps to cancel out the unfortunate effect on Wilde's reputation of his feeble poems, his sentimental stories, and his sensational trial. The letters of Chekhov quoted here are dated: November 2, 1903 and April 4, 1897 respectively. They appear in English in his *Letters on Literature.*

**PAGE 299**        TAKING DRAMA TO MIDDLE-WESTERN FARMERS. What may happen when the playwright attempts to speak directly to the people without compromising his art is shown in the story of Tolstoy and his great play *The Power of Darkness:*

> . . . Stakhovich read it aloud to the peasants who had been invited to hear it. About forty of them came and listened in silence. Only the pantry boy expressed his delight with noisy laughter.
>
> The reading came to an end. Tolstoy turned to his favorite pupil, a middle-aged peasant, and asked, "How do you like it?"
>
> The peasant answered, "I don't know what to say, Count. . . . At first Nikita managed things pretty well, but in the end he slipped up."
>
> This crushing answer caused Tolstoy a deep mental depression. He still held one of the essential factors in a work of art to be its universality and its meaning to the plain people.

The final irony was that this play for the people was chiefly successful in the salons of Petersburg:

> Everywhere the readings met with great success. Finally, on January 27, 1887, Alexander III expressed a desire to hear the play. The stage was set in Count Vorontsov's palace for Stakhovich to read the play before the entire imperial family. . . .
>
> At the conclusion of the fifth act, everyone remained silent for a long time, waiting for the Tsar to speak. At last he said, "A marvelous piece of work!"—*Tolstoy and His Wife,* by Tikhon Polner (New York, 1945).

# AFTERWORD (1987)

# AFTERWORD (1987)

IF THIS BOOK NEEDS CORRECTING, AMPLIFYING, OR SUPPLEMENTing, then, to the extent of my abilities, I have corrected, amplified, and supplemented it in books that followed *The Playwright as Thinker*, which was written in 1944–1945.

I would, however, like to explain why certain changes I made in a 1955 edition are not preserved in the present volume, which restores the original text of 1946. One consisted in the updating of the bibliographical notes: To have continued this process to 1987 would not only make for bulk; it would also fail to match a text written over forty years earlier. Another change consisted in the omission of the original Foreword on the ground that it tended to monopolize the attention of reviewers and others. Today it won't. Even what a reader of today

might find unacceptable in it will nevertheless serve to indicate
the author's point of departure.

A third change made in 1955 is more important. It consisted in deleting the word *naturalism* in many instances and
replacing it with the word *realism*. Let me explain. The book
always had much to do with Bertolt Brecht. He was not by any
means its sole inspiration; nor was I—despite rumors to the
contrary—the first in the English-speaking world to write about
him. I was, however, endeavoring to be the first in that world
to understand him and present him to the public in the right
context and in the right language.

The right context and language, that is, in the milieu I
inhabited, not the milieu he inhabited. In the thirties, Brecht
differed with his Communist comrades in matters of literary
theory, but since it was his aim to win them over, he necessarily
accepted their language and their sense of right context. He
was after all enclosed in their ideology, and even more in their
mentality. Which meant, among many other things, that *realism*
was a sacred word, and, if one wished to differ from the other
realists, one had to argue that one's own position was even more
realistic: it was *really* realistic. Which in turn meant that, for
discussion of the actual issues, the term *realism* lost all value. I
don't mean that none of the current definitions had literary
content. There was such content in Georg Lukacs' essays—for
example, the notion that what is realistic must be not only life-
like in appearance but also typical of a class and an epoch. But
the fact that the word *unrealistic* could be used to send people
to their death or to what later would be called the Gulag seemed
to me to delegitimize even legitimate uses of the word. However
this may be, I made what would otherwise have been the very
curious decision to discuss modern drama at book length without ever using the words *realism* and *realistic*. Well, not quite.
In the foregoing text the words *realism* and *realistic* occur once
or twice in passing. What is not used is the standard distinction
realistic/naturalistic. Rather, we get naturalism with a small *n*
and Naturalism with a capital *N*. Of course, nobody followed

me in this. In numerous discussions I found myself obliged to revert to realism/naturalism, and I ended up making the change just reported in a later edition of *The Playwright as Thinker*.

Brecht read the first edition, and our correspondence about it, itself quite inconclusive, eventually led to his drafting his *Short Organum for the Theatre*. The spiritual distance between us might be measured by the fact that he completely missed my point about realism. "I think I see why you did not use the word *realism*," he wrote me. "*It is still too much of a shock for many.*" For whom was it a shock? I knew mostly people for whom it was a bore or worse. In leftist circles, it customarily led only to a competition in being more realistic than thou. Think how many pages in the past half-century, not just in Russia but in every country with a Communist Party, have been wasted on denunciation of Messrs. A, B, and C for being unrealistic or in awarding prizes to Messrs. D, E, and F for their realism!

Will my restoration of the 1946 text be a shock for many? Hardly. It may just be something I owe to myself. For a second time, the usage I propose (naturalism, Naturalism!) will fail to stick. I didn't stand by it, after all, in my own later work. Yet I recall with relish the polemic force it had in Brecht's lifetime and can only hope that readers too young to recall such things will be able to imagine them.

Not, of course, that all this was what *The Playwright as Thinker* was about. What it was about was . . . But it tells its own story. By this time, certainly, it has meant what it has meant, and you, the reader in 1987, must decide what it is going to mean now. You need not bring a Marxist background to it, nor yet an anti-Marxist background. You need only grant me that, in the words of my late friend Friedrich Heer: "The works of the poets and artists are spiritual games played in space and time. They add their weight to the play of the philosophers and theologians, and act as mediators of invaluable experiences, structures, contents, forms, and materials."

# INDEX

# INDEX

N.B. No attempt has been made to duplicate here all the bibliographical material of the Notes; the index is designed to cover only the main body of the text; it does however include references to the chief topics discussed in the Notes. The index was compiled by Leone Albinson.